Movie Migrations

New Directions in International Studies

Patrice Petro, Series Editor

The New Directions in International Studies series focuses on transculturalism, technology, media, and representation, and features the innovative work of scholars who explore various components and consequences of globalization, such as the increasing flow of peoples, ideas, images, information, and capital across borders. Under the direction of Patrice Petro, the series is sponsored by the Center for International Education at the University of Wisconsin–Milwaukee. The center seeks to foster interdisciplinary and collaborative research that probes the political, economic, artistic, and social processes and practices of our time.

For a list of titles in the series, see the last page of the book.

Movie Migrations

Transnational Genre Flows and South Korean Cinema

HYE SEUNG CHUNG AND
DAVID SCOTT DIFFRIENT

Rutgers University Press
New Brunswick, New Jersey, and London

KOREA FOUNDATION
한국국제교류재단

This publication project was supported by the Korea Foundation.

Library of Congress Cataloging-in-Publication Data

Chung, Hye Seung
Movie migrations : transnational genre flows and South Korean cinema / Hye Seung Chung and David Scott Diffrient.
pages cm
Includes bibliographical references and index.
ISBN 978–0-8135–6998–7 (hardcover : alk. paper)—ISBN 978–0-8135–6997–0 (pbk. : alk. paper)—ISBN 978–0-8135–6999–4 (e-book (web pdf))
1. Motion pictures—Korea (South)—History—20th century. 2. Motion pictures—Korea (South)—History—21st century. 3. Culture in motion pictures. 4. Motion pictures and transnationalism. 5. Motion pictures and globalization. I. Diffrient, David Scott, 1972- II. Title.

PN1993.5.K6C545 2015
791.43095195—dc23
2014035987

A British Cataloging-in-Publication record for this book is available from the British Library.

Visit our website: http://rutgerspress.rutgers.edu

Manufactured in the United States of America

Contents

Acknowledgments

We wish to thank a number of individuals who have read various parts of the book and helped us improve it with their thoughtful comments and suggestions: Nancy Abelmann, Robert Cagle, David Desser, Ted Hughes, Kelly Jeong, Kathleen McHugh, Michael Pettid, and Tim Tangherlini. We would also like to extend our gratitude to Jinsoo An (UC–Berkeley), Andrew Jackson (SOAS, University of London), David Kang (USC), Christina Klein (Boston College), and Hyung-Sook Lee (Ewha Womans University) for inviting us to their campuses to present early drafts of chapters. A generous Professional Development Award from the College of Liberal Arts at Colorado State University made our field trip to Seoul possible in the summer of 2012. We are particularly grateful for the research support from Chung Chong-hwa and Jang Kwang-heon in the Korean Film Archive, who provided invaluable insights into the data presented in the Conclusion. We are also indebted to director Shin Dong-il and actor/activist Mahbum Alam who shared with us not only the backstory of *Bandhobi* (a case study in Chapter Eight) but also their thoughts on the state of multicultural media productions in South Korea. Last but not least, we remain thankful for the love and support of our families in South Korea (Chung Sang Ho, Shim Eunok, Jung Hyeuk, and Kang Taesu) and in the United States (Harry and Donna Diffrient).

The authors and the publisher express their sincere gratitude to the Korea Foundation for awarding a generous publication grant and supporting this project financially.

Chapters One, Four, and Five are expanded and revised versions of Hye Seung Chung's previously published essays: "Toward a Strategic Korean Cinephilia: A Transnational *Détournement* of Hollywood Melodrama," Kathleen McHugh and Nancy Abelmann, eds., *South Korean Golden Age Melodrama: Gender, Genre, and National Cinema* (Wayne State University Press, 2005),

117–150; "*The Man with No Home: Shane* Comes Back in a Korean 'Manchurian Western,'" *Journal of Popular Film and Television*, Vol. 39, No. 2 (Summer 2011): 71–83; and "Reinventing the Historical Drama, De-westernizing a French Classic: Genre, Gender, and the Transnational Imaginary in *Untold Scandal*," *Post Script*, Vol. 27, No. 3 (Summer 2008): 98–114. Chapter Two is an adapted and revised version of David Scott Diffrient's previously published essay "*Over that Hill*: Cinematic Adaptations and Cross-Cultural Remakes, from Depression-Era America to Post-war Korea," *Journal of Japanese and Korean Cinema*, Vol. 1, No. 2 (Spring 2010): 105–127.

Note: The Romanization of Korean names in this book follows the McCune-Reischauer system, which is the academic standard endorsed by the Library of Congress. Exceptions to this rule are names of filmmakers, actors, and political leaders whose spellings are known to English-speaking readers, such as Bong Jun-ho, Chun Doo Hwan, Im Kwon-taek, Lee Byung-hyun, Park Chan-wook, and Park Chung Hee. Whenever Korean authors' works that have been published in English are cited, their names are presented the way that they are printed in source materials. Korean and other East Asian names appear in their native standard, with surname first (except for names printed otherwise in English-language publications). Finally, all quotations from Korean-language sources have been translated by Hye Seung Chung.

Movie Migrations

Introduction

South Korean Cinema's Transnational Trajectories

Standing on a pier that overlooks Hong Kong Harbor, a trio of Chinese jewel thieves, fresh from a burglary that has filled their pockets and inflated their egos, discuss their next potentially lucrative endeavor. Led by a hardened yet charismatic criminal named Chen (Simon Yam), the gang members await the arrival of a fourth crew member, a skilled safecracker named Julie (Angelica Lee) who will play a part in a diamond heist that promises to net them millions of dollars. Once Julie arrives, the Beretta-packing leader informs her that another gang of thieves—a group of outsiders from overseas—will be arriving in the former British crown colony soon, and that they will band together to steal the famed "Tear of the Sun" from a casino in Macao. Significantly, that valuable, one-of-a-kind jewel was itself lifted from an exhibition in Tokyo and is currently in the possession of a Japanese woman, Madame Tiffany (Ye Su-jŭng). The latter character is the mistress of an underworld kingpin named Wei Hong (Ki Kuk-sŏ), and she is carrying the "Tear of the Sun" to one of China's two Special Administrative Regions, a former Portuguese colony that is now among the world's most popular gambling locations. Macao thus eventually replaces Hong Kong as the site of illicit activities, a city of glitzy, kitschy excess that brings together a diverse cross-section of locals, tourists, and transnational migrants.

The previous scene, drawn from a recent example of East Asian blockbuster cinema, might remind readers of the gritty crime thrillers directed by Hong Kong action auteurs, such as Tsui Hark, John Woo, Ringo Lam, Johnnie To, and Andrew Lau. These directors, in their own distinctive ways, have been instrumental in breathing new life into their local film industry and in providing Hollywood with grist for the remake mill, with neo-noir dramas like *City on Fire* (*Lóng hǔ fēng yún*, 1987) and *Infernal Affairs* (*Mou gaan dou*, 2002) being adapted into Quentin Tarantino's *Reservoir Dogs* (1992) and Martin Scorsese's *The Departed* (2006), respectively. However, the nighttime scene described in the opening paragraph comes not from a Hong Kong film, but rather from a South Korean production, an all-star heist flick entitled *The Thieves* (*Todukdŭl*, 2012).

Directed by Ch'oe Tong-hun (Choi Dong-hoon), this border-crossing film is indeed redolent of the works by his Chinese predecessors, owing not only to its diverse cast (Simon Yam in particular, a fixture in Johnnie To's *Full-time Killer* [*Chuen jik sat sau*, 2001], *PTU* [2003], and *Election* [*Hēi shè huì*, 2005]), but also to its dynamic visual style. Filled with spectacularly choreographed set pieces and stunt work as well as humorous yet deadly interludes in which Chinese and Korean characters interact, Ch'oe's commercially successful, stylistically audacious throwback to Hong Kong action cinema captured the imagination of local audiences after its theatrical release in the summer of 2012, eventually becoming South Korea's third highest-grossing motion picture (with 12.9 million ticket sales in the country). But it has also generated positive reviews in places as far-flung as Jakarta, Sitges, Taipei, and Toronto, where it was shown in film festivals and multiplexes before finally making its way to the US market via DVD and Blu-Ray distribution, giving international audiences the opportunity to see what many reviewers were calling a Korean remake of an *American*, rather than a Hong Kong, film.

In fact, among *The Thieves*' many direct homages and indirect allusions, it is Steven Soderbergh's *Ocean's Eleven* (2001) that tends to be singled out by many viewers as the most decisive influence on Ch'oe Tong-hun's stylistic and narrative choices. This intertextual connection between a big-budget Hollywood production and a South Korean crowd-pleaser necessarily situates the latter film in a less-sanctified position: that of a lowly "remake" (intentional or not) that presumably "pales in comparison" to its American antecedent. And yet, by referring to Soderbergh's film as an "originary" text, critics push to the side *Ocean's Eleven*'s status as a *derivative* text, conveniently overlooking its own indebtedness to an earlier motion picture bearing the same title and released in 1960. Directed by the Hollywood stalwart Lewis Milestone and starring members of the famous "Rat Pack" (Frank Sinatra, Dean Martin, Sammy Davis, Jr., Peter Lawford, and Joey Bishop), *Ocean's 11* set the template for many of the all-star heist films that followed it, helping to establish (along with post-war European productions such as *Rififi* [1955], *Bob le flambeur* [1956], and *Big Deal on Madonna Street* [*I soliti ignoti*, 1958]) some of the formal conventions that would be adopted and adapted by Ch'oe Tong-hun in the process of making a Korean variant five decades later. But *The Thieves* is more than merely a Korean variant of a genre that has roots in Hollywood's earliest crime pictures. Although it reproduces many of the tried-and-true visual tropes and narrative formulas associated with Milestone's and Soderbergh's caper movies (including the gathering together of co-conspirators, the "casing" of the place to be robbed, the revealing of plot twists and unexpected setbacks, and the pitting of once-unified group members against one another), *The Thieves* ultimately breaks from cinematic tradition to showcase intercultural encounters and transnational flows.

Moving fluidly from one international location to another and hinging on the sometimes-strained partnerships between Chinese and Korean characters (some of whom pretend to be Japanese), *The Thieves* is very "contemporary" in its cosmopolitanism—its awareness of cultural differences and similarities among global communities as well as its eagerness to transcend national boundaries. But, as we will explain throughout this book, such awareness has been an ingrained feature of South Korean cinema since its golden years of the 1950s and 1960s, despite the country's (clichéd) status as a "hermit kingdom" historically cut off from regional neighbors and other nations. As the latest in a long string of cultural productions concerning South Korea's evolving status as an increasingly "connected" yet deterritorialized "imagined community" (a kind of "virtual nation" held together by mediated communication networks), this film thus crystallizes an enduring feature of the country's cinema, which has long gravitated toward non-Korean sites (and sights) as sources of localized discourse. The localization of heist film conventions in *The Thieves* is therefore tied, perhaps paradoxically, to globalizing trends within the motion picture industry and within South Korean society more generally. Tellingly, the film's principal visual motif—the recurring image of thieves scaling skyscrapers and other buildings by way of a wire facilitating freedom of movement yet preventing deadly falls—is an apt metaphor of local and global connectivity. Beginning with a lengthy sequence in which a cable-swinging cat burglar named Yenicall (Jun Ji-hyun [Chŏn Chi-hyŏn]) breaks into a gallery filled with priceless artifacts, and escalating toward a climax in which another Korean character, Macao Park (Kim Yun-sŏk), flees Chinese thugs while suspended from a similar contraption outside an apartment complex in Pusan, *The Thieves* offers up images of wire-work that hint at South Korea's figurative ties to other cultural contexts and regions, from Hong Kong to Hollywood and beyond, despite remaining tethered to local traditions that are presumably threatened by the presence of global others.

The high-flying acrobatic wire scenes in *The Thieves* also suggest the "escapism and voyeurism" that Kirsten Moana Thompson and other critics see as central to the heist film genre (or what is sometimes referred to as the "caper movie"). According to Thompson, "Heist films afford a powerful screen

FIGURE 0.1. In one of the many action scenes in *The Thieves*, a Korean jewel thief confronts a Chinese gunman while suspended from a wire outside an apartment complex in Pusan.

identification with criminals breaking the law." Thus, "the pleasure of watching stories about illicit worlds and transgressive individuals" is part of this genre's appeal and perhaps one reason for its revived popularity in recent years.[1] By combining the horizontality of border-crossing movement (from Seoul to Hong Kong to Macao to Pusan) and the verticality of edifice-scaling lawbreakers (climbing great heights as they plunge deeper into criminality), the film highlights the fluidity of identity in spaces that are themselves permeable and always shifting. But *The Thieves*, like other caper movies, also "encodes in story form a particular desire to elude the oppressive aspects or limitations of contemporary mass society,"[2] something that makes this South Korean motion picture an especially useful case study in thinking about the utopian impulses of a nation and a citizenry pursuing new social realities that do not always gel with older value systems. As Daryl Lee states, "The genre inscribes a wish-fulfillment for a new social order with the express intention of breaking away from a technologically and institutionally threatening society."[3] It is possible, then, to posit genre conventions associated with the heist film (in particular the "extraordinary robbery of a formidable institution that requires careful planning and the skills of specialists")[4] as a cultural response to the challenges faced by very *real* social actors snared between dueling desires: the craving for change and the countervailing need for stability.

If, as Lee maintains, caper movies "are part of a broader reflection about the role of film artists in consumer societies,"[5] then *The Thieves* can be framed as a metatextual mirror of sorts. Self-consciously, the film nods toward its many non-Korean predecessor texts and pushes to the fore a titular fascination with *thievery*—a metaphor for the act of appropriating or "lifting" elements from earlier motion pictures. Indeed, the title of Ch'oe Tong-hun's film reflexively comments on the predilection for pilfering apparent in the works of *other* cultural producers—globally recognized cineastes (such as the aforementioned Tarantino and Scorsese) who express a "migratory" interest in various national/regional contexts. Such "movie migrations," we hope to explain, are the textual expressions of an extratextual phenomenon, one that maps onto broader transnational flows—of capital, of labor, of technologies, of ideas and values—unique to the era of rapid economic and cultural globalization.

In many respects, the concept of transnationalism has been used by media scholars and cultural critics as a counterbalance to the more monolithic, homogenizing notion of globalization. According to Françoise Lionnet and Shu-mei Shih, "The transnational designates spaces and practices acted upon by border-crossing agents, be they dominant or marginal."[6] This differs from the logic of globalization, which "assumes a universal core or norm." As Lionnet and Shih explain, transnationalism can be thought of as "a space of exchange and participation wherever processes of hybridization occur and where it is still possible for cultures to be produced and performed without necessary mediation by the center."[7] In recent years, the widespread circulation of contemporary South Korean films, as part of the so-called "Korean Wave," is significant because of the country's peripheral status throughout the prior century—a period when it had been dominated by Japanese and American imperial influences, in much the way that an adolescent might be subjected to an older sibling's taunts or commands. Today's rising tide of Korean popular culture, also known as *Hallyu* (the millennial inter-Asia craze for Korean dramas, popular music, films, and celebrities, among other things),[8] has contributed to enhancing cultural solidarity among peripheral nations without the "Big Brother"-like intervention of the global cultural center (i.e. Hollywood). But it has also reintroduced the problem of the "national" in a presumably "post-national" world, one in which geographical and political borders still exist but are said to be permeable.

Until the 1980s, the commonplace understanding of a national cinema as films produced within a particular nation-state and as expressions of a countrywide spirit had been largely accepted without challenge. Over the past three decades, however, the concepts of "the nation" and "national cinema" have been increasingly scrutinized and destabilized by such theorists as Benedict Anderson, Paul Willemen, Ernest Gellner, Eric Hobsbawm, and Andrew Higson. In 1983, Anderson famously defined the nation as an "imagined community," one that is culturally constructed through a variety of mediating forms (including print media).[9] Apart from this theoretical deconstruction of the nation by Anderson and others, geopolitical conditions of the 1980s and 1990s applied further pressure on the conceptual paradigm of the national. Those conditions include the transnational relocation of people as immigrants, exiles, refugees, and guest workers; the weakening of national, economic, and cultural borders with the consolidation of regional and global markets (thanks to the World Trade Organization [WTO], the European Union [EU], the Association of Southeast Asian Nations [ASEAN], the North American Free Trade Agreement [NAFTA], etc.); and the further development of global media channels, which were opened up in heretofore unprecedented ways through satellite technologies and the Internet (materializing Marshall McLuhan's prophesy of humanity consolidating into a "single global tribe" based on electronic interdependence).[10]

In the context of East Asian cinema studies, the advent of globalization and transnationalism introduced an imperative to renew outdated concepts of national cinema. When film studies was first institutionalized in North American universities in the 1960s and 1970s, such classic Japanese auteurs as Kurosawa Akira, Ozu Yasujirō, and Mizoguchi Kenji (who had been making films for decades) managed to ascend the ranks of world cinema canons after their works were held up as essentialized expressions of Japanese culture, aesthetics, and spirituality. However, other East Asian cinemas that subsequently entered the critical-academic pantheon in the United States and beyond since the 1980s (e.g. the Fifth Generation Chinese cinema of Chen Kaige and Zhang Yimou; the Taiwanese New Wave cinema of Hou Hsiao-hsien, Edward Yang, and Tsai Ming-liang; and the Hong Kong art cinema of Wong Kar-wai and Stanley Kwan) cannot be fully grasped within the traditional frameworks provided by "national cinema."

As many scholars have pointed out, these East Asian cinemas are transnational on several fronts. First, upon attaining fame both locally and globally, the previously-mentioned auteurs often pursued and acquired co-production financing opportunities from neighboring countries, as well as from European "suppliers" (particularly France), in hopes of circumventing the political, industrial, and artistic restrictions of their countries of origin. For example, Chen Kaige's epic *The Promise* (*Wu ji*, 2005) is a pan-Asian co-production involving three countries (China, Japan, and South Korea) and pairing Korean superstar Jang Dong-gun (Chang Tong-gŭn) with the Hong Kong actress Cecilia Cheung as the leads. Second, many transnational films textually foreground the act of border-crossing—a movement that finds its extratextual correlative in the flow of talent and creative personnel moving "to-and-fro" (from country to country) as part of an ever-decentralized production process. For example, Wong Kar-wai's *Happy Together* (*Chūn guāng zhà xiè*, 1997) locates and displaces a Hong Kong Chinese gay couple in Buenos Aires, while Tsai Ming-liang's *What Time Is It There?* (*Ni na bian ji dian*, 2001) is set in both Taipei and Paris. Ch'oe Tong-hun's *The Thieves* is simply a contemporary spin on that border-crossing phenomenon, shuttling from one location to another with the greatest of ease. And finally, in terms of the global reception of East

Asian cinema, many films emanating from Mainland China, Taiwan, Hong Kong, and South Korea tend to be more popular in specialized international markets—film festivals and art-house theaters—than in domestic commercial markets. The films of the internationally renowned (and steadfastly controversial) Korean auteur Kim Ki-duk (Kim Ki-dŏk) are exemplary with respect to this trend. For example, his meditative Buddhist fable *Spring, Summer, Fall, Winter . . . and Spring* (*Pom yŏrŭm kaŭl kyŏul kŭrio pom*, 2003) garnered 370,000 admissions in US art-house theaters, breaking all previous box-office records of Korean imports in North America. By contrast, that film was seen by a mere 30,000 theatergoers in its country of origin.

Without wishing to "obscure the question of imbalances of power (political, economic and ideological)" that accompany global cultural exchanges,[11] we wish to follow Olivia Khoo, Belinda Smaill, and Audrey Yue's lead in positing transnationalism as a critical "methodology." In the Introduction of their recently published book *Transnational Australian Cinema: Ethics in the Asian Diasporas*, Khoo, Smaill, and Yue argue that such a self-reflective approach goes beyond the merely descriptive to address the ways in which media scholars themselves might occupy a liminal position vis-à-vis the local and the global. Methodologically, transnationalism assists in meeting a cinematic text *on its own terms*, engaging in a dialogic relationship with its form and content while resisting the fixity that comes from asserting one's own national identity or cultural background too forcefully. Moreover, it aids in the critical unpacking of genre films—ostensibly the most fixed and circumscribed categories of cultural production—which are ultimately shown to be just as fluid and boundless in their solicitation of spectatorial activity as the most challenging or rigorous of art films.

As Christine Gledhill explains, the cross-border circulation of specific categories of cultural production (for instance, "the Italian development of the spaghetti Western which Clint Eastwood then [brought] back to Hollywood" in the 1960s and 1970s) attests to the destabilizing potential of film genres once they are retooled "according to different local and national-cultural interpretations."[12] If, as Miriam Hansen has argued, Hollywood genre productions functioned as the "first global vernacular" upon the US film industry's consolidation of power in the 1920s and 1930s (a time when the influx of immigrant populations ensured some degree of heterogeneity below the surface of what was becoming a monolithic machine of global dominance), then the international circulation of those motion pictures could be said to have informed the "horizon of expectations" that local audiences in various parts of the world bring to the viewing of non-Hollywood films. Thus, Gledhill reminds us, "local film production is pressured to engage or differentiate itself against such expectations, maintaining Hollywood's power of definition. In this context, Hollywood comes to stand for 'popular culture'—obscuring from critical view the existence of an indigenous popular culture which is similarly relegated by the artistic criteria espoused as 'national culture.'"[13] Concluding with the comment that "genericity has broken free from the master genres to create an international pool of protagonists, actions, icons, and performances, capable of multiple configurations and effects to which the genrified 'national' now contributes,"[14] Gledhill clears a rhetorical path for our own undertaking in the following pages, which examine particular uses of cinematic traditions within the South Korean context—a cultural-industrial space that has grown enormously since the first motion pictures were produced in Seoul and other cities beginning in the 1920s (when such colonial-era works as *The Plighted Love under the Moon* [*Wŏlha ŭi maengsŏ*, 1923], *The Nation Border* [*Kukkyŏng*, 1923], *The Story of Chunhyang* [*Ch'unhyangjŏn*, 1923], and *Arirang* [1926] were released). However, it is a space that, perhaps paradoxically, can only be fleshed out by moving *outside* that national context from time to time, taking into consideration the many *transnational* valences of genericity that have come to define "local" productions over the past several decades.

With this in mind, *Movie Migrations: Transnational Genre Flows and South Korean Cinema* examines global genre transformations and the concept of cross-cultural intertextuality through analyses of South Korean melodramas, literary adaptations, comedies, Westerns, historical dramas, monster movies, psychological thrillers, and multicultural films, all of which are comparatively linked to non-Korean counterparts, from Hollywood to Japan and beyond. As the title of this volume indicates, we intend this work as a "migratory" project that focuses primarily, but not exclusively, on South Korean films—separate yet interlocking case studies—so as to illustrate broad, theoretical concerns about cultural flows. By doing so, we hope to bring South Korean cinema (which still remains relatively unknown in US academia, despite its growing influence in regional markets) to the forefront of recent and ongoing debates about globalization and transnationalism. We also aim to revitalize American genre studies, an area of research and critical theory that has long been attached to Hollywood as a kind of signifying nexus.

Many of the major works concerning film genre—Barry Keith Grant's *Film Genres: Theory and Criticism* (1977), Thomas Schatz's *Hollywood Genres* (1981), Rick Altman's *Film/Genre* (1999), and Steve Neale's *Genre and Hollywood* (2000)—have neglected the question of transnational permutations, the necessarily politicized transformation of genres once they are mobilized outside of Hollywood's dominant industrial models and narrative modes. Indeed, a full understanding of genre hybridization and textual pragmatics cannot be achieved without looking beyond US borders and examining the deterritorialized manifestations of a given category of cultural production globally. We aim to reconceive genre as a transnational, transhistorical process, one that involves dialogic hybridity and multiplicity beyond the institutional constraints of any one national cinema, be it American or Korean.

Our conceptualization of the project is partly indebted to an essay written by Christina Klein and published in *American Quarterly*. In that essay, Klein poses the timely question, "Why does American Studies need to think about Korean cinema?"[15] As the author argues, local transformations of Hollywood genre conventions and iconographies, as demonstrated in many of the "Hollywood-inflected films" produced in South Korea, merit the attention of non-Koreanists as significant indicators of the ambivalent relationship between the two nations as well as tools through which to measure the impact of US popular culture's global circulation. Equally noteworthy is what we call the "reverse cultural flow" from South Korea to the United States and other countries (including China, India, and Japan) in recent years. This is demonstrated by over a dozen Hollywood and Bollywood remakes of Korean films in the past few years, including Mohit Suri's *Murder 2* (2011), which was inspired by Na Hong-jin's crime drama *The Chaser* (*Ch'ugyŏkja*, 2008), and Spike Lee's high-profile remake of Park Chan-wook [Pak Ch'an-uk]'s cult film *Oldboy* (*Oldŭ poi*, 2003), as well as the YouTube craze for the Korean rapper Psy's "Gangnam Style" in 2012. That reversal demonstrates an increasing fragmentation of cultural hegemons in a global era.

This book is divided into two main sections. The first part charts the postcolonial implications of multivalent genre flows connecting "the West" to "the East" while examining intertextual points of contact or convergence linking Classical Hollywood cinema (of the prewar and postwar eras) to Golden Age South Korean cinema (of the 1950s and 1960s). The second part of the book, comprised of four chapters and a Conclusion, continues this investigation of genre flows but expands its focus to consider the recent vogue for adaptations and remakes in an age when New Korean Cinema and *Hallyu* have not only gained a strong following among Western art-house patrons but also attracted the attention of Hollywood producers and movie studios eager to cash in on that craze.

Chapter One establishes a theoretical model or base for understanding South Korean cultural producers' borrowings from Hollywood (in the form of imitations, remakes, and restylings)—creative appropriations or moments of strategic "thievery" that we frame as examples of "transnational *détournement*." Literally meaning "turning around," *détournement* is a technique of cultural recycling and political resistance adopted by French Situationists in the 1960s and 1970s. South Korean Golden Age classics produced during the 1950s and 1960s often deflected the romantic excess of Hollywood melodrama by recontextualizing familiar visual tropes and star images in a realistic, postcolonial setting where desperate women could be seen selling their bodies to American GIs and unemployed veterans plotted bank robberies, as illustrated in the neorealist masterpiece *The Stray Bullet* (*Obalt'an*, 1960). This chapter will elaborate some of the cinephilic strategies of generic/textual *détournement* in South Korean Golden Age melodramas, comparing particular visual tropes from *The Stray Bullet* with their more aesthetically and ideologically idealized counterparts in Hollywood "woman's films," such as *Waterloo Bridge* (1940) and *Love Is a Many-Splendored Thing* (1957).

Building upon the theoretical framework established in the preceding chapter, Chapter Two is devoted to an investigation of the neglected genre of *pŏnan yŏnghwa* ("cross-cultural adaption films"). Such American classics as Fox's family melodrama *Over the Hill* (1931) and MGM's aforementioned wartime "weepie" *Waterloo Bridge* were adapted into Korean versions entitled *Over That Hill* (*Chŏ ŏndŏk ŭl nŏmŏsŏ*, 1968) and *Grief* (*Aesu*, 1967), respectively. In these and other adaptations, the process of historical and cultural recontextualization shifts the original semantic elements across syntactic lines, altering their denotative and connotative meanings in the process.[16] For example, *Over That Hill* resituates the Depression-era story of the American original, thematizing the schism between rural parents and city children in an era of state-initiated modernization, overseen by Park Chung Hee's military government (1961–1979).

In Chapter Three we cast a net over South Korean "modernization comedies" of the 1960s, paying attention to films featuring the iconic male star of the era, Kim Sŭng-ho, who was known as the "Emil Jannings of Korean cinema" (a reference to one of Germany's most famous—or infamous—silent-era actors). As a subgenre of film comedy proper, the modernization comedy hinges on clashes between "modern" values (associated, problematically, with American and European customs) and "traditional" Korean values. Those two sets of values strike a delicate balance, the source of much humor in such representative films as *Romance Papa* (*Romaensŭ ppappa*, 1960), *Mr. Park* (*Pak sŏbang*, 1960), *Third Rate Manager* (*Samdŭng kwajang*, 1961), and *Under the Sky of Seoul* (*Sŏul ŭi chibung mit*, 1961). However, that sense of equilibrium ultimately tilts to one side, in favor of the newly ascendant younger generation of the postwar period, as a result of the films' principle settings, their strong foregrounding of a rapidly urbanizing, developing society seemingly content with leaving the past behind. In modernization comedies, the emasculation of the father—his insufficiency, meager wages, and alienation from his sons' and daughters' generation—is a pretext for his ultimate obsolescence or even disappearance (a recurrent theme in Golden Age Korean cinema). Any laughter that might be generated by these comedies of the 1960s is thus "nervous," insofar as melodramatic pathos and social consciousness permeate even the most comic situations and scenarios—a generic marriage, we argue, that is symptomatic of a postcolonial national identity.

Chapter Four explores the "Manchurian Western" genre, a transhistorical phenomenon that first emerged in the 1960s and 1970s but has been given new life in a handful of contemporary productions, most famously Kim Jee-woon (Kim Chi-un)'s recent blockbuster *The Good, the Bad, the Weird* (*Chotŭn nom, nappŭn nom, isanghan nom*, 2008). Set in Manchuria during the 1920s and 1930s, and populated by members of the Korean colonial diaspora (including freedom fighters, hired guns, and peasants), South Korea's Manchurian Westerns are unique. In addition to mixing syntactic variants of the war film, the espionage film, martial arts cinema, and the family melodrama, this most hybridized of cultural forms tends to look down the proverbial barrel not at Native Americans (Hollywood's go-to "bad guys") but at another archetypal enemy—the Japanese Imperial Army—whose representatives often assume the antagonist position within the narrative. In addition to offering an overview of the Korean "Manchurian Western" genre, we will analyze the intertextual linkages between George Stevens' *Shane* (1953) and its cross-cultural counterpart *The Man with No Home* (*Musukja*, 1968), directed by the legendary Korean auteur Shin Sang-ok (Sin Sang-ok). Through scene-by-scene comparisons, we address generic hybridity of the latter text, which blends American Western conventions with Korean melodramatic sentiments. Toward the latter part of the chapter, we investigate how Kim Jee-woon's aforementioned *The Good, the Bad, the Weird* further dilutes conventions of the American Western genre not only by harnessing iconography associated with South Korea's Golden Age productions of the 1960s but also by borrowing from another "bastardized" form of the genre: the Italian spaghetti Western. Taking a cue from its title, we address the "weird" manner in which Kim's film depoliticizes the Manchurian Western's anti-colonial content to cater to a broad demographic of younger audiences throughout the world.

Chapter Five continues our shift toward more contemporary productions, and centers on E. J-Yong (Yi Jae-yong)'s *Untold Scandal* (*Sŭk'aendŭl: Chosŏn namnyŏ sangyŏljisa*, 2003). This unique cross-cultural adaptation of Choderlos de Laclos's 1782 novel *Les Liaisons dangereuses* (*Dangerous Liaisons*) had been adapted for the big screen several times in Europe and America. As the first Asian adaptation, *Untold Scandal* is the most interesting as a site of cultural convergence, creatively recontextualizing the original tale by resituating it within Korea's late Chosŏn period (during the King Chŏngjo era [1776–1800]). A major migratory break from *Untold Scandal*'s source material comes at the point of the Korean film's narrative closure, with the actions of the three romanticized lead characters (Valmont, Marquise de Merteuil, and Madame de Tourvel) departing from the original novel's moralistic ending—a departure as fascinating as director-writer E. J-yong's decision to incorporate baroque-style chamber music (rather than traditional indigenous tunes) as the sonic backdrop for this most unusual example of *sagŭk* (historical dramas). These issues, as well as the specific appeals that *Untold Scandal* holds for different spectators (including fans of Bae Yong-joon [Pae Yong-jun], star of the

Korean Wave drama *Winter Sonata* [*Kyŏul yŏnga*, 2002], which had become a cult sensation in Japan only a few months prior to this film's theatrical release), will be broached in this chapter, which not only charts out the genealogy of the historical drama in South Korean cinema but also points toward the crucial role that *Untold Scandal* played in the genre's recent revival in the domestic market.

While striving to historicize South Korean filmmakers' adoption and subversion of Hollywood genre conventions in the geopolitical context of the Cold War (a period in which US hegemony swept through the Korean peninsula, in ways both obvious and not-so-obvious), our volume will also investigate another important postcolonial relationship: that between Japan and Korea. In Chapter Six we compare and contrast two significant monster movies—one Japanese, the other Korean—that share thematic concerns despite a significant temporal gap separating them. After summarizing the rich history of *kaijū eiga* sparked by the theatrical release of the original *Godzilla* (*Gojira*, 1954), we discuss the critical tendency to assign allegorical meanings to those texts, through symptomatic readings that reveal the metaphorical suggestiveness of the movies as well as the monsters within them. That tendency is also on view in the many written commentaries surrounding director Bong Joon-ho (Pong Chun-ho)'s *The Host* (*Goemul* [*Koemul*], 2006), a Korean variation on the earlier Japanese creature feature that is simultaneously unique and derivative. Unlike the semiotically overloaded title monster in director Honda Ishirō's *Godzilla* (which has been said to represent, in its singular form, the horrors and anxieties of the nuclear age, in particular the threat of the atomic bomb that was prevalent throughout the immediate postwar period), the misshapen creature at the heart of *The Host* is hard to pin down—a literally slippery signifier that squirms away from many critics' grasp. And yet, while it is a closer approximation of what Maria Beville and other horror film scholars might call an "unknowable" or "unnameable" monster, that Thing has been rendered "knowable" and "nameable" through a kind of critical consensus among local (Korean) reviewers, who see its "thingness" as a visual representation of the otherwise unrepresentable horrors associated with the nation's tumultuous past (particularly the period of mass protests known as the *minjung* era of the 1980s).

Another kind of "monster" is on view in director Park Chan-wook's award-winning film *Oldboy*, the title character of which becomes, according to Kyung Hyun Kim, "larger-than-life" after gaining "superhuman agility and strength" while living in captivity as a mysteriously imprisoned salaryman.[17] Seeking revenge for his incarceration as well as the death of his wife, Oh Dae-su [O Taesu] moves from one extreme to another. That word—"extreme"—is significant, insofar as *Oldboy* has been seen as one of the progenitors of the "Asian Extreme" cinema craze among Western fanboys and cinephiles, especially following the film's Grand Prix win at the 2004 Cannes Film Festival and the praise heaped upon it by the festival's Jury President, Quentin Tarantino. Since that time, "extreme cinema" has been used as an umbrella term referring to a variety of films characterized by exploitative or sensationalistic use of sex, violence, and horror/terror. The UK-based Tartan Films (now Palisades Tartan based in the United States) launched the popular "Asia Extreme" brand in 2002 and subsequently distributed numerous Asian horror films, thrillers, and erotica (including Park Chan-wook's celebrated "Vengeance Trilogy," Kim Jee-woon's *A Tale of Two Sisters* [*Changhwa, Hyongryŏn*, 2003], and Japanese auteur Miike Takashi's *Audition* [*Odishon*, 1999]) to British and American markets. Park's 2003 cult sensation *Oldboy* is certainly a part of that phenomenon, but its abduction and detention narrative makes it a much more profound statement about, or at least allegorical evocation of, the US War on Terror and the CIA's practice of extraordinary rendition.

Although the history of rendition (the extra-legal transfer of a detainee to the United States or a foreign government) dates back to 1886, its modern incarnation date can be traced to 1986, when Ronald Reagan authorized renditions to the United States of criminal suspects, but only from locations where the US government is unable to attain custody through normal extradition process. The Clinton administration also practiced renditions of terrorist suspects into the United States for criminal prosecution. After the September 11, 2001 terrorist attacks, the scope and number of renditions expanded significantly to include transfers to third countries for sole purposes of detention and interrogation (with prospects of torture). Within days of 9/11, the Bush administration granted authority to the CIA to conduct these "extraordinary" renditions without preapproval of the White House or the Justice Department.[18] Although the film is seemingly remote from that political context, we argue that *Oldboy*'s underlying themes gain transnational resonance in light of such events. Released in South Korea in the fall of 2003 (in the wake of news reports on prisoner abuses in Guantánamo prisons) and inclusive of an image of 9/11 attacks on the Twin Towers, *Oldboy* is a richly encoded transnational political allegory. As we will demonstrate in the chapter, Park Chan-wook draws an implicit parallel between human rights abuses during the harshest period of the Korean authoritarian past (1972–1987) and those in overseas CIA black sites and US military-operated prisons after 9/11.

In Chapter Eight, we address the latest trend in which ethnic diversity, diasporic consciousness, and new intraregional cultural flows reveal how heterogeneous South Korea has become in recent years. In the past few years, *tamunhwa* ("multi- or plural culture") has become a buzzword in Korean society. Contemporary statistics indicate that approximately 3.1% of the country's population are foreigners—data that does not take into consideration the hundreds of thousands of "illegal immigrants" who are frequently excluded not only from the government's statistical assessments but also from programs that promote (if not actually promise) basic civil and human rights. Despite their peripheralized status as economically deprived, undocumented workers living on the fringes of society and fighting against exploitative labor practices, such individuals have become the focus of several contemporary cultural productions that together comprise an emergent genre: that of *the multicultural film.* Recent Korean multiculturalism films made by liberal young filmmakers—particularly, Sim Sang-guk's *Where Is Ronny?* (*Roni rŭl ch'ajasŏ*, 2008) and Shin Dong-il (Sin Tong-il)'s *Bandhobi* (*Bandubi*, 2009), which will be analyzed in detail in the chapter—tackle such thorny issues as xenophobia, racial discrimination, illegal immigration, and migrant workers' rights. We argue that these films should be understood as "pedagogical films" that advocate inclusion and tolerance and aim to educate Korean audiences about an ethics of "unconditional hospitality," a concept coined by Jacques Derrida.

Finally, in the book's Conclusion we briefly discuss the effects of convergence culture and new technologies in disseminating Korean films and videos to non-Korean audiences in the United States and beyond. Along with Hulu and Netflix (where wide selections of subtitled Korean television shows and/or films are available for instant streaming), YouTube has become a major media exhibition venue where many of the otherwise inaccessible cultural productions originating from South Korea can be instantly accessed. Not coincidentally, that video-sharing platform was largely responsible for transforming Psy, a Korean pop singer, into an overnight global star in the second half of 2012. With over 900 million hits generated in the course of a five-month period, Psy's "Gangnam Style" became the most-watched viral video in the history of YouTube. Less well-known than this music video are the many cinematic classics from South Korea's Golden Age, which are now available on YouTube, including dozens of subtitled motion pictures that the government-subsidized Korean Film Archive has uploaded for purposes of promoting its national cinema. We will conclude our volume with departing thoughts about the impact that increased online distribution and media convergence has had on the present state and future developments of South Korean cinema as "spreadable" cultural products in global digital spaces.

Ultimately, this book is a call for *critical transnationalism*, using film genres as the appropriately mobile vehicles through which to move movie audiences beyond conventional readings of hybridized texts (bearing the imprint of Korean as well as non-Korean influences). Many of the core ideas that we present in this book—ideas related to migrations both literal and figurative—are meant to invite readers to speculate on the prospects of "post-purity cinema" in South Korea, a formally colonized nation once obsessed with racial, ethnic, and cultural homogeneity as a means of resisting (neo)colonial powers as well as the specter of difference that came with each new wave of immigrants looking for opportunities for professional growth and personal well-being. As its government continues to promote multiculturalism as an official policy and its cultural producers seek to expand their overseas markets for the Korean Wave, the cinema of South Korea might be expected to move beyond ethnocentrism and heteronormativity to embrace marginal identities (LGBT individuals, migrant workers, foreign brides, North Korean refugees, etc.) that once were excluded from the public sphere. Only time will tell if such prospects for progressive social and political change pan out.

Part I

From Classical Hollywood to the Korean Golden Age

Cinephilia, Modernization, and Postcolonial Genre Flows

Chapter 1

Toward a Strategic Korean Cinephilia

A Transnational *Détournement* of Hollywood Melodrama

A slight yet significant gesture: a man lights a cigarette with the graceful elegance and the casual demeanor of someone whose cool exterior belies a passionate, romantic streak. He hands another, unlit cigarette to a young woman standing opposite him. She brings it to her lips and leans seductively toward him. Face to face, the couple poses as if on the verge of a kiss. As they slowly draw nearer to each other, the ends of the two cigarettes touch, one lighting the other. By visualizing the convergence of two cultures—one ostensibly bound to tradition, the other representative of modernity—this blissful contact not only seals the pact of their newfound affection but also inscribes, at a deeper level, the complex cultural hybridization bound up in the symbolic image of the romantic couple.

Any American movie fan worth his or her salt will recognize this famous "nicotine kiss" between William Holden and Jennifer Jones as the most memorable scene in Henry King's sweeping East-meets-West melodrama *Love Is a Many-Splendored Thing* (1955), a film that taught would-be-lovers around the world a particularly Hollywood way of igniting both cigarettes and passions. Aficionados of South Korea's cinematic Golden Age, however, might recall a different scene upon hearing the previous description. In place of a picturesque Hong Kong beach, dramatically framed in CinemaScope and populated by a swimsuited twosome, a drab black-and-white apartment in poverty-stricken Seoul might flicker in their minds. This is one of the settings of director Yu Hyŏn-mok (Yu Hyun-mok)'s critically acclaimed *The Stray Bullet* (*Obalt'an*, 1961), a postwar classic that ingeniously rearticulates and recontextualizes the scene in *Love Is a Many-Splendored Thing* by situating its cigarette-lighting couple within a claustrophobic interior. The male hero is not the American correspondent played by Holden, a personification of the escalating US imperial presence in the British crown colony, but rather an unemployed, battle-scarred Korean War vet played by matinee idol Ch'oe Mu-ryong, emasculated by his lack of financial means to court and marry another woman, his movie star fiancée (Kim Hye-jŏng). His partner in this scene (Mun Hye-ran), unlike her Hollywood counterpart (the financially stable Eurasian medical doctor played by Jones), is a struggling part-time college student who earns her tuition by spending four hours a day in a smoky cellar as a factory worker. Counterpoised against Hollywood's star-crossed lovers who whisper sweet-nothings against a swelling musical score, the Korean couple confesses familial loss and destitution while mimetically enacting the romantic Holden-Jones pose accompanied by a soundtrack featuring little more than caged birds chirping offscreen.

Yu's film subtly critiques Hollywood's Orientalist geopolitical imaginary by decisively refusing its fantasy settings and romantic excess. Like French Situationist guru Guy Debord,[1] director Yu mobilizes the technique of *détournement*, whereby the tropes of dominant popular culture are appropriated, rerouted, and reconfigured so as to provoke a counterhegemonic disarticulation of meaning. The Korean *détournement* of the melodramatic scene cleverly registers the squalor and despair of postwar Seoul in which a young, handsome couple is literally caged inside slum walls while their Hollywood counterparts leisurely engage in touristic consumption in exotic Hong Kong and neighboring Macao. *The Stray Bullet* is a remarkably modernist text that not only hybridizes Korean and Euro-American signifiers (costumes, languages, and soundtracks) but also commingles and intermixes Hollywood melodramatic tropes and realist South Korean aesthetics. Golden Age South Korean melodrama diverges from its American equivalent of the Eisenhower era due to the former's focus on ordinary lower-middle and working-class citizens (*sŏmin* or *sosimin*) as opposed to the latter's gravitation toward upper-middle-class bourgeois housewives and widows.[2] In this respect, one could argue that South Korean film melodrama offers a more discursive range of spectatorial positions than that engendered by Hollywood's 1950s family melodrama, which, as Christine Gledhill points out, opens up a cross-class fantasy of identification for petite bourgeois or working-class audiences vis-à-vis screen surrogates basking in "lavish furnishings and consumer goods"[3] whose fetishistic potency represents America's postwar prosperity and abundance. In marked

FIGURES 1.1 AND 1.2. Cross-cultural *détournement*: The "nicotine kiss" scenes from *Love Is a Many-Splendored Thing* (above) and *The Stray Bullet* (below).

contrast, the South Korean society of the 1950s and the 1960s was torn apart by postwar poverty and chaos. Melodrama sided with underprivileged masses suffering social and familial alienation in the shadowy margins of modernization and economic development. Thus, in terms of its aesthetic characteristics and semantic ingredients, South Korean melodrama was seldom divested of its realistic, socially conscious core.

Although many commentators observe the influence of Italian Neorealism and German Expressionism in *The Stray Bullet*,[4] few scholars have pointed out the film's intertextual relationship with Hollywood melodrama. By linking South Korean Golden Age cinema (1955–1972) and Classical Hollywood melodrama within a comparative paradigm, this chapter addresses not only the cross-cultural translation and adaptation of particular scenes and star-images but also South Korean audiences' unique cinephilic fixation on over-looked Hollywood films. Korean audiences' infatuation and identification with Hollywood cinema should be historicized in the postwar cultural context rather than being simply frowned upon as a symptom of US cultural imperialism. The post-Korean War generation's intense nostalgia for sentimental Hollywood melodrama is a significant indicator of the cultural displacement that occurs when spectatorial desire for the "other" operates within a postcolonial setting. Before embarking upon specific comparative case studies, a brief examination of the otherwise discursive cultural forces intermingled within and responsible for the formation of South Korean melodrama will provide a historical backdrop against which to frame intertextual relations.

Origins of South Korean Melodrama: *Sinp'a*, *Han*, and Hollywood

In her book-length study of Korean melodrama, feminist film scholar Yu Chi-na identifies three origins of the genre that figured decisively in the context of an emergent national cinema.[5] The first source is the Japanese *sinp'a* (new school) drama introduced and localized during the colonial era (1910–1945). In the late-nineteenth-century Meiji period, the *sinp'a* drama arose in Japan as a popular alternative to the *kup'a* (old school) drama, kabuki.[6] Set in a modern milieu, it usually features a sentimental plot revolving around family tragedy and heterosexual romance. After Japan's annexation of Korea in 1910, the *sinp'a* drama strongly influenced Korean theater, film, and literature, injecting Japanese theatrical modes of storytelling into the syntactic core of Korean cultural productions. Famous silent *sinp'a* films include *Twin Jade Pavilion* (*Ssangongnu*, 1925), *Arirang* (1926), *Long Cherished Dream* (*Changhanmong*, 1926), and *Fallen Blossoms on a Stream* (*Nakhwayusu*, 1927). During the Golden Age of South Korean cinema in the 1950s and 1960s, the *sinp'a* drama became associated with female audiences, identified by such derogatory nicknames as "handkerchief army" (*sonsugŏn pudae*), "tear gas" (*ch'oerut'an*), and "rubber shoes" (*komusin*: trademarks of married, middle-aged women who migrated to the metropolis from rural areas).[7] The term *sinp'a* is still used by South Korean critics and audiences to derogatorily designate old-fashioned melodramas filled with unlikely coincidences and fortuitous reversals as well as excessive sentimentality.[8]

In addition, Yu and other scholars claim that Korean melodrama hinges upon the national sentiment of *han*, a slippery and subtle term that, depending on context, denotes everything from "resentment" and "lamentation" to "unfulfilled desire" and "resignation."[9] *Han* can be vaguely defined as the deep-rooted sadness, bitterness, and longing sparked by prolonged injustices and oppression. Various scholars have identified the sociopolitical sources of Korean *han* to include: a long history of foreign invasions by the Chinese, the Japanese, and the West; patriarchal Confucian traditions that have silenced and enslaved women for hundreds of years; the inhumane treatment and exploitation of the subaltern class under the feudal caste system as well as during the full-throttle modernization process; and the gross violations of civil rights by successive authoritarian military regimes in the postcolonial period.[10] Indeed, the recuperation of the abiding sense of *han* in South Korean melodrama seems to facilitate our appreciation of the indigenous and dormant forces behind a genre deeply influenced by colonial cultural import. However, overdependence on this elusive, psycho-phantasmic concept for the explication of generic categories intrinsic to a particular national cinema risks generating what can be labeled "critical nationalism." By "critical nationalism," we refer to the attitude of filmmakers, critics, and scholars alike who contend that *han* is uniquely Korean, a concept that almost, if not completely, escapes translatability in other cultural lexicons. Im Kwon-taek (Im Kwŏn-t'aek)—a household name in South Korea and a director whose oeuvre brims with *han*-centric films that aestheticize Korean history, tradition, and culture in melodramatic modes—concisely sums up this position: "*Han* is not a concept that Koreans can agree on. I can't even count the number of books that have been written about *han*. . . . However, *han* is a specific emotion that has profound links to the history of the Korean people, and as such, might be a difficult concept for non-Koreans to grasp fully."[11] The critical overemphasis on such an ambiguous concept as definite marker of Korean-ness contributes to the erection of "imagined [emotional] communities" of the nation and its culture.

From the point of view of genre studies, *han* can be better understood as a historically and culturally specific mobilization of what Peter Brooks defines as the "melodramatic imagination" or "melodramatic mode."[12] *Han* indeed connotes melodramatic affect and sensibility in the Korean context. However, what is unique about Korean *han* is its *context* rather than *affect* in and of itself. The overlooked transnational valency of the concept becomes salient once we examine the etymological roots of this monosyllabic Sino-Korean character. According to a Chinese-English dictionary, "*han* is *hen* ('hate') in Chinese, *kon* ('to bear a grudge') in Japanese, *horosul* ('sorrowfulness') in Mongolian, *korsocuka* ('hatred,' 'grief') in Manchurian, and *hân* ('frustration') in Vietnamese."[13] Although similar concepts exist throughout East and Southeast Asia, only *han* has emerged as a privileged marker of national culture and identity.

Instead of essentializing the uniqueness of Korean melodrama on the grounds of the ontologically uncertain *han*, it is useful to examine how similar concepts function in other national cinemas and how they converge with and diverge from it. For example, in exploring the transnational circulation of filmic *han* as it cross-pollinates into neighboring cultural arenas, attention could be directed to the historical epics and melodramas of Zhang Yimou, Chen Kaige, and other Chinese Fifth Generation filmmakers who anchor their stories in the imagery of suffering female bodies. Is the *han* expressed by the Korean surrogate child bearers in Im Kwon-taek's *Surrogate Mother* (*Ssibaji*, 1986) fundamentally different from the pain and suffering of the Chinese concubines in Zhang Yimou's equally exoto-ethnographic melodrama *Raise the Red Lantern* (*Dà hóng dēnglóng gāogāo guà*, 1991)? Or does the difference lie in the cultural and historical crevice separating these two nations?

One can similarly cast doubt on the concept of *mono no aware* as being distinctively Japanese. Defined by Donald Richie as "sympathetic sadness . . . a serene acceptance of a transient world" and by David Bordwell as "the pathos of things,"[14] *mono no aware* is an underlying emotional chord struck in the meditative family melodramas of Ozu Yasujirō and other Japanese auteurs sensitive to quotidian poetics. It is tempting to argue that *mono no aware* is what distinguishes tranquil Japanese melodramas from their more emotionally intense South Korean counterparts. However, many Japanese audiences appear to have experienced *mono no aware* when they saw Hur Jin-ho (Hŏ Chin-ho)'s *Christmas in August* (*8wŏl ŭi K'ŭrisŭmasŭ*, 1998), a critically lauded pan-Asian success already canonized as a representative South Korean melodrama. According to film critic Deruoka Sojo, many Japanese who compared this film to Ozu's work were surprised to discover that Korean sentiments were, after all, very similar to their own.[15] This dispels prejudiced perceptions about South Korean cinema as alienating and defamiliarizing due to its imagined exoticism and emotive primitivism. The cult status of *Christmas in August* in Japan is such that the film was remade into a Japanese version directed by Nagasaki Shun'ichi in 2005. As evidenced by the Japanese reception of *Christmas in August, mono no aware* as well as *han* can be unraveled as a discursively radiating transnational experience rather than as a uniquely indigenous manifestation of a given culture's resignation to or transcendence of sorrow. Granting that *han* and *mono no aware* have different origins, histories, and connotations, both concepts have been similarly mobilized by critics as the aesthetic purveyors of national identity. If it is true that South Koreans can sense *han* in Zhang Yimou's melodramas and the Japanese can feel *mono no aware* in *Christmas in August*, both concepts need to be reexamined from a critical perspective more attuned to the cross-cultural implications of not one but many melodramatic imaginations.

While many Korean film scholars have emphasized *sinp'a* and *han* as two foundational determinants of South Korean melodrama,[16] the third influence, Hollywood melodrama, remains notably understudied. The unabated influx of American films since the US military occupation (1945–1948) and the Korean War (1950–1953) significantly affected the genre formations of the embryonic South Korean industry. Golden Age melodramas of the 1950s and 1960s register palimpsestic traces of Hollywood's tropes and iconography, which undergo a process of cross-cultural translation or, as Stuart Hall defines it, a "continuous process of re-articulation and recontextualization, without any notion of a primary origin."[17] These visual and aural motifs and semantic elements are recycled and recast in specifically South Korean contexts. South Korean melodrama furthermore complicates American melodrama's entrenched country/city binary as well as its nostalgia for a preindustrial past, both of which, as Gledhill asserts, replaced the class oppositions permeating European melodrama and created the myth of American egalitarianism.[18] Rather than vilifying the city like in early American melodramas (especially those directed by D. W. Griffith), South Korean melodramas represent Seoul as bearing the imprint of modernization—as a polyphonic center that mediates confrontations, conflicts, and compromises among rivaling values and camps: European, American, Japanese, and Korean; tradition and modernity; the ruling class and the working class; male and female; the urban and the rural. Perennial favorite *The Stray Bullet*, for example, does more than simply evoke or copy Hollywood melodramas, specifically Mervyn LeRoy's *Waterloo Bridge* (1940) and the aforementioned *Love Is a Many-Splendored Thing*. Its translation and *détournement* of Hollywood melodramatic scenes lay bare the artificial constructs and ideological spuriousness of larger-than-life romantic trappings that often obscure the disparity of power among various nations, races, genders, and classes.

Waterloo Bridge and Postwar Korean Cinephilia

While relatively obscure in the United States, *Waterloo Bridge* is among South Korean audiences' favorite Classical Hollywood films. According to the Korean Broadcasting System (KBS)'s nationwide survey of "100 Films That Audiences Want to See Again" (conducted in 1996), the ten most requested films were, in order of preference: *Roman Holiday* (1952), *Gone With the Wind* (1939), *Romeo and Juliet* (1968), *The Sound of Music* (1965), *Breakfast at Tiffany's* (1961), *Ben-Hur* (1959), *Waterloo Bridge, Doctor Zhivago* (1965), *The King and I* (1956), and *Casablanca* (1942).[19] The popularity of these films remained strong across generations, from parents who saw them in theaters during the 1950s and 1960s to their children who encountered them through television reruns dubbed in Korean. Considering that 6,523 out of 11,064 participants responded by means of local computer networks (such as Chollian [*Ch'ŏllian*] and Hitel [*Hait'el*]) rather than conventional postcards, it can be inferred that the voice of the younger generation was considerably amplified in the survey. In fact, among the top fifty were a number of 1980s and 1990s films including *Dead Poets Society* (1989, No. 14), *The Shawshank Redemption* (1994,

No. 19), *The Mission* (1986, No. 22), *The Terminator* (1984, No. 24), *Forrest Gump* (1994, No. 25), *The Last Emperor* (1987, No. 26), *Once Upon a Time in America* (1984, No. 29), *Amadeus* (1984, No. 31), *Out of Africa* (1985, No. 32), *A River Runs through It* (1992, No. 37), *Ghost* (1990, No. 38), *Rain Man* (1988, No. 39), *Schindler's List* (1993, No. 40), *Top Gun* (1986, No. 41), *Back to the Future* (1985, No. 44), *Raiders of the Lost Ark* (1981, No. 45), *Braveheart* (1995, No. 47), and *Scent of a Woman* (1992, No. 48). However, the fact that the top ten list consists primarily of Classical Hollywood films clearly attests to South Korean audiences' general preference of what they call "unforgettable classics" over contemporary Hollywood blockbusters. Although *Love Is a Many-Splendored Thing* ranks relatively low on this list (No. 84), its status would likely have been much higher if more fans from the older generation had participated in the survey.

Regrettably (and tellingly), only one South Korean film, Im Kwon-taek's *Sopyonje* (*Sŏp'yŏnje*, 1993), broke into the list, coming in at No. 74. This is not surprising. Attracting record-breaking audiences at the time of its theatrical release, *Sopyonje* became a cultural phenomenon in its country of origin, reviving the popularity of the waning indigenous operatic storytelling art form *p'ansori*.[20] Despite the fact that the survey was conducted before the arrival of South Korean cinema's fin-de-siècle renaissance initiated by a series of box-office hits such as *Contact* (*Chŏpsok*, 1997), *Whispering Corridors* (*Yŏgo koedam*, 1998), *Shiri* (*Swiri*, 1999), *Attack the Gas Station* (*Chuyuso sŭpkyŏk sagŏn*, 1999), *Joint Security Area* (*Kongdong kyŏngbiguyŏk*, 2000), *Friend* (*Ch'in'gu*, 2001), and *My Sassy Girl* (*Yŏpgijŏkin kŭnyŏ*, 2001), it is both curious and disturbing that not a single Golden Age South Korean film appears on a list dominated by Classical and post-Classical Hollywood cinema.

The distinctive characteristics of South Korean cinephilia should be analyzed and contextualized before such preferences are dismissed as the by-product of US cultural imperialism in general and of Hollywood hegemony in particular. For many post-Korean War theatergoers, whose mania for "Dream Factory" products and whose celebration and recognition of the "genius of the system" rivaled that of contemporaneous *Cahiers du Cinéma* critics in Paris, American films offered much more than an entertaining night out with friends and family. With few exceptions, Old Hollywood films, packed with glossy images and blessed with wholesome, innocent characters and story lines, represented the hopes and dreams of poverty-stricken masses in the underdeveloped country. Like the poor Sicilian child Toto (Salvatore Cascio) and his undereducated projectionist friend Alfredo (Philippe Noiret) in *Cinema Paradiso* (1988)—the highest ranked Italian film (No. 11) on the KBS list—cinephilic Koreans managed to endure postwar poverty and hardship in the therapeutic glow of the movie screen. From a political standpoint, it is indeed problematic that audiences were passively sutured into a cross-racial set of identificatory gazes and were often oblivious to the ideological transparency normalizing the implicit white, male subject position. However, the enormous spectatorial pleasures and comfort provided by Classical Hollywood films, as well as the emergence of a cinephilic competency and potential to engage the act of cross-cultural *détournement*, should be recuperated as a critical intervention in the cultural history and memory of the 1950s and 1960s.

In renowned South Korean journalist-writer Ahn Junghyo (An Chŏnghyo)'s novel, *The Life and Death of the Hollywood Kid* (*Hŏlliudŭ k'idŭ ŭi saengae*, 1992),[21] the narrator dreamily reminisces about the period's obsessive theatergoing:

> We chased dreams and escaped the sorrows of our ugly lives through the films. We sought outlets for our anger and longing for happiness at the cinema. Although we missed the early silent era when such screen legends as Greta Garbo, Rudolph Valentino, and the Barrymores reigned, we still had many names to evoke our fantasies: Rudolph Maté, Henry King, Henry Hathaway, Cecil B. DeMille, Frank Capra, George Cukor, Michael Curtiz, Delmer Daves, Edward Dmytryk, Fred Zinnemann, Howard Hawks, Fritz Lang, Jean Negulesco, Mervyn LeRoy, Lewis Milestone, Mark Robson, George Seaton, George Stevens, King Vidor, Raoul Walsh, Robert Wise.... Upon my first encounter with the world of cinema, I was, like a drug addict, unable to resist the magical power of the screen.... For us, going to the movies was a religious act, like going to Mass.[22]

Although the star-struck, auteurist narrator is retrospectively critical of his and his friends' (a group of schoolboys who proudly proclaim themselves the "Magnificent Seven") blind fascination with Classical Hollywood films, which caused them to "misrecognize white faces as [their] own faces" and "misconstrue Indians as [their] enemies and genocidal American and English troops as [their] allies,"[23] the novel unmistakably evinces nostalgia for a bygone era. It was a time when South Korean audiences had access to thousands of North American and European classics, many of them now available only as faded images flitting about in failing memories due to the limited South Korean video and DVD markets. Although South Koreans were so engrossed by Occidental cultural productions that they deemed indigenous films inferior to their Western counterparts, the reception of Hollywood products remained emphatically Korean in terms of canon formation and cross-cultural hermeneutics.

Historically, Koreans have often gravitated toward sad stories centering around star-crossed lovers separated by war, death, or social prejudice—melancholic films, in other words, that demand a certain willingness to withhold ironic judgment in the face of providential coincidences and emotional excess.

Except for *The Sound of Music*, all of the films in the aforementioned top ten list depart from Hollywood's conventional happy endings. Tragic romances—unconsummated due to the intervention of social upheaval, familial opposition, or cruel fate—form the narrative trajectory of many of these films. Although Ahn Junghyo's narrator unfurls an impressive list of favorite directors, South Korean audiences generally flock to star vehicles in lieu of auteur films. Remarkably, yet tellingly, not a single Hitchcock, Ford, or Welles film broke into the KBS 100 list, whereas four romantic comedies starring Audrey Hepburn (*Roman Holiday* [No. 1], *Breakfast at Tiffany's* [No. 6], *Sabrina* [No. 16], and *My Fair Lady* [No. 33]) were included in the top fifty. It is noteworthy that the quoted passage from *The Life and Death of the Hollywood Kid* lists Henry King and Mervyn LeRoy, who directed *Love Is a Many-Splendored Thing* and *Waterloo Bridge* respectively, without a trace of such legends as Douglas Sirk and Nicholas Ray, film melodrama's preeminent auteurs whose combined work is crucial to the academic legitimization and canonization of the genre. Mervyn LeRoy's MGM melodramas and literary adaptations, including *Waterloo Bridge, Random Harvest* (1942), *Madame Curie* (1943), *Little Women* (1949), and *Quo Vadis* (1951), are considered classics by South Korean audiences, while his critically acclaimed Warner Bros. gangster and social problem films such as *Little Caesar* (1931) and *I Am a Fugitive from a Chain Gang* (1932) remain virtually unknown. *Screen* (*Sk'ŭrin*), a leading South Korean movie magazine, described Mervyn LeRoy as "The Father of Melodrama Who Made *Waterloo Bridge*" and referred to the film as one of the five best melodramas ever made,[24] an audacious statement in light of the Western canon's preference for such films as *Stella Dallas* (1937), *Letter from an Unknown Woman* (1948), *Rebel Without a Cause* (1955), and *Imitation of Life* (1959).

Indeed, *Waterloo Bridge* and *Love Is a Many-Splendored Thing* are the archetypal sentimental melodramas popular among South Korean audiences. The older generation of theatergoers who saw these films upon their original release during or not long after the Korean War could easily identify with the tragic stories of two lovers who suffer the separation and loss caused or exacerbated by wars.[25] During the three-year civil conflict, 3 million Koreans were killed, wounded, or missing. Another 10 million people endured familial breakups.[26] This transpired only a decade after the Japanese colonial government mobilized millions of Koreans for labor, military service, and sexual slavery to expedite their war efforts across Asia and the Pacific Islands, dividing countless families and lovers.[27] South Korean audiences wept for Vivien Leigh's Myra, a ballet dancer-turned-streetwalker in *Waterloo Bridge*, just as they shed tears for Jennifer Jones's Han Suyin, a Hong Kong Eurasian doctor who loses her American lover during the Korean War in *Love Is a Many-Splendored Thing*. These unfortunate heroines whose ill-fated lives were ravaged by war, functioned—in the collective spectatorial consciousness—as surrogates for millions of Korean daughters, mothers, and sisters who either lost their fathers, husbands, and sons during World War II and the Korean War or became sex slaves ("comfort women") for the Japanese Imperial Army and prostitutes for American GIs.

The theme of military prostitution, a shadow looming over Korean femininity, plays a pivotal role in *Waterloo Bridge*. Robert E. Sherwood's eponymous play was adapted into three very different studio films over a twenty-five-year period. Director James Whale's pre-Code Universal version (1931) is most faithful to the original story and stars Mae Clark as the heroine. Two MGM remakes followed: Mervyn LeRoy's 1940 film, held dear by South Koreans, and director Curtis Bernhardt's *Gaby* (1956), unanimously panned as the worst of the three despite the endearing, pixie-like presence of Leslie Caron and a revised happy ending. Sherwood's original play is regarded by literary critics as "melodramatic, and . . . as sentimental as the author warns in his preface it is going to be . . . the sophomore's story of the Fallen Woman and the Nice Young Man . . . [which] can in no sense establish a claim to literary distinction."[28] The play's setting is World War I. Myra is an expatriate American chorus girl who is stranded in London and enduring German air raids. After befriending Kitty, a cockney British prostitute, Myra—penniless and desperate—descends into a life of soliciting sexual bargains from GIs on furlough. The chorine-turned-prostitute soon falls in love with an innocent compatriot soldier enlisted in a Canadian regiment, Roy Cronin, who offers tender affection to Myra, mistaking her as a decent girl. Roy is even willing to desert the military to stay with his loved one. Myra persuades him to return to his duties as a soldier, assuring him that she will wait steadfastly for him. After parting with her lover on Waterloo Bridge, where the two first met, Myra, unable to escape her shameful past, invites death by making herself a visible target for German bombers.

Whale's and LeRoy's cinematic adaptations of Sherwood's anti-war play fit conventionally into the category of what Lea Jacobs calls the "fallen woman film . . . the genre [that] is not popular with present-day audiences . . . [but] was a staple of Hollywood melodrama"[29] from the 1920s to the 1940s. Due to its focus on illicit sexuality, the fallen woman genre was subjected to careful scrutiny by the industry and was prone to censorship, which became more systematic after the 1934 installation of the Production Code Administration (PCA) headed by Joseph I. Breen to enforce the Motion Picture Production Code of 1930. Warner Bros., a socially conscious studio known for its founders' pro-Roosevelt political affiliation and sensitivity to working-class interests, first attempted to remake Whale's *Waterloo Bridge*. The PCA discouraged the studio by stating, "We regret to inform you that it is our opinion that this story, as treated in the play, is definitely objectionable from the point of view of the Production Code. . . . The story is objectionable on the ground that it glorifies a prostitute, shows details of prostitution, sympathy is created for acts of prostitution, and the sin itself is not shown to be wrong."[30] When David O. Selznick knocked on the door of the PCA again with the same material in tow, Breen this time forwarded the producer a cable from the British Board of Film Censors that expressed their disapproval of the earlier version: "Film *Waterloo Bridge* submitted for censorship September 1931 considered prohibitive heroine being a prostitute. Film drastically amended to eliminate this characteristic and was passed. Board considers reissue most undesirable."[31]

Once MGM began toying with the project and finally submitted their early draft to Breen's office, the PCA still found the script objectionable on three counts: the details of prostitution; the condoning of prostitution by Roy's mother; and the inclusion of air raids over London, a taboo topic for the British censors. LeRoy and his screenwriters gave the original material a thorough "cleansing" to conform to the PCA's standards and regulations. The details of Myra's descent into prostitution were curtailed and no direct mention of her occupation was made; the dialogue in which Roy's mother condones Myra's past was eliminated; and Myra's death scene was rewritten so that the heroine commits suicide by throwing herself in the path of speeding army trucks rather than being bombed. One of the notable differences between Whale's and LeRoy's versions is the pre-fall status of Myra. As Cam Tolton comments, "Mae Clark's Myra [in the 1931 version] was a cheap chorine packaged much as she was in The *Public Enemy* with James Cagney in the same year. A far cry from the exquisite ballet-hopeful that Myra would become when played by Vivien Leigh. When LeRoy upgraded Myra's cultural status, he upgraded the whole production with her."[32]

Just as Vivien Leigh's Myra is a much more polished, respectable variation of Mae Clark's, Robert Taylor's Roy likewise rose from a humble Canadian soldier to a Scottish aristocrat officer. Leigh's character changed from an American-born chorus girl to an English schoolmaster's daughter who works as a ballet dancer under the stern disciplinary watch of Madame Kirowa (Maria Ouspenskaya). Vivien Leigh's Myra turns to prostitution only after she is unjustly fired, is mistakenly informed of her fiancé Roy's death, and learns that, after months of sickness, her best friend Kitty (Virginia Field) has been supporting her with money earned from streetwalking. As Mary Ann Doane points out, the "situation is an impossible one"[33] because prostitution is unspeakable and unrepresentable in Classical Hollywood cinema. For example, Myra manages to make Roy's mother (Lucile Watson) understand her past by answering "You are naive" to the future mother-in-law's question, "Has there been someone else?" Belatedly discovering Myra's secret after her disappearance and suicide, Roy relieves Kitty of the burden of speaking the unutterable word by saying, "I understand—you don't have to say it."

The American censorship of *Waterloo Bridge* contrasts sharply with South Korean censorship of *The Stray Bullet.* While American motion picture censorship, with its principal of self-regulation that precluded the need for federal restrictions, focused on issues of sexual and religious morality so as to prevent local censorship and church boycotts, Korean films have constantly been subjected to stringent state regulations, whether the colonial government's suppression of anti-colonial, nationalistic films or South Korea's authoritarian, military regimes' (1961–1987) severe censoring of politically subversive subjects. In *The Stray Bullet*, prostitution is unambiguously foregrounded in the narrative and is explicitly named by characters. For the Park Chung Hee (Pak Chŏng-hŭi) regime, which came into power through the May 16, 1961 coup d'état during the original release of *The Stray Bullet*, the threat posed by the film stemmed not from its representation of military prostitution but from its realist critique of social illness and corruption. The anti-communist government banned the film, suspecting a pro-North subtext couched in recurring scenes where the North Korean refugee family's demented matriarch (No Chae-sin) yells, "Let's get out of here!"[34] The ban was not lifted until 1963, when the film was rereleased. Unlike in Classical Hollywood film, prostitution and adultery emerged as normative subject matter in South Korean cinema, culminating in the "hostess genre" cycle of the 1970s,[35] under the acquiescence of dictatorial regimes encouraging sexual subjects to divert the public's attention from political oppression. If the story of *Waterloo Bridge* seems deviant by Hollywood's sometimes-puritanical standards, it is completely normal and familiar to South Koreans accustomed to realistic portrayals of illegitimate sexual relations.

Interestingly, at the time of its original release, *Waterloo Bridge* was not deemed an "impossible text," as contemporary cine-feminists might be predisposed to label it. The film was instead promoted and reviewed as a typical Hollywood romance with top stars. Much publicity has been generated from the fact that this was Vivien Leigh's first starring role after her Academy Award-winning portrayal of Scarlett O'Hara, a compelling performance in *Gone with the Wind* (1939) that turned a little-known British actress into a big-name marquee attraction. The studio also milked what was being touted as the "happiest reunion in Hollywood"—that between Leigh and Taylor, who first costarred in MGM's *A Yank at Oxford* (1938), one of the studio's many productions shot in England. The film additionally marked LeRoy's anticipated return to the director's chair after overseeing the production of *The Wizard of Oz* (1939) and other big-budget MGM projects of the late 1930s.

Although *Waterloo Bridge* is now nearly forgotten or ignored by critics and the public alike in the United States, the film received glowing reviews upon its release. Commentators, for the most part, described the film as a fine love story or a woman's picture, calling it "a persuasive and compelling romantic tragedy that will sweep through for smash grosses . . . adult entertainment, particularly aimed at femme customers" (*Weekly Variety*, May 11, 1940), "a sure-fire woman's picture headed for important coin" (*Weekly Variety*, May 11, 1940), "a beautiful, tender love story that should have special appeal for femme fans" (*Film Daily*, May 16, 1940), and a picture with "deep appeal for women patrons, as evidenced by the extensive use of handkerchiefs at the preview" (*The Hollywood Reporter*, May 11, 1940).[36] Considering this observation of the film's appeal to female audiences, it is peculiar that *Waterloo Bridge* continues to fall by the wayside whenever the feminist film canon is revamped or reformulated. One interesting aspect of the film's American reception is that it did much better at the box office when rereleased in 1944 than it did on its original release in 1940. On October 4 of that year, the *New York Times* reported "astonishment over at MGM these days [concerning] the success being enjoyed by the current reissue of the 4-year-old *Waterloo Bridge*." As the newspaper elaborates, "In thirteen out of the fourteen cities it has played so far, managers of Loew's Theaters have reported grosses ranging from 24 percent to 179 percent above business done by the film when it was brand new."[37]

Even though many reviewers commented on the film's "timeliness" upon its original release in the wake of Great Britain's entrance into World War II (the historical frame of the film encapsulating Roy Cronin's flashback), the United States of 1940 was only a precariously situated yet distant observer of conflicts brewing in the European political arena. By the time the picture was rereleased four years later, its story was no longer foreign or abstract. No doubt, after the Japanese attack on Pearl Harbor in 1941, American audiences could better appreciate the immediacy of a narrative depicting the tragic effects of the war on the lives of sympathetic young men and women. The same was true for South Korean audiences who encountered the film for the first time during the Korean War. Myra—a respectable ballerina who sinks into prostitution for GIs when her fiancé is mistakenly reported dead—is an all-too-familiar figure in the minds of South Koreans: she is the image of the *yanggongju*. As Hyun Sook Kim succinctly defines her: "Historically, the term 'Yanggongju' has referred to Korean women who engage in sexual labor for foreign soldiers. . . . Used derogatorily, it means 'Yankee whore,' 'Yankee wife,' 'UN lady,' and/or 'Western princess.' This epithet, 'Yanggongju,' relegates Korean women working in militarized prostitution with foreign men to the lowest status within the hierarchy of prostitution."[38]

Following the Korean War, US troops became permanently installed in South Korea so as to protect the host country from communist threat from the North. Accordingly, over 1 million Korean women have served as "entertainment hostesses" to accommodate the sexual needs of American military officers and soldiers—VIPs of the South Korean government.[39] Although Vivien Leigh's Myra is not a prostitute for foreign soldiers of different racial backgrounds, her suggestive smile at uniformed GIs carries an unsettling resemblance to that of South Korea's cinematic *yanggongjus*, from the evening gown-clad seductress Sonya (Ch'oe Ŭn-hŭi) in *Hell Flower* (*Chiokhwa*, 1958) to the peasant widow-turned-"UN Lady" Ŏl-lye (Yi Hye-suk) in *Silver Stallion* (*Ŭnma nŭn oji annŭnda*, 1991). Raven-haired, brown-eyed Myra even physically approximates the ubiquitously inscribed filmic *yanggongju* image.

Throughout the cinematic Golden Age, *yanggongjus* were portrayed either as temptresses equivalent to the dangerous, powerful, and sexually promiscuous femme fatales of American film noir or as tragic fallen women forced to sell their bodies due to postwar poverty and familial duties. For *Hell Flower*, director Shin Sang-ok (Sin Sang-ok) cast his wife, Ch'oe Ŭn-hŭi (a Golden Age actress who is best remembered as the chaste widow in *The Houseguest and My Mother* [*Sarangbang sonnim kwa ŏmŏni*, 1961]), against type. In the film, Ch'oe plays an egoistic, decadent *yanggongju*, a bad "spider woman" who lures male characters into her web of deceit and is ultimately punished for her transgression by an avenging husband who kills her. In *The Stray Bullet*, Myŏng-suk (Sŏ Ae-ja), the decent-minded daughter of an impoverished North Korean refugee family, slides into the life of a *yanggongju* when rejected by her disabled Korean War vet fiancé for whom a marriage is too heavy a burden. When her brother Ch'ŏr-ho's wife (Mun Chŏng-suk) gives birth, it is Myŏng-suk's savings earned from military prostitution that pay for the hospital fee, despite the fact that Ch'ŏr-ho (Kim Chin-gyu), in an earlier scene, turned his face in shame when he spotted his sister with an American GI. Myŏng-suk is emblematic of the tens of thousands of postwar Korean women who were forced into military prostitution out of economic urgency.

The pro-democratic, anti-authoritarian, anti-American labor union and student demonstrations that comprised the *minjung* movement of the 1980s and early 1990s instigated a new perception of and interest in *yanggongjus*. Having been long neglected and despised as the lowest of the low, these women emerged as the victimized "sisters and daughters" of the nation enslaved by American imperialists, so long as their legacy was couched within the rhetoric of nationalist activism and political dissidence urging the withdrawal of the US military and the reunification of the Korean peninsula. One case in particular—the brutal rape and murder of a bar woman, Yun Kŭm-i, by Private Kenneth Markle (who stuffed two beer bottles into Yun's womb, a cola bottle into her uterus, and an umbrella into her anus after killing her) in 1992—sparked nationwide rage and stoked protests against the US military. As a convenient corporeal metaphor for the oppressed nation and the disfranchised classes, the *yanggongju* conspicuously haunted the margins of the New Korean cinema throughout the 1980s and 1990s (from *In the Heat of the Night* [*Pam ŭi yŏlgi sok ŭro*, 1985] to *Spring In My Hometown* [*Arŭmdaun sijŏl*, 1998]), a period dominated by intellectual New Wave male directors emerging from the leftist student movement, such as Jang Sun-woo (Chang Sŏn-u), Park Kwang-su (Pak Kwang-su), and Chung Ji-young (Chŏng Chi-yŏng).

The Hollywood "Scene of Misrecognition" vs. the Korean "Scene of Recognition"

Returning once again to the question of intertextuality linking *The Stray Bullet* and *Waterloo Bridge*, we would like to draw attention to two contrasting, yet parallel scenes—one from each film—in which the same event of the fallen woman's accidental encounter with her lover at a place of prostitution is repeated in radically different configurations. Built upon dissimilar gaze structures and moving toward different narrative outcomes, these scenes provide a mutually enriching case study through which to unmask the ideological mechanisms undergirding the construction of a transnational imaginary. In the former, Myra makes her usual trip to Waterloo Station to solicit a customer. She enters the station, sending inviting glances and smiles toward a crowd of arriving solders. When she greets one, saying "Welcome home," the soldier condescendingly responds "Thanks, ducky," and exits. The camera dollies in to a close-up of Myra's face overwhelmed by shame and pathos. Looking blankly into the camera, her sad, trance-like visage suddenly beams with a combination of shock and joy. The following shot cuts to several soldiers walking toward the camera along the platform, a stampeding crowd from which Roy emerges. The point-of-view immediately shifts to Roy, who spots Myra and rushes toward her, frantically calling her name. With climactic orchestral accompaniment, the lovers reunite in each other's arms, gazing at each other adoringly in tightly framed shot-reverse-shots. The officer's excitement and euphoria overflows into a torrent of words in contrast to a speechless Myra who can barely utter, "Roy, you're alive." The miraculously returned fiancé seems unaware of any change in Myra's appearance and status despite her tawdry dress and tell-tale makeup as well as her feeble excuse that she has come to the station to meet "no one in particular."

There are two moments when Roy makes a deliberate effort to *look* at Myra, to subtly fix his gaze on a woman who no longer conforms to the ideal image of virginal heroine. The first moment occurs when he tells her that he cannot believe what has happened: "Darling, let me look at you. I'm not dreaming, am I?" The second instance takes place in the following scene set in a teashop, where they sit and talk. "Let me have a squint at you," Roy says, as he inspects Myra up and down after she improvises the meager excuse that she cannot accompany him to his family mansion in Scotland because she looks unfit and has no decent wardrobe. Although Roy reluctantly agrees with her, stating, "Now I look at you, there is something in what you say," he misreads her dress code as a sign of destitution rather than prostitution. In both cases, Roy's scrutinizing gaze fails, for he does not see what the spectator sees. Oblivious to Myra's dilemma and internalized agony, Roy takes charge and dominates the scene, pouring tea for the sobbing woman, telling her that she will quit her job and marry him, calling his mother to inform her of their impending arrival, and suggesting a trip to the clothing store. Once again, Roy misunderstands when Myra musters courage to say that she cannot go with him. He asks if she has someone else, a suspicion Myra adamantly denies, assuring him, "I loved you. I never loved anyone else. I never shall"—a statement which will resurface during middle-aged Roy's oral flashback in the film's last scene. Roy's momentary doubt evaporates and his ego remains intact due to Myra's oath of platonic devotion, which the unknowing fiancé self-servingly misrecognizes as sexual fidelity.

In the corresponding scene of *The Stray Bullet*, Myŏng-suk, dressed in Western attire, is shown in a deep-focus shot standing alone with her head hung low as she sets up "shop" on a street corner where nightly transactions between Korean women and American GIs take place. The background shows the traditionally coded gate of the Chosŏn Hotel, which displays a bilingual sign. Into the middle distance streams a group of men and women. The "new face" is noticed by a GI who addresses Myŏng-suk in English, fishing for her name. The flirtation between the two is juxtaposed with a long shot of Myŏng-suk's disabled ex-fiancé, Kyŏng-sik (Yun Il-bong), limping toward the scene from afar. Laughing mischievously, Myŏng-suk runs away from the GI who claims her for the evening. The scurrying woman and her Korean lover with crutches bump into each other and fall to the ground. Recognizing Myŏng-suk, Kyŏng-sik flashes a smile, in a rare close-up shot, which quickly turns south into a frown against a grim musical cue. Myŏng-suk's reaction shot is suppressed. The camera stays with Kyŏng-sik's point-of-view as he watches her flee the scene with the American GI chasing after her. The wounded veteran immediately comprehends the gravity of his lover's situation as he stands alone, looking in the direction where Myŏng-suk has disappeared. His horrific recognition is visually accentuated as a *yanggongju*-GI couple emerges from the left side of the frame and crosses the foreground. Picking up his crutches, Kyŏng-sik despondently starts limping away. A bilingual traffic sign is clearly visible in the background, indicating the Korean man's displacement in a space reserved for American masculinity. Kyŏng-sik eventually sinks into a nearby bench, sobbing uncontrollably. The scene of his breakdown is intercut with a shot of an escaped Myŏng-suk, guilty but relieved, leaning against a tree.

These two scenes are symptomatic of the aesthetic and ideological ruptures separating a Classical Hollywood text and a Golden Age South Korean text. In *Waterloo Bridge*, the use of close-ups and shot-reverse-shots are pronounced. As the station scene progresses, shots get tighter and tighter until Myra and Roy look into each other's eyes in a self-contained and flattened romantic

FIGURE 1.3. Roy misrecognizes Myra in a close-up from *Waterloo Bridge*.

space winnowed from its external setting. Background passers-by, though occasionally visible in frame, are conveniently out of focus so that the spectator's attention stays fixed on the main couple. The scene in *The Stray Bullet*, by contrast, extends and maximizes focal depth and suppresses close-ups in favor of long shots so as to accentuate the surroundings in which the characters are situated. As André Bazin argues, the use of deep-focus cinematography "brings the spectator into a relation with the image closer to that which he enjoys with reality" and invites a "more active mental attitude on the part of the spectator."[40] The Korean scene not only reworks a transnational melodramatic trope across more realistic deep-focus shots, which effectively stage simultaneous actions from foreground to background, but also complicates the Hollywood gaze structure. Yet more than reflecting the realist style of the South Korean film, this contrast suggests a greater emphasis on the larger social context of the latter film. *Waterloo Bridge*'s close-ups emphasize the personal psychological crisis of its female character, whereas *The Stray Bullet*'s long shots suggest that the lovers' problem is societal, not merely individual.

The "scene of misrecognition" in *Waterloo Bridge* involves three looking positions: Myra, Roy, and the spectator. Myra initially functions as the subject of the gaze when she accidentally spots Roy after being rejected by a potential customer. Her eyes look vacant in a way that recalls an earlier scene when she peered through a misty and steam-covered window to see Roy who was

FIGURE 1.4. Kyŏng-sik recognizes Myŏng-suk as *yanggongju* in a deep-focus shot in *The Stray Bullet.*

supposed to have left for the front. Because her vision is fuzzy, unstable, and shaky, it reveals the underlying anxiety of looking. This anxiety grows from a psychological split, the gap that emerges when the female subject usurps the privileged position of the "bearer of the look," which, according to feminist film critic Laura Mulvey, belongs to the active male protagonist in mainstream narrative cinema.[41]

When the camera cuts to what she sees, Roy enters the frame and takes control of the gaze. Roy, however, misrecognizes Myra. He sees her as the same innocent girl that he had left years ago. Unlike the soldier who correctly ascertained her role as prostitute and labeled her a "ducky," Roy is incapable of imagining her as erotic spectacle despite her "slutty" makeup and dress. His misrecognition is a form of disavowal. In the narrative logic of Classical Hollywood cinema, it is not possible for Roy to *see* Myra's scene of prostitution, which fortunately transpires prior to his disembarkation. Roy's knowledge must remain inferior to that of the knowing spectator if his own sense of phallic power is to be kept intact. For Roy, the recognition of Myra's prostitution stands for the acknowledgment of his own figurative castration or emasculation. Hence, he disavows her excessively coded sexuality as a prostitute and despecularizes her (as proven by her erasure of lipstick upon his temporary absence) with his nonsexual, paternal gaze and infantilizing attitude. Actual recognition comes much later in the film only after the threat of marrying an ex-prostitute is eliminated, as Myra disappears and is about to commit suicide. Roy maintains his and his family's aristocratic status through her sacrificial act. Myra's death is inevitable because, according to Doane, "the woman associated with excessive sexuality resides outside the boundaries of language; she is unrepresentable and must die."[42]

The man's immediate recognition of his ex-fiancée's status conspicuously distinguishes the parallel scene in *The Stray Bullet* from its Hollywood counterpart. In the Korean "scene of recognition," the gaze structure is much more complicated due to the introduction of a third embedded look commanded by the American GI. Whereas the soldier whom Myra approaches ignores her and passes by, the GI in *The Stray Bullet* aggressively pursues Myŏng-suk, declaring "You are mine for tonight, baby." In actuality, it is the American GI who misrecognizes. He sees Myŏng-suk only as a "new face," another streetwalker, not as someone's daughter, sister, and lover, as the spectator sees her. The ignorant GI aggravates the situation by chasing the woman who has run into her lover at the scene of prostitution.

One notable difference from *Waterloo Bridge* is the excision of the female perspective (except for an insert shot of Myŏng-suk after she flees the scene). Myŏng-suk is literally caught in between two male gazes—that of the GI on the left side of the frame and that of Kyŏng-sik on the right side. After the GI codifies her as a *yanggongju* (whore), the point-of-view promptly swivels to Kyŏng-sik's position as he collides with Myŏng-suk, whom he first identifies as his lover and then as a fallen woman. Quite opposite to *Waterloo Bridge*, it is the disabled Korean fiancé who literally vanishes from the screen after painfully witnessing the white male's appropriation of "his" woman. In *The Stray Bullet* and other South Korean films, the spectral nonappearance of the powerful patriarch and the emphatic focus on the *yanggongju* as a signifier of modernity function not only as an allegory of the (neo)colonized nation but also as a symptom of Korean male trauma precisely because she bears the traces and thus is a reminder of the infiltration and domination of American masculinity in South Korea.

What Kyŏng-sik—already emasculated by his crippled leg—recognizes in the scene is his symbolic castration, the annihilation of his masculinity in a postcolonial space packed with *yanggongju*s and US soldiers. Like Myra in *Waterloo Bridge*, he is an unrepresentable sign that must be eradicated from the narrative at all costs. Myŏng-suk stays on, but she must redeem herself in the end. The only way "guilty" cinematic women (running the gamut from an unfaithful professor's wife Sŏn-yŏng [Kim Chŏng-rim] in *Madame Freedom* [*Chayu puin*, 1956], to the *yanggongju* mother Ŏl-lye in *Silver Stallion*) can redeem themselves is to return to their maternal role, the most honored female function in neo-Confucian society. It is Myŏng-suk who stands by her baby nephew, acting as a surrogate mother, in the penultimate scene after her sister-in-law dies immediately following childbirth. Her eldest brother, the head of the family, is reduced to a "stray bullet" (as a taxi driver describes him), roaming the city aimlessly without knowing which obligation he should attend to first: the crazed mother and his young daughter at home, the younger brother in prison, or the baby son in the hospital. Affectionately gazing at the newborn nephew, Myŏng-suk soliloquizes, "Brother, come back. . . . We can help the baby smile, can't we?" Her hopeful wish for the baby's future implies that she will quit sex work and devote herself to raising her motherless nephew, her surrogate maternalism thus canceling the earlier *yanggongju* image. While in Classical Hollywood narratives conflicts usually develop and are resolved in the tightly circumscribed world of the romantic couple, Golden Age South Korean cinema, for the most part, situates young couples in the thickly woven web of familial obligations. Clashes arise because traditional Confucian values often prioritize the family over heterosexual love. Whereas Myra's unwitting infidelity to Roy is unpardonable from the viewpoint of the sexual mores and Christian doctrines governing individual, man-to-woman relationships, Myŏng-suk's prostitution is forgiven by the family-centric society in light of her willingness to assume maternal duties for the newborn heir and to provide unpaid domestic labor.

From *Aesu* to *Obalt'an*: Transnational Reception and Canon Formation

Many South Korean audiences might not immediately recognize the English-language titles of *Waterloo Bridge* and *Love Is a Many-Splendored Thing.* For them, these films are respectively known as *Aesu* (translated as "Sorrow" or "Grief") and *Mojŏng* ("Affectionate Love"). The Sino-character based titles were originally created in Japan and imported to South Korea along with the film prints. Ahn Junghyo's novel, *The Life and Death of the Hollywood Kid,* elaborates the Sino-Japanization of Hollywood film titles: "Back then, when a foreign film was imported to South Korea, it came with a title made in Japan. . . . We had a hard time distinguishing one Sino-Korean title from the other because many of them sounded alike and their meanings were ambiguous. . . . We confused *Aesu ŭi yŏro* ("Sad Journey Road": *Separate Tables*) with *Yŏjŏng* ("Journey Love": *Summer Time*), *Aesim* ("Sad Heart": *The Eddy Duchin Story*) with *Aejŏng* ("Sad Love": *Wuthering Heights*), and *Param kwa hamkke sarajida* (*Gone with the Wind*) with *Param kwa hamkke chida* ("Fallen with the Wind": *Written on the Wind*)."[43] As Ahn's novel suggests, many postwar cinephiles were also keen on collecting

Japanese film magazines such as *Aeigano Domo* ("Cinema Friend") or *Screen*, which likely affected the South Korean canonization of foreign films and stars. The Japanese-constructed pantheon of Classical Hollywood texts has much in common with its South Korean counterpart as shown in the KBS list. In fact, the enormous popularity of *Waterloo Bridge* seems to be a pan-Asian, rather than exclusively South Korean or Japanese, phenomenon. When former Beijing Film Academy professor Chuanji Zhou visited UCLA to teach a post-1949 Chinese film course in the spring of 2001, he screened *Waterloo Bridge* for curious graduate students, arguing that one can only make sense of emotionally excessive Chinese melodramas after comprehending the affective appeal of this film to Chinese audiences.[44] It would not be an exaggeration or conjectural leap to argue the same for South Korean cinema.

What is unique about the South Korean reception of *Waterloo Bridge* is its centrality to the cultivation of the *Aesu* cycle. The KMDB (Korean Movie Database) website, which is maintained by the Korean Film Archive (KOFA),[45] lists ten films that use the word "aesu" in their titles: *Yujŏn ŭi aesu* (*Hereditary Grief*, 1956), *Aesu* (1959), *Aesu e chŏjŭn t'oyoil* (*Sad Saturday*, 1960), *Aesu ŭi namhaeng yŏlch'a* (*South-bound Train of Sorrow*, 1963), *Aesu ŭi pam* (*A Sorrowful Night*, 1965), *Aesu* (1967), *Aesu ŭi ŏndŏk* (*Hill of Sadness*, 1969), *Aesu ŭi Saenp'ŭransisŭk'o* (*Sad San Francisco*, 1975), *Aesu ŭi hamonik'a* (*The Harmonica of Grief*, 1996), and *Aesu ŭi kobyŏl* (*Sad Goodbye*, date unknown). Inheriting the narrative tradition of *Waterloo Bridge, Hereditary Grief*—directed by none other than the director of *The Stray Bullet*, Yu Hyŏn-mok—recounts a love story between a prostitute and a man from a wealthy family, an amorous affair which tragically yet inevitably culminates with female suicide. *Sad Saturday* likewise features a female protagonist who slides into prostitution after being separated from her lover during the Korean War. She reunites with the soldier, but eventually commits suicide to set him free. The other *Aesu* films are melodramas thematizing tragic love affairs, the exigencies of prostitution, illegitimate motherhood and so on. Besides these films which either cross-culturally adapt *Waterloo Bridge*'s paradigmatic plot or simply borrow its famed title and melodramatic spirit, a number of foreign titles were deemed *Aesu* offspring upon their South Korean release. Two Hollywood tearjerkers, *Daisy Kenyon* (1947) and *Never Say Goodbye* (1956), were retitled as *Aesu ŭi sarang* ("Sorrowful Love") and *Aesu ŭi ibyŏl* ("Sad Goodbye") in an attempt to recapitulate *Waterloo Bridge*'s legendary success. Vivien Leigh's *The Roman Spring of Mrs. Stone* (1961) transformed into *Roma ŭi aesu* ("Sad Rome") in oblique homage to *Aesu*'s leading actress. The German biopic of Clara and Robert Schumann, *Frühlingssinfonie* (*Spring Symphony*, 1983), was renamed as *Aesu ŭi T'ŭroimerai* ("Sorrowful Traumerei [Dreaming]"). More recently the

Graham Greene adaptation, *The End of Affair* (1999), was released as *Aesu*, probably because the film is set in a wartime London and focuses on a fated romance that must end sadly. Most South Korean reviewers of the film did not forget to mention the original *Aesu*.

Indeed, the celebration and recirculation of the same narrative and/or title during the past six decades attests to the fact that *Aesu* (*Waterloo Bridge*) is not simply a single film but a discursive and mobile ur-text melodrama favored as an emotional outlet for South Korean audiences whose tears were shed in the wake of national division, the Korean War, familial separation, political tyrannies, economic crises, and gender and class oppression. The connection between *Waterloo Bridge* and Korean national discourse is further solidified by the film's foregrounding of the Scottish folk song "Auld Lang Syne"—theme music supplying the quixotic yet doleful sonic backdrop against which Roy and Myra dance their last waltz in the Candlelight Club on the eve of Roy's departure for the front. Before the 1948 inauguration of the ROK government, "Auld Lang Syne" provided the melodic foundation for the Korean national anthem, "Aegukka" ("Patriot Song"). Although An Ik-t'ae's newly composed anthem had already been officialized by the time *Waterloo Bridge* was first released in South Korea in 1953, "Auld Lang Syne" must have still carried special meaning and emotional resonance for South Korean audiences who had weathered the colonial years singing "Aegukka."

Now we would like to shift focus back to *The Stray Bullet* and its transnational reception. Although audiences did not vote it as one of their 100 choices in the KBS list, the film is widely considered as an indisputable masterpiece of realist cinema by critics, scholars, and journalists. The Motion Picture Promotion Corporation (now the Korean Film Council)'s 1995 list of the "10 Best Korean Films" consists of (in order): *The Stray Bullet, Piagol* (*P'iagol*, 1955), *Late Autumn* (*Manch'u*, 1966), *Mandara* (1981), *Viva Freedom* (*Chayu manse*, 1946), *A Sea Village* (*Kaet maŭl*, 1965), *The Marines Who Never Return* (*Toraoji annŭn haebyŏng*, 1963), *March of Fools* (*Pabodŭl ŭi haengjin*, 1975), *The Coachman* (*Mabu*, 1961), and *Declaration of Fools* (*Pabo sŏnŏn*, 1982).[46] The 1998 *Chosun Daily* (*Chosŏn Ilbo*) poll of the "50 Best Korean Films" confirms the number one status of *The Stray Bullet*, which is followed by *Mandara, The Housemaid* (*Hanyŏ*, 1960), *Late Autumn, Sopyonje, Why Has Bodhi-Dharma Left for the East?* (*Talma ka tongtchok ŭro kan kkadak ŭn*, 1989), *The Houseguest and My Mother, Piagol, The Coachman*, and *Kilsottŭm* (1985).[47] The film was presented at the 7th San Francisco International Film Festival, an entry that contributed to its domestic rerelease in 1963 after the two-year ban mentioned earlier. According to one-time producer and film historian Ho Hyŏn-ch'an, *The Stray Bullet* did not enjoy an enthusiastic reception in San Francisco.

Ho quotes Yu having said that the Korean situation depicted in his film was difficult for Western audiences to fully understand.[48] Although the film was not commercially successful in South Korea, it appealed to intellectuals in the audience and cinephiles who appreciated its artistic values and political messages.

Sadly, the original print was lost and the film was unavailable for theatrical screenings for many years. Although in the mid-1970s KOFA struck a restored print from an existing copy submitted to the San Francisco Film Festival, this English-subtitled version was not publicly accessible. Instead, director Yu's personal copy of *The Stray Bullet* was circulated in underground campus screenings organized by activist students during the *minjung* period. When the Korean Educational Broadcasting System (EBS), a public broadcaster, aired the film on April 7, 2002, it had to resort to KOFA's subtitled print due to the lack of any alternative version. The same copy (with its unremovable English subtitles) was eventually transferred to DVD and became available in South Korea, ending the film's long absence in the commercial market. Now the film can be instantly accessed online via KOFA's YouTube channel.

Although the film remained virtually inaccessible to the general public in South Korea until recently, *The Stray Bullet* began to creep into the Western art-house canon of East Asian cinema in the mid-1990s. Thanks to the recognition of New Wave Korean cinema in the international festival circuit beginning in the late 1980s and early 1990s (especially the works of Pae Yong-gyun, Park Kwang-su, and Jang Sun-woo), *The Stray Bullet* was given a second chance to travel to North America after its less-than-stellar San Francisco debut in 1963. Packaged as a part of "Three Korean Master Filmmakers: Shin Sang-ok, Yu Hyun-mok, and Im Kwon-taek" (the first major film series in the United States devoted to South Korean cinema),[49] the film was shown in New York's Museum of Modern Art in late 1996. Since then, *The Stray Bullet* has been added to the MoMA Collection and re-exhibited several times. The "Three Korean Master Filmmakers" program was also sent on a cross-country tour through Canada (Montreal, Toronto, Ottawa, and Vancouver) in 1997. *The Stray Bullet* continued to appear in major Korean film events in North America, including the 1998 "Postcolonial Classics of Korean Cinema" festival at UC–Irvine; the 2000 "Korean War: The Last 50 Years" series at UCLA; and the 2002 Korean Film Festival at the University of Wisconsin–Milwaukee. In each of these festivals, the film's English title changed from *An/The Aimless Bullet* to *The Stray Bullet*. The closest translation of its Korean title (*Obalt'an*) would be *A/The Misfired Bullet*.[50] Ironically, the West has finally come to "recognize" *The Stray Bullet*—a text bearing the permanent inscription of transnationalism in its indelible English subtitles—as a masterful work of international cinema over three decades after its initial "misrecognition" in the 1963 San Francisco Film Festival. This belated fixing of the epistemological and cinephilic gaze contrasts drastically with South Korean audiences' immediate canonization of *Waterloo Bridge* as an archetypal melodrama, a recognition that still slips through the consciousness of North American and European critics.

Chapter 2

The Mamas and the Papas

Cross-Cultural Remakes, Literary Adaptations, and Cinematic "Parent" Texts

In 2002, many South Korean newspaper critics who were disgruntled with explicitly derivative genre films and would-be blockbusters like Yun Sang-ho's *R. U. Ready?* (*A Yu Redi?*) and Chŏng Yun-su's *Yesterday* (*Yesŭt'ŏdei*) coined a neologism that has since been pejoratively applied to a variety of productions. The term, "Copywood," connotes mainstream filmmakers' purportedly "parasitic" imitation of Hollywood plots and tropes, which are either lifted wholesale or subtly recalibrated to meet the demands of a domestic audience increasingly accustomed to action, spectacle, aural bombast, and visual sheen.[1] Recent genre productions like Yi Su-yŏn's *The Uninvited* (*4inyong sikt'ag*, 2003), a horror film modeled after *The Sixth Sense* (1999); Yi Chong-hyŏk's *H* (2002), an urban thriller similar to *Silence of the Lambs* (1991) and *Se7en* (1995); and, perhaps most egregiously, Paek Un-hak's *Tube* (*T'yubŭ*, 2003), a blatant knockoff of both *Speed* (1994) and *Under Siege 2* (1995), have drawn the ire of those who believe that Korea's cultural institutions and aesthetic traditions are being displaced or undermined by an inauthentic, homogenous, Hollywood style of filmmaking.

However, few reviewers and journalists have bothered to address the industrial, economic, and artistic motives behind such a practice, not to mention the cultural, national, and political aspects of putting Asian faces and bodies in spaces once primarily reserved for Caucasian Americans. From an industrial and economic perspective, we can see that, in duplicating some of the storylines, narrative strategies, stylistic flourishes, and thematic motifs developed in Hollywood, the South Korean film industry has been able to claim a large percentage of the total market share.[2] This in turn has increased the export-potential of locally produced dramas, action-adventures, comedies, and thrillers in East Asian markets. As Lee Byoungkwan and Bae Hyuhn-Suhck have pointed out, South Korea's screen quota system, which was not strongly enforced until 1993, has steadily "functioned as an appropriate institutional mechanism to protect the Korean film industry from the dominance of US film distribution."[3] Since 2000, it has served as a deeply entrenched protection policy ensuring that domestic product will be showcased in theater programs for 146 days a year, and has remained just one of the ways in which South Korea has stemmed the tide of Hollywood's hegemonic incursion in the country (the quota was eventually reduced to seventy-three days in 2006 due to US trade pressures). By remaking, adapting, imitating, or surreptitiously "stealing" elements from films made across the Pacific, Korean filmmakers engage in yet another tactic that not only has cultural dimensions as well as financial incentives, but also reveals a great deal about spectatorial inclinations (the tastes and preferences of local audiences).

This fundamental irony—the idea that, in order to remain competitive at the box office, South Korean filmmakers have been forced to reproduce the signifying codes and modes of production associated with Hollywood—has not been lost on critics. However, there has not been a sufficient attempt to adduce what makes Hollywood narratives so readily *adaptable* within certain industrial and cultural contexts despite (or perhaps due to) their projection of American values (which, decade-by-decade, have been disseminated exponentially throughout the world via popular culture). Nor has there been any real effort to broaden the hermeneutic horizons of this phenomenon to encompass discussions about noncinematic media (television, literature, painting, etc.) as well as the role of local or foreign spectators in negotiating such dense intertextuality. Cinephilic recognition, a topic discussed in the previous chapter, is a vital component that has thus far been overlooked; as has the value of parody, a deconstructive mode capable of problematizing distinctions between highbrow and lowbrow, the authentic and the copy. Significantly, even highbrow films and idiosyncratic art-house auteurs are not immune to charges of "shameless plagiarism," as evidenced in Tony Rayns's dismissal of Kim Ki-duk (Kim Ki-dŏk)'s *3-Iron* (*Pin chip*, 2004) as a knock-off of Tsai Ming-liang's *Vive l'amour* (*Aiqing wansui*, 1994).[4] As this last example illustrates, weight has begun shifting from the United States to Korea's regional neighbors (China, Taiwan, Japan, and countries in Southeast Asia), which now serve as wellsprings of inspiration for artists whose "originality" is problematically thought to be contingent on the presence of other, less derivative artists.

More germane to this chapter, however, is the absence within critical and journalistic discourses of any historical contextualization that might not only properly frame cross-cultural appropriation as a form of creative adaptation and aesthetic transformation reflecting South Korea's current immersion in postmodernist debates, but also see this trend as only the most recent manifestation of an industrial practice that has long been a part of the country's cultural landscape. Indeed, this "Copywood" craze is nothing new, having existed in less conspicuous yet salient forms since the early 1960s, when Golden Age directors like Shin Sang-ok (Sin Sang-ok), Kang Tae-jin, Cho Kŭng-ha, Yi Sŏng-gu, Pak Sŏng-ho, and Yu Tong-il worked within the technological and ideological constraints of the filmmaking industry while freely adapting Western texts to suit the needs of local audiences. In fact, a handful of productions from that era—most notoriously *Barefoot Youth* (*Maenbal ŭi ch'ŏngch'un*), a 1964 classic directed by another, earlier Kim Ki-dŏk—were deemed "shameless plagiarisms" of preexisting American and Japanese films not long after their debuts,[5] a charge that seems both excessive and inappropriate as a description of cross-cultural appropriation, yet one that is not unlike that leveled against contemporary productions. Moreover, this transnational practice, which we label *pŏnan yŏnghwa* (or the cross-cultural adaptation of non-Korean films), has roots in the country's hybridized literary culture of the colonial period (1910–1945), a time when "Korea's unique modern experience," according to Gi-Wook Shin and Michael Robinson, could not be "broken into discrete Japanese, Western, or Korean parts."[6]

One of the most neglected genres of Korean literature, *pŏnan munhak* literally means "adaptation literature." However, *pŏnan* can be distinguished from the more general term *kaejak* (which also means "adaptation") insofar as the former term connotes the cross-cultural adaptation or reworking of foreign (primarily Japanese and Western) literary works, with Korean names, settings, and historical backgrounds substituting the originals (while the basic plotlines are retained). As Kim Yŏng-min argues, *pŏnan* authors of the early colonial period (such as Yi Sang-hyŏp and Min T'ae-wŏn) contributed to the revitalization of the nation's literary culture through experimental departures from traditional writing styles, genres, and subject matter—a phenomenon inherited by subsequent writers who, rather than merely translate or plagiarize preexisting novels, plays, or short stories, borrowed from them for the purpose of putting "localized" spins on internationally recognized texts.[7] The most notable instances of this practice include Cho Chung-hwan's *Long Cherished Dream* (*Changhanmong*), a 1913 Korean adaptation of Ozaki Kōyō's Meiji-era masterpiece *The Golden Demon* (*Konjiki yasha*, 1897–1902); and Kim Naesŏng's *Pearl Tower* (*Chinjut'ap*), a 1947 radio serial-turned-novel based on

Alexandre Dumas's *The Count of Monte Cristo* (1844–1845).[8] The latter example transports Dumas's famous adventure story of personal vengeance into an entirely different cultural and historical milieu, drawing parallels between the anti-colonial resistance of Korean people during the March 1st Movement of 1919 and the pursuit of anti-monarchist ideals among Bonapartists in the immediate aftermath of the French Revolution.

From the 1910s until the 1950s, *pŏnan* (a term meaning "cross-cultural adaptation") remained a legitimate if critically disparaged category of popular fiction, but eventually slipped into obscurity with the postwar reassertion of nationalist agendas during the Park Chung Hee (Pak Chŏng-hŭi) administration (1961–1979). However, the regenerative transformation of Western and Japanese texts became a staple of South Korea's Golden Age cinema, as exemplified by such films as *A Stormy Hill* (*P'okp'ung ŭi ŏndŏk*, 1960), director Paek Ho-bin's remake of William Wyler's *Wuthering Heights* (1939), and *Grief* (*Aesu*, 1967), actor-turned-director Ch'oe Mu-ryong's remake of Mervyn Leroy's *Waterloo Bridge* (1940), a film discussed in the previous chapter. Utilizing the concept of *pŏnan* intertextuality, this chapter explores the ways in which filmmakers of South Korea's cinematic Golden Age of the 1960s tapped into a vast repository of transnational images and themes borrowed from other cultural and historical contexts, from Depression-era America to postwar Japan. To illustrate Korean filmmakers' unusual penchant for narrative assimilation and cross-cultural adaptation, we highlight a representative melodrama of that era as a convenient case study through which to further adduce the roles that cinematic remakes played in narrativizing the ideals, hopes, and goals of a nation that was itself being "remade" through the implementation of Park Chung Hee's modernization plan, a systematic overhaul of Korean society modeled after Western paradigms yet critical of the latter's moral relativism and materialistic hedonism.

Produced by Park's favorite filmmaker at the time, Shin Sang-ok, and directed by Kang Ch'an-u (who had made the earlier tearjerkers *Daughter and Mother Guitar* [*Monyŏ Git'a*, 1964] and *The Mountain and River Wept* [*Sanch'ŏndo ulŏtda*, 1965]), *Over That Hill* (*Chŏ ŏndŏk ŭl nŏmŏsŏ*) was one of more than 200 South Korean films made in 1968 (when, on average, Koreans went to movie theaters six times a year).[9] Given that number, it is perhaps not surprising that Korean film scholars have thus far overlooked it in favor of more famous examples of 1960s cinematic "artistry," such as *The Stray Bullet* (*Obalt'an*, 1961) and *The Marines Who Never Return* (*Toraoji annŭn haebyŏng*, 1963). This critical neglect reflects an even larger oversight, one that fails to recognize the historical significance of cross-cultural literary adaptations and film remakes, which are inherently suited to comparative analyses of institutional, economic, textual, and thematic material otherwise hermetically confined to a single national cinema. Adaptations and remakes are not merely copies. Nor are they automatically inferior to an "original." Instead, they provide unique intertextual responses to pressing questions about nationhood, citizenship, and collaborative participation in the body politic at particular moments in history.

Appropriately, as a film revolving around generational conflict and filial obligation, *Over That Hill* is itself the youngest "descendent" of what might be called "parent texts." It is, depending on one's national or cultural affiliations, either a remake of *Over the Hill*, a 1931 film produced at Fox Film Studios in the early years of the Depression; or a remake of an earlier Korean remake, also titled *Over That Hill* (*Chŏ ŏndŏk ŭl nŏmŏsŏ*, 1960). The latter film, directed by Pak Sŏng-bok, was released just three months before the nationwide student revolution of April 19, 1960 ousted the autocratic and corrupt Syngman Rhee (Yi Sŭng-man) administration, and is therefore an important stopgap between the American text and Kang Ch'an-u's creative re-imagining of it as a specific response to Park Chung Hee's enforced mobilization of *kŭndaehwa* (modernization) as a socioeconomic corrective to the nation's ills. Significantly, this latter version of *Over That Hill* was produced and exhibited in 1968, the year Park declared his National Education Charter (*Kukmingyoyukhŏnjang*), a famous plan (co-written by philosopher Pak Chong-hong and eventually featured in high school textbooks) that put particular emphasis on national development and anti-communism as necessary components of the state's modernization. This came three years after the Republic of Korea entered the Vietnam War (as an ally of the United States), roughly coinciding with the country's normalization of its diplomatic ties with Japan (on December 18, 1965), an important historical moment that contributed to the slow but steady removal of cultural and political barriers separating these two East Asian nations.

Besides looking west for its narrative and thematic material, *Over That Hill* also looks toward neighboring Japan,[10] where the film's hands-on producer, Shin Sang-ok, had studied art and screened the works of Kurosawa Akira, Mizoguchi Kenji, and Ozu Yasujirō before returning to Korea. In fact, there are numerous similarities between *Over That Hill* and at least three of Ozu's films: *The Only Son* (*Hitori musuko*, 1936), *The Brothers and Sisters of the Toda Family* (*Toda-ke no kyōdai*, 1941), and *Tokyo Story* (*Tōkyō monogatari*, 1953), not to mention Ushihara Kiyohiko's *Where is My Mother?* (*Haha izuko*, 1922). This latter film—an early example of the *haha-mono* ("mother film") genre that later dominated Shōchiku productions of the early 1930s (when Ozu made *A Mother Should Be Loved* [*Haha o kowazuya*, 1933])[11]—was similar to an even earlier William Fox production, a 1920 silent version entitled *Over the Hill to the Poorhouse*, which Ushihara may have seen during his brief tenure in the United States, prior to his exposure to the films of Charlie Chaplin and his other cross-cultural adaptations and remakes of Western texts.[12] These works share a thematic focus on the tenuous love/hate relationship between provincial parents and city children before and after the death of either a mother or a father.

It should be pointed out that the generational as well as geographical schisms so pronounced in each of these films (which are concerned not only with emotional distance but also physical separation) cast in relief an issue central to the study of remakes and adaptations: *fidelity* (or lack thereof) to an ancestral or antecedent text. Given this diegetic as well as extradiegetic focus on loyalty (to one's literal or figurative "parents"), it seems appropriate to ask if the structural isomorphism between South Korean films and their American and Japanese predecessors simply revives the specter of cultural imperialism. Or, as the culmination of several cross-media, cross-cultural "makeovers" and adaptations, do films like *Over That Hill* make a break from the past by using Euro-American and Japanese signifiers as mere pretexts for distinctively Korean texts envisioning the nation's socioeconomic future?

Before discussing the subject of remakes and adaptations in general and the 1968 Korean film in particular, some preliminary comments about its historical context should be made. Rather than delve deeply into the already well-rehearsed history of *kŭndaehwa*, we want to frame the discussion of specific *pŏnan* texts around key institutional, cultural, political, and socioeconomic shifts of the 1960s, when Park Chung Hee's rush to modernize South Korea entailed a radical break from the past even as his government supported films that, while forward-looking in many respects, ultimately endorsed and reestablished Confucian values and patriarchal norms. The many contradictions of that era have not gone unnoticed by Koreanists invested in the history of *kŭndaehwa* and Park's national reconstruction project, which relied on an export-oriented form of industrialization making use of existing or new partnerships with the United States and (later) Japan, from whom scientific, technological, and material resources were procured.

For instance, Kim Eun-shil has already pointed out that "the Korean modernization project . . . sought to simultaneously pursue the material wealth of the west and the spiritual and cultural values of Korea," leaving behind the former's long tradition of liberal democracy while instilling a deep sense of nationalism. Kim's own conception of *kŭndaehwa* accommodates the "ambiguous, various, and multidimensional concepts of time" unique to the 1960s.[13] Although this discontinuity does not entail the eradication of "concrete and empirical time," which has long held sway over traditional historiography, as a spatiotemporal amalgam of elements it can effectively supplant the other's limited range of cultural operations, thereby offering a useful way to conceptualize adaptations and remakes within an intertextual matrix of multidirectional, overlapping, transnational flows. In this way, the 1968 Korean film, although produced chronologically last, becomes a kind of "leading" or "primal" text that unifies meanings and provides a centering framework for examining the structural links between different national cinemas.[14] Nevertheless, before analyzing that work and its connections to Ozu's *Tokyo Story*, we wish to delve deeper into the historical roots of its apparently universal story of self-sacrifice, shifting the focus to three American motion pictures that, despite their significant roles in inspiring Korean filmmakers, are rarely mentioned in critical accounts of the medium.

Will Carleton, William Fox, and the American Roots of a Korean Classic

As previously indicated, the 1931 Hollywood film—a family melodrama directed by Henry King and starring Mae Marsh as the eventually widowed matriarch neglected by her children—was itself a remake of William Fox's 1920 silent version entitled *Over the Hill to the Poorhouse.* Hyperbolically hailed by the studio's publicity department as "The Most Spectacular and Thrilling Psychodrama Ever Staged," this latter film indeed became a cultural phenomenon throughout the Roaring Twenties, running nearly two years in dozens of theaters throughout the United States and instilling a sense of filial piety in men and women who, as Fox described it to his biographer, Upton Sinclair, poured out of theaters "thinking about their old parents and whether they were doing their duty."[15] A one-reeler made in 1908 at the American Mutoscope and Biograph Company predated both films.[16] Of the three American versions, the one directed by Henry King was likely the main source of inspiration for both Pak Sŏng-bok (the director of the 1960 version) and Kang Ch'an-u, not simply because it is the only talkie, but also due to King's reputation in South Korea as an auteur in the same league with Orson Welles, John Ford, and Howard Hawks.

All of these films share a literary point of origin: Will Carleton's 1871 poem "Over the Hill to the Poorhouse." Filled with idiomatic expressions unique to the American South and steeped in Victorian sensibilities (as well as Christian sentimentality), the poem tells in first person the hardships of an old mother whose husband has died and whose six children have abandoned her. Faced with the indifference of her kin, and left with nowhere to go, she heads to a "poor house"—an establishment (usually maintained at public expense) designed to accommodate the homeless. While there is a long tradition of American and British films that incorporate bits of poetic verse into dialogue passages, from *Now, Voyager* (1942) and *Splendor in the Grass* (1961) to *Dead Poets Society* (1989) and *Shakespeare in Love* (1998), considerably fewer works are actually based on familiar poems. Along with a small handful of other films such as *Pippa Passes* (1909), *Enoch Arden* (1911), and *The White Cliffs of Dover* (1945), *Over the Hill* is thus a curiosity insofar as its textual origins lie not in a short story, novel, or stage play, but in a poem—the most evocative and lyrical of art forms (save for music), yet one that seems antithetical to the demands of mainstream filmmaking.

Like the many films that it spawned, the poem was inspired by a preexisting work: in this case, the Hillsdale County Poor House, a mid-nineteenth-century building made of small cobblestones, designed in the Greek revival style, and located in Michigan, where Will Carleton attended college.[17] Commissioned by a local tavern-owner to house the aged members of nearby communities (men and women whose families could not or would not care for them), the Hillsdale infirmary attracted the attention of Carleton, who was so touched by the plights of those inmates forgotten by their families that he wrote the poem. Upon its July 17, 1871, publication in *Harper's Weekly*, "Over the Hill to the Poor House" attracted nationwide notoriety, making Carleton a household name and putting his literary career into high gear. Besides awakening "the nation's moral conscience to the problems of the aged," the poem was even thought to be a catalyst for Social Security legislation years later.[18]

Of all the films that William Fox shepherded through production at his studio, none left such a lingering effect on him as his 1920 version, *Over the Hill to the Poor House.* Fox was proudest of this film not only because, lacking big-name stars and produced on a budget of $100,000, it managed to net an unexpected $3 million during a long theatrical run, but also because its themes reflected the ethical disposition and fierce determination of this avowed family man. In Upton Sinclair's biography of William Fox, the studio mogul recounts how the story was his own idea, albeit one that came from hearing "a young man recite Will Carleton's poem."[19] After reading a volume of the poet's writings, Fox felt sure that "Over the Hill to the Poor House" would be the perfect foundation for a film casting light on the "old people left in institutions through the neglect of thoughtless and selfish children." However, it was not until his wife encountered a seventy-five-year-old man "in broken health and great need and without a friend or relative in the world" that Fox was truly motivated to film such a story. According to Fox, the old man who appealed to the mogul's wife "to get him into a home" had six well-to-do children. Annoyed with their mistreatment of their father, Mrs. Fox wrote a letter to each of the sons and daughters, inviting them to her home. When they arrived, "meeting one another after long separation," they inquired what it was all about.

> Said Mrs. Fox: "I am confronted with a grave problem concerning a worthy old man seventy-five years of age, who appealed to me for help and begged that I provide a home for him, as he hadn't a soul to turn to. In my efforts to have him admitted to a home, I find he has four sons and two daughters." At this point one of the girls was crying with embarrassment and said she knew

> Mrs. Fox was referring to their father. This daughter had lost her husband and the others agreed to contribute money so that the old man could live with her. They all agreed to send their remittances to Mrs. Fox, so that she could be sure the plan would be carried out.[20]

As Sinclair describes it, this is how *Over the Hill to the Poor House* developed in William Fox's mind. So firm was the producer in making this picture that, rather than use a script, he simply recited the scenes that director Harry Millarde would shoot each day.

Although many people involved in the film's shooting felt that the finished product was too preachy and sentimental to capture a large audience, it did better than expected when it was given a trial run at the Astor Theatre in New York. Standing in the lobby after the initial screening, Fox encountered a straggler exiting the theater. In Fox's words, the man

> had the hardest face of any man I had ever seen. He was smoking his pipe, and I asked him for a light. While we smoked, I asked him how he liked the picture. He spoke with a Scotch accent and said: 'I liked it very much, lad, but it's had a terrible effect on me. You see, I'm a seaman—I am only fifty, but I have been out to sea forty out of those fifty years. I ran away from home when I was a lad and never returned or wrote me mither [sic] a line. Ah, but tomorrow I buy me a ticket to go home to Scotland—I am going to see me mither again.'

When Fox suggested to the movie patron that he cable his mother first (as he had been away for so long), the man replied, "I will go home to Scotland, and if she be dead, I am going to kneel at her grave and ask her to forgive me." Reflecting back on this encounter, Fox knew that, if this man was so affected that he would travel 3,500 miles to kneel at his mother's grave, the film "would do much good."[21] A year and a half after the film's September 1920 release, the studio's publicity department learned that "more than 5,000 old men and women had been [reclaimed from homes for the aged and] taken back to live with their children."[22]

After running an entire year in different Broadway theaters, *Over the Hill to the Poor House* was later rereleased in late-September 1921 at the newly built Tivoli Theatre at Eighth Avenue and 50th Street. There it played for another six months, along with another recent rerelease, D. W. Griffith's *Way Down East* (1920). Although, unlike Griffith's now-canonized classic, *Over the Hill to the Poor House* is practically forgotten today, the film was so successful and enduring as a moral fable that its title was often placed above those of John Ford's *The Iron Horse* (1924), Raoul Walsh's *What Price Glory* (1926), and Frank Borzage's 7th *Heaven* (1927) in newspaper advertisements for subsequent Fox productions, such as F. W. Murnau's *Sunrise* (1927).[23] By the end of the decade, though, its status as a classic had begun to wane. After Ford, a contract director at the studio, made his Bavarian World War I drama *Four Sons* (1928), a reviewer at the *New York Times* wrote, "William Fox has another *Over the Hill*," only to follow up this remark with a less sanguine comment about the earlier film's old-fashioned sentiments and "extravagant" incidents, which seemed out-of-step with audiences' modern tastes.[24]

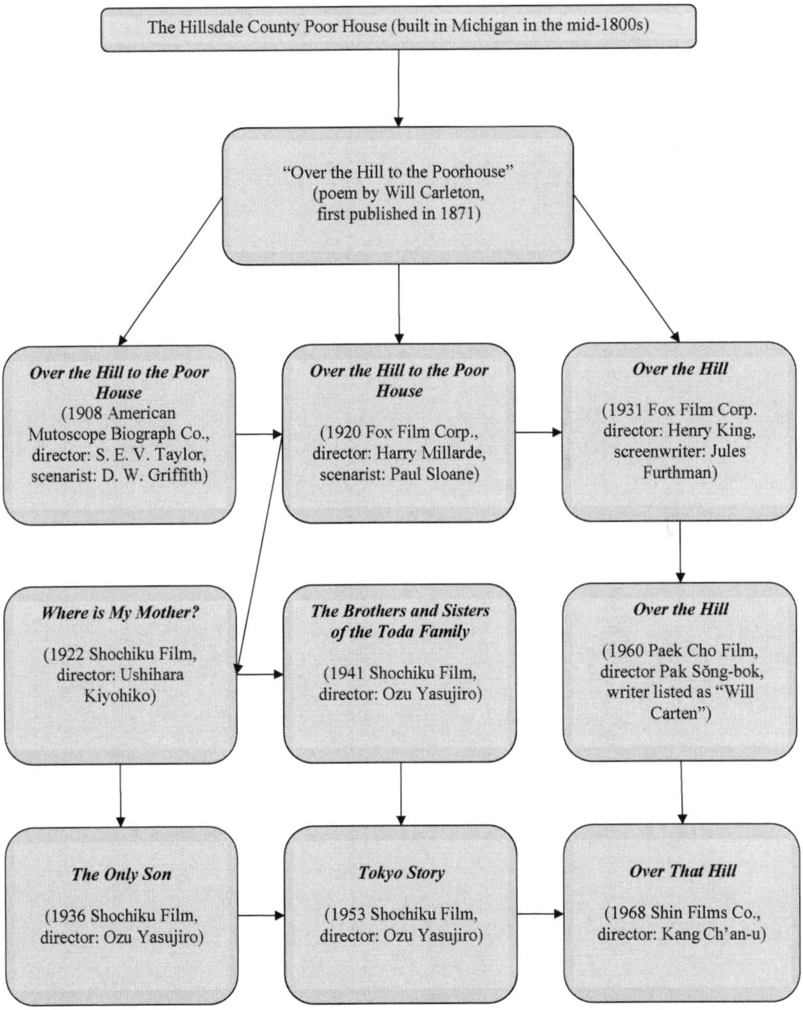

FIGURE 2.1. The legacy of the Hillsdale County Poor House, showing the many films directly and indirectly inspired by Will Carleton's 1871 poem "Over the Hill to the Poorhouse."

Although *Over the Hill to the Poor House* had become an indexical point reference for future stories about families in crisis during the early 1920s, its 1931 remake never really captured the public's imagination. In the midst of backstage musicals, slapstick comedies, and gangster films, a family melodrama dealing with economic hardships and patterned after a sentimental poem seemed either quaintly anachronistic (and lackluster) or a little too uncomfortably close to the socioeconomic conditions outside movie theaters, where an estimated 35 million people (roughly 28% of the population) lacked secure sources of income. Indeed, the same reviewer at the *New York Times* who had earlier dismissed the 1920 version as being inferior to Ford's *Four Sons*, now referred to the 1931 version as an "old sob film."[25] This was unfortunate for Fox, who not only was forced to relinquish control of his own company after a stockholder's meeting that year (an ouster undertaken by the investment banker Harold Leonard Stuart), but also saw his earnings fall "from $10 million in 1930 to minus $4 million in 1931."[26] A successful run at the box office would not have made much difference in terms of Fox's role as studio mogul, yet it would have bolstered his enthusiasm at a time when most companies in Hollywood were beginning to feel the crunch of the Depression. Although remakes were thought to be a pragmatic, economically viable means of keeping production costs low and countering losses incurred by studios like Fox during the Depression, the 1931 film performed poorly at the box office and quickly disappeared from the cultural map, only to resurface years later in South Korea.

Indeed, Henry King's *Over the Hill* was one of several American motion pictures imported into Korea after the 1945 liberation and eagerly consumed by a public hungry for something new. As Yi Hyo-in and Chŏng Chong-hwa point out, the importation of foreign films by companies such as Sinhan Munhwasa and Kisin Yanghaeng was a lucrative business, one that continued during the postwar period and well into the 1960s.[27] After the first revision of the Motion Picture Law in March 1963 and the second revision in August 1966, producer-distributors of so-called "Good Films" (*Usu Yŏnghwa*) were awarded import quotas for foreign films.[28] Along with period pieces and historical epics about legendary heroes, literary adaptations of Western classics fit the "Good Film" criteria by ironically hewing to conservative Confucian values and appealing to the sensibilities of middle-class consumers. Thus it was that American (and to a lesser degree French) texts became doubly ensconced within the South Korean popular imagination as something to be imitated yet reformulated in order to adhere to Park Chung Hee's official policies. It is to those "imitative" texts that we now turn, framing them as exemplary instances of *pŏnan yŏnghwa* leading up to and following the 1968 release of *Over That Hill.*

From *Pŏnan Munhak* to *Pŏnan Yŏnghwa*

Dozens of stories written and first popularized in the United States and Europe made their way across the Pacific throughout the 1960s and 1970s, most notably those of O. Henry and Guy de Maupassant. In 1960 alone there were numerous examples of *pŏnan* intertextuality, including *A Returned Man* (*Toraon sanai*, 1960), an adaptation of Maupassant's short story "The Return"; *A Murder without Passion* (*Chŏngyŏl ŭpnŭn salin*, 1960), based on James Hadley Chase's 1956 pulp novel, *There's Always a Price Tag*; and *K'atch'usa* (1960), a reworking of Leo Tolstoy's 1899 magnum opus *Resurrection*. Cross-cultural adaptations of O. Henry's works include *The Last Leaf* (*Majimag ipsae*), a 1977 omnibus film chaining together three short blackout tales ("A Service of Love," "The Last Leaf," and "The Gift of the Magi") linked by the theme of romantic devotion in the face of economic hardships. Like many Korean adaptations of Western texts, *The Last Leaf* is also connected to an earlier film, in this case *O. Henry's Full House*, a 1952 Twentieth Century-Fox omnibus production featuring the contributions of five directors (including Henry King).

This inter-filmic proclivity to minimize the influence of a literary text (while freely adopting/adapting elements from earlier motion pictures) is not true of Shin Sang-ok's *A Woman's Life* (*Yŏja ŭi ilsaeng*, 1968), however, as it is indebted more to *Une Vie*, Maupassant's 1883 novel, than to French director Alexandre Astruc's same-titled film adaptation of it, made in 1958. Released a decade after Astruc's film, and a mere six years after an earlier Korean version of the same story (Sin Kyŏng-gyun's *Yŏja ŭi ilsaeng* [1962]), *A Woman's Life* similarly charts the downward spiral of a long-suffering maiden whose philandering husband marries her only for money, sponges off his in-laws as a *teril sawi* (a son-in-law taken in by a family) and impregnates the family maid. Both are set primarily in the country, although the heroine in the French version, Jeanne, occupies a remote mansion in Normandy filled with amenities not available to Nan-ju, the main character in the Korean version (played by Ch'oe Ŭn-hŭi), who is still recuperating in the town of Ch'ung-ju from a three-year bout of depression following the death of her forcibly drafted brother during the Pacific War. Because Astruc's film is set in the latter part of the nineteenth century, while Shin's begins in the brief interim between the 1945 liberation and the 1950 outbreak of civil war on the peninsula, it would seem that the former is more faithful to the French original. Yet Astruc chose to adapt only the first half of Maupassant's novel, leaving out its more sentimental passages toward the end in which Jeanne's son takes center stage. Shin's evocation of the spiritual plights faced by both the mother in the country and her initially callous son in the city allows for a less astringent outpouring of lyricism that, for all its *sinp'a*-style excess, is strangely similar in tone to that of Maupassant's story, suggesting a more complete adaptation.

A scene from the beginning of this film illustrates some of the inherent tensions of South Korean adaptations and remakes. The popular Korean song "Spring in My Hometown" ("Kohyang ŭi pom") plays during the credits, which list Guy de Maupassant's name as the source of the film's story. Viewers of the film will no doubt notice that, in addition to that odd sonic and visual juxtaposition, Nan-ju's bright yellow clothing in the scene that immediately follows (in which she is being driven home from a sanitarium) seems anachronistic vis-à-vis the immediate post-liberation era. Instead, it more accurately reflects the period in which this film was made (the late 1960s), when tradition and modernity coexisted as equally vital components in Park Chung Hee's plan for national recovery. In fact, clothing plays a significant role in the film, for it is after Nan-ju's future husband Chong-su (Nam Kung-wŏn) dons one of her brother's outfits that the mother says that he looks just like her dead son. "It's like Tae-jun has come back to life!" the old woman exclaims, a remark that diegetically suggests Shin Sang-ok's extradiegetic revivification not only of Maupassant's *Une Vie*, but also of the earlier Korean adaptation from 1962.

The trend for adapting Western texts likely began with Cho Kŭng-ha's *The Road of Flesh* (*Yukch'e ŭ kil*, 1959). This melodrama, based on Hungarian-born author Lajos Biró's *The Way of All Flesh* (the literary foundation for Victor Fleming's 1927 film of the same name), was itself remade in 1967 by the same director, Cho Kŭng-ha. Both versions recapitulate the themes and basic plot of the earlier film, which focuses on a shamed man who, having left his family out of necessity, can only view his eldest son's professional success from afar. Starring Oscar-winning German actor Emil Jannings, Fleming's silent film has no relationship to Samuel Butler's *The Way of All Flesh*, a semi-autobiographical novel written over the course of eleven years (1873–1884) and published posthumously in 1903. Whereas Butler's text tracks the rise and fall of the Pontifex family, and savagely attacks Victorian hypocrisy and dogmatic religiosity, Fleming's melodramatic tearjerker reasserts the values of a bygone era in its binaristic presentation of the pitfalls associated with big city life and the pastoral pleasantries linked to a nostalgically imbued countryside, which serves as a source of emotional and spiritual nourishment for the male protagonist. As with Will Carleton's poem "Over the Hill to the Poorhouse," which went through three stateside incarnations before being visually and linguistically transmuted as a Korean text beginning with Pak Sŏng-bok's 1960 version, Lajos Biró's story was one that lent itself to numerous adaptations *before* and *after* Fleming's famous film; beginning in 1918, when Cecil B. DeMille made *The Whispering Chorus*, and culminating in 1940, when the Paramount production *The Way of All Flesh* gave Russian-born character actor Akim Tamiroff the opportunity to fill Jannings's large shoes as the failed patriarch of a Midwestern clan.

As one of the comparatively few "paternal melodramas" made during Hollywood's studio system era, this 1940 version of *The Way of All Flesh* may have been anathema to American audiences accustomed to female-focalized tear-jerkers like John Stahl's *Imitation of Life* (1934) and King Vidor's *Stella Dallas* (1937)—two of the many canonical texts favored by Western scholars that either were remade and displaced by subsequent versions (such as Douglas Sirk's *Imitation of Life* [1959]) or were themselves remakes that supplanted lesser-known originals (such as Henry King's *Stella Dallas* [1925]). But for South Korean audiences of the 1960s who habitually immersed themselves in Hollywood films, the self-sacrifices of a down-on-his-luck father out of touch with modernity resonated in a way that suggests some of the complexities and contradictions of that decade. Like Tamiroff's bank employee Paul Kriza, who bids a sentimental farewell to his wife and four children in setting out for an inhospitable New York City only to later realize, after losing his money and becoming a garbage collector in the Big Apple, that the future of the nation is bound up in the sanctity of family, the archaic fathers in South Korea's Golden Age melodramas occupy a pivotal if dislocated place as signifiers of traditional values that must be partially abandoned, partly retained if economic growth and rural development is to be achieved.

Indeed, in many South Korean films of the 1960s, women and (especially) men of the older generation are victims of cruel circumstance, their very presence signifying the legacy of the colonial past. Hence the irony that, having been subjugated by the Japanese, they underwent yet another subjugation at the hands of their children's generation, who benefited from formal education and professional training and came to replace these obsolete figures of premodern Korea. Thus, specific antagonisms were transmuted into a wholesale liquidation of the past, which extended even further to feudal times. Nevertheless, tradition was not simply a set of values entrenched in the feudal period, but something that could, as Gregg Andrew Brazinsky argues, "buttress or inform modernity."[29] By adapting such binaristic concepts as "traditional" and "modern," South Korean intellectuals of the 1960s engaged in a complex form of cultural hybridity that was not far removed from what filmmakers like Shin Sang-ok and Kang Ch'an-u were doing.

In a sense, the adaptations and remakes brought to fruition by these and other cultural producers set textual templates for the ways in which disparate values and concepts (from Confucianism to egalitarianism to nationalism) could be rationally combined. Thus, in the sphere of textual poetics and allegorical narrativity as well as political discourse, the modern was not strictly a unilateral outgrowth of Westernization, but rather a transformative and intertextual process through which non-Korean systems and signs could be retrofitted, contested, or transmogrified into local products. The localizing of stories originally written and filmed in foreign places thus reflected in microcosm the creative recasting and mobilization of ideas that might have been anathema to South Koreans at the beginning of the 1960s, when the country—then one of the poorest in the world—had a per capita GNP of $78. By the end of the decade, however, such maneuvers seemed rational in light of South Korea's speedy economic recovery and assimilation of certain Western values, despite an attendant erosion of institutional democracy and loss in personal freedoms (which, after the 1972 installation of Park's *yushin* ["revitalizing reform"] system of government, were severely reined in).

This thematic focus on fathers is perhaps nowhere more obvious than in *Mr. Park* (*Pak sŏbang*, 1960) and *The Coachman* (*Mabu*, 1961), two award-winning paternal melodramas starring beloved character actor Kim Sŭng-ho, directed by Kang Tae-jin, and released within six months of one another. Although these films will be reintroduced as case studies in Chapter Three, it is worth pointing out that they each spill over with conflicting images of Westernization that connote the apprehensions involved in adapting or remaking American and European texts. For instance, in addition to being a biting indictment of the inhumanity of a modernized city (where automobiles threaten to replace the horse-drawn delivery service of the wifeless, working-class protagonist), *The Coachman* features a scene in which a young woman sticks out her chest and instructs the protagonist's impressionable young daughter (Ŏm Aeng-ran) on how to dress and walk like a Westerner. "Let's step exactly the same," one says to the other, their synchronized steps suggesting a displaced (and doubled) form of emulation.

A less humorous but equally telling scene occurs in *Mr. Park*, in which a future in-law—an upper-middle-class aunt from Hawaii who disputes her nephew's marriage plans—humiliates the title character not only by scornfully informing him that her grandfather had been a respected *yangban* (aristocrat), but also by showing him how to brew Western-style red tea. The failure of this low-wage laborer, lacking in social graces and interpersonal skills, to brew the tea, which breaks apart and clouds the cup, casts in relief the professional success of his son, Yŏng-bŏm (Kim Chin-gyu), who, as department chief for a pharmaceutical firm, represents the newly emergent class of white-collar workers central to the economic transformation of South Korea.

Looking Back, Looking Ahead: *Over That Hill*

As we alluded to earlier, *Over That Hill*'s story centers on a mother and father whose grown children are either disrespectful and selfish or simply unwilling to reciprocate their parents' sacrifices, save for their youngest son, Chi-sŏng (Nam Chin). Although he had to bear the brunt of his father (Ch'oe Nam-hyŏn)'s disciplinary actions from an early age while his two brothers, Chi-ch'ŏl (Nam Kung-wŏn) and Chi-yŏng (Kim Tong-hun), received privileges and were eventually sent to college in Seoul, Chi-sŏng remains devoted to his increasingly insolvent parents living in the country. He not only takes the blame for his father's theft of money (and, as a result, is sent to prison for a year), but also steps in to support his mother (Hwang Chŏng-sun) emotionally and financially following the death of his father, despite having less money than his professionally trained siblings. The father's death results partly from old age, partly from the guilt he feels for having put his son through such an ordeal. When Chi-sŏng returns from a two-year stint in Vietnam, where he had been working not as a soldier but as laborer after his release from prison, he finds that his brothers in Seoul and sister in Inchŏn have abandoned his widowed mother and sent her to a *yangnowŏn*, a "poor house" for homeless or childless old people. In a fit of rage, Chi-sŏng takes a swing at his eldest brother, Chi-ch'ŏl, dragging him and his selfish sister-in-law to the poor house where they find their mother scrubbing floors. The partially reunited family, which includes the repentant eldest son and his wife as well as the youngest son's devoted fiancée (Kim Chi-su), spirit the old woman away from the place, promising to be better, more dutiful children in the years to come.

As indicated in the "Coordinating Plot Points" table, the previous description of the South Korean film largely applies to the American film as well, with relatively minor differences emerging from culturally specific details and stylistic decisions that reflect particular historical contexts. For example, like most early sound films, Henry King's 1931 version trumpets its technology at the very outset of the story, which begins with the crowing of offscreen roosters. This sound initiates the pastoral setting of the narrative as well as Ma Shelby (Mae Marsh)'s ritualistic devotion to housework, which includes cooking breakfast for her daughter (Susan) and three sons (Johnny, Thomas, and Isaac), scrubbing their faces, and hanging the day's laundry out to dry while her husband casually reads the newspaper and smokes his pipe. Yet it also announces the importance of this new technology (which producer William Fox helped revolutionize through his Movietone sound-on-film system) in lending verisimilitude to a story that, while steeped in the Victorian values of the previous century, comes to connote the socioeconomic difficulties faced by men and women during the Great Depression. Just as the precocious young boys want "one more wink" before trudging off to school, so too does the man of the house, Pa Shelby (James Kirkwood), seem less than eager to go to work, saying "I ain't gonna work for nobody unless they pay me what I'm worth." His lazy refusal to contribute to the family's dwindling savings (from which eldest son Isaac [Joe Hackey] steals) only increases their debt, and is what eventually drives him to a criminal act.

In comparison, the South Korean film begins by announcing its own creative use of a still relatively new technology through bold, primary colors and ShinScope (CinemaScope) anamorphic widescreen. Like the sound of roosters

Table 2.1.
Coordinating plot points. (*Italics* indicate overlapping narrative details.)

Over the Hill (Henry King, 1931)	*Over That Hill* (Kang Ch'an-u, 1968)
Mother prepares breakfast and wakes children for school	
The three boys wake their angry father during noisy horseplay	*The three boys wake their angry father while playing marbles*
Eldest son, Isaac, steals some of his parents' money	
The children go to school	*The children go to school*
Youngest son, Johnny, takes the blame for his brother Tommy's misconduct at school	*Youngest son, Chi-sŏng, defends his brother from a bully and is blamed for being a "troublemaker"*
Father reprimands Johnny, sending him to the corner	*Father reprimands Chi-sŏng, scolding and slapping him*
Young girlfriend Isabelle comforts Johnny	*Young girlfriend Ok-i comforts Chi-sŏng*
	Chi-sŏng, who is given an old trumpet by Ok-i's father, begins practicing on the instrument
Roughly twenty years pass by (segue marked by title card)	*Roughly twenty years pass by* (segue marked by sound of trumpet)
Johnny and Isabelle announce their engagement to family on Christmas Eve	
Father tells Johnny (who has been financially supporting his parents) that he has opportunities lined up	
	Ok-i and Chi-sŏng decide to buy a calf (a source of revenue for their future)
	Father has sold property to send his two "good" sons to college in Seoul
	Ok-i and Chi-sŏng sell their calf in order to pay for his father's 60th birthday party, which is not attended by his two brothers in Seoul
	Mother and father take train to Seoul to visit sons
	They arrive at eldest son's western-style house, only to find that his wife is at a "bulgogi party"
	Wife arrives home late at night, complains about the sudden appearance of her elderly in-laws

Table 2.1.

Over the Hill (Henry King, 1931)	*Over That Hill* (Kang Ch'an-u, 1968)
	Father, angry, decides to leave first son's house for second son's house
	Their sightseeing trip to the zoo is cancelled
	Mother and father visit second son and his wife, discover that he is a struggling artist
	They return to the country
	Yŏt-seller-turned-creditor warns that he will take all of the family's belongings if father does not pay debt, threatens eviction
Father steals whiskey shipment; his getaway truck gets stuck in the snow	*Father steals money box, dropping it during his escape*
Johnny catches father in the act of theft, tells him to return home	*Chi-sŏng catches father in the act of theft, tells the old man to return home*
Johnny takes the blame for his father's act and is sent to prison for three years	*Chi-sŏng takes the blame for his father's act and is sent to prison for one year*
Isabelle visits Johnny in jail; he tells her not to wait for him	*Ok-i visits Chi-sŏng in jail; she tells him that her father wants her to marry someone else; she has taken a job in Seoul at a clothing store*
Guilt-ridden father wants to confess his sin to mother, but dies before doing so (off-camera)	*Guilt-ridden father confesses his sin to mother, then dies off-screen*
Mother visits Johnny in prison, counts the days until he is released	*Mother visits Chi-sŏng in prison, counts the days until he is released*
Johnny is released from prison early and surprises his mother; he tells her about a job he has lined up in Alaska	*Chi-sŏng is released from prison, tells mother and Ok-i that he will work two years in Vietnam*
Before leaving for Alaska, Johnny asks elder brother Isaac to take care of mother while he is away	*Before leaving for Vietnam, Chi-sŏng asks elder brother Chi-ch'ŏl to take care of mother while he is away*
Isaac's wife, Minnie, grows impatient with mother-in-law	*Chi-ch'ŏl's wife grows impatient with mother-in-law, tells friends that she is just an old housemaid*
Johnny sends his mother letters with money from Alaska; Isaac intercepts and takes the money	*Chi-sŏng sends his mother letters with money from Vietnam; Chi-ch'ŏl's wife intercepts and takes the money*
Minnie's wife demands that she be sent away	*First son's wife demands that the old woman be sent to his brother's house*
Mother is taken to second son's house in Manhattan; she overhears her daughter-in-law's flirtations with another man	*Mother is taken to second son's house;* she overhears that they are in dire straits financially

(continued)

Table 2.1 *(continued)*
Coordinating plot points. (*Italics* indicate overlapping narrative details.)

Over the Hill (Henry King, 1931)	*Over That Hill (Kang Ch'an-u, 1968)*
Not wanting to cause a rift between struggling husband and unfaithful wife, *the mother leaves*	Not wanting to burden her poor son, *mother leaves for Inchon, where daughter and her rich husband live*
Daughter Susan and husband Ben cannot put up the old woman, due to financial hardships	Intimidated by her son-in-law's uppity mother, the old woman takes bus for yangnowŏn ("poor house" for homeless or childless people)
Isaac convinces mother to stay at a poor house for old people	
Years pass, and Johnny returns home from Alaska	*Years pass, and Chi-sŏng returns home from Vietnam*
Discovering that mother no longer lives with his brother and sister-in-law, Johnny thrashes Isaac, then goes to poor house with Isabelle to fetch her	*Discovering that mother no longer lives with his brother and sister-in-law, infuriated Chi-sŏng drives to yangnowŏn looking for her, dragging Chi-ch'ŏl with him*
Johnny finds his mother scrubbing floors at the poor house; seeing this, he intentionally kicks a water bucket	*Chi-sŏng finds his mother scrubbing floors at the yangnowŏn; running to her, he accidentally kicks over a water bucket*
Johnny, Isabelle, and mother reunite; she asks if Isaac will attend their wedding the next day	*Chi-sŏng, Ok-i, and mother reunite;* Chi-ch'ŏl and his wife ask for forgiveness; they all walk down the road together

crowing in the American film, the first images in this 1968 version usher in a host of associations linked to provincial living. Shots of grassy knolls, rice paddies, and flowers accompany the opening credits, the camera tilting up to reveal treetops so green and a sky so blue as to be a promotional advertisement for Technicolor. This visual correlative to the uplifting score—its music soaring above the full breadth of the scenery—not only sets the emotional tenor of the film, but also differentiates this Arcadian setting from the more destitute conditions in which the American family is initially rooted. Only later, through the use of a transitional device that sends the story forward some twenty years (a title card in the American version; the sound of Chi-sŏng's trumpet in the Korean), is the audiovisual binary inverted.

Unlike the trumpet blast that segues to an advanced time yet unchanged space where living conditions are still rooted in agrarian ways, the title card insert in Henry King's version (which reads, "Moving onward—up the Path of Life. Love and sorrow—tears and laughter, mark the passing years") is both a throwback to the 1920 version and a marker of upward social mobility. For, in the next scene, the members of the Shelby family gather at a new home to celebrate Christmas Eve, their house (largely paid for by Johnny) a noticeable improvement over their first meager dwelling. Although their standard of living appears to have improved, the old couple still struggles to make ends meet. In the American version, the down-on-his-luck father steals crates of whiskey on the night of Christmas Eve, not money in the broad daylight of spring—a fact that surely points toward an earlier era of prohibition in the United States and a more fundamental need for *monetary*, as opposed to material, wealth in an industrializing Korea.[30]

Stepping in to save his father, the son, Johnny (James Dunn), receives a three-year rather than one-year prison sentence, but is released early for good behavior. His post-prison work takes him to Alaska, not Vietnam. Alaska itself is referenced as a place of adventurous expedition and potentially exploitable natural resources; Vietnam is simply a vacation-like space (filled with palm trees and cabanas) where Koreans guzzle Pabst Blue Ribbon beer and get suntans, with no mention of the war. When Johnny confronts his eldest brother Isaac (Olin Howlin), he does not limit his rage to a slap, but literally drags him out into the street where a mob begins to form. At the end of the American film, only Johnny, his fiancée Isabelle (Sally Eilers), and his mother reunite at the site of her menial labor, leaving Isaac and his wife Minnie (Eula Guy) back in town. A sure sign that the South Korean film is a remake of the 1931 version and not strictly an adaptation of Carleton's 1871 poem is the son's kicking of the mother's scrub bucket in both, whether accidentally or on purpose. The mother and son's embrace in the 1931 film is more openly passionate, a carryover from earlier protracted scenes showing the two kissing profusely on the cheeks and lips.

The son's physical expressions of love for his mother at times border on the incestuous and, coming after the death of his father, textually manifest an oedipal configuration that film theorists have argued is extratextually applicable to the study of remakes in general. Insofar as a remake competes economically and culturally with an earlier production or an "original," it has the potential to supplant the latter in the public's imagination. This was the case with John Huston's 1941 detective film *The Maltese Falcon*, the third adaptation of Dashiell Hammett's novel that retroactively diminished the significance of two earlier versions made at the same studio (Warner Bros.): Roy Del Ruth's *The Maltese Falcon* (1931) and William Dieterle's *Satan Met a Lady* (1936). Film critic Andrew Horton invokes the oedipal metaphor in his discussion of *Time of the Gypsies* (*Dom za vesanje*, 1989), Bosnian-born Yugoslav director Emir Kusterica's cross-cultural recasting of Francis Ford Coppola's *The Godfather* (1972), an American classic whose title alone denotes the patriarchal centeredness of familial relations. Not only does this border-crossing Balkan film facilitate the audiences' spectatorial movement—their own "movie migrations"—across cultures; it also, Horton emphasizes, acknowledges the director's efforts to simultaneously replace his cinematic "father"

(Coppola) and, "in choosing to use the same text . . . hold on to childhood and the past."[31]

Similarly, in choosing to remake films by such directors as Henry King a generation after their original theatrical releases, South Korean cultural producers of the 1960s showed how this oedipal trajectory could accommodate the miraculous advancements not only of a young industry vying for domestic audiences and trying out narrative techniques indebted to Hollywood, but also of a nation whose primary templates for modernization, according to most political and economic analysts, came from Japan and the United States. This relationship between three nations, innocently inscribed in the film's opening shots of the three prepubescent boys shooting marbles into a triangle drawn on the floor, is an even more complex problem than the *ménage a trois* union of mother, son, and fiancée in the final reel of King's *Over the Hill.* As both an introduction to the chatty, bratty kids and an entrance point into the story itself, this sequence unique to the South Korean film suggests that the act of remaking a text is, like a game, bound by certain rules and conventions yet ultimately an opportunity for social interaction, self-discovery, and creative play.

Just as the creative reworking of an earlier American or Japanese film is metaphorically signaled by the ludic maneuvers of the marble-shooting Korean boys (whose game comes to a halt when they break a mirror and awaken their father), so too is the gypsy-like mobility of these transnational texts subtly insinuated in the itinerant life of the widowed mother, who shuttles from one place to the next in search of comfort in her old age. Even prior to the death of her husband, the two were sent from the eldest son's Western-style house in a ritzy part of Seoul to the second son's humbler abode downtown. This is the most significant departure from the American version, an extended series of scenes in which both mother and father take a train to the big city to visit Chi-ch'ŏl and Chi-yŏng, who had been noticeably absent at the old man's *hwangap* (sixtieth birthday celebration) back in the village. Once the parents arrive, they quickly discover the sad truth about their two oldest sons.

Although Chi-ch'ŏl, the first son, is an executive in one of Korea's largest companies, he has been idling away his time while Chi-sŏng (the so-called "black sheep" of the family who had always been blamed for his brothers' wrongdoings) continues to slave away at his father's rice refinery. Moreover, both Chi-ch'ŏl's wife ([Chŏn Kye-hyŏn] whose wealthy family secured him an executive position in their firm) and his sullen housemaid are disrespectful toward the old couple, at one point scolding the "absent-minded" mother when she accidentally breaks an American tea set. Coming home late after a night of dancing, drinking, and smoking at a *bulgogi* BBQ party, the wife in particular adopts a caustic attitude, drunkenly complaining to her browbeaten husband about the unexpected presence of these "dirty, shabby, country folks." The mean-spirited daughter-in-law is explicitly coded as a hedonistic consumer of foreign goods, and her upscale yet middlebrow environs are littered with "fine" European furnishings, Japanese electronics, and a print of Da Vinci's *Last Supper* hanging in the stairwell. This, the mother later explains to her confused husband, is *sinsik* ("the new style"), something for which he has neither patience nor concern.

Once the old couple moves from this inhospitable environment to the meager dwelling of their second son, yet another sad truth becomes evident. Having sold most of their property and belongings to send Chi-yŏng to college for a law degree, they find that he is not a judge but, rather, a struggling artist specializing in moodly landscapes and nude portraits. Although Chi-yŏng's vocation would seem to be consonant with that of Tommy (Edward Crandall), the second son in Henry King's *Over the Hill*, there is a significant difference. Wherease Tommy, a struggling artist living in New York with his flirtatious, philandering wife (Claire Maynard), is forced to paint advertisments for his monthly paychecks (at one point saying, "Never thought I'd stoop to this kind of work"), Chi-yŏng specializes in Western-style modern paintings (in Post-Impressionist, Cubist, Fauvist, and Expressionist styles) to earn his living. As if self-reflexively commenting on the imitative nature of remakes, the faux Cezannes, Picassos, and Matisses lining his and his wife's otherwise drab walls are the material correlatives of a textual act that is at once admired (for its creativity) and derided (for its lack of authenticity). The wide-eyed father is so stunned by his son's deceit that he slaps him, calling him a "monster with the face of a human." This moment—an echo of an earlier scene back in the village, in which the father berates his youngest son (who plays "When the Saints Go Marching In" on a hand-me-down trumpet before giving up his musical pursuits)—precipitates the old couple's immediate return to their home in the country. It also hints at a metaphor that will be introduced in later chapters of this book, devoted to monsters both real and imaginary in such films as *Oldboy* (*Oldŭ poi*, 2003) and *The Host* (*Goemul*, 2006).

The section of the film described earlier seems to owe its existence not to Henry King's *Over the Hill*, for which no comparable scenes can be found, but instead to *Tokyo Story*, Ozu Yasujirō's magisterial film detailing the travails of an old couple—Hirayama Shūkichi (Ryū Chishū) and his wife Tomi (Higashiyama Chieko)—who travel by train from quiet Onomichi (one of the few areas in Japan untouched by American bombs) to bustling Tokyo (a city that, like Seoul, had become a thriving if polluted metropolis a mere decade after wartime devastation). Like the Ch'oe parents, the Hirayamas have four children (a fifth child, their second son, Shōji, died during the war). Two of these children live in the capital city. Kōichi (Yamamura Sō), their eldest son, and Shige (Sugimura Haruko), their stingy daughter, are put out by the sudden appearance of the older couple. This unfortunate disruption in their

Table 2.2.
Comparative family structures in the 1931 American film *Over the Hill*, the 1953 Japanese film *Tokyo Story*, and the 1968 Korean film *Over That Hill*.

Family member	*Over the Hill* (US, 1931)	*Tokyo Story* (Japan, 1953)	*Over That Hill* (South Korea, 1968)
Father	Pa Shelby	Hirayama Shūkichi	Mr. Ch'oe
Mother	Ma Shelby	Hirayama Tomi	Mrs. Ch'oe
First son	Isaac Shelby	Kōichi	Chi-ch'ŏl
First son's wife	Minnie	Fumiko	No name given
Second son	Thomas Shelby	Shōji (dead)	Chi-yŏng
Second son's wife	Phyllis	Noriko	No name given
Third son	Johnny Shelby	Keizō	Chi-sŏng
Third son's wife	Isabelle	n/a	Ok-i
Daughter	Susan Adams	Kaneko Shige	No name given
Daughter's husband	Ben Adams	Kaneko Kurazō	No name given

9-to-5 lives (pediatrician Kōichi works at home, as does beautician Shige, who operates an in-house shop called "Ooh-La-La") results in the old couple leaving Tokyo for their home only to end up in Osaka after Tomi becomes sick on the return trip. This is where yet another son—the ill-mannered Keizō (Ōsaka Shirō)—lives and works, his encounter with the parents being initially elided by Ozu (only later, after Tomi has died and Shūkichi has returned to Onomichi, is Keizō shown with his father). Before making that fateful trip (with a stopover at a loud and busy spa in Atami, which, as the old couple muses, "is meant for the younger generation"), the parents are made to feel like strangers in their own children's houses in Tokyo. Besides postponing their outing to a kabuki performance (similar to the Korean parents' canceled trip to the zoo), Shige tells her customers at the beauty salon that the visitors are "friends" from the country; a remark that recalls Chi-ch'ŏl's wife's reference to the old mother as a "housemaid."

In the absence of a sympathetic son or daughter, only one person expresses real compassion for the couple. Like the ever-attentive Ok-i in *Over That Hill*, Noriko (the lonely, widowed wife of Shōji played by Hara Setsuko) thus fills an emotional void and, despite her status as a low-level employee living in a rundown tenement flat, gives money and a backrub to Tomi before the old woman dies. Tomi's death, like that of the father in *Over That Hill*, takes place offscreen; this structured absence, besides heightening the sense of *mono no aware* in the Japanese film and the shared feelings of guilt and repentance in the Korean film, underlines the quiet desperation of people's lives hidden behind the veneer of a modern metropolis.

It might seem odd or critically unorthodox to compare an obscure South Korean production shot in a localized version of CinemaScope and Technicolor to one of the greatest films by a legendary Japanese director, a black-and-white meditation on transience and mutability lauded the world over for its contemplative tone, compositional integrity, and precision at the level of mise-en-scène. After all, *Over That Hill* appears utterly conventional, indicative of South Korean cinema's penchant for emotional excess and cultural appropriation, whereas *Tokyo Story* is a unique, understated exploration of the subtle violence inflicted by children on their parents that eschews the earthy sentimentality of the former. However, apart from their thematic resemblance, it should be pointed out that *Tokyo Story* was similarly inspired by one of the many Hollywood films that Ozu's collaborator and screenwriter, Noda Kōgo, had seen during his formative years before World War II; namely, Leo McCarey's *Make Way for Tomorrow* (1937), a sophisticated tearjerker based on Josephine Lawrence's 1934 novel *The Years Are So Long*.[32] Although film theorist Robin Wood has already pointed out the structural similarities between the two films, he fails to mention that much of McCarey's masterpiece, when synopsized, reads like a facsimile of Henry King's *Over the Hill*. Although neither of the old parents dies in *Make Way for Tomorrow*, the septuagenarians are still split up after the bank's foreclosure on their house and individually sent from one uncaring son or daughter to another, all of whom are "dispersed, separated geographically . . . or by social status."[33] There is even talk amongst the children of sending the mother to the "Idlewyld Home for Aged Women," something that presumably occurs after the film's downbeat final scene in which the two parents resign themselves to permanent separation from one another.

In *Make Way for Tomorrow*, the city of New York is a space of spiritual rejuvenation where, for a fleeting five hours, the older couple rekindles nostalgic memories of youth before their ultimate separation. An encumbrance on the lives of their demanding and ungrateful children, in Manhattan they receive much needed respite. Even some of the city's denizens (including a car salesman and a hotel manager) gladly accommodate the mother and father's requests, rather than further marginalize them. Neither the Tokyo in Ozu's film nor the Seoul in Kang's film is imbued with such ameliorative potential, however. Like their equivalents in *Tokyo Story*, the parents in *Over That Hill* must resign themselves to the truth of their children's lives as well as the alienating nature of the city, which, steeped in Western culture, has driven a wedge between them. Again, the tension between countryside and metropolis, personified in the guise of rural parents and their cosmopolitan offspring, exacerbates the emotional and physical disconnect between the two generations.

Few other themes are so engrained in the structural and scenographic makeup of South Korea's Golden Age cinema as this contrast between city and country, noticeable in everything from Shin Sang-ok's *Hell Flower* (*Chiokhwa*, 1958) to Chang Il-ho's *Mrs. Hwasan* (*Hwasan-daek*, 1968). The latter film is a melodrama in which the titular mother from the country is treated like a stranger in her youngest son's house. Similar to *Over That Hill*, the film shows the old woman returning from Seoul to her village and her eldest son reprimanding his brother's disrespectful behavior. Soon thereafter, she sells off her property in order to clear the youngest son's debt, paving the way for his tearful appeals for forgiveness by story's end. In a way, the binaristic presentations of these two extremes are not unlike what readers encounter in Will Carleton's poems, which were collected together in published volumes entitled *City Ballads* and *Farm Ballads*. Indeed, the sentimentality of Carleton's work actually seems closer in spirit to the 1968 Korean version of *Over That Hill*.

Besides exacerbating the built-in tensions between city and country, tradition and modernity, *Over That Hill* emphasizes the importance of both parental grace and filial piety (*hyo*) to the maintenance of a well-ordered family unit, each reciprocally bound to the other despite traditional Korea's emphasis on the latter. According to Clark W. Sorensen in his anthropological study of Korean peasant households, greater obligation resides with the children, who are to respect and take care of their parents in old age. Filial piety is thus what Sorensen calls an "ethical imperative" instituted through Confucian systems of thought and behavior that maintain the "patrilineal household structure."[34] While this obligation falls most "heavily on eldest sons," who inherit the bulk of household estates, the film ironically inverts the traditional schema. For it is the eldest son, Chi-ch'ŏl, who—having split from his natal household in the country and set up a nuclear family in the city—leaves filial responsibilities to his younger brother. Chi-sŏng, who would normally be expected "to find the city especially attractive as a source of livelihood" (since, as Sorenson points out, he is "entitled to only a small inheritance"), gives up his one true passion in life—playing the trumpet—to pitch hay on his off-days and financially support the family.[35] Chi-ch'ol's lack of productivity and his wife's lifestyle of copious consumption provide the basis for the film's most savage critique, directed toward all those who would either turn their backs on the past or take their eyes off the future.

Coincidentally, the title of Sorensen's book, *Over the Mountains Are Mountains*, which derives from a famous Korean saying (*san nŏmŏ san*) meaning "one hardship after another," is similar to that of the film. Although listed on the Korean Film Archive's website as "Over the Ridge," and based on a preexisting

FIGURE 2.2. An emblem of filial piety, Chi-sŏng plays the trumpet in an early scene of *Over That Hill.* He will later have to give up this instrument in an effort to financially support his family.

work known as *Over THE Hill*, the English translation that we have opted to use—*Over THAT Hill*—is a more accurate approximation of the Korean title (*CHŎ ŏndŏk ŭl nŏmŏsŏ*). In the American English vernacular, someone who is "over the hill" is said to be past his or her prime, on that downward slope that leads to obsolescence. Often used pejoratively to designate anyone who is too old to be of much use in a capitalist, production-oriented society, the expression would thus seem to be applicable to the Korean film as well. However, this semantic shift from the nonspecific article "the" to the adjectival marker "that" not only particularizes the place and space of socioeconomic transformation, but also puts a specific goal before the viewing public of the Park Chung Hee era.

Thus, in a subtle departure from the original, the title of Kang's film, which replaces "the" with "that," keeps the interrelated themes of old age and obsolescence intact while incorporating the more sanguine idea that South Korea's economic prosperity could be—*would be*—achieved through the collective efforts and personal sacrifices of every contributing family member. Like a shibboleth of the Park Chung Hee administration (reminiscent of the Herbert Hoover administration's 1932 slogan, "just around the corner," denoting the promise of prosperity awaiting millions of Americans), the words "over that hill" suggest both an awareness of the struggles involved in turning postwar South Korea from a decimated landscape of poverty and underdevelopment into a thriving industrial complex, as well as an optimistic determination to surmount any obstacle on the path to national recovery. Thus, while this cross-cultural film adaptation looks back to the past for its many sources of inspiration, it also looks ahead and imagines a future when differences can be put aside for the sake of the nation. "Hope lies just over that hill," the film seems to say—an idea that surely appealed to audiences of that uncertain period.

Chapter 3

The Nervous Laughter of Vanishing Fathers

Modernization Comedies of the 1960s

Beginning November 6, 2008, the Korean Film Archive (KOFA) in Seoul, along with the Goethe-Institut Korea, co-hosted a ten-day retrospective comparatively showcasing the works of the Weimar-era German actor Emil Jannings (1884–1950) and the Golden Age South Korean film icon Kim Sŭng-ho (1917–1968).[1] While star-centered retrospectives are not uncommon in South Korea and Europe, the pairing of these two male stars from different countries and eras warrants at least passing interest among cinephiles with or without in-depth knowledge of either actor or film industry. The most obvious connection between these two heavy-set, avuncular stars is that Kim Sŭng-ho starred in two separate remakes of Emil Jannings's silent feature *The Way of All Flesh* (1927), which also served as the title of the KOFA retrospective of Kim and Jannings. Unfortunately, the print of the original film, directed by Victor Fleming, as well as the print of the first Korean remake, directed by Cho Kŭng-ha in 1959, have both been lost. As a result, the KOFA retrospective screened only the second remake, shot in color and CinemaScope, and originally released in 1967.

As discussed in the previous chapter, the original *The Way of All Flesh* is a sentimental silent melodrama in which a middle-aged family man who is carrying his bank's securities on a train is seduced by a blonde swindler (Phyllis

Haver) and is robbed of everything in his possession. In a desperate attempt to restore the stolen securities, the banker struggles with the woman's partner in the railroad yard and accidently throws the crook in the path of the rushing train. When the mangled body of the crook is misidentified as that of the banker, the man deprived of everything starts his life anew as a bum. Twenty years later, now a trash collector in the park, the estranged ex-banker hovers around his former home, where his family celebrates Christmas. Without revealing his identity to his wife, son, and daughter, who do not recognize him, the lonely, fallen man vanishes into the snowy night.

We cannot help marvelling at the familiarity of this tear-jerking narrative in the collective Korean melodramatic imagination. As Nancy Abelmann puts it in her anthropological study *The Melodrama of Mobility: Women, Class, and Talk in Contemporary South Korea*, "The rapidity of post-Korean War development has made for many stories . . . in which small turns of fates—like the 'pointer of a railroad switch' or the 'casual encounter' . . .—spiral into great tragedies or enormous social divides."[2] Moreover, the male melodrama of *The Way of All Flesh* perfectly encapsulates the predominately downbeat, tragic star persona of both Emil Jannings and Kim Sŭng-ho, who often portrayed emasculated, displaced, abused characters rather than conventionally dashing, handsome heroes. Offscreen, both actors also made unfortunate political choices that would haunt them and negatively affect their careers. After winning an Oscar for Best Actor for the combined strength of his performances in *The Way of All Flesh* and *The Last Command* (1928), the heavily accented Jannings was forced to give up his Hollywood career with the advent of talkies and returned to his homeland. Once universally lauded for his combined naturalistic and expressionistic acting style (a hybridized trait epitomized by his performances in F. W. Murnau's silent masterpiece *The Last Laugh* [*Der lezte Mann*, 1924] and Ewald André Dupont's equally innovative psychosexual drama *Variety* [1925]), Jannings, upon returning to Germany, soon lost favor with many critics. There, during the Third Reich, the repatriated actor starred in a series of Nazi propaganda films including *The Ruler* (*Der Herrscher*, 1937) and *Uncle Kruger* (*Ohm Krüger*, 1941). Named by the Minister of Propaganda Joseph Goebbels as the "Artist of the State" (*Künstler des Staates*), after the German defeat in World War II, Jannings was eventually exiled in Austria with no hope of resuming his career in the film industry.

Kim Sŭng-ho, on the other hand, supported the corrupt regime of Syngman Rhee (Yi Sŭng-man)—a freedom fighter-turned-first President of the Republic of Korea who ruled the country for twelve years (1948–1960) with an iron fist—and was actively involved in the reelection campaign for the octogenarian autocrat. The fraudulent reelection of Rhee on March, 15, 1960 led to mass student demonstrations known as the April 19 Revolution (simply known in South Korea as *Sa-Il-Gu*, or 4.19), which successfully toppled his regime. The day after the uprising, angry citizens and students burnt down Kim's house in protest against the famous actor's public endorsement of Rhee in political rallies during election time.[3] By 1960, Kim was already a prolific, veteran actor who had appeared in approximately 100 films (over one-fourth of the 360 total films comprising his expansive filmography), a key player in the booming domestic film industry of South Korea. However, the political controversy momentarily put a cap on his career as the Korean Screen Actor's Association expelled Kim Sŭng-ho from the trade union in consideration of public opinion.[4] Unlike Jannings, Kim was allowed to come back to the screen after a hiatus of a few months as the industry recognized his irreplaceable talents and contributions. The returned actor's artistic legitimacy was further solidified by three Best Actor Awards from the Asia Film Festival (at the 7th, 8th, and 10th ceremonies) for his lead roles in *Romance Papa* (*Romaensŭ ppappa*, 1960), *Mr. Park* (*Pak sŏbang*, 1960), and *Romance Gray* (*Romaensŭ kŭrei*, 1963). Although Kim Sŭng-ho successfully dodged political crisis in the wake of the April Revolution of 1960, his attempt to transition from actor to producer in 1967 failed miserably and Kim was arrested for overdrafting sixty-six bounced checks the following year. One month after being released from police custody, on December 1, 1968, Kim passed away prematurely at the age of fifty as a result of his chronic high blood pressure and heart condition.[5]

Given the fact that, to a certain extent, Kim's life story mirrors that of Emil Jannings and his character in *The Way of All Flesh*, one can associate the actor with *melodrama*, the most popular genre in South Korean cinema of the 1950s and 1960s. While Kim Sŭng-ho starred in many melodramas in the mode of *The Way of All Flesh* (as alluded to in the previous chapter), this chapter foregrounds a different genre: "modernization comedy." We define the modernization comedy as a subgenre of film comedy, one whose humor mainly derives from the clash between stereotypically traditional/Korean and modern/Western values and lifestyles, contextualized in a rapidly urbanizing, developing society. Kim Sŭng-ho, a much-loved yet publically stigmatized actor from that Golden Age period, gained fame for his habitual appearance as a middle-aged, heavy-set, good-hearted father figure who personified the "*sŏmin*" (common or little people) of his time. Indeed, Kim was a ubiquitous presence in such modernization comedies as *Romance Papa, Mr. Park, Third Rate Manager* (a.k.a. *A Petty Middle Manager, Samdŭng kwajang*, 1961), *Under the Sky of Seoul* (*Sŏul ŭi chibung mit*, 1961), and *Romance Gray.* In these films, the actor plays vulnerable patriarchs, each struggling to maintain his position as the family head while his legitimacy (as bread-winner, as rule-maker, and so forth) is constantly being undermined by various factors: (1) his inability to keep pace with the speed of modernization; (2) his meager wages, which are insufficient in supporting the needs of the family; (3) his alienation from the younger generation; and (4) his complicity with outdated feudal customs, such as concubinage and herbal medicine, or implicit connection to the colonial past. Kim's persona accords with and is symptomatic of a recurrent theme in Golden Age South Korean cinema, namely the emasculation (and eventual disappearance) of the traditionally encoded father.

In an article entitled "The Time of the Modern, The Time of Nation," film scholar Kim Sŏn-a argues that 1960s Korean cinema foregrounds the "son's generation" as the subject of modernization and nation-building while relegating paternal and female others to the background. Having been subordinated to both Japanese and American domination, the cinematic father thus turned into an obsolete relic lacking phallic power, someone whose existence was dependent on and defined by the piety of sons and sons-in-law, the newly ascendant male generation in charge of national reconstruction.[6] As such, modernization comedies induce nervous laughter at the expense of disempowered, anachronistic fathers who are ill-adapted to social change and new customs. This is precisely why their various comic situations and scenarios are both charged and diluted by social consciousness and melodramatic pathos. According to Kelly Jeong, "a tragic, failed patriarch or a comic, bumbling father" embodied in Kim's persona "invokes nostalgia, forgiveness, and sympathy for his human frailties even when he fails or, rather, especially because he fails."[7] Moreover, as Jinsoo An argues in his doctoral dissertation on South Korean Golden Age films, despite the infusion of melodramatic circumstances of "misfortunes or individual drawbacks," these films tend to offer a "clear and happy [resolution wherein] the young patriarch rescues his father from the downfall and restores stability and harmony to the family."[8] Read as social and political allegories, paternal comedies of the early 1960s "reflect and refract the pervasive social anxiety, alienation, despair, and powerlessness that characterize the years prior to the arrival of the Park Chung Hee regime (1961–1979) and its powerful state nationalism."[9] Jeong likewise situates Kim Sŭng-ho's films in a historical context, stating, "The desire for a strong ethnic nation, one that suppresses the chaos and instability of the times, surfaces in movies of this era in an attempt to reestablish the emasculated father, the figure who possesses the symbolic phallus."[10]

Another Korean film scholar, Yi Hyŏ-in, succinctly sums up some of the common father–son dynamics and modernization themes present within 1960s Korean films, including textual examples to be discussed in this chapter:

1. Fathers must be symbolic figures to uphold patriarchy (*kabujangje*) but they are unfit to accomplish the era's imperative: the modernization (*kŭndaehwa*) project.
2. Capitalists and intellectuals are objects of envy for power holders of the military regime.

3. Sons can be reckless and risky but they are alternative forces to lead the era's modernization project.
4. Women are passive assistants to "Korean-style modernization" ([whose characteristics include] hard work, honesty, fairness, Confucian ethics).
5. Korean modernization epitomizes the fissure as it encompasses both Western-style modernization and Confucian patriarchal order.[11]

These five thematic characteristics will be explored and expanded upon in our analysis of key texts and case studies that reveal the inherent ideological orientation of modernization comedy as a Korea-specific yet transnationally mobile (and thus contradictory) genre. At once rooted to the past and pointed toward the future, this category of cultural production can be said to represent the nation as a whole. If it initially seems unnecessary to add yet another neologistic expression to the already bloated body of critical terms comprising genre studies generally (and comedy film studies more specifically), our hope is that a clearer picture of the stakes involved in unmasking and indeed *naming* the otherwise hidden or unspoken aspects of gender and class relations in South Korea comes into focus through the establishment of modernization as both the *content* and *form* of historically important motion pictures concerned with the plight of "little people." This chapter, then, focuses partially on cinematic representations of the trials and tribulations faced by everyone from white-collar salarymen to blue-collar laborers, the so-called *sŏmin* who populate the many films under consideration and who struggle to make ends meet while growing accustomed to rapid postwar social change in a country where "modernization" is synonymous with "progress."

From *Sŏmin* Dramas to "Modernization Comedies"

In her analysis of director Shin Sang-ok (Sin Sang-ok)'s *Romance Papa* and director Kang Tae-jin's *Mr. Park*, Nancy Abelmann dubbed the genre comprising these films as "melodrama of social transformation," a category that hinges upon a "creative tension between patriarchy, namely the excesses of male privilege and power, and the dislocation of men on account of radical social transformation."[12] These films center on the theme of the "staging of patriarchy," which creates ambivalent situations of both "humorous antics" and "pathetic machinations."[13] On the other hand, Jinsoo An defines the same text *Romance Papa* as an example of "family comedy films," which "often place the protagonist in melodramatic predicaments, although such moments are contained within the larger narrative frame of laughter and happy ending."[14] This generic interchangeability shouldn't come as a surprise as most examples of what we call the "modernization comedy" are hybrid genre films that can be broadly designated as "*sŏmin* (little people) drama," an equivalent to *shomingeki* (little people film, also known as *shōshimin eiga*) of postwar Japanese cinema. As Donald Richie points out, "In a sense, all Japanese cinema became, for a season, shomingeki. All films were about the 'little people' because, for the time being, everyone was 'little,' poor, just scraping by. As Arthur Nolletti reminds us, 'The shomingeki was actually a broad, all-inclusive genre. . . . [A]s such it was able to accommodate an often wide and disparate range of material and moods, among them farce, light comedy, lyricism, social criticism, and melodrama. . . .'"[15] Transnationally dislodged from its Japanese context, Richie's description is particularly useful in helping to frame the cultural logic of generic permeability in *Romance Papa* and other South Korean modernization "(melo-) dramedies" discussed in this chapter.

Directed by the legendary Golden Age auteur Shin Sang-ok, *Romance Papa* stars Kim Sŭng-ho as the titular patriarch who loses his insurance agency job and maintains the pretense of continued employment in order not to lose face in front of his family. In the theatrical prologue sequence, Kim directly addresses the audience, staring straight into the camera and introducing his character as "Romance Papa." According to him, his children coined this nickname because of his alleged "senility" (*nomang*), although he is only fifty-two years old. Throughout the first few scenes of the narrative, the ineffectual patriarch's authority is constantly challenged by his five children, whose material needs cannot be satisfied by his low salaries. When her father fails to give her money to buy hiking pants, the second daughter (To Kŭm-bong) complains that her college classmates own fancy luxury items such as cars and pianos, not to mention pairs of hiking pants. Likewise, after being denied allowance money for window shopping, her nineteen-year-old brother (Sin Sŏng-il) chimes in, "There's no dad like my father with no skills [to provide for his family adequately]." While the mother scolds her children for being disrespectful, the father takes these criticisms silently with a benevolent grin on his face. When the couple is left alone, the wife (Chu Chŭng-nyŏ) criticizes their children, "They conclude that you are an incapable man. Moreover, they think that they're victims of their dad's incapability." Instead of siding with his wife, the father accepts his children's verdict with graceful resignation, stating, "They're right. I am incapable." When his son and daughter playfully begin to shout their protest slogan ("give me money, time, and freedom") behind closed doors, however, the titular character humorously deflects the family tension by repeating their slogan and telling the offscreen children that he has no such things, not even for himself.

Gently mocked and blamed by his demanding children, Kim's father-figure is a metaphorically "vanishing" patriarch who nevertheless refuses to be relegated to the margins without first challenging younger men: he wages a bet with his eldest daughter's meteorologist boyfriend (Kim Chin-gyu) about the likelihood of a rain shower and engages in a wrestling match with the aforementioned son who, unbeknownst to his parents, is captain of his high-school wrestling team. Although Romance Papa luckily wins the weather bet, thanks to his sensitive, arthritis-afflicted joints, he is knocked down by his athlete son in the wrestling match and ends up spraining his neck.

From his iconic fedora hat to his rendition of a favorite song (a Korean spin on the American minstrel song "My Old Kentucky Home"), nearly everything about Kim's character is out of fashion and behind the times. Tellingly, one of the most prominent props in the mise-en-scène of the film's main setting—the family common room (*maru*) which opens to the asphalt utility yard—is an oversized antique clock visible in the background. This object is a family hand-me-down, chiming frequently, that used to belong to the patriarch's father. As if representing its owner's temporal lag, the clock fails to keep time punctually and is habitually causing problems due to its technical faults. For example, in one scene, Romance Papa grumbles, "When it's one, it rings five times. When it's five, it rings one time," to which his wife responds, "The clock is old like you." After the titular character's forced early retirement three quarters into the film, the narrative swiftly shifts from the comic mode to the melodramatic mode, providing a new lens through which to understand his vain attempts to find a new job and his aimless daytime wandering throughout the city to kill time. Despite his efforts to conceal his desperate situation from his family, his wife and children eventually become privy to his "staging of patriarchy," yet go along with the charade while raising the much-needed family income through piecemeal work and part-time jobs. The film closes with a heartwarming birthday party for the father, who is presented with the valuable gold pocketwatch that he had earlier pawned out of economic desperation and which his family has since retrieved. With the return of the watch, his most proud possession and a symbolic reference to his need for temporal adjustment, Romance Papa restores the façade of his patriarchal power through the help of his understanding, loving family.

While in *Romance Papa*, Kim Sŭng-ho plays a managerial, middle-class patriarch (who nevertheless suffers from capitalistic exploitation and diminishing social power), in other films he was cast as a proletarian protagonist who overcomes a masculinity crisis in a similar fashion as his petit bourgeois counterparts.[16] For example, in Kang Tae-jin's critically acclaimed 1961 family drama *The Coachman* (*Mabu*), a follow-up to the director's *Mr. Park* and winner of the Silver Bear Award at the 1961 Berlin International Film Festival, Kim is an anachronistic carriage driver, not only unable to keep pace with modern means of transportation but also out of step with his children's rebellious generation of anti-authoritarians. Once again, he is the apotheosis of traditional Korean fathers who were being replaced by their sons' generation. Kim's character Ch'un-sam, a poor widower with four children, stakes

FIGURE 3.1. The oversized antique clock in the background is a recurrent visual reminder for the titular character's need for temporal adjustment in *Romance Papa*.

his hopes for a better life in the future of his eldest son (Sin Yŏng-gyun), who is preparing for the national bar exam. One day, the coachman is involved in a traffic accident and breaks his leg, which has been run over by an automobile. The driver of the car who is responsible for his injury is none other than his boss (Chu Sŏn-t'ae) who, rather than apologize, blames his employee for the accident. After this misfortune, the crippled coachman is reduced to the status of a child, someone who has to be taken care of by his family. When he is fired by the callous coach owner, who is responsible for his injury in the first place, the law-student son pleads, albeit unsuccessfully, on his father's behalf and protests the unjust treatment.

The coachman's romantic interest, Suwŏn-daek (Hwang Chŏng-sun), a maid in the coach owner's household, assists him financially behind his back with her hard-earned savings. In an earlier bar scene, we learn from a conversation between Ch'un-sam and his friend that he became a coachman after his father's death while being exiled in Manchuria during the colonial period. In other words, his vocation is not only a throwback to the premodern past but also a shameful reminder of a colonial history that must be overcome if a new modern nation is to be built. The film's dénouement resolves this national imperative by showing the family happily reunited in snowy downtown Seoul, where they receive long-awaited news that the eldest son has passed his bar exam. Reminiscent of the dénouement in *Romance Papa*, the father thus regains his nominal power via male bonding with his dutiful, upwardly mobile son, who is capable of leading the family down the road toward modernity and presumed wealth.

Taking a Back Seat to Modernization: Political Satire and the Generation Gap in *Third Rate Manager*

Less well-known than *Romance Papa* and *The Coachman*, Yi Pong-rae's 1961 film *Third Rate Manager* is an underrated masterpiece that epitomizes the concept of "modernization comedy." According to film historian Yi Yŏng-il, the comedy genre had been marginalized in Korean film history until the late 1950s, when an unprecedented number of comedy films were released before the genre started to decline again throughout the 1960s. Yi categorizes Korean comedy films of that period into three groups: situation comedy, dialog-centric "sound comedy," and slapstick comedy.[17] According to this classification, *Third Rate Manager* belongs to the second group, whose humor primarily derives from satiric and witty dialogue.

The film's director, Yi Pong-rae, studied literature at Rikko University in Japan and worked as the head of the cultural section for the *Tokyo Times* before returning to the homeland after the end of the Korean War and forming a modernist poets' group called "The Second Half" ("Hubangi," which would later be used as the name of Yi's production company responsible for making *Third Rate Manager*). After writing a couple of screenplays, the poet debuted as a film director in 1959 with *The Condition of Happiness* (*Haengbok ŭi chogŏn*), which tells a story of a war widow (Yi Min-ja) betrayed by a boyfriend who has been posing as a university student to swindle her money on the pretext of paying for tuition. The broken-hearted woman finds solace in a courtship with her landlord's son, a good-hearted widower, and the two lonely souls plan a better future together. From his debut feature forward, the writer-director Yi Pong-rae exhibits both biting satire of the inhumane capitalist system and warm affection for humble yet resilient *sŏmin*—a thematic preoccupation discernible throughout his oeuvre. In a career that includes such witty, humanistic films as *Salary Man* (*Wŏlgŭp chaengi*, 1962), *Angry Cosmos* (*Songnan k'osŭmosŭ*, 1963), *Apron* (*Haengju ch'ima*, 1964), and *Wealthy Man Mr. Hwang* (*Map'o sanŭn Hwangbuja*, 1995), *Third Rate Manager* stands out as Yi's greatest achievement, a remarkably sophisticated, progressive comedy fusing cosmopolitan sensibilities with social consciousness.

It is important to point out that the film was produced and released during an interim democratic period sandwiched between two dictatorships: that of Syngman Rhee (who lost power in the April 19 Revolution) and Park Chung Hee (Pak Chŏng-hŭi who rose to power with a military coup of May 16, 1961).

Under the leadership of the relatively mild-mannered, US-educated Prime Minister Chang Myŏn, the South Korean government adopted a new parliamentary system and was undergoing democratic reform when *Third Rate Manger* was released in early May 1961. The film's creative personnel fully took advantage of increased artistic freedom under a new democratic regime in the wake of the April Revolution. At the mid-point of this film's narrative, the titular manager's son, a college student named Yŏng-gu (Pak Sŏng-dae), tells his girlfriend, "Freedom to eat, freedom to speak. That is the freedom of the mouth. Who's going to take that away?" The explicit foregrounding of the mouth's "freedom," *through spoken dialogue*, is significant as *Third Rate Manager* was, along with Yu Hyŏn-mok's realist masterpiece *The Stray Bullet* (*Obalt'an*, 1961) and Kim Ki-yŏng's transgressive hothouse thriller *The Housemaid* (*Hanyŏ*, 1960), a product of the short-lived Second Republic's democratic reforms, which fostered a relaxed environment where filmmakers could tackle sensitive topics such as poverty, class oppression, US military prostitution, political corruption, and the culture of bribery. Although the student-led April Revolution of 1960 overthrew Syngman Rhee's authoritarian government and made democratic reform possible, *Third Rate Manager* does not back down from taking satirical jabs at the revolution itself. In the opening sequence of the film, the grandmother of the family (Pok Hye-suk) asks her granddaughter (To Kŭm-bong), a new office girl on her way to her first day at work, to buy her a handbag as she will get her first paycheck. The granddaughter laughs and says that she will get paid on the last day of the month. Disappointed, the geriatric woman grumbles, "The same was true for your grandfather. I guess even the April 19 Revolution could not change that." Such disillusionment is shared by her daughter-in-law (Hwang Chŏng-sun), who complains to an electricity bill collector, "Does it make sense that you don't provide power and yet bill the customers? . . . That's why I call politicians 'thieves.' They promise electricity, water, and lower taxes. And they change their words after being elected." Later in the film, the extended Ku family consisting of three generations—grandparents, Mr. Ku and his wife, and their adult children, Yŏng-gu the college boy and Yŏng-hŭi office girl—celebrate Mr. Ku's promotion to manager (after working for twenty-five years) with a *bulgogi* BBQ party. In this scene, the father is informed that his son is dating a girl and disapproves of it, insisting that "Students should just concentrate on studying." The college boy rebels, saying, "You shouldn't ignore students. We started the April 19 revolution." The unimpressed father responds, "The Revolution has nothing to do with your romance business (*yŏnae*)."

The disparaging or nonchalant remarks about the youth-led April Revolution on the part of the grandmother (a figure who represents the colonial period) and the father and mother (characters personifying the Syngman Rhee era) are significant as they express the earlier generations' ambivalence toward post-revolution social change being ushered into Korean society, most significantly, empowerment of the next generation as an enabler of democracy, modernization, and economic development. The grandmother who is "over the hill" and with no economic power slyly comments that the April 19 Revolution was not that groundbreaking after all, as compensations for ordinary white-collar workers are still delayed a full month to serve the interests of management/capitalists. Her sister-in-law, a middle-aged housewife, blames politicians as a whole who, regardless of their party affiliations and the democratic revolution, nonetheless fail to deliver on campaign promises.[18] On the other hand, Mr. Ku, the head of the family, admonishes his son for using the revolution as an excuse to justify his neglect of study. The father's intuition is on the mark as Yŏng-gu is previously shown cutting his classes to flirt and ice skate with his girlfriend, whom he calls "après" (after), a postwar neologism referring to sexually liberated women lacking traditional values of femininity and chastity. To viewers with foreknowledge of actor Kim Sŭng-ho's predicament after the April Revolution (as a campaign aide in Syngman Rhee's Liberal Party [*Chayudang*]), his character's indifference toward the student movement in the scene has greater extradiegetic meaning.

What is unique about *Third Rate Manager*, though, is that the film focuses less on Mr. Ku's generation gap with his playboy son than on his complex relationship with his daughter, Yŏng-hŭi, who joins Samch'ŏlli (Three Thousand Miles) Logistics, a transportation company that the titular patriarch has been serving for a quarter of a century, as an office clerk when the film opens. On her first day at work, the tomboyish daughter witnesses her father's humiliation in front of the short-tempered executive director Song (Kim Hŭi-gap), a second-in-command in the company. When the executive hears of the news that one of the company trucks was involved in an accident, Song calls the in-company cafeteria and summons Mr. Ku at lunch. Without hearing out his employee, Song scolds Ku as if he were a child, blaming him for having lunch at a time of crisis and neglecting his duty. To the embarrassment of her father, Yŏng-hŭi is at present in the scene as the new recruit has been brought to the office to offer a formal greeting to the executive. Soon enough, the misunderstanding is dispersed and the atmosphere lightens up as Ku reports to the executive that the accident was minor and resulted in no damage to the truck. In the ensuing scene, the father takes his daughter to the company rooftop, where they have a heart-to-heart conversation, something that would normally be reserved between a father and a son in South Korean family dramas. The father timidly confides, "From the beginning, I've never liked the idea of us working at the same company. . . . I was afraid that if we worked together, you would soon find out the kind of life I have in the company." He also begs his own daughter not to relay the episode to the family, saying that "If you tell, I'll lose face as the head of our family." Gently ridiculing her father for being "too shy and fainthearted," Yŏng-hŭi agrees to keep his shame confidential in exchange for a small bribe: a new handbag. Although the underpaid, overburdened father delays his answer to the daughter's demand, in a subsequent scene, he himself is paid a bribe which will partly be used to pay for Yŏng-hŭi's handbag.

The scene in question takes place in the home of Executive Director Song's mistress Myŏng-ok (Yun In-ja), an unemployed dancer. Song coerces Ku to form a social dance club on the second floor of the branch office that the latter is in charge of. The ostensible purpose of such a club is to "improve and modernize the company staff's spirit" and to help them "keep pace with the times." However, the executive quickly reveals his real motive: to find part-time employment for his mistress who is bored during the day. At the demand of Myŏng-ok, the executive contributes 10,000 won ($10), which is handed to Ku in a bribe envelope (*ch'onji pongt'u*). In a later scene, Mr. Ku is shown dancing with Myŏng-ok, telling his awkward partner, "Modern men must learn how to dance." When Ku clumsily bumps into another dancer, a younger employee steps in and snatches the dance teacher away while the older man watches helplessly. The young man seems eager to learn Western dance and to become a "modern man," whereas Mr. Ku is apparently uncomfortable and displaced. Throughout the film, Mr. Ku is caught between two acts—the staging of patriarchy and the staging of modernization—which are achieved partly through bribes deriving from the same source, Executive Director Song's deep pockets. Both acts are a cover-up operation to conceal male failures or weaknesses—lack of authority at work in the case of Ku and an illicit, polygamous relationship in the case of Song. Ironically, the so-called modernization project, the social dance club, is mired in backward customs such as bribery and concubinage. The aforementioned promotion is a reward to Mr. Ku for assisting and protecting his boss's private life (Ku is promoted to the welfare department manager, a third-class post overseeing fraternity, recreation, and health of employees). Ultimately, the titular manager is punished for his complicity as Song lies to his jealous, husband-beating wife (Sŏk Kŭm-sŏng) that Myŏng-ok is Ku's mistress. The fib nearly destroys Ku's marriage until the wife learns the truth in a raid of Myŏng-ok's house, where she accompanies Song's wife and awkwardly encounters a naked executive director (instead of her own husband) in the bathtub.

The film's dénouement highlights the reconciliation of Ku and his wife, who dine out alone for the first time in twenty-five years. In an upscale, Western-style restaurant, Ku compares the relationship between husband and wife to that of a driver and his assistant (conductor) in a communal taxi. The husband explains, "If the driver and conductor are on bad terms, their passengers will feel nervous. That's why we should always be united in spirit. . . . That is especially true for people like us who have no connections or money." The wife smiles and agrees. Then, the high-spirited husband insists that they go for a drive like a newlywed couple (despite his wife's comment that it is unfit for "old people" like them). The final scene shows the happy, middle-aged couple in the backseat of a taxi. Like a child, the husband seeks his wife's endorsement, "Isn't this seat nice?" The offscreen driver asks the couple, "Where are you going?" The husband replies, "Just go around and step on it. Let's go. Step on it." The camera cuts to a final long shot of the taxi rushing forward toward a deserted, suburban road.

Although much happier and more upbeat than the tragic ending of Emil Jannings's *The Way of All Flesh, Third Rate Manager* closes on an ambiguous note as the head of the family is literally relegated to the backseat after declaring himself as a driver in the preceding scene. If the speeding taxi in the final shot is a metaphor for the nation on the road to rapid industrialization and modernization, Ku's generation is no longer in the driver's seat. It is a time for the son's generation, represented by Kwŏn O-chŏl (Pang Su-il), Yŏng-hŭi's love interest and coworker with high moral standards and integrity. Unlike Ku, who protects Song's illicit affair with Myŏng-ok (who happens to be Kwŏn's cousin), the righteous young man persuades the kept woman to break off with the married executive and start a straight life. A former captain of his college basketball team, Kwŏn is physically fit and intellectually ambitious (his dream

FIGURE 3.2. *Third Rate Manager* closes on an ambiguous note as Manager Ku and his wife are relegated to the backseat of a speeding taxi, which symbolizes the nation on the road to modernization.

is to study in France). In the scene immediately preceding the restaurant scene, the formerly combative, screwball couple—Kwŏn O-chŏl and Yŏng-hŭi—shares a Hollywood-style kiss, suggestively captured behind the back of Kwŏn who forcefully pulls a resistant Yŏng-hŭi into his arms and presses her into romantic submission. Kwŏn's imitation of Hollywood leading men's grand gesture (reminiscent of Clark Gable's impassioned kiss of Vivien Leigh in Victor Fleming's *Gone with the Wind* [1939]) further distinguishes the young man from his future father-in-law, Ku, whose meek expression of affection for his wife is awkward and infantilized.

Although Ku is Kwŏn's superior by rank in the workplace, the older man's impotence in the presence of his son's generation is evident in an earlier scene when the manager visits the young recruit's boarding house. The purpose of this visit is to persuade Kwŏn to break off with Myŏng-ok, who Ku mistakenly believes, based on a false rumor, is cheating on his boss with the younger man. A panicked Ku pleads desperately to Kwŏn, saying, "I beg on my knees like this. . . . I endured everything to become a department manager just like our ancestors did for thirty six years under the Japanese rule. Suppose I lose my job now. My son is still a college student and then there are my old parents. Please, have mercy on me." Although the misunderstanding quickly dissipates as Kwŏn discloses his kinship to Executive Song's mistress, the titular manager's previously-quoted line reveals his undemocratic, oppressed relationship with the employer which, to him, is akin to the colonial master.

If we approach this scene from a star studies framework, it can be interpreted as Kim Sŭng-ho's autobiographical confession for his inglorious servitude to the past corrupt regime of Syngman Rhee. As a future leader of the company/nation, Kwŏn is Ku's counterpoint on several fronts. Unlike the overweight, clumsy manager, the young recruit is endowed with a fit, agile body and advanced athletic skills that are put to good use to win a friendly basketball match with a competitor company's team. Rather than following the path of regressive office politics established by his seniors, prone to brownnosing, flatteries, briberies, and extortions, Kwŏn pursues self-improvement and Western/European education as means to achieve his future goals. In short, the young man epitomizes ideal values associated with "Korean-style modernization," such as "hard work, honesty, fairness, [and] Confucian ethics."[19] Although not as morally upright as Kwŏn, his love interest Yŏng-hŭi shares his dream of Western modernity as she is seen exercising on her bed while uttering the English words, "one, two, three," in the film's opening scene. When asked by her grandma what she is doing, the new office girl uses an English word, "smart" (which she translates as "slim or sexy"), to describe her fitness objective.

The habitual use of this and other foreign phrases by the younger generation confuses the grandparents, who are unfamiliar with "new style" (*sinsik*)

FIGURE 3.3. The Korean screwball romantic couple, O-chŏl (left) and Yŏng-hŭi (right), shares the dream of Western modernity in *Third Rate Manager.*

words, and induces comic situations of intergenerational misunderstanding (for example, Yŏng-hŭi's grandmother misunderstands "smart" as "pomade"). In fact, the film's dialogue incorporates many contemporaneous examples of popular neologisms, such as "oversense," "old miss," "sabasaba," "après," and "que sera sera"—borrowed vocabulary that often creates new meanings in the Korean context. For example, "oversense" means oversensitive; "old miss" means a spinster; "sabasaba" ("mackerel" in Japanese) means bribery; as mentioned earlier, "après" ("after" in French) means a sexually liberal post-war woman. Thus, the film's foregrounding of linguistic hybridity and cross-cultural malapropisms not only reminds us of postcolonial theorist Homi Bhabha's famous phrase "imperfect mimicry,"[20] but also draws attention to the fact that postcolonial modernity in 1960s Korea is a unique mixture of Koreanness, Japaneseness, Americanness, and Europeanness. As Chungmoo Choi points out, Korean films of the 1960s often mobilize "discontinuous and hybrid images" in order to capture "the non-synchronous and fractured nature of Korean society that is caught in the contradictions of post-coloniality."[21]

A Clash between Old and New: *Under the Sky of Seoul*'s Dueling Masculinities

The production and release of socially conscious motion pictures such as Yi Pong-rae's *Third Rate Manager* and Yu Hyŏn-mok's *The Stray Bullet* (the latter analyzed in Chapter One) would have been impossible without the temporary abolishment of state film censorship and the creation of the National Motion Picture Ethics Committee (*Yŏnghwayunri chŏngukwiwŏnhoe*) in August 1960, four months after the April Revolution. In an attempt to separate its operation from the draconian censorship principals of Syngman Rhee's Liberal Party, the new civil organization—the first of its kind in South Korea—pledged its commitment to the "anti-authoritarian, [politically] neutral, and democratic" regulation of motion pictures.[22] These liberal ideals were short-lived, however, as Major-General Park Chung Hee assumed power with the May 16 military coup (known as *O-Il-Gu*, or 5.16), immediately suspended the Ethics Committee, and formally revived direct state control of film production, regulation, and exhibition with the enactment of the first Korean Motion Picture Law in 1962. Under the new law, Park's regime further centralized the film industry and enforced stringent "double censorship" rules (pre- and post-production) reminiscent of colonial-era regulations. State-controlled Korean censorship differed fundamentally from its American counterpart implemented by the Production Code Administration (PCA), beginning 1934.[23] A creation of the Motion Picture Producers and Distributors of America (Hollywood's trade organization), the PCA based its authority solely upon carefully laid-out, self-regulatory codes and had no power to penalize violating producers except for denying certificates of approval to their films. The South Korean military government, on the other hand, could arbitrarily ban the production and exhibition of domestic films. In addition, while the PCA's preemptive, pro-industry censorship mainly targeted the issues of sex and morality that might provoke local censorship and church boycotts, Korean state censorship aimed at suppressing any politically subversive content and influencing producers to cooperate in propagandizing official national discourses such as militarism, anti-communism, and rural enlightenment (*Saemaŭl* or New Village movement).

The second Motion Picture Law of 1966 mandated that when a film project falls under any one category specified in the list that follows, the Minister of Public Information can prevent the production and exhibition of such film:

1. Films that do not treat the national flag or anthem in a respectful manner.
2. Films that might profit the enemy countries or any country that is in conflict with the Republic of Korea.

3. Films that depict riot and massacre scenes that might disturb public order and safety.
4. Films that depict religion as object of sarcasm, mockery, or hatred and which treat religious rituals in a slanderous way.
5. Films that justify or encourage superstition.
6. Films that depict democratic education in a slanderous way.
7. Films that depict law-abiding citizenry or court of law in a slanderous way.
8. Films that depict legitimate executions or enforcements of law in a negative way or which depict law-enforcing officers as incompetent and powerless figures.
9. Films that justify crimes or depict crimes in an excessively detailed way.
10. Films that justify the humiliation and torture of kinsfolk.
11. Films that depict scenes of killing, torture, lynching, or violence in an excessively cruel way.
12. Films that might encourage suicide.
13. Films that expose sexual organs (e.g. female breasts) in an excessively lustful way, or which depict costumes, motions, gestures, and other behavior or language in a sensual or lustful way (for fear that films might do harm to sexual morale).
14. Films that justify rape, adultery, or prostitution.
15. Films that treat historically great men or events in a misleading and twisted way.
16. Films whose titles (including translations of foreign writings) or dialogue is of questionable taste or does not match up with the content of the film.
17. Films that plagiarized other films' content or theme songs.
18. Films that make exaggerated or false propaganda or introduce other makers' products in a misleading and twisted way (this applies only to advertisement of films).[24]

Some of the these clauses entail universal moral concerns of censorship (religion, sexuality, and violence) shared by different national film industries. However, the fact that the first three rules exclusively focus on political and ideological issues hints at the *real* priorities of the military government. It is notable that the second clause echoes the hard-lined, still-extant National Security Act (*Kukka Poanbŏp*) of 1948, under which anyone who praises or encourages enemy states (No. 1 of which remains North Korea) can be subject to prosecution and imprisonment.[25]

Unlike *Third Rate Manager* which took full advantage of the permissive regulation standards of the nongovernmental Motion Picture Ethics Committee, Yi Hyŏng-p'yo's debut film, *Under the Sky of Seoul,* was produced after the May 16 coup and released in December 1961. The film was produced by Shin Sang-ok's new company, Shin Films, a vertically integrated studio which would become a major force in domestic filmmaking over the next decade and half (under the protection of Park Chung Hee's regime until 1975, when Shin's filmmaker's permit was abruptly cancelled due to his fall-out with the regime). At this early stage of the collaborative relationship between Park's regime and Shin's production company, the new government ordered the deletion of any scenes or lines with political relevance from *Under the Sky of Seoul*.[26]

Politically cleansed and devoid of direct allusions to social upheavals, *Under the Sky of Seoul* tells a universal tale of intergenerational male rivalry and a clash between tradition and modernity. The precredit montage—a series of establishing shots of the titular city, accompanied by the sound of upbeat, modern orchestral music—immediately foregrounds the film's central theme by juxtaposing aerial shots of busy intersections and modern office buildings with those of traditional Korean houses (*hanok*) with tilting roofs in a quiet residential neighborhood. The camera cuts to a long shot of the alley where two diametrically contrasting buildings face one another across the street: a low-slung traditional Korean house with a horizontal sign in classic Chinese, indicating an oriental medical clinic, and a two-story Western-style building with a vertical sign in Korean, indicating a modern obstetrics and gynecological clinic. Suddenly, a voice-of-god narration steals into the soundtrack: "The sun starts to shine on the roofs in Seoul. Today, old age and new age stand shoulder to shoulder in this alley. Dream, love, laughter and tears of Seoul can be felt here." The narrator introduces two young characters who are gazing at one another flirtatiously across the street: Kim Hyŏn-ok (Ch'oe Ŭn-hŭi), a beauty salon owner and widow, and Dr. Ch'oe Tu-yŏl (Kim Chin-gyu), a widowed gynecologist. The smiling doctor on his roof top is hailed by an off-screen character who shouts "Hey!" The camera cuts to a low-angle shot of Kim Sŭng-ho, garbed in traditional *hanbok* (Korean dress), who looks up at the young doctor dressed in a Western-style doctor's gown and suit and scolds him, "Stop looking at other people's windows every day." The narrator introduces the meddling man as "Hyŏn-ok's father, Kim Hak-gyu. A grumpy old man of Oriental medicine." The over-protective father orders his daughter to close the window screen, to her disappointment. After the daughter and the doctor withdraw, the Oriental medicine man is joined by his sidekicks and best friends: Pak Chusa (Hŏ Chang-gang), a fortune-teller, and No Mong-hyŏn (Kim Hŭi-gap), a realtor, both of whom are tenants in his business establishment. When the insulted father complains about Dr. Ch'oe's daily stare at his daughter, No says it is called, in a "new-style" expression, *yŏnae* ("free love" or "romance"), a half-joking comment that provokes Kim's indignation and rebuttal.

The exposition scene quickly sets up the "oriental medicine man" Kim's antagonism against the "Western medicine man" Ch'oe, who happens to be courting his daughter despite his disapproval. The two male characters represent opposing values and ideologies: premodern tradition vs. modernity, the East vs. the West, and the old vs. the young. The herbalist/acupuncturist Kim resents Dr. Ch'oe, a modern ob/gyn, and openly calls him an "enemy" for "invading [his] turf of thirty years" and taking his customers away. Dr. Ch'oe, on the other hand, regards the stubborn senior as "childish" and jokingly calls him a "dictator" to Kim's daughter when the two would-be-lovers are left alone. The two men's rivalry intensifies when the local tavern owner's daughter, Chŏm-rae (To Kŭm-bong), visits Kim's oriental medicine clinic (*hanŭiwŏn*) with her mother (Hwang Chŏng-sun). On their way to the clinic, the mother expresses her confidence in traditional medicine to her sick daughter, saying, "Internal illness can be better cured by oriental medicine than by common Western medicine." Her good faith dissipates quickly, however, when Dr. Kim diagnoses that Chŏm-rae has been pregnant for a few months. The proud mother takes offense and blames the oriental herbalist for slandering her virgin daughter. Unbeknownst to Dr. Kim (as well as her mother), Chŏm-rae has been secretly dating his college-educated yet unemployed son Hyŏn-u (Sin Yŏng-gyun) and is carrying his baby. In order to keep their illicit relationship confidential, Chŏm-rae lies to her mother that she saw Dr. Ch'oe and that the young doctor vouched that she is not pregnant. When Chŏm-rae's mother returns to Kim's clinic to humiliate him and threatens to take a trip to the police station, the oriental medicine man's hatred of the other doctor reaches a peak. He yells at his absent rival across the alley, "You, swindler! You, thief! What do you know about medicine? A doctor of medicine? If you are a doctor, I am a doctor's grandfather."

To get even with his foe, Kim reports Ch'oe to the police for performing what the former mistakenly suspects is an illegal abortion. When the older man raids the young doctor's clinic along with a police officer, it turns out that the suspected abortion has been performed legally in order to save the life of the mother who is suffering from tuberculosis. The police officer reprimands Kim, addressing him as *yŏnggam* (a derogatory appellation for an old man), and warns him, "If you falsely accuse Dr. Ch'oe again, it is you who will be arrested." After his plan to remove his rival has been foiled, Kim complains about the "immoral law" to his friends, Pak and No, and asks who makes laws. As the most worldly member of the trio, Pak replies that it is lawmakers in the National Assembly who are in charge. The comic-relief character No mischievously encourages Kim to run for a seat in the National Assembly or city council in order to change laws. Kim's vanity gets the better of him and he prematurely declares, "I'll send anyone immoral to jail. . . . I'll change all immoral laws in this country." In the latter part of the film, when Kim finds out that

Ch'oe is running for city council, he decides to run against him out of spite and jealousy. The young doctor withdraws his candidacy close to the election date out of respect for the father of his love interest. By that time, the patriarch has squandered his entire family fortune as well as his daughter's beauty salon property on the election campaign. When dismal election results are broadcast on radio (Kim gets a mere eight votes from his immediate family, his closest friends, and his "enemy," Dr. Ch'oe), the shamed protagonist is unable to face his family and leaves home after writing a suicide note. Dr. Ch'oe comes to the rescue by not only paying for the family's debt, but also treating Kim after he gets into a traffic accident while trying to run away from his daughter, who had spotted him on the road. Finally, the stubborn father accepts Chŏm-rae and Dr. Ch'oe as his daughter-in-law and son-in-law, and reconciles with his estranged son whom he had expelled from home after finding out about his relationship with the tavern owner's daughter. The film's final shot focuses on the proud, happy grandfather who is babysitting his grandson (Chŏm-rae and Yŏng-gu's baby) while the rest of his family is occupied offscreen with Chŏm-rae and Yŏng-gu's wedding reception. Despite the upbeat, nondiegetic music and Kim Sŭng-ho's trademark smile, the final shot leaves a bittersweet aftertaste as the father is seen alone and physically separated from other family members.

While not explicitly satiric, in terms of taking potshots at the contemporaneous political climate and corporate corruption (in the vein of *Third Rate Manager*), *Under the Sky of Seoul* is nevertheless infused with implicit social criticism, which was sufficiently diluted to pass the new military government's censors. Kim's wife (Han Ŭn-jin) goads her husband to pay for his son's bribe to prospective employers. She estimates that they should pay at least 200,000 won ($200) for him to find employment. The wife adds, "You need money for everything." When Kim decides to run for city council, he persuades his skeptical wife by telling her, "If I get elected, I will make big money," a suggestive remark that implies political corruption within a "bribe culture." In his election campaign, with the help of his publicity manager (a local radio repair shop owner play by the slapstick comedian Ku Pong-sŏ), Kim brands himself as "a true patriot for all his life and real representative of people" who is dedicated to "justice." Such hypocritical political slogans would have been met with a jaundiced perspective among contemporaneous theatergoers who were watching the film one year after the presidential election scandal, which led to the April 19 Revolution and the temporary ousting of Kim Sŭng-ho from the film industry. Compared with the protagonists of *Romance Papa* and *Third Rate Manager*, Kim's character is much more caricatured, flawed, and unreasonable: he is prone to uncontrollable rage, petty jealousy, illogical obstinacy, and narcissist illusions. In particular, his blind hatred for Dr. Ch'oe verges on being pathological. In sharp contrast, Dr. Ch'oe, a member of Seoul's new social elite, is perpetually polite, logical, composed, and compassionate. The film's narrative leaves no doubt in the viewer's mind as to who—or, rather, *which generation*—should lead the family and larger community (and, extending it further, the society and nation). Nevertheless, the film reintegrates Kim into the family unit and respects his nominal status as the head of the household while simultaneously foregrounding his distance from the rest of the family in the final shot.

Despite all the insults he has endured in the past, Dr. Ch'oe gracefully greets Kim with the appellation "father" (*abŏji*), adding "father-in-law (*changin*) is father, too" in the penultimate scene set in Kim's room where the recent traffic accident victim is nursed by his wife and visited by his two stooges. Moments before Ch'oe's appearance at the door with a familial greeting, in front of his wife and friends, the stubborn old man puts on an act of continued animosity against the young doctor, who has saved his family's finance as well as his own life. Kim's attitude, however, reverses after being called "father." The camera pans right from a medium shot of Kim's daughter and Dr. Ch'oe at the door to a close-up of Kim in the foreground, who begrudgingly endorses his future-son-in-law with the reply, "That's true [that father-in-law is father, too]," and bursts into nervous laughter connoting both joy and embarrassment. This shot is significant as Kim is hailed to the foreground through Dr. Ch'oe's act of acknowledging their kinship (by marriage).

Throughout the film, Kim's figure is often positioned in the background in medium shots to connote his familial alienation and social marginalization. For example, ten minutes into the film, a medium shot shows Kim eating on a separate table in the background while his wife and daughter share another table in the foreground. The conversation focuses on the daughter's marriage prospect with Dr. Ch'oe, her suitor, which the father adamantly opposes despite his wife's approval. The film's mise-en-scène visually accentuates the mother and daughter's alliance against the obstinate man, who is literally behind them in both a spatial and temporal sense. In the same scene, Kim is reprimanded by his wife for being a cheapskate with children, despite the fact he had "spent a fortune on mistresses" when he was younger, and when they were better off. The embarrassed husband, with a guilty expression on his face, awkwardly changes the subject to his son's absence at dinner.

Similarly tiered staging is repeated in a scene where Chŏm-rae's mother, after discovering the truth of her daughter's pregnancy, raids Kim's house at night to blame Hyŏn-u for ruining her daughter as well as his parents for arranging a "family date" with a prospective bride (from a wealthy family) for their son. When the camera dollies in to a medium shot of the paper-paneled door of Kim's room, Chŏm-rae's mother sits on the threshold step in front and Kim's wife stands off-frame in the adjoining family room (with an edge of her *hanbok* skirt barely visible on the far-right side of the frame).

FIGURE 3.4. In *Under the Sky of Seoul*, Kim Sŭng-ho's character is often positioned in the background to connote his familial alienation and social marginalization.

The man of the house is recessionally located in the background, behind the bamboo screen of the open door, which he holds up to lend an ear to the agitated visitor's speech. When the tavern woman accuses the Kim family for neglecting her and her daughter because of her lowly profession, Kim's daughter silently enters the frame from the left (standing in the yard) and is foregrounded as the principal listener of the older woman's complaints. In contrast with her parents who remain silent, the daughter intervenes and pacifies the self-pitying woman with comforting words: "We didn't know that. Now we understand, so please go back home. This doesn't help. Let's talk about ways to solve this problem." While the daughter is coping with the problem, her father in the background is seen closing the bamboo curtain and withdraws from the scene altogether. The camera cuts to the interior of his room while Chŏm-rae's mother continues to whine offscreen about her daughter's ruined life. Then the father is shown sitting in the background with an angry expression on his face, while his son in the foreground keeps his head down in shame. After the visitor's departure, the father and son enter into a heated argument in which the rebellious offspring scorns the older man's insistence on class superiority over Chŏm-rae's family. At this point, the insulted father kicks his only son out of their home. Throughout the entire fight scene, the father is situated in the background or behind his son's back, once again attesting to his inability to accept the social changes of a modern time when class equality and free love/marriage are taken for granted by a younger generation.

Directed by Yi Hyŏng-p'yo, who was trained to make newsreels at the United States Information Service (USIS, later USIA or the Unites States Information Agency) and who worked as an assistant director on the Paramount-produced

Korean War docudrama *Cease Fire!* (1953), *Under the Sky of Seoul* at times exudes the influence of Western/American culture, in particular its appropriation of Hollywood soundtrack songs such as "I Whistle a Happy Tune" (from Twentieth Century-Fox's 1956 musical *The King and I*) as well as the theme music of Columbia's *The Bridge on the River Kwai* (1957). However, as a transitional film made during the early months of Park Chung Hee's new military regime, which ruled the nation under an emergency junta (called the Supreme Council for National Reconstruction), *Under the Sky of Seoul* prefigures some of the "enlightenment" (*kaemong*) themes to be adopted by Shin Sang-ok and his fellow producers to assist the Park Chung Hee government's public information goals. Chief among them is the "crackdown on superstitions" (*misin t'ap'a*), as evidenced by the fifth clause of the 1966 Motion Picture Law, quoted earlier, as well as the seventh clause of the original 1962 Motion Picture Law, which more broadly prohibits films that "respect superstition."[27]

In *Under the Sky of Seoul*, Kim's friend and tenant, fortuneteller Pak, is the person who represents adherence to anachronistic superstitions, something that would not have jibed with the new government's modernization (*kŭndaehwa*) objectives. Although he is a sympathetic, if also somewhat dubious and backstabbing, character, the legitimacy of Pak's profession is openly challenged by his friend Kim, who discredits his claim of knowledge in Indian philosophy (Pak is a self-proclaimed expert of Indian philosophy who has never been to the Subcontinent). Moreover, the film includes a witty subplot that tweaks the absurdity of "matchmaking fortunetelling" (*kunghap*) based on the horoscope, which is still used by some Korean parents to screen potential mates for their children. One day, Pak is visited by a young couple who have come for matchmaking fortunetelling. The would-be bridegroom is candid about his disbelief in such a superstition, but he nevertheless passes a bribe (10,000 won [$10]) to the fortuneteller, asking him to give them a good fortune when he brings his superstitious mother the following morning. After the couple leaves, the would-be bride returns alone and gives the fortuneteller another bribe of 10,000 won, this time demanding that he give them a bad fortune. Later that day, the future mother-in-law also visits the fortuneteller's shop and offers 10,000 won, asking him to tell a bad fortune when she comes with her son and the girlfriend the following morning. Having received three bribes with contradictory requests, the fortuneteller is at loss as to which lie to tell. His co-conspirator Kim concocts a scheme to skirt this impossible situation and eventually tells a lie to the returning customers, informing them that the fortuneteller suddenly died of a heart attack that morning. Later, the plan backfires and Pak is chased by the couple in slapstick fashion when he accidently runs into them at a marketplace. This comic segment of the film mocks matchmaking fortunetelling as an illogical superstition and delegitimizes such practices, providing an enlightenment message of the new government's anti-superstition policy, which would be officially written into a list of film regulation principals in 1962 and again in 1966.

Redefining the Family in Contemporary South Korean Cinema

Although Kim Sŭng-ho's popular persona of the 1960s is of a sentimental father figure who struggles to keep up with the rapid speed of modernization and barely maintains his symbolic post as the family patriarch thanks to the filial respect of the son's generation, cinematic fathers of his generation are perhaps more fortunate than some of their contemporary counterparts. In New Korean cinema of the 1980s and 1990s, fathers were often absent, dead, or replaced by surrogate paternal figures as exemplified by Park Kwang-su (Pak Kwang-su)'s *Chilsu and Mansu* (*Ch'ilsu wa Mansu*, 1988) and Im Kwon-taek (Im Kwŏn-t'aek)'s *Sopyonje* (*Sop'yŏnje*, 1993). This formula of the "absent father" is persistent in South Korea's new millennium cinema, including *Tae Guk Gi: The Brotherhood of War* (*T'aegŭkki hwinallimyŏ*, 2004), *Silmido* (2004), *My Brother* (*Uri hyŏng*, 2004), *Mr. Gam's Victory* (*Sup'ŏ sŭt'a Kam Sa-yong*, 2004), *When I Turn Nine* (*Ahopsal insaeng*, 2004), *Sympathy for Lady Vengeance* (*Ch'iljŏlhan Kŭjassi*, 2005), *Family Ties* (*Kajok ŭi t'angsaeng*, 2006), *Bandhobi* (*Pandubi*, 2009), *Mother* (*Madŏ*, 2009), and *Pieta* (*P'iet'a*, 2012). In these films, absent fathers are replaced by brothers (*Tae Guk Gi, My Brother*), colleagues (*Silmido, Mr. Gam's Victory*), friends (*Bandhobi, When I Turn Nine*), and "phallic" mothers (*Sympathy for Lady Vengeance, Family Ties, Mother*, and *Pieta*).

Family Ties, a film whose Korean-language title—*Kajok ŭi t'angsaeng*—literally translates as "Birth of a Family," stands out in the context of new familial and generational formations in recent South Korean cinema. Directed by Kim T'ae-yong, whose debut film *Memento Mori* (*Yŏgo koedam tubŏnjje iyagi*, 1999) gained notoriety as a high-school ghost story which openly challenged societal gender norms through explicit lesbian themes, *Family Ties* is likewise noteworthy for the way that each of its three internally demarcated yet interwoven stories focuses on a female relationship. Significantly, the latter film culminates with a symbolic scene in which a father figure is shut out of the house by his disapproving sister. Prior to that point, the man in question—a good-for-nothing ex-convict named Hyŏn-ch'ŏl (Ŏm T'ae-ung) who is introduced in the film's first episode—has brought a much older bride named Mu-sin (Ko Tu-sim) to the house of his sister Mi-ra (Mun So-ri). Despite her discomfort, Mi-ra shows tact in concealing her disapproval of the newlyweds until Mu-sin's stepdaughter from a previous marriage shows up and Hyŏn-ch'ŏl asks her to admit the little girl into her household. After a quarrel with his sister, the irresponsible man disappears without a word, deserting his bride as well as the girl who is technically his "daughter."

Later, in the film's final episode (which focuses on the romantic struggles of Ch'ae-hyŏn [Chŏng Yu-mi], Mu-sin's grown stepdaughter, now a college student), it is revealed that Mi-ra and Mu-sin have formed a family of sorts, one that is comprised of two mothers and a daughter who is not a blood kin, without the presence of a husband/father figure. While the two mothers are making kimchi with their daughter and her boyfriend in the garden, Hyŏn-ch'ŏl (who had been out of touch for over a decade) makes a surprise visit with a new, noticeably pregnant, girlfriend in tow. The sudden appearance of the unwelcome visitors shocks Mu-sin, a wronged wife, threatening the well-being of the unconventional, matriarchal family. Quick-witted and resolute, Mi-ra intervenes and lures her brother and his guest outside of the house for a private talk, only to shut the door on them. This literal expelling of Ch'ae-hyŏn's nominal father figure is allegorical of a broader transformation of the family structure in South Korean society and cinema over the past half-century, since the heyday of Kim Sŭng-ho and his beloved father figure in modernization comedies.

It is noteworthy that *Family Ties* was released a year after the anachronistic *Hoju* system, a patriarchal means of securing the man's place as "master of the family," was ruled unconstitutional for violating gender equality by the Constitutional Court of Korea. Originally imported from Japan during the colonial period, the *Hoju* system was abolished in January 2008, seven months after the film's release and three years after the National Assembly reformed South Korea's Civil Act (*Minbŏp*), in March 2005. Under the old system, men were privileged as the legal head of the family. The order of succession for the lifelong *Hoju* post was (1) son, (2) unmarried daughter, (3) wife, (4) father's mother, and (5) daughter-in-law. Following a father's death, the eldest son traditionally inherited that role. Once married, daughters were removed from their fathers' family registries (*hojŏk*) and transferred to those of their husbands. The *Hoju* system denied children's adoption of the mother's surname or a stepfather's surname and required the signature of the biological father on legal documents concerning children even after parents got a divorce and despite the fact that children might be living with their mother.

Thus, *Family Ties* is a timely film that envisions the redefined Korean family after the abolishment of the *Hoju* system, an outmoded means of curtailing the rights of women (mothers, wives, and daughters) that bore the traces of Japanese colonial influence. If that system provided the legal grounds for the nominal patriarchal power of Kim Sŭng-ho's postwar generation, its abolishment in recent years opens up new possibilities for the cinematic re-imagination of family and parenthood in South Korea. With its ironic title, *Family Ties* celebrates a loosening of traditional patrilineal ties and lends cinematic substance to the emergence of new/alternative familial dynamics and social formations, thus completing the long process of paternal "vanishment," if not complete banishment, initiated by 1960s modernization comedies.

Chapter 4

Once upon a Time in Manchuria

Classic and Contemporary Korean Westerns

In the closing seconds of George Stevens's magisterial Western *Shane* (1953), after a violent barroom showdown that leaves a hired gun from Cheyenne dead, young Joey (Brandon De Wilde) beseeches the titular hero not to leave his parents' homestead. The plaintive words of the teary-eyed boy—"Come back!"—echo through the valley below the Teton Mountains, which Shane (Alan Ladd) ascends on horseback to the accompaniment of composer Victor Young's swelling score. Although those memorable words continue to reverberate among many American fans of the Western genre, who similarly desire the hero's return, Korean movie audiences of the postwar period had only to wait fifteen years before a localized version of this timeless story appeared on the big screen.

Produced in 1968, legendary Korean director Shin Sang-ok (Sin Sang-ok)'s "Manchurian Western" *The Man with No Home* (*Musukja*, a.k.a. *Homeless*, or *The Wanderer*) is a creative reworking of Stevens's film, one that stars the most popular Korean actress of that era, Ch'oe Ŭn-hŭi, as a farmer's wife whose role is analogous to that of Jean Arthur in the original. A comparative scene-by-scene analysis of these two films underscores the specific semantic/syntactic/pragmatic variations (to borrow Rick Altman's terminology) in the Korean Manchurian Western. Specifically, the significant changes made by director

Shin and his screenwriter in terms of landscape, images of femininity and masculinity, the confrontation between the hero and the villain, and the theme of surrogate paternalism highlight how American Western conventions are mixed with and diffused by Korean melodramatic sentiments in *The Man with No Home*.

The expression "Manchurian Western" refers to a cycle of 1960s and 1970s South Korean action films set in Manchuria during the 1920s and 1930s, a space that is populated by members of the Korean colonial diaspora (consisting of disparate groups, such as peasants, bandits, freedom fighters, and hired guns). Reminiscent of contemporaneous variations of the Western genre produced in the United States and throughout Europe, such as the "professional Western" (*The Magnificent Seven* [1960], *The Wild Bunch* [1969], etc.) and the "spaghetti Western" (including Italian director Sergio Leone's famous "Man with No Name" trilogy consisting of *A Fistful of Dollars* [1964], *For a Few Dollars More* [1965], and *The Good, the Bad, and the Ugly* [1966]), the moral compass of the Manchurian Western is difficult to pinpoint. Its narratives are ambiguous, to say the least, filled as they are with heroes who are stateless outlaws, not righteous sheriffs. However, what distinguishes the Korean Western from its American and Italian counterparts is its nationalist message: the Japanese Imperial Army normally assumes the antagonist position, and bandits or mercenaries conveniently turn out to be undercover guerrillas. While retaining certain scenographic elements of the classic Western (horses, guns, saddles, frontier houses, etc.), the Manchurian Western is revealed to be a hybrid genre mixing characteristics of the war film, the espionage film, the martial arts film, and the family melodrama.

Alternatively dubbed the "continental film" genre (*taeryukmul*) or an example of "Manchurian action" (*Manju hwalgŭk*), this Korean variation on the Western genre was inaugurated by Chŏng Ch'ang-hwa's *The Horizon* (*Chip'yŏngsŏn*, 1961), a pioneering work that is believed to be permanently lost (no original negative is said to exist), and Im Kwon-taek (Im Kwŏn-t'aek)'s debut film *Farewell Tuman River* (*Tumanganga chal itgŏra*, 1962). Like the American Western, which has its roots in pioneer literature published prior to the twentieth century, the Korean counterpart has undergone subtle yet significant transformations, with its emphasis shifting from the collective heroism of independence fighters to the personal quests of lone wanderers or outlaws toward the "mature" period of the genre in the late 1960s to the early 1970s. Representative films from the latter period include Im Wŏn-sik's *Yŏng* (1968), Shin Sang-ok's *The Man with No Home*, and Lee Man-hee (Yi Man-hŭi)'s *Break the Chain* (*Soesasŭl ŭl kkŭnŏra*, 1971), the latter serving as a major source of inspiration for Kim Jee-woon (Kim Chi-un)'s recent blockbuster hit *The Good, the Bad, the Weird* (*Chotŭn nom, nappŭn nom, isanghan nom*, 2008), a film that will be analyzed in detail toward the latter part of this chapter.

Western Genre Theory and the Curious Case of the Manchurian Western

Before discussing the culturally specific transformations of the Western genre in South Korean cinema, it will be helpful to take a brief tour of the scholarship concerned with this perennial Hollywood genre in order to provide a theoretical springboard for the ensuing textual analysis. Dubbed by the film historian Thomas Schatz as "the richest and most enduring genre of Hollywood's repertoire,"[1] the Western has been central to the work of many genre theorists (especially that of Edward Buscombe, Andrew Tudor, and John G. Cawelti). Early conceptual treatment of the Western was influenced by Claude Lévi-Strauss's structuralist methods of studying cultural myths as binary oppositions. Theorists of the Western became increasingly obsessed with reading the genre in terms of thematic binaries of the frontier mythology, including those pitting the wilderness against civilization, the individual against the community, nature against culture, the West against the East, the garden against the desert, cattlemen against homesteaders, cowboys against Indians, and schoolmarms against dancehall girls.

Schatz traces the transformation of the genre, moving from (1) the classic formula of the late 1930s to the 1940s (e.g. *Stagecoach* [1939], *The Westerner* [1940]) to (2) the "psychological" Western of the late 1940s and the 1950s (e.g. *Pursued* [1947], *Blood on the Moon* [1948], *High Noon* [1952]) to (3) the "professional" Western of the 1960s and the 1970s (e.g. *The Magnificent Seven, The Wild Bunch, Butch Cassidy and the Sundance Kid* [1969], *The Shootist* [1976]). He also argues that the Western morphed into a nostalgic and self-reflexive mirror of itself in its late stages, as in *The Man Who Shot Liberty Valance* (1962) and *The Shootist*—both films deconstructing the myth of the genre and its hero.[2] Drawing upon the theoretical writings of Christian Metz, Schatz contends that genres pass through clear stages, a linear process that segues from the *experimental* stage (when conventions are isolated and established) to the *classical* stage (when they are accepted and understood by audience) to the *refinement* stage (when formal and stylistic details are embellished) to the *baroque* stage (when mannerist or self-reflexive/metatextual elements come to the fore, and when the form of a film becomes its "content").[3]

Critiquing Schatz's assumption of generic evolution, Tag Gallagher asserts that self-reflexivity and self-consciousness existed even during the silent period. This can be exemplified in the last close-up frontal shot of the bandit firing his gun at the audience in Edwin S. Porter's *The Great Train Robbery* (1903). Gallagher finds Schatz's argument of "internally generated evolution specific to the western genre" historically unverifiable.[4] Not only does evolution-based theory gloss over the historical evidence of pre-World War I Westerns, but it also negates the *cyclical* nature of genres. In his essay "Questions of Genre,"

Steve Neale further problematizes Schatz's paradigm, which presupposes a textually-based evolution without consideration of the ways in which industrial and sociocultural contexts contribute to transformations. Neale argues that genres should be understood as "processes [that] are marked fundamentally by difference, variation, and change" and which are prone to hybridity.[5] For instance, *The Great Train Robbery*, now considered to be the first Western film, was promoted as a "melodrama, chase film, railway genre, and crime film, rather than [a] western" upon its original release.[6] Genres are not static, but always in flux, prone to transformation, inherently temporal and thus bound to historicity. Neale calls for a genre criticism rooted in the Russian Formalist concept of the *dominant*, seeing genres constructed through a complex "interplay between canonized and noncanonized forms of representation and between canonized and noncanonized genres."[7] Mel Brooks's comedy Western *Blazing Saddles* (1974) exemplifies Neale's emphasis on hybridization and the dominant. Although the subgeneric element of comedy can be found in studio-era Westerns of the 1930s–1940s, comedy and parody emerged as a generic dominant of many post-studio period Westerns, as in *Cat Ballou* (1965), *Support Your Local Sheriff!* (1969), *The Apple Dumpling Gang* (1975), *Goin' South* (1978), and *The Frisco Kid* (1979).

Ideologically-oriented critics such as Virginia Wright Wexman and Brian Henderson have reinterpreted the Western from gender-specific and racial perspectives—issues previously dismissed by structuralists. In her book chapter "Star and Genre: John Wayne, the Western, and the American Dream of the Family on the Land," Wexman points out how the Western, based on the imperialist myth of "Manifest Dynasty," normalizes masculinity and whiteness as characteristics of Americanness. Accordingly, the woman is reduced as the bearer of a male heir in a "dynastic marriage" for the perpetuation of patrilineal ownership of land, and Indians and Mexicans "become objects of colonialist domination . . . subordination or extermination."[8] In "*The Searchers*: An American Dilemma," Henderson sees the tale of bigotry and revenge in Ford's 1956 film as an allegory of racial conflicts between whites and blacks in 1950s America. The film was released in the wake of heated debates surrounding the *Brown v. Board of Education of Topeka* case, in which the Supreme Court ordered desegregation of public schools. Henderson points out that Ford and his scripter racialized the Martin Pawley character (Jeffrey Hunter) from a full white in the original story to one-eighth Cherokee, intentionally creating a racial conflict between antihero Ethan Hawks (John Wayne) and his adopted kin.[9] In contrast to Schatz's romantic analysis of the last shot of Ethan's exclusion from the frontier community as "an appropriate farewell for Wayne, Ford, and the genre itself,"[10] Henderson reads it as an embodiment of "the figure of the white Southerner [who] often functions as a scapegoat on the race question."[11] When we critically position the film within the context of its production and initial dissemination as a national and social allegory of 1950s America, Ethan represents an old-generation Southerner with Confederate values,[12] someone who shares no space in the integrated frontier home (a metaphor for the new America of the Civil Rights era), which welcomes biracial and bicultural members such as Martin and Debbie Edwards (Natalie Woods), Ethan's abducted and eventually rescued niece who has been raised by Comanches. Subsequently, the changing tenor of racial discourse in American cinema and society since the post-studio, post-Civil Rights era contributed to the appearance of a cycle of pro-Indian Westerns demythologizing classic Westerns' stereotypes of Indians as savages and subhumans and revisiting the history of the West from victims' perspectives. Instances of the latter include *Geronimo* (1962), *Tell Them Willie Boy Is Here* (1969), *Soldier Blue* (1970), *Little Big Man* (1970), *Ulzana's Raid* (1972), *Dances with Wolves* (1990), *Black Robe* (1991), and *Geronimo: An American Legend* (1993).

As William McClain argues in his article "Western, Go Home! Sergio Leone and the 'Death of the Western' in American Film Criticism," the Western genre is perhaps the purest distillation of American values that cinema as a cultural institution has given us, a truly "national genre" that, in the final analysis, is "irremovably and fundamentally American."[13] It is precisely because of the primacy of the Western in the construction of national mythology and identity that many homegrown critics seem to have resented the Italian appropriation of this uniquely American film genre in the late 1960s, when Leone's aforementioned "Man with No Name" trilogy received stateside releases. Perhaps American critics during that decade should have been more forgiving of Leone's spaghetti Westerns, which are comparatively "authentic" evocations of the American frontier in the second half of the 1800s and which retain a certain degree of historical verisimilitude despite the occasional mixing of Roman Catholic iconography, including monasteries and priests.

Unbeknownst to these niggling naysayers, these guardians of national culture of the 1960s, the Western genre was being more radically hijacked, mutated, and decontextualized by filmmakers of South Korea's Golden Age cinema (1955–1972). Along with Hollywood melodramas such as Mervyn LeRoy's *Waterloo Bridge* (1940) and *Random Harvest* (1943), classic American Westerns from the likes of Fred Zinnemann, director of *High Noon*, and George Stevens, director of *Shane*, were enormously popular among South Korean theatergoers of the 1950s, when the public was hungry for escapist entertainment to cope with emotional and financial hardships in the wake of the civil war. In his semi-autobiographical novel *The Life and Death of the Hollywood Kid* (*Hŏlliudŭ k'idŭ ŭi saengae*, 1992), the renowned journalist-writer Ahn Junghyo (An Chŏng-hyo) vividly describes his and others' intense love of all things Hollywood in postwar South Korea: "Absorbing diverse models of life manufactured in Hollywood . . . we came to believe that the wide plains of the American West were our beautiful, lost home from some previous life. Denying our poverty-stricken home and dirty streets, we came to mistake the screen world as our idealized reality."[14] However, the popularity of American Westerns waned in South Korea in the 1960s. According to the film historian Yi Yŏng-il, such Hollywood Westerns as *The Alamo* (1960), *4 for Texas* (1963), and *Major Dundee* (1965) underperformed at the Korean box office.[15] Instead, spaghetti Westerns, including the films comprising Leone's "Man with No Name" trilogy and the entries in Sergio Corbucci's *Django* (1966) series, were among the most popular foreign imports along with the James Bond series being produced in Great Britain and the Hong Kong action films being made by Shaw Brothers and other companies throughout the 1960s. The mass influx and widespread popularity of Italian Westerns even led to the momentary strengthening of import restrictions for the genre on the part of Park Chung Hee's military regime.[16] According to Yi, spaghetti Westerns shocked Korean audiences because of their focus on obsession, revenge, and violence unmotivated by morality and the pursuit of justice, unlike their American cousins.[17]

The first Italian Western import, *A Fistful of Dollars*, was released in South Korea in 1966. Not coincidently, it is around this time that the Manchurian Western genre began to undergo an important transformation, with its previous emphasis on nationalist agendas or missions (including the fight for independence) starting to diminish or be diffused. In his doctoral dissertation, "Popular Reasoning of South Korean Melodrama Films (1953–1972)," Jinsoo An argues that the Manchurian action genre functioned to revitalize masculinity in 1960s Korean cinema, a cultural space in which disempowered and humiliated patriarchs—the casualties of modernization—had a ubiquitous presence particularly in the context of family melodramas and modernization comedies (which we discussed in the previous chapter). In contrast to that representational schema, the early Manchurian Western, according to An, depicts Korean men as "romantic, assertive, adventurous, competent, intelligent, and muscular."[18] Although they might be temporarily lured into "such romantic activities as gambling, drinking, womanizing, and fighting," these heroes are ultimately and single-mindedly devoted to "a grander and more altruistic goal, i.e. the fight for the nation's independence."[19]

Transporting its protagonists and viewers to a diasporic space—the multiethnic frontier—of Manchuria during an era of colonization, the Korean Western typically portrays Japanese military forces as a collective threat pitted against the "good guys," that is, Korean resistance guerrillas and spies. Thus, it expands and localizes traditional thematic binaries in the American Western (the wilderness vs. civilization, lawmen vs. outlaws, cattlemen vs. homesteaders, cowboys vs. Indians, etc.) to accommodate new settings and different historical/cultural contexts. According to An, there were two political and ideological factors which influenced the rise of this particular genre in the early to mid-1960s. First, the ongoing controversy surrounding Korean filmmakers' plagiarism of Japanese motion pictures, on top of the dominance of American films in South Korea, called for the reinstatement of anti-Japanese, nationalist narratives. Second, South Korea's integration into the US-dominated "triple alliance security system" of the region, as a partner in the wake of the much-protested normalization of diplomacy with Japan in 1965, necessitated a cinematic response in the form of old-fashioned nationalism.[20]

In the Cold War context of the 1960s, it is curious that cinematic antagonisms were renewed against an old foe, one that had just morphed into South Korea's new ally. It is possible to hypothesize that, while dressed in Japanese military regalia and uniforms, the enemy stood in for North Korean, Chinese, or even North Vietnamese communists in the collective imaginary of South Korean theatergoers living in an anti-communist nation-state whose troops were fighting side-by-side with Americans in Vietnam between 1965 to 1973. In any case, the transnational flow of the American Western genre within South Korea during the authoritarian Park Chung Hee era (1961–1979) provided Koreans an opportunity to screen the (doubly) displaced national imagination in a Manchurian setting with multicultural (American, Chinese, and Japanese) iconographies or visual tropes. Just as the mythical West of the nineteenth century was cinematically constructed as an imaginary haven for Americans weathering the Depression or, decades later, as an allegorical means of deflecting political crises during the Cold War era, the Manchurian wilderness of Korea's colonial past seems to have satiated the escapist fantasies of local audiences under military dictatorship.

Showing No Shame in "Koreanizing" *Shane*: Shin Sang-ok's *The Man with No Home*

Also known as *Homeless* and *The Wanderer, The Man with No Home* represents the second phase of the Manchurian Western genre (encompassing the years between the late 1960s and the early 1970s), which is characterized by the presence of a lone hero, a focus on apathy to national resistance, and a prevalence of personalized conflicts. The director of this 1968 film, Shin Sang-ok, is a legendary figure who in 1960 had established Shin Films, the first Korean company modeled after Hollywood studios. Shin Films produced approximately 150 motion pictures over the course of ten years, a figure which accounts for 10% of the total output of the industry during that period. Although best known for his technically polished melodramas such as *The Houseguest and My Mother* (*Sarangbang sonnim kwa ŏmŏni*, 1961) and historical dramas such as *King Yŏnsan* (*Yŏnsangun*, 1961) and *Women of the Chosun Dynasty* (*Ijo yŏin chanhoksa*, 1969), Shin's diverse filmography is composed of war films, comedies, literary adaptations, ghost and horror films, and murder mysteries.

Promoted as an "Oriental Western" on its original theatrical release, *The Man with No Home* is an exemplary work that epitomizes Shin's generic prowess, his ability to mix elements of the Western, melodrama, martial arts action, the gangster film, and the war film.

Most interestingly, the film is a fascinating reworking of the American classic *Shane*, which remains one of the most beloved Westerns in South Korea, as evidenced by the Korean Broadcasting System (KBS)'s 1996 nationwide survey of "Films That Audiences Want to See Again" (which we referenced in Chapter One of this book). Stevens's film ranked No. 56, the highest among Westerns. The only other Westerns on the list are *The Good, the Bad, and the Ugly* (No. 58), *High Noon* (No. 71), and *Gunfight at the OK Corral* (No. 75).[21] Given older Korean audiences' predilection for sentimental melodrama (a subject explored in Chapter One), it is not surprising that *Shane*—a film whose subplot involves a forbidden, unspoken love between married woman Marian Starrett (Jean Arthur) and the titular drifting gunman—ranked so high. Both *The Man with No Home* and *Shane* begin with the arrival of a lone rider at a frontier house in the wilderness and end with his disappearance into the sunset. The dramatic core of both films is the mysterious drifter's friendship and intergenerational bonding with a little boy whose mother he falls in love with early on. In both films, the boy's father heroically leads a group of farmers in their fight against a gang of greedy villains, risking his own life in the process. In both films, the titular wanderer intervenes and eliminates the villains with his fast-draw skills (while the father is temporarily incapacitated or mortally wounded). The dénouement of each film shows the self-sacrificing gunman quietly leaving for the sake of the woman he loves as well as her son. Despite this similarity in the two films' basic narrative structure, their settings, iconography, and subplots are considerably different. Specifics of the Korean adaptation of the mythical and romantic narrative of *Shane* will shed light on some of the syntactic and pragmatic necessities involved in transforming a story of frontier homesteaders in 1880s Wyoming into a tale of Korean colonial diaspora in 1930s Manchuria.

Genre theorist Rick Altman interprets categories of cinematic praxis as complex textual operations based on interplays between semantic and syntactic variants. The semantic elements include "common traits, attitudes, characters, shots, locations, sets," or as Altman puts it "the genre's building blocks," while the syntactic line refers to the structures into which these elements are arranged and put to use.[22] In his book *Film/Genre*, Altman introduces a third idea, that of pragmatics, to his genre theory. Defined as the "user factor," pragmatics acknowledges "multiple users of various sorts—not only various spectator groups, but producers, distributors, exhibitors, cultural agencies, and many others as well." Altman goes on to say that pragmatic analysis "recognizes that familiar patterns, such as genres, owe their very existence to multiplicity."[23]

From their opening shots, *Shane* and *The Man with No Home* display syntactic similarities and semantic dissimilarities. Produced at Paramount Pictures, *Shane* begins with a Technicolor credit sequence that fills the screen with breathtaking shots of the Teton Mountain valley, photographed in Jackson Hole, Wyoming. As the film's co-producer Ivan Moffat states, "The central part of the action, the Starrett homestead, is throughout the film seen in the huge geographical context of the Teton Mountains. You can see the whole realm around it. You see exactly where it is in the whole landscape . . . the huge expanses of mountains. So it gives [the film] the context of physical and geographical reality."[24] Shot in a wide, anamorphic format (2.35:1) and featuring the slightly less-resplendent hues of Korean Technicolor (Han'guk Ch'ŏnyŏnsaek), *The Man with No Home* takes a diametrically opposite approach. The Korean Western, in fact, obfuscates the physical and geographical reality by opening with out-of-focus blurry images of a lone horseman. Throughout the credit sequence, set during dusk, low-key lighting prevents the audience from discerning details of either the setting or the human figure approaching from a distant point on the horizon. The only clue of the film's ostensible Manchurian location derives from the lyrics of its Korean-language title song, which goes,

> Riding away in the wilderness is one man.
> Today he is in northern Manchuria, tomorrow in the East,
> Floating and floating again years after leaving the hometown.
> Into the sunset does he ride away.
> Such is the man's life.

Even after the sequence transitions into daytime, the mountainous landscape remains nondescript, with no specific natural or architectural landmarks.

In his interview with the film critic Kim So-hŭi, Shin Sang-ok identified Anyang Film Studios, the biggest production facilities in Asia to date (established in 1957), as the location used for shooting both interior and exterior scenes of *The Man with No Home.*[25] However, his former production manager, Pak Haeng-ch'ŏl, recollects differently. According to Pak, the film's primary exterior location was Chŏrwŏn in Kangwŏn Province, a border territory which used to belong to North Korea in the late 1940s, before the Korean War. As additional locations, Pak named Cheju Island, Korea's miniature version of Hawaii some sixty miles off the southernmost coast of the peninsula; and Py'ŏngt'aek in Kyŏnggi Province, home to Camp Humphreys, a US military installation, and the setting for CBS's perennial Korean War dramedy *M*A*S*H* (1972–1983).[26] In other words, various Korean landscapes from northernmost borders to southernmost islands stood in for the imaginary Manchurian valleys and plains. This representational strategy

FIGURE 4.1. *Shane*'s credit sequence shot in Teton Valley.

FIGURE 4.2. The out-of-focus opening of *The Man with No Home*.

can be conceived of as intraregional Orientalism, South Korea's mimicry of the typical Hollywood mode of depicting the East as a culturally nonspecific, interchangeable geography of alterity. This is one of the reasons why the Manchurian Western is critically disparaged in Korean film historiography. The film historian Ho Hyŏn-ch'an, for example, argues that "the

Manchurian film was not historically researched and it was rarely based on facts at all. So it was referred to as a transnational film."[27] As the feminist film critic Soyoung Kim points out, instead of portraying Japanese-controlled Manchuria as a kind of show window displaying East Asian signs of modernity through multiethnic registers, the Manchurian Western genre reduces the place to a lawless, rural backdrop for Korean guerrillas, ironically imitating Hollywood's one-dimensional representation of Korea as a primitive frontier in American war films made during the Cold War era, such as *The Steel Helmet* (1951), *Fixed Bayonets!* (1951), *Battle Hymn* (1957), *Men in War* (1957), and *Pork Chop Hill* (1959).[28]

The size and surroundings of the homestead in *Shane* and *The Man with No Home* differ as well, particularly at the level of their respective characters' living standards within the two households. The Starrett homestead consists of a main cabin and an adjoining stable as well as a spacious yard where the family dog, chickens, calves, and cows roam freely. In the background are majestic mountains and the surrounding area is patched with green grass and water, which provides nourishment for the Starrett family's livestock as well as occasional wild visitors (mostly deer and elk). Smoke puffs from the chimney of the main living quarter, signaling that its hearth is in full operation. In sharp contrast, the Manchurian homestead might more accurately be described as a "straw-roofed shack" (*ch'oggajip*, a Korean term for a "poor, makeshift home") in a barren wasteland. There are no visible signs of life, botanical or bestial (although attentive viewers might spot a reined horse to the side of the house in one shot). This is a familiar yet different type of house combining a straw roof—a fixture of the Korean rural landscape—and Mediterranean-style white brick walls, familiar to fans of Italian Westerns like *The Good, the Bad, and the Ugly*. The wooden well in front of the house where the wanderer drinks water is also reminiscent of a similar structure in *A Fistful of Dollars*, a film that was introduced to Korean audiences only two years prior to the release of *The Man with No Home*.

These contrasting images of home attest to the radically different evocations of the past in the American and Manchurian Westerns. As Douglas Pye points out, in American film and literature, "If the West was seen as a potential Eden, the garden of the world, it was also seen as the wilderness, the great American desert. The life of the frontier was both ennobling because it was close to nature, and primitive, at the farthest remove from civilization."[29] The opening of *Shane* introduces the Starrett homestead as an ideal American home surrounded by picturesque native landscapes. Victor Young's lyrical title music has the capacity to evoke feelings of nostalgia for the Old West as a pristine reserve for American national identity. In *The Man with No Home*, on the other hand, the familiar yet foreign shack is a space of exile and signifies the figurative and literal loss of home (as the lyrics of the doleful title song inform us, it has been years since the main character left his hometown in Korea).

In the romanticized world of *Shane*, land is free for Wyoming homesteaders. Under the 1862 Homestead Act (Act of May 20, 1862), any adult individual could claim freehold title up to 160 acres of underdeveloped land outside of the original thirteen colonies.[30] As Joe Starrett (Van Heflin), the leader of homesteaders, explains in the film, "You got to pick your spot, get your land, your own land. A homesteader . . . can sure grow grain and cut hay and what with his garden and the hogs and milk, he'll make out all right." The lofty ideal of free ownership of land among small farmers in *Shane* contrasts sharply with the dead-end situation faced by poor Korean immigrants in Manchuria, who were given two choices: to act as slaves for Chinese landlords or to flee to the mountains and become nomadic "fire-field farmers." In an article entitled "Peopling the Japanese Empire: The Koreans in Manchuria and the Rhetoric of Inclusion," Barbara J. Brooks quotes a 1920 report by a Japanese journalist who blamed the Governor-General of Korea (*Chōsen Sotokufu*) for "misleading poor Korean farmers into believing they could find a land of opportunity for wet-rice cultivation in Manchuria when in fact many were at the mercy of 'crafty and unscrupulous' Chinese landlords, lacked capital to begin farms, and had no food or even warm clothes in the cold winters. Their impoverished circumstances led them to 'a policy of desperation': falling in with others in plots against the Japanese authorities."[31] The mass-scale relocation of farmers from colonial Korea to Manchuria was thus a part of the colonial project, which protected the economic interests of big landlords and Japanese development companies and sought to absorb uncultivated land under state control.

By 1944, the number of Koreans living in northern China reached approximately 2 million.[32] Although Korean immigrants were barred from land ownership in China and Manchuria (unless they became naturalized as Chinese citizens, an option discouraged by the Japanese colonial authorities), some impoverished peasants fled to the mountains and became *hwajŏnmin* ("fire-field farmers") who, according to the historian Bruce Cumings, were "the poorest but the freest of Koreans during the Japanese period." Cumings elaborates their lifestyle, stating, "*Hwajŏn* (fire-field) farmers sometimes worked extremely steep slopes, where even tilling by hand would be difficult. . . . They worked the fields for three to five years and then moved on. They grew millet, barley, and soybeans, sometimes potatoes and buckwheat. They usually had exhausted their harvest by spring, and lived all summer 'on berries, nuts, mushrooms, herbs and roots.'"[33] The nonvegetated, scorched field on view in *The Man with No Home* suggests that the occupants of the shack may be *hwajŏnmin*, a term that conjures up images of exile, austerity, hardship, and desperation.

The most notable commonality between *Shane* and *The Man with No Home* is the immediate bonding between the titular character and the little boy who eventually looks up to the former as a kind of surrogate father. In the opening moments of *Shane*, it is through Little Joey's perspective that we see the buckskin-clad drifter approaching the Starrett homestead. After asking Joe's permission to cut through their property, Shane turns his attention to the shy boy sitting on the fence. Shane asks Little Joey, "Hello, boy. You were watching me quite a spell, weren't you?" Joey replies with his head down, "Yes, I was." Shane quickly breaks the ice, encouraging the boy with compliments: "You know, I . . . I like a man who watches things go on around. It means he'll make his mark someday." In fact, the child turns out to be quite observant and predicts Shane's talents in gunplay as he shows the stranger his rifle and tells him, "Bet you can shoot." The quick-draw artist with a six-shooter holster answers with modesty, "A little bit." After wrongly suspecting Shane to be one of the Ryker gang, a villainous group of cattlemen who are bent on harassing and expelling a small group of homesteader families from their grazing territory, Joe amends his earlier take by inviting the friendly stranger to share supper and stay overnight (to the delight of his son). The next day, Joey makes an early morning visit to Shane in the stable, pleading with him to stay and teach him how to shoot. Shane complies and joins the Starrett homestead as a farmhand.

From this point forward, Joey's loyalty is split between his biological father (Joe Starrett) and his surrogate father (Shane). The subtle competition between the two men is suggested from the first day of Shane's employment when Joey asks his father, "Pa, you guess Shane will teach me to shoot?" The threatened father asserts his parental right, saying, "I'll teach you myself once I get the time," but he reluctantly admits that he is probably not as good a shooter as Shane is. Noticing the boy's growing attachment to Shane, his mother warns him, "Don't get to liking Shane too much. He'll be moving on one day, Joey. You'll be upset if you get to liking him too much." Later, the boy tells Marian Starrett, "Mother, I just love Shane. I love him almost as much as I love Pa. That's alright, isn't it?"—a confession Shane overhears outside of the room. As Thomas Schatz observes, Shane mediates "both the rancher-homesteader conflict and the boy's confused notions of his ideal father figure. Although Starrett is the bravest and most capable of the homesteaders . . . he is basically a farmer of rural sensibilities and simple values. Starrett is no match for Shane in either Joey's or his wife's eyes."[34] Joey's idolization of Shane culminates in the final shootout scene, which is focalized through his perspective (and which will be addressed later).

The child in *The Man with No Home* is six-year-old Myŏng (Kim Chŏng-hun), a more gregarious and cheerful version of Joey. In much the same way that Joe Starrett initially suspects Shane of being a Ryker spy and points a gun at him, Myŏng's mother greets the titular drifter Chang (Sin Yŏng-gyun) with hostility by firing at him from offscreen. After assuring her, "I am not a suspicious person. I am just a wanderer," Chang provocatively satiates his thirst by drinking from the family well outside of the house. Innocent and trusting, Myŏng approaches the stranger (whom he initially mistakes as his daddy) and befriends him immediately. The inquisitive boy asks the hero, "Where are you from?" Chang answers, "From yonder." The boy then inquires, "Where are you going?" Chang replies, "This way." During this brief encounter, Chang imparts fatherly advice to Myŏng, saying: "A man should be brave." This comment is reminiscent of the similarly paternal care given by Shane to Joey.

It is also notable that in *Shane*, it is Joe Starrett who asks the titular hero where he is heading. Just like Chang, Shane equivocally replies, "One place or another. Someplace I have never been." As the two adults converse, Joey silently listens with interest while admiring Shane's six-shooter gun hanging on the chair. Direct communication between Chang and Myŏng in the absence of the latter's biological father facilitates a stronger bonding between the man and the child on their first meeting. In fact, Myŏng succeeds in persuading his cautious mother to trust the stranger and share their food (a few simple buns), something that Marian does in *Shane*. After the death of the boy's

FIGURE 4.3. Shane encourages shy Joey.

FIGURE 4.4. Chang bonds with cheery Myŏng.

father, Chang takes over his role and escorts Myŏng and his mother to the latter's hometown. The two adults enter into a heated quarrel, however, when Myŏng's mother suspects Chang again and resists his innocent approach, which she has misinterpreted as a sexual advance. An offended Chang admonishes her, reaffirming his priority of concern for the boy: "Did you think I'm the kind of scum that would follow you, lusting after your body? It's because of your husband's dying wishes and my affection for Myŏng, who was kind to me at first sight." Much later, when Chang proposes to the widow in the farming village where they have temporarily settled, he begs her to let Myŏng be *their* son and let him be called "father," once again privileging his surrogate paternalism over the desires associated with heterosexual coupling. Like Joey, Myŏng also functions as a go-between mediating the relationship between Chang and his mother—whose communications are at times suppressed because of misunderstandings and/or shyness—thus bringing the reluctant couple closer together in their common love for him.

Perhaps Jean Arthur's Marian Starrett and Chŏe Ŭn-hŭi's Hwa-yŏng constitute the most intriguing pair from a comparative standpoint. From the opening scene, Marian is depicted as a peacemaker and her aversion to gun violence is repeatedly expressed in dialogue throughout the film. She is introduced as an ordinary homemaker who hums tunes while cooking in the kitchen, a domestic counterpoint to the outdoor work being performed by the men in her life. Like Joey, Marian takes an instant interest in Shane (which is emphasized in a medium shot of her catching a glimpse of the handsome hero through the window) and influences her husband to invite the mysterious stranger heading north for dinner and, later, overnight. Marian's attraction to Shane is expressed through the extra care that she takes in preparing their meal, which her simple husband finds unusual: "Say, we're kind of fancy, aren't we? Our good plates and extra fork." When distributing slices of dessert pies, she gives one to Shane first and to her husband, Joe, second, and even forgets her son's piece until being reminded, "What about me, Ma?" After dinner, Shane praises her cooking politely: "That was an elegant dinner, Mrs. Starrett," a compliment she receives with visible satisfaction. Earlier in the film, Joe also tells Shane: "My place ain't very much yet, but I'll tell you one thing: my wife sure can cook." In a later scene set at Grafton's General Store, we see her fascination with new jars, a further indicator of her role as a domesticator. Marian is representative of what Matthew J. Costello calls "the civilizing woman" of the Western who "seeks to end violence and endorse the community."[35] Indeed, she intervenes in Shane's teacher-like demonstration of shooting techniques to her son, declaring her pacifist philosophy, "Guns aren't going to be in my boy's life. We'd all be much better off if there wasn't a single gun left in this valley, including yours."

Chŏe's Hwa-yŏng in *The Man with No Home* is introduced in a way that clearly contrasts her American forerunner. She is a tough frontier woman who brandishes a rifle as a means of singlehandedly protecting herself and her boy during her husband's absence. She threatens Chang with two warning shots and refuses to curb her vigilantism even after hearing his words of good faith. Unlike Marian, who treats Shane with an elegant, full-course dinner complete with apple pie, the Korean woman flatly tells the nearly starved drifter that she has no food for him and orders him to go away. Unlike the well-lit window shot through which we are introduced to Arthur's soft facial features and curly blond hair—Hollywood's "ideal" version of femininity accentuated by flowers and plants outside the window panel—the counterpart window shot in *The Man with No Home* features a medium-close-up shot of Ch'ŏe, an iconic Korean female star of the 1960s, who is presented here as a potentially dangerous woman with stoic facial features and straight dark hair. At least in this introductory scene, she is more in line of what Costello calls "the dark woman who understands the [Western hero] and the need for violence."[36] Although Hwa-yŏng gradually reveals herself to be a feminine, maternal figure, compared to Marian she is a much darker woman, literally and figuratively. While the love between Shane and Marian is expressed only through glances and handshakes, after her husband's death, the widowed mother of *The Man with No Home* is nearly raped by a Chinese general and passionately pursued by Chang, who embraces Hwa-yŏng despite her apparent discomfort at his proposal (which she initially blocks, telling him, "Don't say anything," and virtually rejects by saying, "I have Myŏng"). The romantic trajectory of the narrative is interrupted only when high-fevered Myŏng is heard moaning in pain. The red background and chiaroscuro lighting in this proposal scene are reminiscent of a similar scene in Douglas Sirk's maternal melodrama *All That Heaven Allows* (1955), depicting the unsuccessful proposal made by Rock Hudson's young gardener Ron Kirby to Jane Wyman's wealthy widow Cary Scott, a woman who is overly concerned about the opinions of her local community and her children. In the figure of Hwa-yŏng, one can see a kind of cross-cultural fusion of the civilizing woman and the dark woman of the American Western, someone who represents domestic values as a mother and wife but is simultaneously worldly about the perils of the Manchurian frontier and is not above resorting to violence to protect herself and her family.

The nature of the threats to the community in the two films is also a worthy subject of investigation. In *Shane*, the primary threat derives from the greedy local ranchers, the Ryker brothers, who resent and intimidate homesteaders whose properties are in the way of their open grazing range and irrigation lines. The Rykers resort to common bullying tactics, insulting homesteaders with such slurs as "pig farmers," "sodbusters," and "squatters." They vandalize crops and houses and threaten their opponents into packing up and leaving their homes. On noticing the extraordinary fighting skills and physical prowess of Shane in the local saloon, the cattle baron Rufus Ryker (Emile Meyer) attempts to recruit him to his side, offering him double the salary that Starrett is paying. Shane flatly rejects his offer and proves his loyalty to the Starretts. When one of the local homesteaders, the hot-tempered Southerner Stonewall Torrey (Elisha Cook, Jr.), is killed by the notorious Cheyenne gunslinger Jack Wilson (Jack Palance), who was hired by the Rykers, the tension between the two groups intensifies. As the leader of homesteaders, Joe Starrett takes it upon himself to face Rufus Ryker and Wilson by himself, a suicide mission his wife desperately tries to avert. Despite his wife's

FIGURE 4.5. The homemaking "civilizing woman" Marian Starrett.

FIGURE 4.6. The gun-toting "dark woman" Hwa-yŏng.

tearful plea to move out and avoid trouble, Joe shows a courageous determination to carry out his mission to protect his own and his fellow homesteaders' properties. Thus, he represents what Costello calls "the virtuous individual," another character type of the law-and-order subgenre of the Western, who is willing to meet "the threat to community even with the potential for death that it entails."[37]

The husband/father character in *The Man with No Home*, Sam-man (Ch'oe Sŏng-ho), functions in a similar way. In this Korean spin on *Shane*, the threat is a group of mounted bandits under Nŭng-ch'ŏng's leadership. The bandits are extortionists drawing heavy "military taxes" from compatriot peasants, and Sam-man is leading a revolt to evade unjust taxation. It is particularly noteworthy that these bandits are called *yugŏkdae* (translated as "guerrillas"), insinuating their connection to the independence movement. Instead of showcasing solidarity between peasants and guerrillas in collective resistance against Japanese colonial forces, *The Man with No Home* delves into the internal fragmentation of the diasporic community in which diverse factions and interests are pitted against one another (or shown taking advantage of one another). Sam-man returns home after spending three days asking for help from other guerrilla groups to no avail. Like Marian, his wife pleads to the noble husband to abandon his impossible mission:

> You fought enough for farmers. They have land and they will harvest crops in the fall. But you don't have anything left despite your bloody fight to protect them. I plead to you. Let's leave and become farmers ourselves. Think of Myŏng. Do you want to make him a guerrilla, too?

Sam-man is unmoved, however, and tells her, "Darling, loyalty means everything to me. I still have my men to think about."

At this point, Chang returns to the house to warn the couple about Nŭng-ch'ŏng's impending raid. Earlier that day, after getting water and meager food from the farmhouse, Chang is captured by Nŭng-ch'ŏng's men and taken to the guerrilla leader who is torturing Sam-man's men by burying their bodies from the neck down. Like Rufus Ryker, the chief villain Nŭng-ch'ŏng is impressed with the hero's quick-draw skills and tries to recruit him. Unlike Shane, Chang accepts the offer with one stipulation, saying, "I am expensive." Nŭng-ch'ŏng capitulates and invites him to his quarters, where he treats his starved new recruit to a feast. The bandit leader orders his newest hire to get rid of Sam-man, the father of the little boy with whom Chang had bonded earlier. Instead of carrying out the order, Chang dashes to the farmhouse to save the family. He persuades Sam-man to leave, stating,

> I was a guerilla who tried to protect farmers and I even lost my home. I overheard outside and your wife is right. Leave with your child. . . . Your enemies are watching for you around every corner and farmers are hiding without breathing. Do you want to die alone like a dog? It's silly to protect farmers in this situation. Farmers live cleverly and they leave land after they die. But what will you leave?

He ends his speech with the simple yet telling remark, "I was a farmer's son, too." Sam-man agrees to flee with his family, but he is forced to give up his gun when his wife and child are taken as hostages by Nŭng-ch'ŏng and his underlings. While Chang is occupied fending off Nŭng-ch'ŏng's other men on the opposite end of the hill, Sam-man faces a grim, drawn-out death at the hands of sadistic Nŭng-ch'ŏng, who shoots him multiple times (in the leg, the shoulder, the torso, and the hands) at leisurely intervals, forcing his victim to crawl desperately on the ground toward his gun for revenge only to thwart his attempt with another shot. Held by Nŭng-ch'ŏng's underlings, Sam-man's wife and son are forced to helplessly witness this atrocious scene of his slow, agonizing death.

A Showdown of Genres: The American Western vs. Korean Melodrama

This prolonged, torturous death scene is what separates *The Man with No Home* most radically from the classical narrative and sanitized violence of *Shane*. It is when the narrative of *The Man with No Home* shifts both semantically and syntactically, causing melodrama to emerge as the dominant mode. Thus, the Manchurian Western serves as an excellent example of the *dominant* which, as elaborated by Steve Neale and discussed earlier in this chapter, can be defined as an interplay between "canonized and noncanonized genres."[38] In the context of America's Eisenhower-era cinema, the Western exerted a slightly more "dominant" role in mainstream cinema than melodrama, and the sentimental, repressed love story in *Shane* was largely submerged under the classical genre formulation of the Western. In the context of South Korea's 1960s cinema, the Manchurian Western was an anomaly, a marginal genre (or subgenre) which was often mixed with other more-canonized genres such as action, melodrama, and martial arts. Although Western elements interrupt the dominant mode of melodrama in this death scene, when Chang belatedly comes to the rescue and eliminates the menace of Nŭng-ch'ŏng by outgunning him and most of his underlings, the intervention is "too late" (a temporal mode often associated with melodrama, which evokes excessive affect and pathos) rather than "on time" (more typical of the Western and the chase film, which usually leads to a satisfactory dénouement in which family and community well-being as well as law and order are restored, albeit at the expense of the lone Westerner who is simply incompatible with "civilization" as it has been normatively conceived).

In *Shane*, the titular hero steps in on time to prevent Joe from entering into a suicidal showdown with Ryker and his hired gun Wilson. Rightly, Shane calls it "my kind of game" and hits Starrett in the head with a gun, knocking him unconscious. After giving Marian instructions on how to help her husband regain his consciousness, Shane acknowledges that this will be the last time they will see each other. They share friendly handshakes, suppressing their mutual romantic longings. In typical Hollywood fashion, the husband and child recede into the background in soft focus, directing spectatorial attention to the unconsummated romantic couple in the foreground in sharp focus. *The Man with No Home* develops in a completely different fashion when the father/husband dies tragically, entrusting his wife and child to the stranger in his final minutes: "Please take my wife and Myŏng to their hometown." Just as the collective clash between ranchers and homesteaders boils down to the dramatic proxy duel between two third-party gunslingers (Shane and Wilson), *The Man with No Home* ultimately displaces the larger intradiasporic struggle between farmers and bandits/guerrillas within a familial tragedy schema. Unlike the showdown in George Stevens's film, wherein Little Joey functions as a proud spectator of Shane's lightning-fast draws (which put an end to the evil that has swept through the valley), Myŏng and Hwa-yŏng become traumatized eyewitnesses of the slow, painful death of their beloved—harkening back to a familiar, familial narrative of the dark colonial era. Exaggerated sadism on the part of the villain Nŭng-ch'ŏng, combined with the extreme agony and vengefulness of his victim, the profuse tears shed by Sam-man's wife and son, and the over-the-top nondiegetic music that not only accompanies but *accentuates* these visuals, result in a complex constellation of "foreign" elements that would simply have no place in a classical Western like *Shane.*

In this defamiliarizing or "weirding" process (to invoke once again the title of a recent Manchurian Western, *The Good, the Bad, the Weird*), American Western conventions are mixed with and diffused by the dominant mode that is Korean family melodrama. In fact, the remaining two-thirds of the film intermixes semantic and syntactic variants of multiple genres including the family melodrama, the road movie, the gangster film, martial arts action, the samurai film, and the war film. Traditional Western iconography ultimately reemerges in the film's final scene. However, its syntactic use is radically different from that in classic American Westerns. Chang returns to the rural village after one year of solitary wandering to reconnect with Myŏng and his mother (who he thinks have been waiting for him according to a promise made at the point of his departure). To his dismay, Chang finds that Myŏng and Hwa-yŏng have moved on and started a new life with the rich Chinese landlord Mr. Sa. Hidden behind a tree in the garden of Sa's residence, Chang vicariously witnesses their comfortable, luxurious life with a servant, good food, and silk garments, which he could not provide. His face momentarily brightens when Myŏng runs toward him, calling, "Uncle, where have you been?"—a happy reunion anticipated by a fleeting flash-forward in an earlier scene. However, Chang sadly realizes that the greeting was intended for Mr. Sa, into whose arms the boy dashes.

In *Shane*, the hero leaves and disappears into the sunset despite Joey's repeated pleas: "We want you. . . . Mother wants you. . . . Come back!" This ending satisfies rather than frustrates audience expectations since, as Schatz points out, the incompatibility between the lone, antisocial hero and the community becomes increasingly pronounced in mature Cold War-era Westerns of the 1950s such as *Winchester '73* (1950), *High Noon, The Searchers*, and *Rio Bravo* (1959).[39] Thematic binaries of the frontier mythology—the wilderness vs. civilization, the individual vs. the community, nature vs. culture, the West vs. the East, the garden vs. the desert—can be told and retold, precisely because the Western hero refuses to settle down and continues his wandering ways, seeking the next community, the next villain, and the next adventure. In contrast, in *The Man with No Home*, Chang leaves and disappears into the sunset because he is unfit or inadequate to be Myŏng's father and Hwa-yŏng's husband, and another foreign man eventually takes his place during his absence (despite the fact that he became a fugitive from the law due to the sacrificial act he performed to raise Myŏng's medical fees). Thus, his departure is not a part of the national myth of rugged individualism and frontier masculinity, but an act of self-sacrifice on the part of the colonial male whose masculine, paternal, and financial legitimacy is under siege on all fronts. In this way, Chang and other troubled heroes in 1960s Manchurian Westerns share something in common with the fathers and husbands at the center of that decade's modernization comedies (discussed in the previous chapter).

Thus far, virtually all major theories of film genre, whether those indebted to Schatz's evolutionary, ritual model; Neale's quest for historically-specific generic regimes; or Altman's linguistically-inspired semantic/syntactic/pragmatic approach, have neglected the question of transnational permutations—the necessarily politicized "poaching" or *détournement* ("hijacking" or "rerouting") of genres once they are mobilized outside of Hollywood's dominant industrial models and narrative modes. Indeed, a full understanding of genre hybridization and textual pragmatics cannot be achieved without looking beyond US borders and examining the deterritorialized manifestations of a given genre globally. In that respect, *The Man with No Home* proves to be a fascinating case study not only for its value in terms of contributing to the ongoing examination of Shin Sang-ok as a filmmaker as well as the further development of Korean film historiography. Shin's pragmatic reworking of Stevens's beloved mid-century Western *Shane* erects the kind of scaffolding that is needed to build new theories and spark discussions of genre as a transnational, transhistorical process, one that involves cultural hybridity and dialogic multiplicity beyond the constraints of any one national cinema, be it American or Korean.

The Comeback of the Manchurian Western and a Return to Colonial Modernity

Long forgotten in the popular memory and marginalized as a footnote in Korean film historiography, the Manchurian Western made an unexpected comeback in 2008, with the release of two films: Kim Jee-woon's big-budget action blockbuster *The Good, the Bad, the Weird* and Ryoo Seung-wan (Ryu Sŭng-wan)'s more modest espionage comedy *Dachimawa Lee* (*Tach'imawa Yi*). Prior to its domestic release in July, following a prestigious world premiere at the Cannes International Film Festival, the former film attracted attention as it not only cost an unprecedented $17 million and was shot in the Gobi Desert in Dunhuang, China, but also brought together the three biggest male stars of the South Korean film industry—Jung Woo-sung (Chŏng U-sŏng), Lee Byung-hyun (Yi Pyŏng-hyŏn), and Song Kang-ho—who take up the titular roles as "the good," "the bad," and "the weird." Although this all-star revival of the Manchurian Western received mixed reviews for its emphasis on spectacle, entertainment, and nonstop action, the film garnered nearly 7 million admissions and became the tenth-highest grossing domestic film of all time as of 2008. To capitalize on a renewed public interest in this anomalous genre of national cinema, between August 21 and August 31, 2008, the Korean Film Archive held a special retrospective of fifteen Manchurian Westerns, including the aforementioned Golden Age films such as *Farewell Tuman River, The Man with No Home*, and *Break the Chain.*

As a genre revisionist reminiscent of New Hollywood auteurs of the 1960s and the 1970s (such as Robert Altman, Francis Ford Coppola, Brian De Palma, and Martin Scorsese), the director/writer Kim previously experimented with horror (*The Quiet Family* [*Choyonghan kajok*, 1998], *A Tale of Two Sisters* [*Changhwa, Hongryŏn*, 2003]), comedy (*Foul King* [*Panch'inkwang*, 2000]), film noir (*A Bittersweet Life* [*Talch'omhan insaeng*, 2005]), and vampire film *Coming Out* ([short, 2001]). Having openly acknowledged his indebtedness to both the spaghetti Western and the Manchurian Western of the 1960s and the 1970s in various local media interviews, Kim explains his authorial inspirations for *The Good, the Bad, the Weird* in the video interview available on the Region 1 DVD:

> I've always wanted to take on the Western genre. But while I was doubting whether that's ever possible in Korea, the thought of Song Kang-ho [the comic actor who plays the Weird] shooting two guns in a Western came to mind. That's how it all started. To show a truly entertaining genre film. To go beyond the limits. Everything stemmed off from there.... *The Good, the Bad, the Weird* is a unique Korean Western.[40]

Although the English end credits of the film's US/international release print explicitly identifies the film as an "Oriental Western by Kim Jee-woon," like its Golden Age predecessors, *The Good, the Bad, the Weird* is a hybrid genre film which intermixes comedy, martial arts fantasy, adventure, and action along with the Western, which serves as its dominant generic orientation.

Semantically, Kim's film incorporates familiar visual tropes of the Western such as horses, saddles, guns, rifles, camp fires, desert landscapes, fast-draw duels, and trains. However, it denaturalizes these semantic elements by "weirding" them with "matter out of place" (generic anomalies) such as sunglasses, pilot hats, Chinese costumes, bamboo structures, paper lanterns, scooters, motorcycles, machine guns, army jeeps, Big Band music, movie theaters, and opium dens. Syntactically, the narrative centers on a multiparty hunt for a stolen treasure map and culminates with a three-way quick draw duel involving the titular characters: a stoic bounty hunter (the Good), a cold-blooded hit man (the Bad), and a bumbling train robber (the Weird). Not surprisingly, the central villain is eliminated by narrative's end. Prior to that, the circular camera movement and alternating extreme close-up shots of the three antiheros in the showdown explicitly pay homage to Sergio Leone's *The Good, the Bad, and the Ugly*. As in classic Manchurian Westerns, *The Good, the Bad, the Weird* introduces an indigenous syntax which foregrounds the conflict between the Japanese colonial authority and Korean independence fighters. As a new, revisionist Western, though, Kim's film shies away from the clear moral dichotomy dividing the colonized and the colonizer, the victim and the victimizer, and good and evil.

Toward the beginning of the film, Yun T'ae-gu (a.k.a. the Weird, played by Song Kang-ho), a petty Korean bandit in Manchuria, robs a train full of multinational passengers including Sir Kanemaru (Yi Hang-su), chief of Japanese Imperial Bank, who is carrying a map that supposedly reveals the burial spot of lost Qing Dynasty treasures. Prior to the fortuitous raid on Kanemaru's first-class carriage, Yun, disguised as a Chinese snack seller, nonchalantly passes by a scene of great national import without displaying any interest or sympathy. Ignored by his apathetic compatriot, an independence activist in the background who desperately chants a political slogan and displays a forbidden Korean national flag is forcefully taken off of the train by Japanese soldiers. After stealing the treasure map from Kanemaru and fleeing Pak Ch'ang-i (a.k.a. the Bad, played by Lee Byung-hyun), an assassin working for the double-crossing traitor Kim P'an-ju (Song Yŏng-ch'ang) who schemes to steal the map back from the Japanese after selling it to him, Yun is captured by the bounty hunter Pak To-wŏn (a.k.a. the "Good," played by Jung Woo-sung), a mercenary hired by an independence movement group. Just like the relationship between Blondie (Clint Eastwood) and Tuco (Eli Wallach) in *The Good, the Bad, and the Ugly*, a temporary alliance is formed between the Good and the Weird against the Bad, a psychotic killer who ruthlessly eliminates his employer after failing his mission to retrieve the map. Ironically, the villain chastises the traitor for "selling off [his] country" after stabbing him to death while playing Glenn Miller's "Moonlight Serenade" on a gramophone in the background.

Between chaotic races and chases, Pak To-wŏn and Yun T'ae-gu have a peaceful night together by the campfire in the desert. Gleefully anticipating the awaiting treasures, Yun confides his dream to his captor/partner, saying, "If we find a big treasure there, whatever it may be, you know what I'll do with it? Wanna hear what my dream is? I'm going back [to Korea] and buying me some land. I'll build a house and raise some cows, horses, and sheep. And some dogs and chickens too." Pak responds, "Why buy land when your country's stolen?" Once again demonstrating his lack of commitment to the nationalist cause, Yun replies, "For folks like us, it's the same living under nobility or the Japs." In a later scene, set in an opium den run by a Korean expatriate named Sŏ Chae-sik (Son Pyŏng-ho) who identifies himself as "a fighter for independence" but turns out to be a Japanese collaborator, Yun reaffirms his disregard for the nation's grand narrative. As Sŏ starts giving him a lecture on Japan's imperial ambition to take over Gando, home to many Korean expatriates in China and former territory of the ancient Korean Kingdom of Balhae (in order to persuade the bandit to submit the treasure map for the sake of Korean independence), Yun expresses his boredom and confusion: "You are talking about such things as territory and foreign relations. I don't know any of that. [It] gives me a headache."

In the original Korean ending (which was cut out of the film's international release, including the US version), after surviving the three-way duel the Weird is seen burying the corpse of the Bad along with dynamite, which the former offers as a belated reparation for chopping off the latter's finger in a violent confrontation in Korea years earlier. In the midst of this makeshift burial at the site of the underground ruins, Japanese troops encroach upon the scene, aiming their guns down at the Korean bandit. Quick-witted, the Weird ignites the dynamite in his hand, pretending to be a suicide bomber. A threatened commander of the Japanese army gives his troops a retreat order, cursing "Damn Korean!" The situation is humorously ironic as the most apolitical character (with no apparent sympathy for the Korean independence cause) is misidentified by colonizers as a militant freedom fighter willing to sacrifice his own life for his nation/people. Prior to the troops' arrival, the Weird accidentally finds a bag of diamonds from the pocket of the dead man who had stolen the jewels from his traitor-boss. In other words, the lucky bandit indirectly benefits from the corrupt wealth accrued at the price of betraying one's own country. Unlike the Good, who single-handedly guns down many Japanese soldiers during the climactic chase scene (in a detached style reminiscent of the outlaw hero the Ringo Kid [John Wayne]'s cool gunplay during the Apache raid scene in John Ford's 1939 film *Stagecoach*), the Weird does not harm colonizers but outwits them by posing as a "terrorist" only to scare them away.

While the Good and the Bad are, by proxy, affiliated with freedom fighters and traitors respectively, neither of them cares about politics and both are propelled by monetary interests and/or desire for personal vengeance. As the Good tells the Weird in the campfire scene, "Even if you have no country, you still gotta have money." Although the Weird comments to his bounty-hunter partner, "You're the most cold-hearted Korean I ever met," the former is the most realistic character, someone who repeatedly neglects impractical actions or speeches fueling nationalistic sentiments throughout the narrative. This lack of well-defined thematic binaries and ideological oppositions—core characteristics of the Western genre—is partly why the film frustrated several local critics. For example, the critic Yi Hyŏn-gyŏng labels it an "action roller coaster" which lacks substantial themes beyond gunplay and chases, while Soyoung Kim expresses her disappointment at the film's focus on "action for the sake of action."[41] Despite the film's apparent eschewing of deep thematics and political subtexts, its unequivocal rejection of the colonial era's nationalist historiography is arguably the most significant generic experimentation of Kim's film. This trait puts the film on equal standing with a group of recent "colonial modernity" films that collectively offer a re-interpretation of the colonial era beyond the conventional dichotomous binary of Japanese oppression and Korean resistance. Initiated by the sports comedy *YMCA Baseball Team* (*YMCA Yagudan*, 2000), several recent films across different genres, including the comedies *Radio Dayz* (*Radio Deijŭ*, 2007) and *Once Upon a Time in Corea* (*Wŏnsŭ ŏp'on ŏ t'aim*, 2008), the romantic drama *Modern Boy* (*Modŏn poi*, 2008), the biopics *Rikidozan: A Hero Extraordinaire* (*Yŏkdosan*, 2004) and *Blue Swallow* (*Ch'ŏnyŏn*, 2005), and the horror film

Epitaph (*Kidam*, 2005), showcase the ability of cultural producers to resist nationalistic sentiments in favor of everyday lives and the practices of ordinary people—individuals who participate in the construction of colonial modernity as much as government officials do.

This assortment of films constitutes a collective cinematic response to the scholarly call by Gi-wook Shin and Michael Robinson, who insist on challenging "the simplistic binary of colonial repression/exploitation versus Korean resistance," a binary that persisted in many postcolonial Korean films set during the Japanese colonial era.[42] As the authors argue:

> In the nationalist perspective, the colonial state as agent of change delegitimizes the 'modern' itself. . . . Colonialism intervened in Korea's path to modernity, but this did not automatically make Koreans mere passive recipients of modernity. Koreans participated directly and indirectly in the construction of a unique colonial modernity—a modernity that produced cosmopolitan . . . without political emancipation. Colonial modernity possessed liberating forces and a raw, transformative power, and it affected the more nuanced forms of domination and repression in the colony. Its sheer complexity must be recognized.[43]

The Good, the Bad, the Weird indirectly participates in the process of reevaluating colonial modernity by depicting not only the permeable lines between resistance and collaboration (for example, showing an "independence fighter" in an opium den who turns out to be a Japanese spy), but also the nonnationalistic professional pursuits of colonial diasporic subjects as represented by Korean mounted bandits (members of the so-called "Tri-Nation" [*Samg'uk*] gang) who join forces with other nationalities/ethnicities such as Han Chinese, Manchus, Mongolians, and white Russians. It is telling that, when asked by the Good why he came to Manchuria, the Weird responds, "I came to live a new life," positioning the frontier as a land of opportunity and adventures rather than exile and hardships, unlike in *The Man with No Home.*

Thus, Kim Jee-woon's de-nationalized, revisionist Western is a timely cinematic contribution to the ongoing process of re-imagining the legacy of colonial history from multiple perspectives. As Shin and Robinson point out, Japanese colonial hegemony "provided 'space' for groups to reconstruct their own being—some took an oppositional stance, others reformed, still others supported colonial hegemony."[44] In the words of the Weird, the film subtly conveys the popular sentiment of a majority of colonial citizens whose concerns for daily survival far outweighed the master narrative of a stolen nation. As a genre film, albeit a "weird" one, *The Good, the Bad, the Weird* both succeeds and fails by injecting the kind of authenticity and verisimilitude (achieved through ten-month-long location shooting in the Gobi Desert) that was lacking in classic Manchurian Westerns and destabilizing clear-cut thematic/moral binaries. Ultimately, it is a significant "migratory" film that attests to the resilience and adaptability of the Western genre in a global context beyond its presumed "home territory" of the United States.

Part II

From Cinematic Seoul to Global Hollywood

Cosmopolitanism, Empire, and Transnational Genre Flows

Chapter 5

Reinventing the Historical Drama, De-Westernizing a French Classic

Genre, Gender, and the Transnational Imaginary in *Untold Scandal*

As South Korean cinema continues to attract international recognition and pan-Asian fandom, talented young filmmakers have creatively experimented with different genres, reinventing formulaic conventions through aesthetic and technical innovation, mature themes, and poignant social commentary. Despite the increasing diversification and hybridization of contemporary South Korean films, three particular genres labeled "box office poison" had been, until recently, avoided by producers and film companies: the costume drama, the sports drama, and the animal film.[1] This aversion to outdated or unproductive genres was challenged in 2003. The five top-grossing Korean films that year were, in order of box-office statistics: *Memories of Murder* (*Salin ŭi ch'uŏk*), *My Tutor Friend* (*Tonggap naegi kwawŏi hagi*), *Untold Scandal* (*Sŭk'aendŭl: Chosŏn namnyŏ sangyŏljisa*), *Oldboy* (*Oldŭ poi*), and *Oh! Brothers* (*O! Pŭradŭsŭ*).[2] As a period piece set during the Chosun (Chosŏn) era as well as a cross-cultural adaptation of Choderlos de Laclos's 1782 novel *Les Liaisons dangereuses* (*Dangerous Liaisons*), *Untold Scandal* is an anomaly in this group of thrillers or comedies set in contemporary times. Between 1996 and 2002, only three epic-scale warrior films set in the ancient tribal or medieval Koryo periods—*Bichunmoo* (*Pich'ŏnmu*, 2000), *The Legend of Gingko* (*Tanjŏkbi yŏnsu*, 2000), and *The Warrior* (*Musa*, 2001)—made the list of each year's top ten domestic releases, otherwise dominated by action blockbusters, gangster films, comedies, and horror films all set in the present day or in the not-too-distant postcolonial past (during the last sixty years). This box-office trend clearly attests to contemporary Korean audiences' preference for films set in modern milieus over historical dramas set in Chosun (1392–1910) or earlier dynastic eras.

This does not mean, however, that the historical drama (*sagŭk*) has traditionally been a marginalized genre in South Korean film history. In this chapter, we apply the term *sagŭk* broadly to designate both fictional and factual narratives set in Chosun or earlier dynastic eras, following the popular conventions of journalistic and critical discourses. Other scholars such as Jinsoo An distinguish between two terms: "period" drama films (*sidaegŭk*) and historical drama films (*sagŭk* or *yŏksagŭk*). We agree that there should be a distinction between the first group, based on folkloric or fictional stories set in premodern times, and the second group, which narrativizes official histories of the nation. Im Kwon-taek (Im Kwŏn-t'aek)'s international festival entries such as *Surrogate Mother* (*Ssibaj*, 1986) and *Chunhyang* (*Ch'unhyangdyŏn*, 2000) can be situated within the former group while biopics of royalty, such as Chŏng Ch'ang-hwa's *Lady Chang* (*Chang hŭibin*, 1961), Shin Sang-ok (Sin Sang-ok)'s *Prince Yŏnsan* (*Yŏnsang'un*, 1962), or Pak Chong-wŏn's *Eternal Empire* (*Yŏngwŏnhan cheguk*, 1995), are examples of the latter category. Strictly speaking, then, *Untold Scandal* is an example not of the historical drama (*sagŭk*), but of the period drama (*sidaegŭk*) because it does not involve the lives of real-life historical figures. However, various Korean-language newspaper reviews, which we will reference in this chapter, categorize *Untold Scandal* as an example of *sagŭk*. The Korean Film Archive's recently published book on 1960s and 1970s cinema (*Hang'uk yŏnghwasa kongbu*, 2004) also applied the term to refer to both types of films. Therefore, we have opted to mobilize the term *sagŭk* in an inclusive rather than exclusive manner, while acknowledging the equally legitimate alternative use of this generic category.

As film scholar Soyoung Kim points out, the film industry's postwar reconstruction was greatly indebted to two box-office hits of the mid-1950s: *The Story of Chunhyang* (*Ch'unhyangjŏn*, 1955), an adaptation of perennial *p'ansori* literature centering on an interclass love story against a mid-eighteenth century backdrop, and *Madame Freedom* (*Chayu puin*, 1956), another adaptation based on Chŏng Pi-sŏk's contemporaneous newspaper series-turned-novel about the scandalous affairs of a married woman.[3] In other words, historical and modern melodramas held equal appeal to post-Korean War moviegoers. Indeed, the 1960s was not only the Golden Age of South Korean cinema but also a heyday for historical films, spawning such important works as *Lady Chang*, *Prince Hodong* (*Hodong wangja*, 1962), *Queen Dowager Inmok* (*Inmok taebi*, 1962), *Koryo Funeral* (*Koryŏjang*, 1963) as well as a number of films directed by legendary director and producer Shin Sang-ok, including *Chunhyang* (*Sŏng Ch'unhyang*, 1961), *Prince Yŏnsan, Tyrant Yŏnsan* (*P'okgun Yŏnsan*, 1962), *The Sino-Japanese War and Queen Min* (*Ch'ŏngil chŏnjaeng kwa yŏgyŏl Minbi*, 1965), *Eunuch* (*Naesi*, 1968), and *Women of the Chosun Dynasty* (*Ijo yŏin chanhoksa*, 1969). The 1970s witnessed a precipitous decline of the genre due to competition with the emergent rival medium of television. As the historical drama became a generic staple within the domestic context of television viewing, audiences no longer felt a need to go to theaters to see stories of royal families and historical figures readily available for private consumption at home at no additional cost.

Given this reconfiguration, it should not be surprising that a genre so proficient at propagandizing national heroes was co-opted to serve the interests of Park Chung Hee (Pak Chŏng-hŭi)'s authoritarian regime (1961–1979) and thus transformed into a vehicle for coercing the citizenry into personal sacrifices for the sake of state-initiated modernization and development. Accordingly, historical biopics focusing on strong male leaders, such as *Sacred Hero Yi Sun-sin* (*Sŏngung Yi Sun-sin*, 1971), *A War Diary* (*Najung ilgi*, 1977), and *Great King Sejong* (*Sejong taewang*, 1978), were produced in line with the government's cultural policies. During the 1980s, two particular strains of the genre reemerged, targeting radically different audience groups: The first of these were adult-oriented "*t'osok ero*" dramas,[4] or soft-porn films using premodern settings as a pretext for staging tantalizing erotic spectacles, such as *Ŏudong* (1985), *Mulberry* (*Ppong*, 1985), and *Pyŏn Kangsŏe* (1986); the second were international festival-oriented historical melodramas centering on the deep-rooted sadness and resentment (or *han*) of long-suffering, beautiful women victimized by a monstrous Confucian patriarchy, such as *Spinning Wheel* (*Yŏin chanhoksa mulleya mulleya*, 1983), selected in the 37th Cannes Film Festival's "Un Certain Regard" section, and *Surrogate Mother*, which garnered the Best Actress Award in the 44th Venice Film Festival.

Up until the recent, post-*Untold Scandal sagŭk* boom leading to the emergence of such box-office hits as Yi Chun-ik's queer-themed *King and the Clown* (*Wang ŭi namja*, 2005), Kim Han-min's CGI-filled *War of the Arrows* (*Ch'oejongbyŏnggi hwal*, 2011), and Ch'u Ch'ang-min's *The Prince and the Pauper*-inspired *Masquerade* (*Kwanghae: Wangi twoen namja*, 2012), historical dramas were largely absent from the New Korean Cinema scene, which, since the 1999 release of *Shiri* (*Swiri*), had been dominated by such pan-Asian blockbusters as *Joint Security Area* (*Kongdong kyŏngbiguyŏk*, 2000), *Friend* (*Ch'ingu*, 2001), *My Sassy Girl* (*Yŏpgijŏkin kŭnyŏ*, 2001), and *Tae Guk Gi: The Brotherhood of War* (*T'aegukki hwinallimyŏ*, 2004). However, there were notable exceptions, such as Im Kwon-taek's *Chunhyang* and *Chihwaseon* (*Chihwasŏn*, 2002), two vibrant, self-orientalizing epics that apparently pleased international film festival programmers and juries far more than they did domestic theatergoers. In other words, prior to the recent renovation and revival of the genre as a "new" film form catering to contemporary local audiences' aesthetic tastes and social concerns, *sagŭk* productions primarily served as "heritage commodities" (to borrow the words of Yun Mi Hwang), wherein historical narratives are packaged and marketed globally to meet the converging interests of the state's ideological directives and the industry's quest for both profit and prestige.[5]

The Question of Genre: Is *Untold Scandal* a Historical Drama?

Untold Scandal is a unique film that does not conform to any of the previous trends or subgenres of historical dramas. Given its Western and contemporary flavors, one might even question whether or not this film is a historical drama at all. As a cross-cultural adaptation of Choderlos de Laclos's 1782 novel *Les Liaisons dangereuses* (*Dangerous Liaisons*), *Untold Scandal* depicts Chosun aristocratic culture in a very unconventional way. In lieu of royal families, famed artists, or oppressed feudal women, the clandestine libertine sexcapades of the ruling *yangban* class come into narrative focus. Laclos's novel had already been adapted for the big screen several times in Europe and America, dating back to Roger Vadim's *Les Liaisons dangereuses 1960* (France, 1959), which transformed the eighteenth-century setting into a chic, jazz-soaked Parisian society of the late fifties. Subsequent versions of the epistolary narrative include Stephen Frears's *Dangerous Liaisons* (US/UK, 1988), Milos Forman's *Valmont* (France/US, 1989), and Roger Kumble's *Cruel Intentions* (US, 1999), a teen-pic which transported the setting to modern-day New York. As the first Asian adaptation, *Untold Scandal* is perhaps the most audacious and creative of them all insofar as it shrewdly recontextualizes the high society drama by shifting its setting from pre-Revolution France to the late Chosun period in Korea (during the King Chŏngjo era [1776–1800]), when strict Confucian gender rules mandated that, after the age of seven, members of the opposite sex no longer associate with each other outside familial and conjugal relations. More recently, Korean director Hur Jin-ho (Hŏ Chin-ho)'s Chinese-language film *Dangerous Liaisons* (2012), which pairs the regional superstar Jang Dong-gun (Chang Tong-gŭn) with the mainland Chinese star Zhang Ziyi and the Hong Kong actress Cecilia Cheung, can be cited as an example of a transnational co-production. Set in Shanghai (the so-called "Paris of the Orient") in 1931, this latest adaptation of the French novel is an excellent example of transnational East Asian cinema, which brings together directorial and acting talents as well as funding sources from different regions (South Korea, mainland China, Hong Kong, and Singapore) and which directly targets pan-Asian audiences.

Despite its perceived commercial disadvantage as a period piece, *Untold Scandal* broke all previous opening records of domestic films to date by garnering 1.1 million admissions in the first four days of its theatrical release in 2003. Newspaper reviewers busied themselves accounting for this miraculous success. The September 25, 2003 issue of *Chosun Daily* (*Chosŏn Ilbo*) declared that "no historical drama like this had been produced before," adding that, in fusing dissimilar cultural and historical elements, the film effectively heralds "the possibility of a modern historical drama." Likewise calling the film "a historical drama unlike previous historical dramas," the October 6, 2003 issue of *Sports Chosun* (*Sŭp'och"ŭ Chosŏn*) predicted the impending fever for similar productions that shirk generic formulas and clichés. This prediction materialized when another "fusion" historical drama, *A Jewel in the Palace* (*Taejanggŭm*, 2003–2004), a fifty-four-episode MBC television series hybridizing the elements of traditional Chosun court melodrama with modern cooking and medical shows, became the biggest hit of Korean television to date (garnering a 54% rating) and earned the appellation "national drama." Other unusual historical films in the tradition of *Untold Scandal* include *Blood Rain* (*Hyŏl ŭi nu*, 2005), a graphic murder mystery set in 1808, and *The Duelist* (*Hyŏngsa*, 2005), a postmodern martial art/detective/love story which uses the Chosun setting as an excuse for its director Yi Myŏng-se's stylistic experiments with color, movement, and texture. The most noteworthy outcome of the revived boom of historical dramas, however, is *King and the Clown*, a political satire-meets-queer love story set during the reign of notorious tyrant King Yŏnsan (1494–1506). Despite its unconventional subject matter (street performance art and homosexuality) and lack of big stars, this modest period piece ended up becoming the highest-grossing domestic film to date. As Kyung Hyun Kim points out, *Untold Scandal* was responsible for not only "changing the perceptions of investors who had thought that period films were not commercially viable," but also freeing filmmakers from the dictates of historical accuracy and authenticity. As Kim puts it, "Sagŭks were no longer required to get the historical details right" because "the virtuality rendered in [new historical dramas] is a Korea that insists on blurring the boundary between the way things really were and the way things are remembered, or the way things now appear in our consciousness."[6]

In his *Cine 21* article dated October 14, 2003, film critic Sim Yŏng-sŭp identified *Untold Scandal* as a comprehensive "gift set," intermixing Korean audiences' favorite genre elements: comedy, melodrama, and erotic drama.[7] He went on to compare the film to an "Apgujŏngdong antique" (an allusion to Seoul's richest area, south of the Han River) and a "myŏngp'um" (foreign brand product). For another critic, Hwang Hye-jin, *Untold Scandal* is a "fusion historical movie" which blends traditional/historical and modern/contemporary elements.[8] All of these reviews share the view that *Untold Scandal* is a "new," "modern," and "contemporary" historical drama, departing from preexisting genre conventions at both stylistic and thematic levels. Echoing yet modifying that critical consensus, we argue that this film's unique appeal lies in the fact that it addresses contemporaneous attitudes toward sexual mores and (anti) melodramatic sensibilities despite its Chosun-era setting. More specifically, *Untold Scandal* is a revisionist melodrama brimming with irony and cynicism, one that mocks and parodically reframes the *sinp'a*-style sentimentalism and Confucian values that are so central to traditional historical dramas.

Director-writer E. J-yong (Yi Chae-yong) differentiates his film from previous historical dramas by using a classic Western text as source material, further embellished by a soundtrack comprised of baroque-style chamber music (composed by Yi Pyŏng-u). Explaining his initial inspiration for the film, E. J-yong states that he often listens to Bach's music, and "at one point an image came into [his] mind—the image of people wearing *hanbok* [traditional Korean clothing] combined with Bach's music."[9] His initial interest in combining "Western classical music with a Korean traditional drama" led him to search for story material that fit his vision of cultural hybridity. He opted to adapt the French novel *Dangerous Liaisons* because, to him, it was a "timeless story like the Greek tragedies" centering on basic human emotions such as "love, revenge, hate [and] betrayal" that could be easily translated to different cultural contexts.[10] Although the film's concept essentially formed as a cross-cultural experiment juxtaposing heterogeneous, conflicting elements on both sonic and visual levels, E. and his collaborators made painstaking efforts to recreate the props, costumes, architectural facades, and interiors as historically accurate as possible, investing nearly half of the total production cost ($4.5 million) toward art direction. Finally, E. pushed forward his cross-cultural intentions by devising an English-language title (Korean title: *Scandal*) for his adaptation. The title alone immediately imparts an impression of the film's "myŏngp'um" (foreign brand) quality, capsizing spectatorial preconceptions regarding traditional historical dramas.

Untold Scandal's ostensible claim to historical authenticity is stressed in the opening credit sequence. Against undulating red silk, a close-up image of a picture book entitled *Record of Cho's Scandalous Affair* fills the screen. An offscreen narrator's hand opens the volume, which consists of introductory text and sexually explicit paintings (*ch'unhwa*). Accompanied by the graceful polyphony of baroque music, a voiceover intones:

> Most of the characters in these illustrations are promiscuous and immoral. So much that one is led to doubt whether they had indeed existed. It is widely

> known that Chosun was founded on Confucianism, whereby men must be virtuous gentlemen and women to be modest ladies. So these characters are more unlikely found in Chosun. Even though the contents here have been proven to be based on a true story, the names of the characters may be pseudonyms. So be advised not to raise issue with anyone, or with the family. If you have weak self-control or feel nervous about this, close this book and erase it from your mind right now. Written in the year 1792 and published in 1803.

The spoken narration ends against the close-up of a portrait of a naked woman, a cross-cultural image inspired by Édouard Manet's nude painting *Olympia*, which shocked Parisian society when first exhibited in 1865. The camera pulls back to show a live model on the left side of the frame and a painter working on the nude study with his back turned on the right side. Cross-cut with interior shots of the creation of this explicitly evocative painting (culminating with an act of intercourse between the nude model and the painter) are exterior shots of a traditional Confucian ritual, featuring indistinguishable *sŏnbi* (noble scholars) dressed in simple white robes and black hats and a woman in a voluminous white dress with red flower embroidery topped with opulent head ornaments.

From the very introduction, the two libertine protagonists—Cho-wŏn (Bae Yong-jun [Pae Yong-jun]), a notorious playboy who takes pleasure recording his sexual conquests in paintings, and his cousin and first love Lady Cho (Yi Mi-suk), a conniving vamp who hides her cruel intentions under the mask of a virtuous noble lady—are seen breaking away from the Confucian order: the former by irreverently engaging in a clandestine sex act during the

FIGURE 5.1. Unscholarly conduct: Korean Valmont Cho-wŏn undermines Confucian decorum through his provocative nude paintings.

memorial rite and the latter by publicly displaying colorful embroidery on her dress, not to mention bold red lipstick, thus challenging the monochromatic visual economy of the ancestral ritual. The credit sequence culminates with the image of the two rebellious characters indifferently crossing paths in a garden, leading to a blood-red screen carrying the stylized inscription of the film's self-contradictory title: *Scandal: Love Affair of the Chosun Dynasty.*

E. J-yong's credit sequence departs from the original epistolary novel in an interesting way: Choderlos de Laclos's text opens with a fictional publisher's forward followed by a fictional editor's preface. Unlike E.'s narrator, Laclos's publisher expresses doubts about the authenticity of the material, in this case a collection of letters turned over to him (note that E. has opted for paintings in lieu of letters, thus foregrounding the visual ontology of cinema): "A number of [these] characters are so immoral that it is impossible to imagine them living in this century, this philosophical century in which, as we all know, universal enlightenment has made all men so honourable and all women so modest and reserved. In our view therefore, if the adventures here related have any basis in truth, they can only have occurred at other times and in other places."[11] It is noteworthy that, while E. J-yong's cinematic narrator emphasizes the anomalous nature of promiscuous characters on the basis of the story's conservative Confucian society setting (Chosun), Laclos's publisher stresses the mismatch between libertine deviancy and the Age of Enlightenment. Both E. and Laclos make excuses for their stories and characters, thinly veiling their satiric authorial intentions behind apologetic façades. Laclos's original novel is an ambiguous text that at once both criticizes the decadent, morally corrupt *ancien régime* of pre-Revolutionary France and promulgates the eighteenth-century values of libertinism, "viewed as a part of the Enlightenment impulse to free the individual from the constraints of traditional social authority," such as the Church and the moral establishment.[12]

As many critics and commentators have pointed out,[13] Laclos's novel has an oblique feminist edge in its characterization of the Marquise de Merteuil, the rebellious female protagonist who resents the sociopolitical disenfranchisement of her sex and gender-biased double standards regarding promiscuity and is determined to subjugate and punish men. Laclos apparently attempted to appease the censors and cultural conservatives by punishing his heroine (through ostracism, financial ruin, and facial disfigurement), obscuring the exact dates of letters (years are identified as 17—), and even questioning their authenticity through the voice of a fictional publisher. However, the subversive power of his novel to call accepted social and ethical standards into question continues to render the text as adaptable to and transmutable within diverse temporal and cultural contexts.

As Richard Frohock argues, "[T]he continual adaptations [of Laclos's novel] do not result from an abiding interest in dramatizing the decadent aristocratic culture of pre-Revolutionary France; rather, filmmakers are drawn to this eighteenth-century narrative because of its usefulness as a basis for examining and critiquing contemporary culture."[14] E. J-yong's *Untold Scandal* is no exception. The director telescopes the French novel and the Chosun setting to offer a critical commentary on the contradictory social values (both liberalized and conservative) of post-IMF Crisis South Korea. For this reason, the film is clearly an example of a contemporary melodrama disguised as a historical drama. Whereas Laclos deliberately sought to obscure the specific temporal setting of his novel, E. explicitly situates his film during the era of King Chŏngjo, a reform-minded monarch who ushered in a cultural renaissance and abolished discrimination against secondary sons (born to concubines of commoner or slave origins) through the fair employment of scholars regardless of their birth status. During his rule, pragmatism (*silhak*) blossomed, Catholicism (*ch'ŏnjugyo*) was imported, and Pak Chi-wŏn's satiric travel essays, *Yŏlha Diaries* (based on his trip to China in 1780), were published, enlightening the views of many progressive intellectuals. The Chŏngjo period is thought to be Chosun's last opportunity to implement autonomous modernization, an effort that failed due to the reactionary backlash of conservative literati-officials (*sadaebu*).

Although director E. J-yong obsessively insisted on the historical authenticity of props and costumes (often shown in fetishistic close-ups), his film pushes the important sociopolitical and cultural developments specific to the period to the background. This can be seen as a convenient excuse for juxtaposing such modern goods as a telescope and a rococo-style clock with traditional Korean objects as well as staging scenes of nighttime Catholic masses, where the playboy Cho-wŏn openly approaches the chaste widow Lady Chŏng (a.k.a. Lady Sook: Jeon Do-yeon [Chŏn To-yŏn]) unfettered by restrictive Confucian decorum. Despite its appeal to Euro-American audiences, one can thus claim that *Untold Scandal* defamiliarizes the audiovisual properties of Orientalist film by incorporating random close-ups of Western objects as well as an anomalous Baroque-style soundscape. This estrangement effect inverts the Orientalist gaze and channels through a kind of desire for the Occidental *other* on the part of Korean audiences. In addition, modern speech patterns and humor in *Untold Scandal* further differentiates the film from earlier historical dramas. All these factors considered, *Untold Scanda*l is a groundbreaking film which does not conform to the existing standards of either historical drama or Orientalist film.

From Self-Orientalism to Cosmopolitanism: The US Marketing of Korean Historical Dramas

In her book *Primitive Passions: Visuality, Sexuality, Ethnography, and Contemporary Chinese Cinema*, Rey Chow proposes the concept of "the Oriental's orientalism" to account for ethnographic trends prevalent within the Fifth Generation's cinematic output of the 1980s and early 1990s. In her analysis of director Zhang Yimou's international successes, such as *Judou* (1990) and *Raise the Red Lantern* (*Dà hóng dēnglóng gāogāo guà*, 1991), Chow observes,

> Zhang is showing a 'China' that is at once subalternized and exoticized by the West.... If orientalism, understood in the sense [Edward] Said uses it, is in part a form of voyeuristic aggression, then what Zhang is producing is rather an exhibitionist self-display that contains, in its very excessive modes, a critique of the voyeurism of orientalism itself.... In its self-subalternizing, self-exoticizing visual gestures, the Oriental's orientalism is first and foremost a demonstration—the display of a tactic.[15]

While Chow's revisionist view of Orientalism as a self-scrutinizing practice is persuasive, we argue that "the Oriental's orientalism" should be understood within the larger context of global exhibition, distribution, promotion, and consumption of world cinemas rather than be framed as a purely textual set of self-reflexive representational strategies. As Edward Said reminds us, "Never has there been such a thing as a pure, or unconditional, Orient; similarly never has there been a nonmaterial form of Orientalism, much less something so innocent as an 'idea' of Orientalism."[16] When applied to East Asian films as symptomatic case studies, it is nearly impossible to separate images of Orientalism from the material and institutional dimensions of global exhibition, distribution, and promotion, activities that occur not just in the West but in other spaces as well.

One of the foremost practitioners of "the Oriental's orientalism" among South Korean filmmakers is Im Kwon-taek, not surprisingly one of the most well-known Korean auteurs abroad (along with Bong Joon-ho [Pong Chun-ho], Hong Sang-soo [Hong Sang-su], Kim Ki-duk [Kim Ki-dŏk], Lee Chang-dong [Yi Ch'ang-dong], and Park Chan-wook [Pak Ch'an-uk]). Two years prior to awarding Im the prestigious Best Director Award for *Chihwaseon*, a biopic of a nineteenth-century Korean painter Chang Sŭng-hyŏp, in 2002 (an honor he shared with P. T. Anderson, the director of *Punch-Drunk Love*, that year), the Cannes Film Festival committee nominated the Korean veteran director's ninety-seventh feature *Chunhyang* as Korea's first official competition entry into the festival. Based on a beloved folktale which had already been adapted into more than a dozen filmic versions in both North and South

Koreas, Im's *p'ansori*-version *Chunhyang* presents a colorfully-packaged, effervescent "gift-set" of Korea's traditional cultures, folk arts, and ethnographic landscapes, mobilizing images that make the sparkling promotional films of the Korea Tourism Organization look pale in comparison. Like its period-piece predecessors *Surrogate Mother, Adada* (1988), and *Sopyonje* (*Sŏp'ŏnje*, 1993), *Chunhyang* displays a "self-subalternizing, self-exoticizing" bundle of visual tropes that festoon the nation's identity with aestheticized feudal imagery embroidered around a beautiful yet suffering female body.

It is hard to detect any parodic or critical intent in this or any other examples of Im Kwon-taek's self-orientalization. In our view, self-orientalism in Im's films is not mobilized to "quote" or critically contain Western Orientalism in a self-conscious way so as to underscore its voyeuristic visual politics (as Chow argues for the Fifth Generation Chinese filmmakers), but rather to supply competitive products for Orientalist film institutions of the West (i.e. international film festivals and art-house theaters). In South Korea, *Chunhyang* was not only a box-office flop (grossing a modest 240,000 admissions upon its domestic release), but it also sparked scandal and controversy because of its fleeting shots of the young actress Yi Hyŏ-jŏng undressed. Moreover, many domestic audiences felt that Im had failed to provide a new interpretation of gender and class issues underscored in the time-honored tale of interclass romance between a courtesan's daughter and an aristocrat's son under the Chosun Dynasty's stringent caste system. As Hyangjin Lee points out, in the eyes of Korean audiences, "[*Chunghyang*] forgoes populism in order to create a new identity for global film audiences who embody the high sense of artistic experience. . . . Korean-ness, which was widely recognized by the judges at Cannes, could not help *Chunhyang* avoid the widespread indifference of Koreans."[17] In the West, however, *Chunhyang* has been successfully promoted and consumed as a lavish Orientalist epic. After its acclaimed debut in international film festivals (including the Hawaii International Film Festival, the Asia-Pacific Film Festival, the Fribourg International Film Festival, and the Singapore International Film Festival), *Chunhyang* was imported to the US market by independent distributor Lot 47 Films in January 2001, becoming the first Korean film to receive nationwide (if still limited) theatrical release.

A brief exploration of what Gregory Lukow and Steve Ricci have termed "intertextual relay"—referring to the promotional, verbal, and pictorial depictions of films circulated in advertisements, trailers, stills, reviews, posters, and so forth[18]—will help illustrate the discursive modes of Orientalism attending the US release of *Chunhyang* in this age of globalization and transnational capitalism. One striking example of the film's Orientalist promotional disposition can be found in its trailer, one part of a larger intertextual relay of meaning that can also be referred to as a "paratext" (borrowing the language of Gérard

Genette and Jonathan Gray).[19] Not only does the trailer provide a colorful and exotic montage of travelogue-like spectacles, but its male voiceover delivers an out-and-out catchphrase of the Orientalist imaginary: "It will take you to a place where you've never been." Moreover, New Yorker Films' *Chunhyang* homepage contains excerpts from media reviews, unanimously praising the film as "a dazzling epic" (Jonathan Rosenbaum of the *Chicago Reader*); "[an] astoundingly beautiful Korean production" (David Sterritt of the *Christian Science Monitor*); "an almost childlike delight for the eyes" (Elvis Mitchell of the *New York Times*); and "a three-ring circus of visual pleasure, showing us the beauty of Korean garments, customs and national character" (Desson Thomson of the *Washington Post*).[20] These comments, splashed across the distributor's website, collectively and paratextually call attention to the ostensibly overpowering visual pleasure provided by the film, expanding feminist film theorist Laura Mulvey's gendered dichotomy of mainstream cinema's gaze structure to incorporate ethnographic and Orientalist specularity.[21] The film's US promotional poster as well as its Region-1 DVD jacket unmistakably genders the Orient with a dominating close-up image of the bare-shouldered Asian woman (situated between her lover, shown in medium-shot on the upper left side, and a *p'ansori* performer, shown in long shot on the lower right side). She coyly casts her eyes down in a seductive gesture to provoke the Western spectator's curiosity for exotic-erotic others.

At a first glance, the US marketing of *Untold Scandal* appears to warrant a similar accusation of self-orientalization and exoticization of the East. Kino International (now Kino-Lorber)'s webpage for *Untold Scandal* cites excerpts from print-media reviews that position E.'s film as another Orientalist cinematic feast, best exemplified by Derek Elley's endorsement of the film in the pages of *Variety*: "It's a ten-course treat for the eyes and the ears. . . . An elegant, witty game of seduction."[22] However, there is a key discrepancy between the overseas marketing of *Chunhyang* and that of *Untold Scandal*. In the former case, the enlarged close-up of the titular heroine's face and bare shoulders receives disproportionate attention compared to the image used for its South Korean counterpart. On the cover of the South Korean DVD (released by Taewon Entertainment), Chunhyang can be seen playing a traditional musical instrument (*kayagŭm*) next to her lover who has his arm around her in an intimate medium shot, which features the two figures as equals (they are the same size). The foregrounding of exotic-erotic Oriental female bodies for the pleasure of the Western male gaze is a familiar, predictable practice in the US marketing of foreign films across different national and generic contexts.

Compare, for example, the South Korean and US one-sheet posters of the action blockbuster *Shiri*. The original domestic poster features a medium long-shot of the South Korean protagonist (Han Sŏk-gyu) and the North Korean antagonist (Ch'oe Min-sik of *Oldboy* fame) facing each other against a dark, abstracted background. In contrast, the US poster foregrounds the mysterious profile of a long-haired Asian woman in a revealing black evening dress with a gun in her hand. Only the bottom half of her face can be seen; the top half is concealed, ostensibly to mask the identity of the elusive North Korean female sniper played by Yunjin Kim (Kim Yun-jin), whose growing fame in the United States can be attributed to her role as the Korean castaway Sun in ABC's cult TV show *Lost* (2004–2010). Both the hairdo and scandalous party dress of the woman in the publicity shot are manufactured for the US market and have no visual presence in the film's action-filled narrative. The poster further supports the illogical logic of Orientalism by stripping cultural specificity away, replacing it with a nondescript, blurry background consisting of blue-tinted skyscrapers and red-tinted urban traffic. A caption above the film title reads "The Asian hit comes to America," an exceedingly generic way of paratextually framing *Shiri*'s distinction as a Korean blockbuster.

Given this and countless other examples of shameless marketing practices, whereby East Asian films are presented to a global public through the deceptive image of scantily dressed "Oriental women" (falsely enticing curious audiences who might come to the film with "wrong" expectations), it is surprising that the US poster of *Untold Scandal* is the same as that of the South Korean poster, which will be discussed in detail shortly. The only difference is the written copy in English. At the top of the poster is a quote from Elvis Mitchell of the *New York Times*: "A viciously purring comedy of sexual conquest." Above the film's title can be found an explanatory subheading for uninformed Western audiences: "Based on the French classic *Les Liaisons dangereuses*. Set in 19th Century Korea." Kino International, the North American distributor of *Untold Scandal*, plays on art-house theater patrons' familiarity with the original literary classic and appeals to their appreciation of the European/French tradition of sex farce. In other words, unlike in the case of *Chunhyang*, the cosmopolitan characteristics of *Untold Scandal* are underscored so as to market the film to "upscale," "well-read" American audiences. Ironically, the film succeeded in the Korean market because of its very status as an Occidental narrative barely hidden beneath an Oriental shell, something that both overseas and domestic publicity departments sought to exploit as part of their efforts to expand its commercial appeal.

"Did You Connect?": Gender Politics and Cross-Cultural Transformations

Untold Scandal's theatrical poster (reprinted on the South Korean release DVD cover as well as in US promotional materials) conveys the ethos of sexual and cultural politics in the narrative. On the left, actress Yi Mi-suk's Lady Cho is shown wearing a lavish, red-tinted wig decorated with metal pins, multicolored *hanbok* (in purple, red, green, white, and dark brown) and ornate jade trinkets along her waist. Seated next to her is Cho-wŏn, played by actor Bae Yong-joon who recently achieved phenomenal stardom in Japan, Hong Kong, Taiwan, and China due to the pan-Asian popularity of the KBS television drama *Winter Sonata* (*Kyŏul yŏnga*, 2002). In the poster, Bae's bare chest is clearly visible through the open front of his dark gray robe. Actress Jeon Do-yeon's Lady Chŏng, shown crouching with her back turned in the lower center of the frame, demurely stares at the camera, her bared shoulders leaning toward Cho-wŏn. Upon close scrutiny, one notices that the three stars in traditional attire are posing on a European-style velvet canapé or settee. The dimly lit space displays black wallpaper with an abstract modern pattern, another "alien" element in the supposedly Chosun-era interior. Along with pieces of traditional furniture in the background is yet another item of Western antiquity: a rococo-style golden clock with standing legs. Across an otherwise empty space in the upper portion of the frame runs a line of the enigmatic publicity copy, asking the viewer, "Did you connect?" (*t'onghayŏtnŭtya?*).

This seductive image featuring the popular threesome is thus punctuated with a rhetorical solicitation, the textual inscription and apparent ambiguity of which provoke further questions in the minds of curious spectators. Who connects with whom or what? Is this connection strictly sexual or libidinal? Or is it instead linked to the cross-cultural, intertextual relationship between Choderlos de Laclos's epistolary novel and E. J-yong's cinematic adaptation? Is it perhaps a spectatorial connection between the genre of historical drama and contemporary audiences? Newspaper reviews focused on the latter interpretation, reframing the question to ask, "Did *Untold Scandal* connect to contemporary times?" Although the film was favorably received by most local critics as well as audiences, a few detractors answered negatively to the previous question. One critic in particular, Chŏng Sŏng-il, criticized the film for turning recalcitrant and uninhibited individuals (Cho-wŏn and Lady Cho) into passive agents of "Chosun-style melodrama" in its sentimental ending.[23]

However, one could make the counter-argument that *Untold Scandal* indeed did succeed in connecting to contemporary spectators and their social milieu, not only for its liberalized sexual politics involving extramarital affairs and transgressive female desire, but also for its nostalgic ending, which evokes South Korean audiences' collective memory of an "innocent" past implicitly associated with the 1980s (via the recasting of Yi Mi-suk's earlier screen image). In other words, E. J-yong's film consolidates two seemingly contradictory trends within the national cinema after the 1997 financial meltdown known as the IMF Crisis.[24] The first consists of a series of sophisticated yet provocative melodramas featuring modern-day "Madame Freedoms" who actively seek sexual pleasure and personal fulfillment outside the confines of marriage and domesticity. Examples of this include E. J-yong's debut film *An*

FIGURE 5.2. The US promotional poster for *Untold Scandal.*

Affair (*Chŏngsa*, 1998), *Happy End* (*Haep'i endŭ*, 1999), *Marriage Is a Crazy Thing* (*Kyŏlhon ŭn, mich'in chitida*, 2002), and *A Good Lawyer's Wife* (*Parammnan kajok*, 2003). The second cycle is comprised of nostalgia-imbued films which narrativize and literally put into motion a collective desire to return to more innocent, less materialistic times, specifically the 1970s and 1980s (before

South Korea became a bastion of global capitalism and mass consumption). Examples of this latter trend include the previously-mentioned *Friend*, as well as *Peppermint Candy* (*Pakha sat'ang*, 2000), *Failan* (*P'airan*, 2001), *Conduct Zero* (*P'umhaeng chero*, 2001), *Bet on My Disco* (*Haejŏk, disk'o wang toeda*, 2003), and *Once Upon a Time in High School* (*Maljuk kŏri chanhoksa*, 2004).

All three of the main characters in *Untold Scandal* are figures whose modern sensibilities pose a threat to Confucian patriarchal order in one way or another. Based on Laclos's Marquise de Merteuil, Lady Cho is the childless wife of Lord Yu (Na Han-il). According to Confucian doctrines, she is culpable for the primary sin (failure to produce a son) of the infamous "seven offenses" for divorce (*ch'ilgŏ chiak*),[25] and as such, is in an extremely vulnerable, unstable position. She has no power to oppose her husband's decision to take a sixteen-year-old concubine (*sosil*) to continue the family line. Although she is an outwardly obedient wife who volunteers for the prenuptial education of her husband's second wife So-ok (Yi So-yŏn), she secretly schemes and plots her revenge by inviting her promiscuous cousin and accomplice Cho-wŏn (a cross-cultural reformulation of Vicomte de Valmont) to impregnate the virginal bride-to-be as a wedding present to the brother-in-law. Cho-wŏn, however, turns down the offer, calling it too easy. He has another plan of his own: to seduce Lady Chŏng, whose virtuous nine-year widowhood has been honored with the erection of a Gate of Chastity (*yŏlnyŏmun*) by the state.

Although Lady Chŏng is modeled on Laclos's Madame de Tourvel, the two virtuous women are fundamentally different insofar as the former is a virgin-widow (whose husband died before their wedding night) and the latter is a happily married woman (whose husband is temporarily away on business). Although Lady Chŏng may at first appear to be a traditional Confucian woman who cherishes chastity and faithfulness to her (dead) husband, she is, in fact, as much a woman of modern consciousness as Lady Cho. Lady Chŏng is a Catholic convert who regularly attends nighttime masses where the two genders and different classes commingle. Like Lady Cho, she is a well-read, enlightened woman who transcribes religious texts for fellow converts and takes pleasure in learning about China in recently published books. While Madame de Tourvel, a devout Catholic, agonizes over the conflict between her faith in both God and marriage and her desire for Valmont, Lady Chŏng oscillates between Confucian and modern subjectivities.

When Cho-wŏn first approaches her in the garden of her aunt's house where he has visited as a guest, Lady Chŏng refuses to speak to him directly and informs him, by way of her maid, that it is improper for him to socialize with a woman of her status. Cho-wŏn tries to persuade her, appealing to her Christian beliefs: "Are you not an enlightened person who is willing to do good unfettered by customs and prejudices?" Whereas the Church, as a symbol of the conservative establishment, is an archenemy to libertine principals in the original novel, Lady Chŏng's affiliation with Catholicism in *Untold Scandal* is an embodiment of her modern subjectivity—i.e. her egalitarian class consciousness and belief in gender equality. Lady Chŏng is thus a defiant woman who risks her safety to practice a Western religion forbidden by the law of the land. It is also noteworthy that Cho-wŏn takes advantage of her charitable disposition and lays the groundwork for his seductive overtures by donating money to the Catholic congregation to which Lady Chŏng belongs. In other words, the church becomes a facilitator, rather than an obstacle, for their romantic union, reversing its position in Laclos's novel and earlier film adaptations. However, Lady Chŏng ultimately chooses romantic love over her religion when she commits suicide after Cho-wŏn's death, thus violating a fundamental doctrine of Catholicism.

If Lady Chŏng rebels through, and then against, her religion, Lady Cho expresses her resistance to Confucian gender norms not only by engaging in extramarital affairs herself but also by instructing her husband's future concubine, So-ok, to follow her example. After So-ok falls in love with the neighboring young nobleman Kwŏn In-ho (Cho Hyŏn-jae) and is deflowered by Cho-wŏn, Lady Cho shares words of wisdom with her inexperienced apprentice: "Common people do not know this, but all the ladies of nobility have a secret lover or two of their own." Surprised, So-ok asks, "Is that true? Then what about women's duties told from the books?" "Books are books," Lady Cho boldly replies, "but reality is different. Just as a woman's reality is to wed a man she doesn't love. Everyone does it and everyone knows it but no one speaks of it."

It is an unlikely yet audacious hypothesis that every Chosun lady of nobility took a secret lover or two outside the marriage. Common and acceptable for married men, adultery for Chosun women was one of the aforementioned "seven offenses" punishable by expulsion or divorce. In extreme cases, culpable women were punished by death. In 1423, for example, an adulteress—the wife of a high official who had copulated with one of her distant relatives—was decapitated as a warning against future offenses.[26] Defying moral, religious, and judicial principals of her society, Lady Cho is a dangerous femme fatale, not only because of her own infidelity but also because of her influence on innocent young people. Rather than instilling the codes of morality and womanly tasks (as a dutiful wife and wise mother) in her husband's second wife under her supervision, Lady Cho directly mocks the gender constrictions and instructions in Confucian texts. Lady Cho also seduces naive Kwŏn In-ho and uses him as a pawn for her ruthless revenge against her husband and Cho-wŏn.

Lady Cho as played by Yi Mi-suk, an actress in her forties who exhibits remarkable youth and sexual charisma, is more indicative of the contemporary "Missy" phenomenon than aristocratic femininity of Chosun Dynasty. As a neologism of the 1990s introduced by a department store marketing team, the Missy is a consumer-oriented new ideal for young housewives who seek to maintain the appearance of unmarried women and subscribe to a lifestyle in which culture, technology, sports, and leisure can be freely enjoyed. Popular culture has exploited the commercialized images of the Missy as not only a fashion leader and model consumer but also a sexually liberated woman who enjoys extramarital affairs to fill the vacuum of a boring marriage and compensate for the demands of motherhood.[27] Although Yi was often cast as provincial and earthy characters in films of the 1980s such as *Whale Hunting* (*Korae sanyang*, 1984) and *That Winter Was Warm* (*Kŭhae kŏul ŭn ttatŭt haetne*, 1984), when she returned to the screen after an eleven-year hiatus with E. J-yong's 1998 debut feature *An Affair*, she seemed to epitomize the sexy and elegant, if stereotypical, Missy. Having married a renowned plastic surgeon and mothered two children during her absence from the entertainment industry, Yi surprised audiences with her ageless beauty and new persona.[28]

In her comeback role, Yi Mi-suk plays So-hyŏn, an ordinary yet stylish housewife-mother who falls in love with a considerably younger man (Yi Chŏng-jae) who happens to be her sister's fiancé. Yi quickly became a role model and the object of envy for many Korean women in their forties. *An Affair* was extremely popular with middle-aged female audiences who flocked to theaters in groups to see an idealized screen surrogate indulging in a romantic liaison with an attractive young man while leaving husband and home behind at the end without punishment or recrimination. One scene in particular, in which So-hyŏn sneaks out of a tedious commemorative ritual at her in-laws and enjoys a brief rendezvous with her lover in time to return before the end of the ritual, delighted many married women who shared similarly stressful familial obligations as daughters-in-law.[29] Although not as sympathetic as So-hyŏn in *An Affair*, Lady Cho likewise parlays her rebellious attitude toward suffocating Confucian customs into an emotional outlet for contemporary audiences familiar with the history of female oppression.

As it did in Laclos's original novel, the dénouement of *Untold Scandal* reestablishes the status quo by eliminating those who refuse to conform: Cho-wŏn is stabbed to death by Lady Chŏng's avenging brother-in-law and Lady Chŏng takes her own life after her lover's death. When Lady Cho's scandalous affairs are exposed to the world through the posthumous publication of Cho-wŏn's obscene paintings depicting the diabolic duo's promiscuity, her embarrassed in-laws clandestinely send an assassin to her chamber only to find that she has already fled. The final scene of the film shows a deglamorized Lady Cho, now in a commoner's shabby dress, sailing for China. In an earlier scene, Lady Chŏng proposes that she and Cho-wŏn go to Beijing, where they can live as a married couple with little concern for social censors. Cho-wŏn agrees but later coldly breaks off with Lady Chŏng to prove to his cousin-accomplice that he is not genuinely in love with her. Disheartened by the loss of her love, Lady

Chŏng falls gravely ill. Only after he realizes his true love for Lady Chŏng does Cho-wŏn turn down Lady Cho's "reward," sending a letter and a beautiful portrait to seek the forgiveness of Lady Chŏng. Out of jealousy, Lady Cho informs Kwŏn In-ho—So-ok's admirer—of the affair between her husband's concubine-to-be and Cho-wŏn. For his own revenge, Kwŏn in turn informs Lady Chŏng's brother-in-law about the affair between Cho-wŏn and his sister-in-law, an act that leads to Cho-wŏn's murder.

It is noteworthy that *Untold Scandal* decisively romanticizes all three lead characters and their actions at the point of narrative closure, departing significantly from the moralistic ending of its cross-cultural literary source. After he is mortally wounded in a duel with the Chevalier Danceny whose lover he has impregnated, Laclos's Valmont spends his final hours plotting revenge against the treacherous Marquise de Merteuil. He hands the Marquise's letters over to Danceny, one of many victims of her machinations, and instructs the public circulation of the incriminating evidence. E. J-yong's male protagonist, however, dies as a tragic romantic hero, not a vengeful libertine. Having been fatally stabbed in the back, Cho-wŏn desperately attempts to travel to the Kanghwa Island where Lady Chŏng resides, a trip the dying man is unable to complete. As he draws his last breath on the beach, a lovesick Cho-wŏn confides to his servant how much he misses the virtuous woman. After the death of his master, the servant steals and sells Cho-wŏn's picture book (revealing Lady Cho's licentious misconduct) for selfish monetary gain.[30] Therefore, unlike Valmont, Cho-wŏn is not culpable for his accomplice's disgrace and expulsion.

Out of the four prior screen adaptations, Stephen Frears's *Dangerous Liaisons* and Roger Kumble's *Cruel Intentions* particularly romanticize Valmont's death, the circumstances of which remain unclear in the original novel (where it is reported by a third person who was not present in the duel). In the former film, haunted by the flashback of ecstatic lovemaking with Madame de Tourvel (Michelle Pfeiffer), guilt-ridden Valmont (John Malkovich) manipulates his own death in the duel and entrusts Danceny (Keanu Reeves) with his final message of love for Tourvel. In the latter film, Valmont (Ryan Phillippe) sacrifices his life in order to save Annette (a teenaged version of Tourvel played by Reese Witherspoon) from a traffic accident. In both narratives, Valmont ultimately deserts his libertine principals and finds redemption in true love—an interpretation inherited in E. J-yong's film.

Tellingly, in Hur Jin-ho's Mandarin-language version of the tale, *Dangerous Liaisons*,[31] a big-screen adaptation released in 2012, Jang Dong-gun's wealthy playboy Xie Yifan is the softest and luckiest Valmont of them all. After being shot in the back by the Chinese Danceny, Dai Wenzhou (Shawn Dou), on the chaotic streets of Shanghai where patriotic protestors are chanting anti-Japanese slogans and disseminating political fliers, Jang's Valmont rushes toward the apartment of Zhang Ziyi's Madame de Tourvel. It is there, near the home of his distant cousin Du Fenyu (a socially conscious widow from Japanese-occupied Manchuria) where he finally succumbs to the fatal gunshot wound. Initially rejected by the heartbroken Fenyu, who had refused to let him in, a teary-eyed Yifan is able to confess his love behind closed doors, saying, "I finally understand how happy I was with you. I found out too late." Moved by his sincere words, Fenyu opens the door and follows Yifan's bloody trail to a snowy courtyard where the dying man has collapsed. The Chinese Valmont whose dying wish had been to see her one last time takes his last breath peacefully in the arms of the woman he loves. To top off this "softened" dénouement, the film's Marquise de Merteuil—Cecila Cheung's businesswoman Mo Jieyu—is the only villainess who avoids a social downfall in all of the adaptations of Laclos's novel. Her sole punishment is the loss of Yifan, the only man she has truly loved, a loss that she grieves privately in her mirror-filled bedroom.

In an epilogue set one year later, this Chinese version of *Dangerous Liaisons* ends on an upbeat note, showing Fenyu reminiscing about a happy moment with Yifan while teaching a hopeful song to a group of refugee children. As Kate Taylor explains in her review of the film for the Canadian newspaper *The Globe and Mail*, "both the perpetually smiling Cheung [and] the mischievously charming Jang . . . offer performances that seem far too pretty to render the dastardly amorality of their characters. That failing is then intensified by Hur's melodramatic handling of the story's final scenes, which threatens to turn the piece from devastating social critique into tear-jerking romance." Taylor concludes by stating that the Korean filmmaker's Chinese production "is lovely rather than wicked."[32]

In Laclos's novel, Madame de Tourvel faces a much harsher demise: she withdraws to a convent after her breakup with Valmont, plunges into delirium, and passes away in extreme physical agony and spiritual repentance. More sentimental than Laclos's original (although much less so than Hur's adaptation, which was not only snubbed by Taylor but also dubbed as a "deluxe soap opera" by a reviewer for *The Hollywood Reporter*),[33] E. J-yong's film grants a dignified death to Lady Chŏng, who willingly takes her own life as a means of ensuring a heavenly reunion with her beloved, suggested by her voiceover while walking into the half-frozen lake: "I told you that we were not destined to be together in this world. But up there who would say otherwise if we say we're married?" Perhaps Lady Cho receives the most radically different treatment of them all. Humiliated and bankrupt, Laclos's Merteuil is afflicted with smallpox, terribly disfigured, and loses one eye. As one character reports, "[H]er illness had turned her inside out and [now] her soul was showing in her face."[34] Duplicitous and cunning to the end, the Marquise flees Paris for Holland with diamonds and other valuables in her pockets, leaving a huge sum of debts to the family. In sharp contrast, Lady Cho's mask is lifted only to reveal a soft, sentimental side. Having fallen into the life of a humble, unadorned expatriate with few possessions, Lady Cho finally sheds her cynical veneer and callous demeanor. Her tender feelings for her first love are expressed when she takes out the dried wild bellflowers, which had been preserved in her handkerchief. Accompanied by plaintive nondiegetic music, inserted flashbacks momentarily take us back to earlier scenes in which Cho-wŏn presented the flowers to her with a compliment on her beauty and in which she and Cho-wŏn (along with Lady Chŏng) shared a boat ride in the picturesque garden. A gust of wind cuts short the grieving woman's melancholic reminiscence and blows away the fragile memento. Lady Cho raises her hand toward the sky in a vain attempt to hold on to the last trace of Cho-wŏn's affections. The camera tilts to the sky where the flowers have disappeared, bringing the film to a poetic end. This transfigurative softening of the unremorseful French heroine, as well as the evocation of the Korean actress's less sophisticated, makeup-free screen image of the 1980s, are indicative of the cross-cultural maneuvers necessary to recast gender politics specific to post-IMF South Korea.

The IMF Crisis left an indelible trauma in the collective male psyche, resulting in massive layoffs, the widespread unemployment of white-collar workers, and considerable reduction of the middle-class population. The aforementioned cycle of nostalgia films attempted to allay or overcome male anxieties generated by the financial crisis as well as disempowerment in the face of super-adaptive professional women who gained prominence in a globalized postmodern society. A frequent strategy for the restoration of male subjectivity is either extolling militaristic culture and masculine bonding under the authoritarian regimes of the 1970s and 1980s or idealizing traditional images

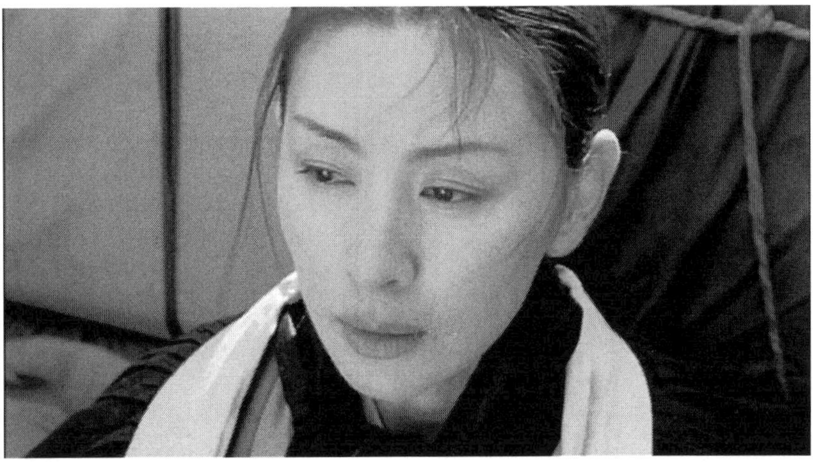

FIGURE 5.3. Actress Yi Mi-suk's makeup-free face in the final scene of *Untold Scandal* evokes the star's innocent screen image of the 1980s.

of women who stand by their men at all costs. A parallel trend to the temporal displacement connoted by nostalgia is spatial escapism, something personified by the iconic and habitually repeated image of expatriating, migratory Korean characters, as seen in the final scenes of *An Affair, Asako in Ruby Shoes* (*Sunaebo*, 2000), *Bungee Jumping of Their Own* (*Pŏnjijhŏmpŭ rŭl hada*, 2001), and *Take Care of My Cat* (*Koyangi rŭl put'akhae*, 2001). *Untold Scandal* follows in this tradition with a romanticized final image of self-imposed exile from the conformist homeland in crisis. Some domestic critics have complained that many of E. J-yong's films end with his characters escaping the homeland (to Brazil in *An Affair*, to Alaska in *Asako in Ruby Shoes*, and to China in *Untold Scandal*).[35] However, his films are prismatic reflections of the current zeitgeist of post-IMF South Korean society, in which financial pressure and educational zeal push many Koreans into immigration or overseas studies. Taking all of these factors into consideration, *Untold Scandal* can be understood as a complex allegory of contemporary South Korea, where conservative and liberalized sexual values coexist, where postmodern discontent is transformed into nostalgia for the past, and the desire for expatriation increasingly mounts as a result of social frustrations and institutional constrictions.

Transnationalizing Nostalgia

Untold Scandal's final scene of exile, migration, and nostalgia provides an excellent opportunity to showcase the multilayered spectatorial positions embedded in a transnational text. Local Korean audiences seem to have been concerned less with the romanticization of Laclos's vile heroine than with the "de-Missifying" of actress Yi Mi-suk and the evocation of 1980s screen memories. In an interview printed in the October 6, 2003 issue of *Sports Chosun* (*Sp'och'ŭ Chosŏn*), Yi attests to this reaction by stating, "Many fans told me that the last scene of *Untold Scandal* reminded them of my performances twenty years ago in such films as *Whale Hunting* and *Winter Wanderer* (*Kŏul nagŭnae*, 1986)." Intentionally or not, E.'s revisionist ending has apparently conjured up the collective cultural memory of Korean audiences who remember Lee's younger image of innocence and naturalness.[36] However, Asian audiences smitten with the Korean Wave (*Hallyu*) likely pay closer attention to the final close-up of regional superstar Bae Yong-joon, whose signature smile is cross-cut with a shot of Lady Cho mourning the loss of her love. For middle-aged and elderly Japanese female audiences—main players of the phenomenal "yon-*sama*"[37] craze in their country—it is Bae's cross-media star persona in their favorite twenty-episode television series *Winter Sonata*, a sentimental eulogy for first love, that evokes nostalgia for *their* lost time of youth and pure love, not the image of Yi Mi-suk, a little-known actress in Japan. For the septuagenarian Nomura Hisa and other elderly fans of Bae Yong-joon,

Winter Sonata furthermore induces "a sense of nostalgia . . . [for] the 'good old Japan' . . . [because] the characters hold ancestors in great veneration and respect their family members."[38]

Ironically, both Korean and Japanese audiences may experience a similar nostalgia for the "good old days" (implicitly associated with the 1980s, Yi Mi-suk's heyday as one of the most popular young actresses of Korean cinema as well as the temporal setting of *Winter Sonata*'s early episodes centering on high school romance) in the final minutes of *Untold Scandal*, mediated through the images of two different stars, one local and the other regional. For Western audiences, though, who know neither of the two stars and remain relatively unaffected by the *Hallyu* phenomenon, a dynamic inter-Asian cultural flow of the new millennium, the Korean ending merely de-westernizes the French heroine and reinstates traditional virtues of Confucian femininity.[39]

As an East-meets-West text of hybridity and transnational valences, *Untold Scandal* holds both universal and culturally specific appeals for divergent spectatorial groups. For literary critics and adaptation specialists, it is a welcome addition to the ever-increasing list of derivative works (including stage plays, operas, films, and television mini-series) based on Laclos's canonical epistolary novel. For aficionados of exotic Asian costume dramas, E. J-yong's stylistic mise-en-scène offers a visually sumptuous, chromatically saturated, ethnographic feast ostensibly designed for Western eyes and the Orientalist imagination. For diehard devotees of the Bae Yong-joon cult, their idol's daring transformation from a wholesome, if bland, televisual protagonist to a promiscuous Don Juan on the big screen, freely indulging in carnal pleasures, may be the film's foremost attraction. For many South Korean audiences, *Untold Scandal* has not only contributed to reviving a once-popular yet waning genre of their national cinema, but also sparks nostalgic memories of veteran actress Yi Mi-suk, whose triumphant comeback in the late 1990s ironically coincided with the newfound popularity and growing reputation of South Korean films both at home and abroad.

Chapter 6

From *Gojira* to *Goemul*

"Host" Cities and "Post" Histories in East Asian Monster Movies

In 2006, a half century after its initial stateside theatrical release, director Honda Ishirō's pioneering monster movie *Gojira* (1954; retitled *Godzilla: King of the Monsters* for its 1956 premiere in the United States) was joined by a contemporary, cross-cultural updating of the perennial Japanese film genre known as *kaijū eiga*. Directed by the talented Korean filmmaker Bong Joon-ho (Pong Chun-ho) and starring celebrated actor Song Kang-ho as a struggling snack vendor forced to rescue his adolescent daughter from a gigantic, lizard-like denizen of the Han River, *Goemul* ([*Koemul*], which literally translates as "Creature" or "Monster") quickly became a box-office sensation in South Korea, selling over 13 million tickets before going on to generate rave reviews at international film festivals (from Hong Kong to Edinburgh to Vancouver).[1] After being given the English title *The Host* for its US distribution, Bong's hyperkinetic monster movie developed a cult following among fans of the genre while reminding audiences of the stylistic dynamism and thematic complexity of contemporary Korean cinema in general. Oscillating between scenes of sudden terror, when the savage title creature threatens to destroy everything in its path (wreaking havoc throughout Seoul), and moments of mounting familial crisis, when the good-hearted yet dim-witted protagonist, Kang-du, strives to bring his bickering siblings and aging father together in unified pursuit of his missing daughter, the darkly comic film is a visceral yet discombobulating mixture of postmillennial anxieties. Those anxieties, linked to the long history of US military presence and bureaucratic mismanagement in South Korea, are subtly suggested by the film's English-language title and therefore tied to its transnational distribution and reception.

With its dialogic ability to denote parasitic feeding while connoting a country or area that provides services for a competition or event (as Seoul did in 1988, the year South Korea hosted the Summer Olympics), the term "host" is thus doubly evocative, a fitting indexical referent that brings additional sociopolitical relevance to the film's "David-vs.-Goliath" scenario. As explained by Christina Klein in a recently published essay about director Bong Joon-ho (who, in interviews, has downplayed the influence of the original *Gojira* and its many Japanese-language sequels), such a conflict between an alternative version of "the Korean national" (represented by "figures of social and economic marginality and failure") and "the global American other" (personified by cross-eyed scientists and bossy morticians) can only result in a literally combustible confrontation on the streets of Seoul, a space historically linked to mass protests and political rallies during the *minjung* movement era of the 1980s and presented to the audience of *The Host* as a place of combined finality and renewal in the film's penultimate scenes.[2] Those scenes, which are designed to spark a range of spectatorial emotions (from fear and apprehension to relief and sadness), invite the viewer to reflect on the potentially contradictory meanings of the misshapen monster itself—a computer-generated creation that can be said to stand in for the missing colonial, postcolonial, and neocolonial culprits: Japan and the United States. As we shall see (or not see), the monster is there but *not there*, an absent presence (or what Kyung Hyun Kim refers to as a "depthless surface") whose intrageneric ties to Japanese creature features and allegorical links to US techno-military domination only partially fade away once it meets a fiery end on the banks of the river from which it came.[3]

In this chapter, after gesturing toward the long history of *kaijū eiga* in Japan (summarizing, in the process, the main strains of critical reception attending Godzilla films), we cast light on some of the textual features of *The Host* that most decisively situate it within Korean and non-Korean traditions of screen monsterdom. Following this investigation into the film's cross-cultural entanglements with other monster movies, including the earlier Korean film *Tae koesu Yonggari* (1967, retitled *Yonggary* for its stateside release), we shift into an assessment of the tactics employed by Bong Joon-ho in his celebrated efforts to both serve and subvert genre conventions. As a director who readily admits to being somewhat politically disengaged, preferring the movie theater to the voting booth, Bong is perhaps representative of a new, relatively young generation of cinephiles and cineastes whose collectively shared interests and individual goals (as both consumers and directors of mainstream genre pieces) run counter to the historical project undergirding many South Korean films of the 1980s and 1990s. Taking the final passages of *The Host* as a sign or symptom of that political disengagement, we question whether a reversal of that trend is possible in a so-called post-historical world where time and space have dissolved and "master narratives" related to nationhood have been emptied of meaning.

Drawing on Jean Baudrillard's philosophical musings about the seemingly ceaseless process of virtualization in contemporary life, a point in time when media images and other forms of simulacra provide our only proof—tenuous though it may be—that a reality beyond the symbolic realm once existed, we test the applicability of the prefix "post" in both academic and nonacademic discussions of cinema. This prefix paradoxically inscribes finality or a sense of completion in even the most fragmented and seemingly incomplete of national histories, suggesting that the future of Korea as a divided nation (torn apart by a war that, even today, lacks an official end) has been permanently preempted by a past forever linked to globally circulating media images. The problems involved in cinematically narrativizing the past are compounded by the fact that, apart from Bong, few contemporary South Korean filmmakers seem genuinely interested in the sociopolitical issues faced by earlier generations—issues related to workers' rights, national division, and the ever-widening divide between the wealthy and the poor.

For his part, Bong injects subtle references to previous decades and, according to Darcy Paquet, showcases destructive acts as a way of evoking "memories of previous disasters that would be familiar" to most Korean audiences—tragic events such as the structural collapses of the Sŏngsu Bridge in 1994 and the Samp'ung Department Store in 1995, the death of two schoolgirls after a 2002 run-in with a US armored vehicle, and the Daegu subway fire of 2003.[4] He furthermore turns his camera toward members of the underclass whose devalued social status and peripheral positioning in other mainstream features belie their centrality to South Korea's recent economic growth and industrial development (dubbed, not coincidentally, "the miracle of the Han River"). But he also parasitically feeds on the ghosts of earlier "hosts," latching onto the iconography associated with Japanese monster movies and leaning on the technology provided by a US-based visual effects team—the true heart and soul of the virtual beast.

Ultimately, Bong's paradoxical investment in and rejection of the historical project is representative of broader patterns in South Korean cultural production over the past ten years. As such, any charge brought against the filmmaker as a purveyor of post-historical attitudes about the nation must also be leveled at his equally renowned contemporaries—Park Chan-wook (Pak Ch'an-uk), Kim Jee-woon (Kim Chi-un), and E. J-yong (Yi Chae-yong)—who likewise undo genre conventions and tap into a vast repository of transnational images while turning their backs on the collective traumas of the Chun Doo Hwan (Chŏn Tu-hwan) era (1980–1988).

Godzilla and the Cinematic Roots of Japanese "Anti-Americanism"

Collective traumas, particularly those related to the 1945 bombings of Hiroshima and Nagasaki, certainly informed the earliest allegorical tales to emerge in the immediate postwar context of Japanese film production. However, besides Kurosawa Akira's *I Live in Fear* (a.k.a. *Record of a Living Being, Ikimono no kiroku*, 1955) and a handful of contemporaneous documentaries on the subject,[5] only one Japanese film from the early-to-mid1950s really mined the widespread paranoia related to future atomic attacks. That production—a rather bleak, black-and-white monster movie—has been the subject of dozens of critical studies in the English language alone, a testament to its longevity as a polysemic text that continues to inspire academic writers as well as armchair enthusiasts with an interest in *kaijū eiga*. Produced in 1954 by the Tōhō Motion Picture Company, *Godzilla* remains the most famous example of *kaijū eiga*, initiating a cycle of Japanese monster movies that would enjoy popularity both at home and abroad in the decades that followed. According to Donald Richie, the postwar monster movie can be subdivided into two junior categories, each facilitating a kind of indirect engagement with the specter of the Bomb, with the fear that future atomic warfare might destroy more cities (including Tokyo). Those two subgenres—"creature-from-the-deep" films and "visitors-from-outer-space" films—have continued to exert sway on the popular imagination of Japanese and non-Japanese audiences since the Cold War era.[6] *Godzilla*, like *The Host* fifty years after it, falls under the "creature-from-the-deep" umbrella, although many of its sequels—including, perhaps most famously, *Invasion of the Astro-Monster* (*Kaijū daisenso*, 1965)—incorporate iconography familiar to fans of alien invasion films.

Readers who have not seen the original film or any of its twenty-eight sequels will nevertheless likely have an idea about its basic storyline and/or its title character, owing to the latter's global iconicity over the past six decades. *Godzilla* concerns an amphibious, genetically altered dinosaur—part allosaurus, part stegosaurus—from the Jurassic era, one that is released from its long hibernation by the American government's H-bomb testing in the Pacific. As many historians have noted, this plot element directs the audience's attention to the film's historical context, in particular to the March 1, 1954, detonation of a fifteen-megaton hydrogen bomb close to the Bikini Atoll in the Marshall Islands.[7] A small Japanese fishing vessel, *Lucky Dragon 5* (*Daigo Fukuryū Maru*), was in the vicinity of the radiation fallout, trawling for tuna

160 kilometers from the test site. Six months later, after reports of radiation exposure among the boat's crew were confirmed, its chief radio operator died. Because his death was linked to the nuclear explosion, a wave of anti-American sentiments washed over Japan, intensified by the paltry sum ($4,000) paid by the US government to the man's widow.[8] This tragic event reminded many World War II veterans and civilians of the terrible cost of that earlier conflict, unleashing pent-up feelings of anger or disappointment and leading to the formation of the Council against Atomic and Hydrogen Bombs and, a few years later, the signing of the 1963 Limited Test Ban Treaty. While no direct references to the war or the Bomb could be presented in Japanese film during the US military's seven-year occupation of the country between 1945 and 1952 (as part of the Allied powers' censorship of local productions), the Lucky Dragon Incident of 1954 brought the specter of another Hiroshima and Nagasaki to the forefront of the popular imagination, a fear of what *might* happen that soon filtered into the first few films to deal with that event.

The brainchild of Tanaka Tomoyuki, a producer at Tōhō who would go on to secure financing for all of the sequels until 1995, *Godzilla* was thus a product of its time, distilling widespread attitudes among the movie-going populace about contemporaneous political events. As Chon Noriega argues in his assessment of the film, *Godzilla* transfers onto the titular beast "the role of the United States in order to symbolically re-enact a problematic United States–Japan relationship that includes atomic war, occupation, and thermonuclear tests."[9] Although this psychoanalytically informed reading of the monster as a manifestation of long repressed social anxieties is now generally accepted as a viable sign of the film's allegorical heft (its weightiness as a politically astute commentary on US–Japan relations), Tanaka had no such designs on the picture during the preproduction stage. However, he did express concern about the suffering of *hibakusha* (surviving victims of the atomic bombings) in interviews after the film's release.[10]

It was during the early stages of preproduction when Tanaka hired renowned science fiction author Kayama Shigeru to flesh out his sketchy ideas about a monster invading Japan. Kayama is believed to have modeled his *Godzilla* script after the basic storyline of *The Beast from 20,000 Fathoms*, a 1953 Warner Bros. film featuring the stop-motion pyrotechnics of Ray Harryhausen. The titular beast in the Hollywood production is a dinosaur awakened from its long Arctic slumber by a nuclear bomb test. Freed from its icy hibernation, the Rhedosaurus eventually makes its way to New York City, where it demolishes skyscrapers and is met by a large military unit. The US troops blow a bazooka hole in the beast's throat, but with the unfortunate result of unleashing a prehistoric germ that contaminates the public. This plot element, not to be found in the Japanese film, would eventually be echoed by a narrative conceit of *The Host*, which concerns in part the supposed spread of a virus among people who have come into contact with the monster.[11]

Another American source of inspiration for Tanaka and Kayama was RKO's *King Kong* (1933), a Depression-era monster movie given a US rerelease in 1952 and shown in Japan soon thereafter. Tanaka, who had been thinking about combining a *King Kong*-style story with the then-pressing fears about radiation, encouraged the screenwriter to fuse these elements in a way that would resonate with Japanese audiences. Kayama, who conceived the sea monster as a cross between two very different animals, came up with film's title, *Gojira*, which combines the words *gorilla* and *kujira* (Japanese for "whale").[12] Assisting Kayama throughout the developmental stages were co-screenwriter Murata Takeo, who had directed Japan's first 3-D film, *The Sunday that Popped Out* (*Tobidashita nichiyobi*, 1953); special-effects artist Tsuburaya Eiji, who was forced to scrap his original octopus design in favor of a dinosaur-style monster suit; and director Honda Ishirō, who had been a second unit director and assistant director at Tōhō on over a dozen pictures prior to that. Perhaps more than any other member of the crew, Honda had a personal connection to the themes in this film. During the Second World War he had witnessed the US firebombing of Tokyo and, as an ex-soldier on his way home to that city in 1946, saw firsthand the devastating effects of the atomic bomb when he passed through decimated sections of Hiroshima.[13] For Honda and millions of other Japanese, the notion of a nuclear holocaust fed into apocalyptic fears that were very *real*, not confined to the realm of science fiction or horror films.

As Thomas Schnellbächer states, "*Godzilla* is actually a highly politicized film—not because it espouses a particular political creed, but because it raises political issues that are conveyed all the more effectively through stylization and the resulting suspension of disbelief."[14] Echoing this sentiment, Mark Siegel argues that "Godzilla's misplaced revenge, his enormity, his excessive violence, and his inhumanity reflect perfectly the attitudes towards the nuclear holocaust that are to this day expressed by Japanese when questioned about the event."[15] As we shall see, this tendency among reviewers and historians to *name the unnameable*, to essentially contain a monstrous thing through critical and categorizing discourses, nullifies its potential as a truly disruptive—indeed *destructive*—force. Maria Beville explains that "it is not the monster itself, but the systematic characterization of the monster within a given culture that reflects societal fears and anxieties that are revealing of a cultural moment. The monster itself flees from our cultural control, but a remnant of it is left behind to mirror the basic fears and anxieties that erupted in the original encounter with monstrosity."[16] Because few movie monsters are as semiotically saturated as Godzilla, its "thing-ness" (i.e. its capacity to invoke primal fear as a marker of absolute difference, beyond long-established cultural associations and historical references) is harder to access than that of the unnamed title creature in *The Host*—a point to which we will return later in this chapter.

Since many readers are familiar with the storyline in the original film, we will not devote much space to a recounting of the plot points leading up to Godzilla's spectacular destruction of Tokyo and its eventual death at the hands of a scientist armed with an Oxygen Destroyer (a fantastical weapon distinct from the more down-to-earth devices, including street signs and Molotov cocktails, harnessed by Kang-du [Song Kang-ho] and his siblings in *The Host*). It does bear noting, however, that the Japanese metropolis is not the only densely populated space on view in the film. Odo Island, off the coast of Japan, is also featured, with its panicked inhabitants fleeing *en masse* after the reptilian monster emerges from its hibernation. Armed with radioactive breath and a powerful tail that can wipe out skyscrapers with a single flick, the beast eventually lays waste to sections of Tokyo while the city's denizens search frantically for a way to destroy it. Among those individuals are Dr. Serizawa (Hirata Akihiko), an eyepatch-wearing scientist; Yamane Emiko (Kōchi Momoko), his emotionally fragile fiancée; Ogata Hideto (Takarada Akira), a naval officer who falls in love with Emiko; and Dr. Yamane (Shimura Takashi), Emiko's levelheaded father, who has been a mentor to Serizawa over the years. As Jerome F. Shapiro notes in his study of Japan's atomic bomb cinema, "the all-important Japanese mother figure appears to be absent from the Yamane family."[17] That maternal absence is also a conspicuous part of the South Korean film's fractured family dynamic, something that Bong perhaps sought to redress (or unwittingly balanced out) in his subsequent feature, the dramatic murder mystery *Mother* (*Madŏ*, 2009). In addition to the four main adult characters in the Japanese film—notably, three men and a young woman caught between them (similar to the familial dynamics on view in *The Host*)—there is a boy who, having been orphaned by Godzilla's destruction, is taken on by Emiko and her father as their ward. As will be elaborated later in this chapter, *The Host* too includes a scene in which an orphaned boy is saved by one of the protagonists, and his presence in the film's final scene is perhaps meant to compensate for the absence of Kang-du's dead daughter Hyŏn-sŏ (Ko A-sŏng).

Subsequent Japanese monster movies produced in the 1960s and 1970s, including the *Gamera* series (launched by rival company Daiei in 1965), would expand not only the spatial field (showing several other cities and regions, such as Kyoto, Nagoya, Yokohama, and Okinawa, being partially destroyed by a variety of fantastical creatures) but also the range of familial relationships on view, bringing mothers and professional women into the fold while supplementing the original film's imaging of orphaned children with additional signs of youth culture. For instance, director Banno Yoshimitsu's *Godzilla vs. the Smog Monster* (*Gojira tai Hedora*, 1971), the eleventh film in the series, hinges on the threat posed by an alien life-form that feeds on the Earth's pollution, and features a nine-year-old boy named Ken (Kawase Hiroyuki) who trusts that the once-antagonistic, now-benevolent Godzilla will save Japan from this gluttonous consumer of garbage. The first sign of the smog monster's insidious presence arrives when a grizzled fisherman discovers an unusually large saltwater tadpole in Suruga Bay. In an early scene of the film, he hands the thing over to Ken's father, a marine biologist named Dr. Yano (Yamauchi Akira), and together they, along with Ken's mother (a nurturing housewife, played by Kimura Toshie), watch a breaking TV news story about even larger creatures wreaking havoc in the bay. The film's heavy-handed environmental message, associating monstrosity with toxicity, is ironically "polluted" by the hallucinatory imagery (much of it animated) and psychedelic scenes of dancing teenagers and twentysomethings littering the narrative. Another young character is added to this family unit: a teenaged neighbor of the Yanos' (Yukio, played by Shiba Toshio) whose main reason for being in the narrative—prior to getting lethally slimed by the smog monster—is to bring a degree of "hipness" to the proceedings while once again reminding audiences of the generational schisms underlying contemporary life in postwar Japan. Moreover, the presence of the two boys signals how decisively the *Godzilla* series had shifted away from the dark waters of the 1954 original film toward brighter, more crowd-pleasing, if also *juvenile*, themes by the end of the 1960s. As William M. Tsutsui states, "the first film was specifically intended for adults, but by the 1970s, eight-year olds were the primary market Tōhō sought to capture."[18]

Unlike the more fantastical, family-oriented spectacles that came in its wake, the original *Godzilla* has a semi-documentary feel, especially in scenes set in a hospital where survivors of the monster's rampage are shown nursing their wounds and grieving the loss of family members. With the gradual introduction of additional monsters in Tōhō's films of the Shōwa period, such as *King Kong vs. Godzilla* (*Kingu Kongu tai Gojira*, 1962), *Ghidorah: The Three-Headed Monster* (*San daikaijū: Chikyū saidai no kessen*, 1964), *Godzilla vs. The Sea Monster* (*Gojira, Ebirâ, Mosura: Nankai no daiketto*, 1966), and, perhaps most notoriously, *Son of Godzilla* (*Kaijūtō no kessen: Gojira no musuko*, 1967), such socially relevant themes took a backseat to cheesy visual effects and campy action.[19] It is true that pro-environmental, anti-greed messages could still be found in these films. And, yes, exploitative corporate leaders, villainous industrialists, corrupt politicians, and other authority figures increasingly bear the brunt of responsibility for either unleashing the monsters or failing to adequately protect the populace. But Godzilla itself—once a representation of American military might in the age of the H-bomb, according to many critics—by the late 1960s had transformed into a Muppet-like mascot of Tokyo, protecting the people of Japan (children in particular) from alien invasions and folkloric foes.

Seoul as Cinematic "Host" in *Yonggary*

In the midst of this second stage of Japanese monster movies, which followed in the wake of the original *Godzilla* and its 1955 sequel, *Gojira no gyakushū* (*Godzilla Raids Again*), the South Korean film industry tried its hand at the genre, producing one motion picture whose notoriety as a "knockoff" has only increased over the years. That film, *Tae koesu Yonggari*, was produced and released in 1967, at the height of the East Asian creature-feature craze. Given the English title *Yonggary: Monster from the Deep* for its brief international release, the movie, directed by the Golden Age filmmaker Kim Ki-dŏk, features many of the sights and sounds associated with its Japanese predecessors, including a dinosaur-like destroyer of cities who is awakened by an earthquake, the result of a nuclear test (this time from nearby Communist China). Audiences familiar with the 1965 film *Gamera*, concerning a giant prehistoric tortoise that emerges from the earth after an atomic blast in the Arctic, will notice many similarities between the two monsters, both of whom are susceptible to cold temperatures, and both of whom take a friendly interest in children. But what sets the Korean film off from its Japanese predecessors is a shift in emphasis from the spectacle of a marauding monster to the spectacle of a nation in the throes of high-tech development. Indeed, as Theodore Hughes points out, South Korea not only is shown to be "in full possession of a space program," but is also home to plentiful cars, highways, and suburban spaces "that seem very much in line with what we might expect in 1960s Pasadena or Cape Canaveral." Industrial and technological development, therefore, is "an already accomplished fact" in *Yonggary*, which furthermore "follows statist anticommunism in its portrayal of the monster as something more than degraded other."[20]

For all of its shoddiness as a science-fiction/fantasy film revolving around a man in a rubber suit (one in which the nozzle at the back of the monster's throat is clearly visible whenever it breathes fire onscreen), *Yonggary* nevertheless demands attention for its cross-cultural recontextualization of *kaijū eiga* iconography and anti-nuclear tropes, not to mention its panoramic presentation of Seoul as a contradictory cityscape combining signs of modernity and architectural vestiges of old Korea—a place where newer buildings appear hollow while national landmarks like Namdaemun (which would eventually be a target of vandalism and arson, burning down on February 10, 2008) display relative solidity. Indeed, scenes of the gasoline-drinking, fire-breathing, spike-tailed marauder crashing into buildings in downtown Seoul are noteworthy for what does *not* get knocked down. As Alison Peirse and Daniel Martin state in the Introduction of their edited collection *Korean Horror Cinema*, despite *Yonggary*'s simulacra-like indebtedness to *Godzilla* ("not least the creature's

FIGURE 6.1. A scene from the 1967 monster movie *Yonggary: Monster from the Deep,* an early forerunner of *The Host,* which similarly foregrounds river and sewer imagery.

visual design"), "the film is distinctly Korean both in its setting (Seoul) and its strong element of tragic melodrama."[21]

Eventually, the title monster in *Yonggary* is sent to his knees after a noxious ammonium powder is released from a helicopter being piloted by the film's protagonists, including an astronaut and a scientist from the National Space Research Center. Joining them for the ride is the young boy who had earlier befriended the beast (the unlikely pair at one point—surely the most surreal scene in the film—dancing to a rock-n-roll version of the traditional song "Arirang"). Because of his sensitivity to Yonggary, the child asks his adult companions if such a malicious method is necessary. Why subject the creature to so cruel a treatment, so ignominious a death, he inquires, only to be reminded that they have no choice. Audiences might also raise the question of whether such a method is appropriate given the monster's proximity to the Han River, which will no doubt be polluted by the lethal chemicals as well as by the blood that now flows from the backside of the hemorrhaging beast. Significantly, the reptilian creature's bellowing wails during the penultimate scene, as he flails around after being doused with chemicals, not only remind us of similar moments in *Mothra vs. Godzilla* (*Mosura tai Gojira*, 1964) and *Godzilla: Tokyo S.O.S.* (*Gojira tai Mosura tai Mekagojira Tōkyō Esu Ō Esu*, 2003), when the goddess moth gives the prehistoric dinosaur a pollen-like dusting, but also anticipate the climactic moments in *The Host.* In the latter film, the South Korean government, prompted by the World Health Organization and the US military, deploys ominous pods containing a chemical called Agent Yellow, which billows out onto the monster as well as the protestors gathered at the banks of the Han River.

Many of the film critics who have written about *The Host* have called attention to this penultimate scene's political undertones. The images of

FIGURE 6.2. An ominous pod dumps a chemical called Agent Yellow near the banks of the Han River. This scene in *The Host* recalls a similar moment in the 1964 Japanese monster movie *Mothra vs. Godzilla*, when the moth gives the prehistoric dinosaur a pollen-like dusting.

demonstrators confronting police forces on the streets of Seoul, combined with an overt reference to Agent Orange (an herbicidal weapon used by the US military during the Vietnam War), ensure that the film's allegorical meanings are right there on the surface, impossible to miss. However, because Bong Joon-ho is a director invested primarily in genre deconstruction (and less in the ideological implications of his stories), the aforementioned images—in particular, the vision of a monster twisting in agony after breathing in the noxious chemicals—are part of the film's post-historical project, its attempt to divest the past of its politicized meanings. By subjecting oneself to the seemingly unending litany of monsters on view in *kaijū* films, some of whom topple and twitch pitifully along the banks of rivers (which might be further polluted by those government-issued chemicals), a spectator is perhaps less likely to read the aforementioned scene in *The Host* as anything more than an intertextual nod to its Japanese (and Korean) predecessors. In fact, the many bridges on view in this contemporary film, reminiscent of those displayed in *Godzilla* films of the Shōwa, Heisei, and Millennium cycles,[22] are suggestive of the generic linkages being made between motion pictures from different time periods and industrial contexts.

Similarly, *Yonggary*'s many scenes set in sewers or other subterranean spaces, where the inquisitive tyke searches for access to the title creature, are evoked in the more recent Korean film. It is notable that significant portions of Bong's first three features transpire in and around open gutters, murky drain systems, and underground spaces that are, on one level, indicative of the director's impulse to tell stories from the underbelly of Seoul, while, on another level, a nod to semantic elements found in the early South Korean monster film *Yonggary*. Hye Jean Chung refers to the underground sewage system in *The Host* as an "uncanny, liminal space," a simultaneously familiar and defamiliarized contact zone where reality and fantasy converge.[23] As we shall see, liminality is a theme that Bong has explored in his other feature-length films, as well as a concept that lends itself to discussions of the monster as a slippery, indefinable thing that only becomes "definable," or *nameable*, through critical discourse. Ultimately, although Jung Ji-youn argues that *The Host*'s origins "cannot . . . be found in Korean film history,"[24] and while Bong Joon-ho can be accused of pilfering images and tropes from earlier Japanese productions (including the anime film *WXIII: Patlabor the Movie 3* [*Weisuteddo Sātīn Kidō Keisatsu Patoreibā*, 2001]),[25] the director's perhaps-unwitting call-backs to *Yonggary* hint at a set of narrative and generic traditions that are "homegrown," specific to South Korea as a liminal—or "in-between"—nation.

Genre, Naming, and the Unknown

Bong Joon-ho is a member of an unofficial collective, a loosely knit group of filmmakers thought to be largely responsible for South Korea's recent cinematic renaissance, which can be traced back to 1999. That was the year when director Kang Je-gyu (Kang Che-gyu)'s action-filled spy film *Shiri* (*Swiri*) was released, topping box-office records and giving new hope to the *chaebŏl* (conglomerate)-led film industry in the aftermath of the IMF Crisis. What Korean film historians often forget, or fail to reference when assessing the hits and misses of the previous decade, is that another big-budget spectacle flooded movie screens in 1999, albeit with considerably less critical or commercial success. That film, director Sim Hyŏng-rae's Hyundai-financed *Yonggary*, was a remake of the Golden Age trash-classic of the same title, a contemporary updating laden with digital effects in place of the original's cheesy "suitmation." Significantly, it features scenes in which members of disparate social groups come together at a time of *international*, rather than strictly national, crisis (including the title creature's first attack, aimed at a hodgepodge of different people, from evangelist preachers and doomsday prophets to profit-driven salarymen and industrialists stuffing themselves with food). Despite its campiness, this science-fiction film, which was retitled *Reptilian* for its limited US release, might be more indicative of things to come in the increasingly transnationalized sphere of postmillennial cultural production, owing not only to the fact that the film's cast was largely American (including actors Dan Cashman, Bruce Cornwell, and Dennis Howard), but also to the presence of non-Korean cities, which play host to the computer-generated monster, itself a palimpsest-like trace of the (cinematic) past. However, as Nikki Lee states, the "poor sound and special effects" of this CGI production turned off all but the most devoted genre enthusiasts,[26] who had to wait more than a half-dozen years before Sim Hyŏng-rae returned to movie monsterdom with the more successful *D-War* (a.k.a. *Dragon Wars*, 2007), a film about the mythical dragon Imugi that stars Hollywood actors (such as Robert Forster and Jason Behr) and is set primarily in modern-day Los Angeles.[27]

Although, at first glimpse, the previous decade's mainstream auteur films directed by Park Chan-wook, Kim Jee-woon, E. J-yong, Im Sang-su, and Ryoo Seung-wan (Ryu Sŭng-wan) seem to owe little to *Shiri* and practically nothing to *Yonggary*, these two productions, along with other chart-topping genre films released in 1999, such as the suspense thriller *Tell Me Something* (*T'el mi sŏmtting*), the teen comedy *Attack the Gas Station* (*Chuyuso sŭpkyŏk sagŏn*), and the horror remake *The Ring Virus* (*Ring*), set the template for subsequent developments in the realm of previously undervalued categories of filmmaking, with science fiction, fantasy, and horror in particular getting a boost thanks to *Resurrection of the Little Match Girl* (*Sŏngnyangp'ali sonyŏ ŭi chaerim*, 2002), *Save the Green Planet* (*Chigu rŭl chik'yŏra*, 2003), *Natural City* (*Naech'urŏl sit'i*, 2003), and *A Tale of Two Sisters* (*Changhwa, Hongryŏn*, 2003), among others. As such, since 1999, several visionary directors have enriched an already diverse cultural tradition through genre experimentation, benefiting from an increasingly liberalized yet profit-driven system of production facilitating freedom of expression (and, in Bong's case, right to final cut).

"Freedom," it turns out, is the operative term, for it not only means autonomy and relative control over one's own work, but also connotes a kind of liberation from the past. As the critic Jung Ji-youn states, the new breed of Korean filmmakers "were the beneficiaries of a cultural diversity somewhat removed from the political gloom of modern Korean history. They had the freedom of no longer needing to talk about politics, labor, class or liberation through film."[28] This idea is echoed by the comments of E. J-yong, director of *An Affair* (*Chŏngsa*, 1998), *Asako in Ruby Shoes* (*Sunaebo*, 2000), and *Untold Scandal* (*Sŭk'aendŭl: Chosŏn namnyŏ sangyŏljisa*, 2003), who stated in an interview, "Filmmakers from the 1980s and 1990s, like Park Kwang-su [Pak Kwang-su], Jang Sun-woo [Chang Sŏn-u], and Chung Ji-young [Chŏng Chi-yŏng], carry a great burden on their shoulders, in terms of history and politics. So they make very 'heavy' films, and they can't free themselves from the weight of their generation's social issues. But the directors in my generation feel free from such pressures. They pursue individual interests, rather than make films that speak for Korean society."[29] In the context of postmodern South Korean cinema, the pursuit of "individual interests" might translate as a problematically inward turn, a retreat into one's personal tastes or cinephilic fixations on films of the past. However, the past itself, as a reservoir of historical memories and collective traumas, becomes secondary to the primary goal of genre diversification and deconstruction, with even the most "allegorical" of genres—science fiction, fantasy, and horror—being stripped of their potential to gesture toward the political.

In the years since the 1980 publication of Vivian Sobchack's genre-defining book *The Limits of Infinity*, science fiction cinema has been upheld by media scholars as a creative means of "enhancing or disseminating political, social and economic opinions," even when the global postwar environment has necessitated the subtle calibration of themes "so as not to upset the delicate status quo that had been achieved at the end of World War II."[30] These words, taken from Samara Lee Allsop's critical assessment of *Godzilla*, highlight the capacity of science fiction narratives to spark symptomatic readings in which conceptual messages or repressed ideas that are involuntarily divulged by a film are revealed to have an ideological component. In the first sentence of her analysis, Allsop states outright that *Godzilla* is "a metaphor for the nuclear age, a popular monster movie hiding a cleverly crafted critique of modern science and its precarious relationship with Japan."[31] Not insignificantly, Allsop's word choice—"hiding"—suggests that a symptomatic reading of *Godzilla* as a politically astute commentary on then-pressing concerns about atomic warfare is actually *made difficult* (but not impossible) due to the monster movie's generic trappings as well as its widespread popularity. She seems to suggest that, just beneath the jagged skin of the film, which was epidermally overlaid with increasingly cartoonish iterations and sequels in the years following its 1954 release, is an anti-nuclear message that has become rote, so accepted in the academic community that she herself can comfortably make the statement that "Godzilla is *obviously* anti-war" (italics added).[32]

It is the "obviously" part of that declaration, repeated elsewhere throughout the critical literature surrounding *Godzilla* and other monster movies, that gives us pause, prompting us to ask if the prescriptive nature of such hermeneutic activity risks turning the past into a "post," a taken-for-granted sign of history's narrative exhaustion. This rhetoric is somewhat reminiscent of Kyung Hyun Kim's statement that, in *The Host*, "the monster of the Han River is *surely* both the allegory and the emblem of loss—of both national sovereignty and clean water." As Kim states, "The monster that ultimately results from this toxic waste thus serves as an apocalyptic message about Korea's downward spiral, in terms of both environmental disasters and the country's continuing subordination by US military forces."[33] Before returning to *The Host*, which will be examined through contextualizing comments as well as textual analysis in the second half of this chapter, we would like to momentarily linger on the film's original Korean title (*Goemul*), which literally translates as "monster"—a conceptual cornerstone of the horror film genre.

According to Noël Carroll, horror films comprise an epistemological genre, for "they are predominantly concerned with knowledge as a theme."[34] The monsters at the heart of so many horror stories threaten to rupture "the order of things," and thus have to be brought into cognitive and narrative alignment as *knowable* unknowns (as "readable" signs) if fear or dread is to be alleviated. Simply put, "the point of the horror genre . . . is to exhibit, disclose, and manifest that which is, putatively in principle, unknown and unknowable."[35] Following Carroll's lead, scholars with an interest in horror (including Robin Wood and Barbara Creed) have positioned the monster as an essential component of the genre—an otherwise unnameable "thing" defined, ironically, by its very lack of definition, its indeterminacy as an abject source of psychological or physical peril. An elusive signifier, the monster is therefore not only unnameable but also unknowable, frustrating epistemological efforts to pin it down even as it threatens to pin its victims down. However, it would seem that the titular creature at the heart of Bong Joon-ho's film is both *knowable* and *nameable*, at least to many local audiences who are able to see past the "postness" of *The Host* and access its historical frames of references.

As Nikki Lee states, *The Host* "invites multiple readings," prompting certain audiences to "read the movie as a political satire of the US government's recent military campaigns (its 'war on terror') and its relationship with the South Korean government." According to her, "because this movie's monster is unnamed and lacks overt symbolic connotations—it does not serve an allegorical, nationalist function—the meanings audiences take away from *The Host* are multifaceted, not one-dimensionally nationalistic."[36] However, when spectators look at the monster they are in fact *looking through the monster*, looking past its "thing-ness" (its excessiveness and abnormality) in search of metaphorical meanings relevant to their own real-world experiences as historical subjects.

If genre is to be conceived as means of artificially arranging "real life" into a particular aesthetic form, then its partial undoing provides opportunities to imagine a way of reclaiming, or renarrativizing, the past, to poke holes in the Symbolic and let the Real bleed through. Because the Real, according to Slavoj Žižek and Glyn Daly, "cannot be directly represented [but] . . . can nonetheless be alluded to in certain figurative embodiments of horror-excess,"[37] the very *unnatural* nature of the film's fantasmatic beast—the physically amorphous title creature in *The Host*—is worth exploring here. Its Frankensteinian mishmash of body parts (including an umbrella-like mouth that, to quote one critic, "seems to *peel* open in many directions at once") is indicative of the film's generic hybridity.[38] Combining pathos and thrills, gross-out moments and guffaws, *The Host* is a decidedly "monstrous" text, one that threatens, like most spectacles, to *consume the consumer*; or, at the very least, to figuratively sweep us away much like the monster does to Kang-du's ill-fated daughter Hyŏn-sŏ. Tellingly, many of the non-Korean critics reviewing this film seemed to have gotten swept up in the categorizing impulse to define, exactly, what the monster is, saying that it is everything from "a weird reptilian thing, a tortoise-like version of H. R. Geiger's original Alien" to "part frog, part fish and wholly a man-made nightmare."[39] Scott Foundas, writing for *LA Weekly*, refers to the monster as "an acrobatic, swift-moving mass of slithery flesh that looks like the love child of the alien from *Alien* and Charlie the StarKist tuna."[40] Humorous though this discourse is, it highlights how the seemingly indescribable monster itself was the product of several creative contributors from around the world, including local game designer Chang Hŭi-ch'ŏl (who did the initial sketches for the creature design), New Zealand's Weta Workshop (which took care of creature modeling), John Cox's workshop in Australia (responsible for the film's animatronic sequences), and the California-based Orphanage (where visual effects were completed).[41]

Building upon a Western literary and philosophical tradition that includes the work of Kant, Hegel, and Žižek, Maria Beville argues that the "Thing" is a "locus for the symbolization of the 'Real,'" although she acknowledges that "symbolization will always and ultimately be incomplete." "This," she concludes, "is the fundamental paradox of the unnameable. It is the intimation of something that can never be known." Beville goes on to say that "the monster, once it has been categorized, is no longer a monster." That is, once a monster is codified (e.g. as a "werewolf," a "vampire," a "zombie"), "it becomes part of a systematized site of fear. It enters a schema with rules for how the monster can be contained and repelled and which delineate its existence in a most basic way."[42] With that in mind, it will be helpful to compare the local reception of *The Host* to its global reception, looking in particular at the discursive clusters of meaning that congeal around the term "monster," which assumes different cultural and political valences depending on context.

FIGURE 6.3. A Frankensteinian mishmash of body parts, the monster in *The Host* is ultimately unnameable and unknowable, despite efforts by critics to claim it as an allegorical figure.

A Contextual Framework

From the kinetic espionage blockbuster *Shiri* to the brutal combat film *Tae Guk Gi: The Brotherhood of War* (*T'aegŭkki hwinallimyŏ*, 2004), several of the most high-profile box-office hits in South Korea have failed to garner commercial success or critical attention in the United States. Instead, the works of international festival favorites Kim Ki-duk (director of *Spring, Summer, Fall, Winter . . . and Spring* [*Pom yŏrŭm kaŭl kyŏul kŭrigo pom*, 2003] and *3-Iron* [*Pinjip*, 2004]) and Park Chan-wook (of *Oldboy* [Oldŭ poi, 2003] fame) remain the most widely praised examples of Korean auteurism. One notable exception to what appears to be an American indifference to Korean blockbusters is the unprecedented widespread interest generated by *The Host*, the second highest-grossing South Korean film of all time after the naval epic *The Admiral: Roaring Currents* (*Myŏryang*, 2014). The former film garnered 13 million admissions in a country of approximately 49.8 million people.

It is not surprising that this particular film drew the attention of American audiences over a raft of other Korean blockbusters, which thematize inter-Korean relations and national division and which spill over with excessively melodramatic premises and culturally specific political allusions. The latter elements might be alienating or confusing to non-Korean audiences, many of whom are unfamiliar with the tragic touchstones of modern Korean history. By contrast, as both a black comedy and an ecological disaster movie featuring a monstrously large amphibian wreaking havoc along the Han River in Seoul as well as a dysfunctional family unit struggling to remain intact amidst the attacks, *The Host* mixes a variety of stylistic flourishes and narrative conventions drawn from Hollywood genre films, from Steven Spielberg's *Jaws* (1975) to Jonathan Dayton's *Little Miss Sunshine* (2006). Moreover, not since director Pae Ch'ang-ho's *Deep Blue Night* (*Kipgo p'urŭn pam*, 1985)—the highest-grossing domestic film of the 1980s, one that depicts the disillusionment of illegal immigrants in Los Angeles—has a contemporary Korean motion picture so prominently featured Americans and evoked an idea of what "America" is (or, rather, what many Koreans might believe America to be, drawing on concepts traditionally linked to its globally disseminated national character).

The film not only won accolades but also aroused controversy in South Korea as well as the United States, but for very different reasons. At home, debates sprang up around the issue of market diversification, since this special effects-driven blockbuster was saturation-released by Showbox Entertainment in a record number of theaters (and was shown on 620 screens, 40% of the total number in South Korea). Several industry personnel and movie critics voiced concern about the possible negative effects such distribution strategies might have on Korean film culture, with the survival of small, art-house films being uncertain. Following its stateside premiere at the AFI Fest in Los Angeles in November 2006, *The Host* was likewise criticized on the other side of the Pacific by a few critics and bloggers, not because it was perceived to be "monopolizing" Korean screens but, rather, due to its alleged anti-American content.

Supporting evidence for this anti-American allegation can be found in the film's prologue scene, set six years prior to the narrative's time period, in the United States Forces Korea (USFK) Headquarters in Yongsan (located in central Seoul). The incident depicted in this opening scene is based on a true environmental crime committed in 2000 by Albert McFarland, an American mortician and USFK employee. In February of that year, McFarland forced his Korean underling, against the latter's protest, to dump 480 large bottles of past-its-prime formaldehyde down a drain leading to the Han River. McFarland ended up as headline fodder and landed in a Korean court, where he was given a two-year suspended sentence. The US military's protection of McFarland (who retained his job at USFK despite the scandal) and the mortician's dismissive attitude toward the country's court system demonstrated by his absence from the first trial (he only showed up for the appeal) further enraged Korean citizens. In a manner that recalls the original 1954 monster movie *Godzilla*, Americans are depicted as being responsible for unleashing a giant, mutated animal on an unsuspecting populace, destroying, if only by proxy, the lives of innocent Asian civilians. While the radioactive Japanese monster is awakened as a result of the American H-bomb test, in *The Host* the enormous catfish-lizard, a fearsome carnivore that feeds on human flesh, emerges out of the Han River, which has been contaminated by toxic embalming chemicals originating from the US Army base.

Even if the first American character to appear in *The Host* is based on a real person (McFarland), one can reasonably argue that the film features grossly caricatured representations that, in their excessiveness, exceed the requirements of genre storytelling, including a cross-eyed mad scientist (Paul Lazar) who, halfway through the story, tampers with the quarantined Korean protagonist's brain under the pretext of finding a virus spread by the mutant. Perhaps most heavy-handed is Bong's inclusion of a sinister conspiracy plot involving the US military, which spreads false rumors about a virus and sprays toxic chemicals (not so subtly named "Agent Yellow") alongside the Han River so as to cover up its own culpability. The United States government is portrayed as an irresponsible, puppet-string-pulling imperial power that unilaterally interferes with South Korea's domestic affairs and determines the fate of ordinary citizens during their time of national crisis. It is even suggested, near the end of the film, that the US military is (mis)using Koreans as scientific test subjects. That scene shows Agent Yellow being dumped onto a group of demonstrating citizens who have gathered along the river to protest the US deployment of chemicals and whose biological response (bleeding from their ears and noses) is closely monitored by American scientists in protective suits. This plotline, tracing the US government's pursuit of its own national interests under false pretenses, offers up a thinly veiled political satire on the American invasion of WMD-free Iraq.

Before returning to these and other scenes as sites of hermeneutic elasticity, and in order to fathom just how insidiously the so-called "anti-Americanism" of the film seeps into the pores of thin-skinned reviewers, it is necessary to contextualize its themes within the larger history of Korea–US relations. Although limited space prevents a thorough assessment of this topic, we wish to survey a few pivotal events that had detrimental effects on many Koreans' perception of the United States government and military. The first American betrayal of Korea took place in July 1905, when President Theodore Roosevelt sanctioned the Japanese control of Korea in exchange for the US's monopoly in the Philippines (through the Taft-Katsura Memorandum). After nearly four decades of apathy toward Korean affairs, the East Asian country had resurfaced onto the map of American foreign policy by the time the Truman administration proposed to the leaders of the Soviet Union an arbitrary division of the peninsula on the eve of the Japanese surrender in August 1945. The ostensible purpose of the division was to disarm the Japanese in the two separate occupational zones, but the real reason was America's fear of losing Korea to Soviet influence. The subsequent failure of the Joint Soviet-American Commission to reach an agreement on the question of reunification led to the 1948 establishment of two separate, ideologically opposing regimes (the Republic of Korea in the south and the Democratic People's Republic of Korea in the north) following three-year American military rule of the southern half of the peninsula. As the Cold War historian Bruce Cumings puts it, the Republic of Korea was "more an American creation than any other postwar regime in Asia . . . [and the United States] is the country that has defined South Korea's existence since 1945."[43]

The most common interaction between Americans and Koreans since 1945 has been that between US military personnel and their local subordinates. In Hollywood's Korean War films (such as Samuel Fuller's *The Steel Helmet* [1951] and Douglas Sirk's *Battle Hymn* [1957]) and the long-running CBS dramedy *M*A*S*H* (1972–1983), American military personnel are often represented as benevolent saviors of South Korean men, women, and children. What is omitted in this self-congratulatory representation is the darker side of South Korea's protectors. In fact, in several contemporary South Korean films set during the war (such as *Silver Stallion* [*Ŭnma nŭn tollaogi atnŭnda*, 1990] and *Spring in My Hometown* [*Arŭmdaun sijŏl*, 1998]), American GIs are portrayed negatively as rapists, womanizers, or even killers. The rape or sexual exploitation of Korean women by American soldiers during and after the war is a recurring theme in nationalist literature and the New Wave cinema of the 1980s and 1990s, which benefited from relaxed political censorship in the wake of partial democratization in the late 1980s. One real-life case in particular—the brutal rape and murder of a bar woman, Yun Kŭm-i, by Private Kenneth Markle in 1992—sparked nationwide rage and protests against US military. More recently, an explosion of nationalistic rage reoccurred after two fourteen-year-old Korean schoolgirls had been killed by a US military minesweeping vehicle in June 2002 and the two American soldiers responsible for the accident were acquitted of negligent homicide charges by a lenient military jury (under the State of Forces Agreement [SOFA], US soldiers stationed in South Korea are immune from criminal prosecution in Korean courts).

The director of *The Host*, Bong Joon-ho, attended college between 1988 and 1992, a transitional period when many democratic reforms were being introduced, gradually putting a halt to three decades of military dictatorships and giving way to new civil rule. As a Sociology major attending Yonsei University and as a student activist, Bong viewed US military hegemony in South Korea critically, adopting a jaundiced position informed by events of the recent past, including the Kwangju Uprising of May 1980 (a massacre of an estimated 2,000 revolting citizens in the city of Kwangju by Chun Doo Hwan's military regime). More than any other, that event is responsible for the rise of anti-Americanism in South Korea, due largely to the US government's alleged backing of Chun's operation (on the grounds that General John Wickham, Jr., US Commander of the Joint Forces, authorized the release of some ROK Army units under his control for the crackdown in Kwangju). As a film director, Bong has a more personal reason to be resentful of US cultural imperialism, despite his professed infatuation with Hollywood cinema since childhood. As of July 2006, the same month that *The Host* was released, the Screen Quota system—a domestic film protection policy which required exhibitors to show local films 146 days a year—was halved, unleashing fierce protests within the Korean film industry and among civic groups as the Korean government succumbed to Washington's ongoing "free trade" pressure (to protect Hollywood's interests in the tenth largest market for American movies).

Regardless of this circumstantial evidence pointing to anti-American biases, *The Host* is a nuanced film whose ideological stance is not a simplistic jeremiad, in the way that many Hollywood blockbusters and television shows are. Examples range from Michael Bay's *Armageddon* (1998) to the Fox ticking-clock series *24* (2001–2010), in which middle-class white male protagonists serve as saviors of the entire communities and even the world. Bong's film features unlikely heroes, focusing on the misadventures of the dysfunctional Park clan. At the head of the family is the habitually melodramatic grandfather (Pyŏn Hŭi-bong), a survivor of the Korean War who lived through decades of military authoritarianism, and who attempts to solve crises by resorting to "old-school" (anachronistic) methods, including bribery. Nam-il (Pak Hae-il) is a hard-drinking former student activist, whose revolutionary fervor has morphed into a general disillusionment with Seoul's materialistic society. His sister, Nam-ju (Bae Doona [Pae Tu-na]), is an Olympic Bronze medalist, a professional archer whose boyish femininity does not adhere to conservative gender ideals. Completing the clan is Hyŏn-sŏ, a thirteen-year-old girl, and Kang-du, her father, a dim-witted snack vendor who plies his trade along the riverside and who initially seems to have no purpose in life beyond eating and sleeping. His paternal instincts are awakened, however, when his precocious child is grabbed by the monster and deposited into a sewer where she is stored, like human prey, for later feasting.

Although the United States' military-industrial complex remains a kind of spectral background presence in *The Host*, the film satirizes various functions of Korean society: its government, its police, its media outlets, its corporate-run health care providers, and even its political activists and civil groups, all of whom are equally ineffectual, untrustworthy, and bumbling during a time of crisis. Debating whether or not *The Host* is anti-American is in some ways a US-centric approach, one that necessitates unpacking the Korean text from a "Western" perspective. When one pays closer attention to the underlying messages and themes of Bong's film, both the amphibian monster (the invader) and the American empire (the official defender) turn out to be Hitchcockian MacGuffins designed to distract the audience's attention from deeper collective anxieties, doubts, and contradictions of a young civil democracy in the shadows of its not-so-distant authoritarian past.

A Textual Reading

The first scene of *The Host* is presented as a prologue, set six years prior to the main action. Inside the US army base at Yongsan, a young medical assistant is told by his American superior to dump dozens of useless bottles of formaldehyde down the drain of a laboratory sink. The Korean lackey, who understands the environmental hazards posed by such a careless action, initially voices his concern, but eventually acquiesces. Tellingly, this first shot of the film presents, through purely visual means, a false image of intercultural parity between the two lab workers. In long shot, they are positioned on either end of the frame—a symmetrical composition that suggests that they work as equals. However, the mise-en-scène is soon unbalanced by the film's second shot, which cuts to a medium-close-up of the Caucasian doctor asserting his authority and communicating his disgust with the dirtiness of this seemingly spotless facility.[44] "I hate dust more than anything," he tells Mr. Kim, a statement that assumes connotative suggestiveness if one considers the definitions of "dust" provided by the cultural historians Joseph Amato and Jeffrey Burton Russell.

According to Russell, dust is "a mixture of dead insect parts, flakes of human skin, shreds of fabric, and other unpleasing materials."[45] Amato puts a poetic spin on the subject, stating that dust, for centuries, represented "an omnipresent boundary . . . between the visible and the invisible," and that it remains "the first and most common measure of smallness."[46] Like its brethren, dirt, it is the antithesis of cleanliness, sanitation, and order—an "inchoate state of being, and thus a type of moral defilement," according to Mary Douglas.[47] Like Amato, Douglas (the author of the 1966 book *Purity and Danger*) acknowledges the lowly status of dust and dirt, both of which hint at pollution, contamination, and contagion—themes that are prominently featured in the film's climactic scenes, when a powdery cloud of toxic chemicals descends on both the rampaging monster and the human demonstrators who protest the use of Agent Yellow. Thus, following the causal logic of *The Host*'s bookending scenes, dust begets dust, and the purity being sought by the American doctor at the beginning of the film is itself impossible to attain once he sullies the waters of the Han River with cast-off chemical pollutants.

Besides marking the frontier between the seen and the unseen, dust is like dirt in the sense that it is "matter out of place," a famous expression coined by Douglas in her aforementioned text that might very well apply to the incongruous ways in which sundry genre elements are brought together in this and other culturally hybridized films. Moreover, the monster itself, once it eventually leaves its watery home and takes to land, is dust-like in its incompatibility with its surroundings—a reptilian blot on the urban landscape that is as incongruous as it is deadly and unruly. The film's prologue thus establishes not only the origins of the creature, a mutation spawned from military hubris and scientific misjudgment, but also the asymmetrical relationship between US and Korean forces, with the latter taking their cues from the former. The irony of the American character's solution to "the problem of dust" (i.e. putting additional matter out of place by dumping chemicals into the Han River) is the first of many instances when bureaucratic mismanagement and inept bungling lead to potentially catastrophic ends. The prologue concludes once the toxic liquid is carried directly into the Han River; a preposterous notion, no doubt, but one that serves to remind audiences that an underlying layer of comedy lies just beneath the surface of this frequently shocking film.

Many Korean audiences will likely read this first scene in *The Host* as a reference to a similar incident that occurred at a military facility in Seoul. When Bong saw news coverage of the aforementioned McFarland case, he immediately thought it would make a good opening sequence of his dream project involving a monster and the Han River. Tellingly, the North American DVD release of *The Host* begins with printed text on a black screen: "February 9, 2000." Then come the words, "Mortuary, 8th US Army, Yongsan Camp." This English-language text provides a fitting frame of reference for audiences not already attuned to the film's historical context. Significantly, while the contextualizing impetus of that onscreen text depends on both temporal and spatial markers (e.g. a date as well as a location), *time precedes place.*

The same organization of contextual information occurs in the film's second scene, which, after a slow dissolve, begins with the words "June 2002, Han River." Two fishermen discover a small, misshapen creature in the water, although the manner in which Bong films this scene (in long shot and extreme long shot) prevents the audience from seeing what these men see. Instead, we hear that the tiny creature "makes your skin crawl" (*chinggŭryŏwŏ*, which more accurately translates as "It's repulsive")—words uttered by one of the fishermen as the thing slivers away below the surface of the water. For audiences, the monster remains an unseen and, indeed, *unknowable* thing throughout these introductory moments. The film's third scene, which begins with the onscreen text "October 2006, Han River Bridge," builds on the preceding moment by offering a vantage of the river from atop a bridge—a place where a suicidal man, about to jump, hesitates when he catches a glimpse of the creature below. A point-of-view shot, accompanied by the salaryman's comment that "something dark is in the water," shows a semi-circle slice in the currents, but nothing more. As rain pelts the surface of the roiling water, we are left with a desire *to see* the source of his hesitation and fear, to bear witness to something—indeed, some (monstrous) *thing*—that is there but not there.

Following these suspense-laden early scenes, the ensuing introduction of Kang-du—the film's protagonist who is first shown snoozing in his *maejŏm* (snack shack) parked on the bank of the Han River—might come as welcome comic relief for some audiences. But it ironically delays the payoff of visual satisfaction that awaits spectators drawn to the strategically withheld sight of the monster. Attentive viewers will notice that, amongst the clutter of fast food items arranged around the dozing merchant, plastic cups bearing Walt Disney insignia and imagery are visible. This icon of American cultural hegemony and global kid culture is thus well-placed, visually and narratively, as a signifier of Western influence, a theme established in the preceding prologue at Yongsan and further elaborated in subsequent scenes involving direct as well as indirect US participation in South Korea's local issues. Additionally, we are tempted to read this nod to Disney products as a reminder that parent–child dynamics are central to *The Host*'s narrative of attempted rescue and salvation, something for which the American film studio's cinematic output—specifically its animated features (such as *The Little Mermaid* [1989], *Beauty and the Beast* [1991], *Aladdin* [1992], and *Pocahontas* [1995], which hinge on father–daughter relationships)—is well-known.[48] The cheap commercial goods filling Kang-du's snack shack, which will eventually be raided by two young orphan boys seeking refuge from the marauding beast, are therefore a reminder of the economic and cultural transactions that bind strangers together, if only momentarily. Not insignificantly, another cultural signifier can be spotted among the visual debris in this scene, a plastic balloon in the shape and image of a Godzilla-like dinosaur. This perhaps-unintentional reference to *The Host*'s cinematic precursor from Japan pricks the senses, punctum-like, once Kang-du's daughter, Hyŏn-sŏ, makes her first appearance in the film. Walking toward her father (who busies himself by eating dried squid legs), Hyŏn-sŏ remains out of focus, as does the green dinosaur balloon. Here, once again, the liminal space between the visible and the invisible is brought forth as a metaphor for both cultural and generic indeterminacy.

Another, seemingly trivial moment deserves mention: a brief passage of dialogue between Kang-du and his father, who likewise makes his first appearance in this scene, this calm interlude before the proverbial storm. Discovering that his son has been secretly eating the legs of dried squid intended for paying customers, the old man chastises him, asking "Why touch other people's things?" This question, in addition to the fact that a squid that is one leg short can be thought of as an "unnatural" thing (similar to a "mutation"), gestures toward the subtle self-reflexivity built into this monster movie. As a film that appropriates cultural signifiers from antecedent texts, *The Host* is not unlike its artificially blond-haired protagonist, in terms of "touching other people's things" and selling Koreanized versions of US and Japanese cultural products to an audience hungry for "local goods."

Running eagerly toward his daughter, the barefooted snack vendor clumsily trips and falls to the ground, another seemingly insignificant moment that not only helps to sketch in this likeable yet dopey character but also encourages a reading that acknowledges parallels between Kang-du and the ungainly monster, which will likewise take multiple spills as it awkwardly adapts to land movement. Many critics have already pointed out the similarities between the protagonist and the title creature, which David Edelstein refers to as a "mandibled squidlike reptile."[49] Although other analogies have been proffered by reviewers in their quest to nail down exactly what the misshapen creature is (e.g. "guppy-like," a "mutant fish-toad," a "hyper-steroidal tadpole," a "lethal lump of goo," a "catfish on acid"),[50] Edelstein's allusion to the tentacled cephalopod that Kang-du ingests links monster and man, the latter eventually imitating the former when, in a subsequent scene, he demonstrates to a police officer how Hyŏn-sŏ was carried away by the squid-like monster. Quarantined behind a plastic sheet in a holding zone set up for people who had been exposed to the creature, Kang-du tells the disbelieving officer "I am the monster" before putting a cell phone in his mouth and spitting it back out. His tragic pantomime not only relies upon practical "tools" like a cell phone (which he uses to represent Hyŏn-sŏ) but also foregrounds the need for metaphor in communicating the unthinkable, the unspeakable. However, Kang-du does speak, saying "I ate her." From her first appearance in a scene showing her father eating dried squid to her final appearance moments after being pulled, lifeless, from the belly of the beast, Hyŏn-sŏ serves a narrative function as the measurement of Kang-du's success (or lack thereof) in overcoming his own failings as an inefficient, marginalized member of the working-class, a man thrust from the social periphery to the center of media attention once his exploits are reported by television news.

While Kang-du is wrongly depicted by local news reporters as a rogue villain on the run and a threat to national security, another individual is portrayed as a hero. That character, a Caucasian American man named Donald (David Anselmo), is present during the scene in which the monster makes its first onscreen appearance. That scene demands scrutiny not only for the way that Bong Joon-ho stages cross-cultural cooperation in the face of calamity, but also for its incorporation of another nationality (besides the United States) at a site of narratively embedded spectatorship. As onscreen surrogates for this film's audience, the men and women lined up alongside the bank of the Han River cast their collective gaze at the creature as it drops from Wŏnhyo Bridge and swims toward them. Among these internal spectators are the members of a Pakistani family, a conspicuous inclusion that is metatextually remarked upon by Kang-du. At the very moment when the onlookers toss beer cans, candy wrappers, and other trash into the river (polluting it much as the scientist had done earlier), the protagonist turns to a fellow spectator and asks him: "Pakistan? You came from Pakistan?" *The Host*'s self-consciousness as a film about cross-cultural interactions and media spectatorship itself is further emphasized when Bong cuts away from the action along the river bank (where the monster wreaks havoc) to show Kang-du's father and daughter inside the *maejŏm*, watching an archery competition on TV. Notably, the channel they are watching is MBC/ESPN, a joint venture between sports providers from South Korea and the United States, respectively, which suggestively registers the film's own culturally hybridized status. One of the contestants in the match is Kang-du's sister, Nam-ju, who steadies her aim at a bull's-eye target only to ultimately fail as a result of "taking too long to release" her arrow. This idea of failure related to a temporal deadline (time running out) is certainly applicable to the struggles faced by the multigenerational Park family, all of whom must overcome historical obstacles if they are to come together as a unit. Moreover, the common complaint (among some genre enthusiasts as well as general audiences) that monster movies "take too long" to show the unknowable thing, the hideous creature that serves so many allegorical purposes (in the minds of many critics), is met with a sharp rejoinder in *The Host*, which gives the viewer what it presumably wants—a full-on shot of the monster—a mere fourteen minutes into the narrative.

Because the film's preceding scenes relied upon spectatorial surrogates to do the work of looking at the monster for us, foregrounding the latter's terrifying effects on characters who can see what we cannot, anticipation for the "big reveal" is likely a palpable experience for first-time viewers, despite the relatively short amount of time the director takes to fulfill his end of the generic contract. In fact, unlike other contemporary monster movies, including the 1998 and 2014 Hollywood-produced reboots of the *Godzilla* franchise (which take forty-five minutes and one hour, respectively, before finally showing the title creature on screen), *The Host* wastes little time in revealing what other films conceal. As stated earlier, that revelation also leads to the introduction of a character named Donald, a similarly coifed bystander who lends Kang-du a hand in attempting to protect others from the monster's wrath. While it is noteworthy that Bong strategically places a minor yet sympathetic American character into the fray (someone who manages to save a few Koreans trapped in a trailer), this seemingly positive image registers as a spoof of sorts, tweaking Hollywood's self-aggrandizing proclivity to depict white male rescuers in Third World contexts. Although Donald appears to represent the United States in all of its altruistic "righteousness," Bong intended the character to be a copy of Hollywood's one-dimensional sidekick minorities who are cast as formulaic counterpoints for racialized villains. In a local interview, Bong admitted to imitating the representational strategies of James Cameron's *True Lies* (1994), an action film that features a scene in which a "good Arab" (supporting character) helps Arnold Schwarzenegger's protagonist defeat a Middle Eastern villain.[51] The director's quiet yet acute cynicism about South Korea's own submissive attitude toward its neocolonial "master" is seen in an onscreen television news report at the midpoint of the film, lionizing the heroism of Donald (who subsequently dies after losing his arm) with no mention of Kang-du, the working-class hero who has equally contributed to the dangerous mission.

In his August 11, 2006, interview with the Korean newspaper *Chosun Daily* (*Chosŏn Ilbo*), Bong Joon-ho posed a provocative question: "If Hollywood can constantly depict other nations as villains, then why can't the US become the object of satire in the films of other nations?"[52] Rhetorical though it might be, his inquiry assumes legitimacy in light of persistent negative stereotypes of Koreans on the big and small screen, from ruthless North Korean communists in John Frankenheimer's *The Manchurian Candidate* (1962) and superstitious farmers in numerous *M*A*S*H* episodes to rude, mercenary Korean American merchants in Spike Lee's *Do the Right Thing* (1989) and Amy Sherman-Palladino's *Gilmore Girls* (2000–2007). In his November 1, 2006 interview with the *Los Angeles Times*, Bong further defended his film by stating, "The movie makes many comments on the US presence in Korea but I think US audiences will actually enjoy it. . . . After all, my movie is just entertainment, fun. It's about a monster. And the political message is very soft, especially compared with your own movies, like *Fahrenheit 9/11*."[53]

FIGURE 6.4. In this scene from *The Host*, an American character named Donald lends Kang-du a hand in trying to protect Korean picnickers from the monster's wrath. After he is injured, Donald is held up as a hero in local and international news reports.

Despite Bong's modesty, *The Host* is not merely "light entertainment" but a clever sociopolitical satire disguised as a Hollywood-style monster movie (complete with CGI-effects supplied by the San Francisco-based company Orphanage). One of the funniest scenes in the film occurs after the first monster attack, when a public funeral is held for family members of victims and the Parks—grandfather, father, uncle, and aunt—mistakenly believe that Hyŏn-sŏ has been killed by the monster (at this point, both the family and the audience are led to believe that the girl is dead). A high-angle shot captures the writhing bodies of the four bereaved adults, who cry hysterically and roll around uncontrollably on the floor. It is clear, from this moment forward, that what this film satirizes is not only US imperialism and the impotency of the Korean government as well as its law enforcement agents, but also the excessive sentimentality associated with melodrama, a genre that often alienates many viewers. In another scene, one set at night in the *maejŏm* where the Parks rest after a futile attempt to find the monster, the old patriarch tells a tearful story of his youth, a time of poverty and hardship, to his indifferent adult children, who are seen dozing off in comic (non)reaction shots. His tale is the kind that overtly conjures up the Korean national sentiment of *han*, the deep-rooted sadness deriving from prolonged injustice and oppression. The old man's story provides a meta-narrative of Korean melodrama, one that would be familiar to viewers of veteran director Im Kwon-Taek (Im Kwŏn-t'aek)'s *Kilsottŭm* (1985) and *Sopyonje* (*Sop'yŏnje*, 1993). South Korean cinema has indeed come a long way since the release of those films, arriving at a point where filmmakers are now able to reflect upon the medium's history in a critical and even comical fashion.

With that in mind, let us return to the aforementioned funeral scene, in which Kang-du, his siblings, and his father mourn the apparent death of Hyŏn-sŏ in a gymnasium full of grieving families. In several interviews conducted after the release of *The Host*, Bong expressed a devilish delight in situating the excessively emotional protagonists in close proximity to corpses, the grotesquely comic wailings of the former casting in relief the cold silence of the latter. When asked why such a mixture of extremes occurs in *The Host*, Bong responded that he finds catastrophes to be both frightening and risible. Referencing the structural failure and collapse of the Samp'ung Department Store in 1995, which resulted in over 500 deaths, the director admitted to feeling shocked and deeply saddened upon hearing the news. Those feelings were soon mixed with bemusement when he learned that looters flocked to the disaster site, looking to lift golf clubs and other luxury items out of the store's import section. As Bong has stated, "When an extreme catastrophe like that takes place, tragedy and comedy always come together. It's inevitable, because people are out of control."[54] In this respect, it is not difficult to discern the reasons for his play with extreme emotional juxtapositions in *The Host*, a film in which a little girl's funeral (ostensibly the saddest moment in the movie) is comically inflected—her hysterical family members rolling on the floor with exaggerated displays of sorrow and pain. What is difficult to determine, at least for some audiences, is this film's precise political leaning. Mike D'Angelo, writing for *Esquire* magazine, states that the film "offers something to both sides of this country's fractured body politic." The Left, he argues, will find much to seize upon in the film's prologue as well as subsequent scenes showcasing military mismanagement and American hubris. On the other hand, the Right "will appreciate Bong's family values, as the main narrative involves a layabout father who enlists his own dad and both siblings to help him save his young daughter."[55] In the end, though, the traditional, extended Korean family is replaced by a surrogate father-son duo: Kang-du and his adopted son Se-ju (Yi Tong-ho).

As a way of wrapping up this chapter, we would like to gesture toward the ending of *The Host*, a quiet scene in which Kang-du watches television with his newly adopted son, previously a homeless orphan boy, after the titular monster has been killed. While a spokesperson from the US Senate Committee of investigation on the virus scandal (a sinister conspiracy involving the US military, which spreads false rumors about a virus and sprays toxic chemicals alongside the Han River to cover up its environmental crime) addresses news correspondents on TV, Se-ju asks his adopted father to turn off the program, which he finds boring. Being unable to locate a remote, Kang-du irreverently turns off the monitor with his foot, silencing the US official who is in the middle of admitting American culpability regarding this incident. Ordinary neocolonial subjects thus direct indifference, rather than hostility, toward the global hegemon. Despite being labeled as "anti-American" by some stateside critics,[56] *The Host* pushes its depoliticizing impulse to the extreme in its anticlimactic ending. To paraphrase Bong Joon-ho's own words, the ending is intended to showcase not only the distance between the United States and ordinary Koreans (who remain oppressed by the former imperial power without recognizing it) but also the Korean public's tendency to personalize disasters and make meaning of them within one's familial unit rather than directing the blame to the system, the nation, and history.[57]

As the little boy's comment insinuates, what matters to average Koreans is to "focus on eating," not the grand narratives of the *minjung* era wrapped in the rhetoric of "American imperialism," "neocolonial occupation," and "national liberation." However, this act of turning off the television (and by extension, the American voice of authority) could be said to crystallize the ethos of "post-historical" politics, a politics of indifference and disengagement, offering in the process a third subject position distinct from the two other subjectivities represented by Kang-du's family members. On the one hand, at various points throughout *The Host* we are witness to the melodramatic or sentimental subjectivity of his father, who survived the Korean War and endured other hardships (and whose misty-eyed recollection of the past induces sleep in his disengaged children during a brief repose between moments of monster hunting). On the other hand, we have the politicized subjectivity of Kang-du's slightly older, college-graduated brother who participated in the student movement of the *minjung* era (and whose throw of a Molotov cocktail at the monster noticeably fails in the film's penultimate scene). How to interpret Kang-du's final act of turning off the television is the challenge that is laid before us. What cannot be denied is that, ultimately, *The Host* is a complex, perhaps contradictory, monster film that subverts expectations and leaves the viewer ambivalent, if not confused, about its political messages.

Chapter 7

Extraordinarily Rendered

Oldboy, Transmedia Adaptation, and the US War on Terror

Few South Korean films have received as much critical attention in recent years as *Oldboy*, director Park Chan-wook [Pak Ch'an-uk]'s 2003 adaptation of a Japanese manga series of the same title (*Oorudo Boi*, written by Tsuchiya Garon and illustrated by Minegishi Nobuaki). After snagging the Grand Prix award at the 2004 Cannes Film Festival, this grisly mystery thriller—the second entry in Park's "Vengeance Trilogy" (following *Sympathy for Mr. Vengeance* [*Poksu nŭn na ŭi kŏt*, 2002] and preceding *Lady Vengeance* [*Ch'iljŏlhan Kŭjassi*, 2005])—became a talking point for professional reviewers and cult movie fans alike, disparate groups that either bemoaned its "aesthetic relativism" and cynical nihilism or cheered its director's virtuosic skills as a pulp auteur.[1] Referred to as "one of the iconic works of New Korean Cinema"[2] as well as an example of "Asian Extreme" filmmaking (which we discussed briefly in the Introduction), *Oldboy* has also popped up in several scholarly essays and book chapters, generating a range of interpretations that attest to its polysemic potential as a text of multiple, contradictory meanings. Before proceeding with our own analysis of *Oldboy*, we wish to turn our attention to prior written work about the film in hopes of summarizing and synthesizing local (Korean) and international (non-Korean) perspectives, ultimately pushing beyond those antecedent writings so as to frame its unique yet "borrowed" visual aesthetics and allegorical characteristics as a post-9/11 cultural production. In doing so, we shall briefly compare Park's film to its source material (Tsuchiya and Minegishi's eight-volume manga series) and then situate it as the crucial link in a chain of transnational signifiers ranging across multiple cinematic and noncinematic texts (including two cross-cultural remakes produced in India and the United States, respectively: director Sanjay Gupta's Bollywood production *Zinda* [2006] and Spike Lee's Hollywood production *Oldboy* [2013]).

Critical Perspectives on *Oldboy*

In assessing the copious amount of critical literature surrounding *Oldboy*, one begins to see how a kind of collective hermeneutics has transformed Park's film into a decidedly *symptomatic* text, demonstrable evidence of South Korean cinema's capacity to gesture toward real-world social and political issues within the constraints of genre filmmaking. Much of that literature hinges on the film's central narrative premise, which involves a blustery businessman named Oh Dae-su [O Tae-su] (Choi Min-sik [Ch'oe Min-sik]) being kidnapped and detained for fifteen years in a prison that looks more like a dingy hotel room than a jail cell. The circumstances surrounding Dae-su's mysterious incarceration as well as his eventual release and pursuit of personal justice (in the form of retribution aimed at the man responsible for his miserable state) have served as the interpretative lynchpin for several scholars whose own search for meaning mimics—or takes its cue from—that of the protagonist. Tellingly, in his analysis of *Oldboy*, British film scholar Terence McSweeney alludes to the cultural fantasies being enacted in it, a kind of collective wish-fulfillment on the part of Koreans who project their own "powerlessness and inability to play an active role in the history of their country" onto the figure of Dae-su, who moves from a claustrophobic form of solitary confinement to an emancipated state of "being in the world" that, ironically, necessitates an equally conformist allegiance to the dictates of capitalistic consumption in a simulacra-filled society (where appearances matter but are misleading).[3] Thus, the inexorable movement of this goal-driven narrative, which culminates with a confrontation between Dae-su and his twisted tormentor (a wealthy industrialist named Lee Woo-jin [Yi U-jin] played by Yu Chi-t'ae), lays out a trajectory of transformation and resolution that resonates with various audiences, from local moviegoers to international critics who first encountered the film in situational contexts far removed from South Korea.

As McSweeney states, "Dae-su's decisive actions," including his violent attacks against the many henchmen hired by Woo-jin, "are perhaps what many have fantasised about."[4] His remark echoes a similar statement by Liese Spencer, who argues that "it is tempting to see *Oldboy* as representing the return of the repressed on a national as well as universal level: an acting out of fantasies that was impossible under the old regime."[5] Both observations capture the allegorical potential of motion pictures that use genre conventions as vehicles for political commentary and/or social change (even if, as in the case of Park Chan-wook, no such goal was intended). And yet, McSweeney, like others, attempts to shift focus away from the surface violence of the film so as to call attention to *Oldboy's* "sensitive meditation on memory, trauma and social alienation on the divided peninsula,"[6] themes that are expressed in scenes that demonstrate the difficulty an individual might have in remembering moments from the past that continue to haunt other people in the present. After alluding to many of the national traumas that played out in Korea over the course of the twentieth century (from Japanese colonization to civil war to political assassinations to prolonged periods of martial law under authoritarian regimes), McSweeney suggests that the divided country "inhabits a permanent state of post-memory," and that grievances of the past have been handed down, generation to generation, albeit in aesthetically manipulative ways that often take the "sting" out of historical events.[7]

"You must remember me," says a teenaged girl named Su-a (Yun Chin-sŏ) seconds before falling from a bridge in one of the film's many flashback sequences. That comment, delivered by the suicidal character to her brother Woo-jin (who, as a high-schooler, failed to save her from slipping from his hands into the river below), conjures the previously-mentioned critical compulsion to pin *Oldboy* to both the colonial and postcolonial pasts, an endeavor shared by McSweeney and other scholars who argue that the film "gives representation to what otherwise remains unrepresentable: the excessive force of global capitalism itself, the absent cause of history."[8] These words, derived from Joseph Tomkins and Julie A. Wilson's article, "The Political Unconscious of Park Chan-wook," indicate that "the logic of revenge" in Park's thematically cohesive trilogy is simply a narrative rehearsal for the very *real* class antagonisms acted out in Korean political life, wherein the representatives of global capitalism (embodied in the guise of corporate elites like Woo-jin) pull the strings of people less fortunate, less powerful, than themselves.

According to Kyung Hyun Kim, the theme of vengeance in this and the other two films comprising Park's trilogy "is carefully restricted to the realm of the personal, rarely ever entering the public domain: it always aims at other individuals and almost never against state institutions."[9] However, that theme attains special salience as a sign of real-world grievances experienced by Koreans who have felt politically disenfranchised and socially marginalized despite the spread of democratic reform since 1987 (the year of South Korea's first free direct presidential election since 1972, and not coincidentally the time immediately preceding Dae-su's imprisonment). It is telling that the period of greatest social and political change in modern-day South Korea is held in abeyance as an offscreen historical referent, something that transpires *outside the frame*—beyond the walls of Dae-su's motel-like jail cell—and thus is something that the protagonist has no direct (unmediated) memory of. Indeed, as we will elaborate later, those years encapsulating the hero's incarceration (between 1988 and 2003) are significant precisely because they are treated as *media representations*, as fleeting images that flit briefly across the screen of a television inside Dae-su's private prison.

Further evidence of *Oldboy*'s symptomatic status can be found in Kelly Y. Jeong's reading of the film, which, according to the author, provides revelations "about the culture of contemporary South Korea" as an illustration of "its globalized, materialistic and metropolitan nature."[10] Jeong echoes the work of Tomkins and Wilson when she states that this film, like *Sympathy for Mr. Vengeance* and *Lady Vengeance*, "depicts capitalism as a malevolent, irresistible force that allows one to buy anything, be it a sentence in a private prison, police authority or a human organ" (the latter is a reference to a hand that Woo-jin buys). What sets Jeong's essay apart from the many other critical perspectives is her sustained focus on the fluidity of identity in the film, gesturing toward Dae-su's recourse to assuming a "feminine position" vis-à-vis Woo-jin (by voluntarily cutting off his own tongue, an act of symbolic castration, in the penultimate scene).[11] In fact, she extends that metaphor to encompass the range of ways in which Koreans "can assume different identities through their blogs, role-play computer games, and Internet clubs, not to mention actually transform their physical self through the immensely popular and widely accepted cosmetic surgeries."[12] In a way, Jeong's emphasis on real and virtual transformation connects with Tomkins and Wilson's notion that Dae-su's physical training in the internment center (wherein the once-flabby businessman's body changes, gradually, into a killing machine) is the outward expression of his "regenerative process," one that is accompanied by "trenchant psychological self-examination" and which is ironically indicative of a utopian strain in Park's overarching conceptualization of the individual as inherently prone to improvement.[13] Korean film critic Kim Young-jin likewise calls attention to *Oldboy*'s celebration of individual heroism, stating that Dae-su, after a long period of imprisonment, "has been born again . . . from a common, everyday man into a solitary hero"—a regenerative/utopian impulse that is prominent within many masculine, or male-oriented, genres (such as action-adventure and the Western).[14]

The aforementioned critical discourses collectively demonstrate *Oldboy*'s capacity to trigger responses about its connection to the "world outside" the film, to the sociocultural conditions that gave rise to feelings of angst, disenfranchisement, and disillusionment so effectively registered on the face of Dae-su as he succumbs to a form of servitude and literal imprisonment only figuratively hinted at in the guise of a salaryman. However, as Steve Choe explains, "Park's images do not *straightforwardly* signify a profilmic world 'out there.' . . . Rather their relationship to the known world is much more allegorical. His films give way to parables about revenge and vengeance, rather than mimetically depicting 'real' people with whom the spectator should identify [emphasis added]."[15] In the second half of this chapter, we will probe this notion put forth by Choe, moving beyond the confines of local or national contexts to examine "real world" events—including the United States' expansion of overseas interrogation sites and imprisonment of suspected terrorists in prisons at Guantánamo, Abu Ghraib, and Bagram—that lend additional meanings to *Oldboy*'s story of revenge. But before tackling such topics, we wish to turn to the film's source material, a series of comic books that originated not in South Korea but in Japan—the two countries linked not only transnationally but also transtextually.

From Manga to Film: Transtextuality and the Question of Cultural Loss

Earl Jackson, Jr.'s article, "Borrowing Trouble," offers one of the few attempts to locate the intertextual and intercultural flows of meaning connecting Park Chan-wook's film and the Japanese manga that inspired it (author Tsuchiya Garon and illustrator Minegishi Nobuaki's aforementioned *Oorudo Boi*, originally published 1996–1998). His effort to tease out "the sociopolitical . . . [and] psychohistorical implications of the transformation of the Japanese manga into the Korean blockbuster" illustrates how the process of "intercultural textual adaptation" is bound to result in discrepancies at the levels of form and content.[16] From a formalistic angle, there are many differences between the eight-volume manga series and the South Korean film that it inspired, including (most obviously) the former's use of black-and-white drawings and the latter's use of color cinematography—the source of many critics' interpretation of *Oldboy* as a revenge thriller whose visual aesthetics communicate a great deal about its underlying themes.[17]

As a sequential art form in which stories unfold over a series of pages and panels, comic books (and, by extension, graphic novels) demand a certain phenomenological investment, a willingness to engage physically as well as cognitively with a cultural artifact despite its singular emphasis on the visual. Flipping from page to page, scanning panels from left to right (or, in the case of Japanese manga, right to left), the consumer of comic books must literally take possession of the thing, holding and/or touching it as part of the participatory contract. Furthermore, he or she is asked to assume an active role in ascertaining causal relations among plot points within an image-based narrative that he or she co-constructs (along with the "author"). The reader does this by filling in the gaps, connecting otherwise discrete and visually demarcated images—the largely rectangular panels that are separated by white spaces and often arranged on the page as if on a grid. According to David E. Low, those spaces, known as "gutters," are significant sites of "meaning-making." As he states, "Recognizing the relationship of panels to the page and panels to each other is crucial, for it is the basis for understanding the language of comics."[18]

Because "each panel is dependent upon the reader linking it and its semiotic content—through her or his interpretive imagination—to the panels around it," the comic book requires an informal apprenticeship before its subtleties as an art form are apparent.[19] What "apprenticeship" connotes here is a period of "training" in which the reader's competency with the medium's codes and conventions increases through prolonged exposure. As interstitial gaps, as fractures of space and time that must be surmounted before a cohesive diegetic world can be said to exist, the gutters are thus a distinguishing feature of comic books, playing host "to much of the magic and mystery that are at the very heart of [the medium]."[20] Once a reader has acclimated himself or herself to its form, only after he or she has gained the literacy level required to make sense of it, the comic book can be said to "come alive," with once-static drawings now figuratively endowed with a sort of virtual animation marked by character movement and narrative progression. Such inference-making "gutterances" (to borrow Low's language) might likewise occur when a person watches a motion picture, particularly in those rare cases (such as Chris Marker's twenty-eight-minute classic *La Jetée* [1962]) when motion itself has been halted, frozen into a series of still frames whose consecutive presentation mimics that of manga's sequential storytelling.

Cuts, fades, dissolves, and wipes—as editorial transitions between shots in motion pictures—can similarly be thought of as "spaces invested with content,"[21] even if a spectator's phenomenological engagement with a film differs considerably from a reader's relationship to a comic book. According to Noël Carroll, film editing "encourages the viewer to infer the meaning of a sequence of shots, finding the best possible explanation for the sequence. The grounds for inference are varied and numerous. They include several types of narrative considerations, sensuous and thematic comparisons and contrasts, as well as linguistic and conceptual evocations. These grounds serve as inductive premises, which, when combined with the particularities of the film itself and its broader historical context, yield hypotheses about the meaning of the shot linkages."[22] Inductive reasoning, triggered by the associative logic of a single cut, is what leads viewers of *Oldboy* to make cognitive leaps while watching key scenes.

An example occurs at the end of the film's most famous sequence—a lengthy, horizontally scrolling shot (tracking the hero's movement from left to right) that shows Dae-su fending off a horde of attackers with a mere hammer. Once that two-and-a-half-minute unbroken take comes to an end, the writhing bodies of Dae-su's defeated foes can be seen behind his shoulder as he waits for the elevator to arrive. When it does, the doors open to reveal yet another set of thugs. A medium close-up shows at least seven men inside the elevator, casting their collective gaze at the smiling protagonist while holding steel pipes as readied weapons. Suddenly, this image cuts to a long shot inside the parking garage downstairs. Elevator doors open to reveal a pile of bloodied bodies within it, some of which spill forward as Dae-su exits, dropping his hammer on the way out. Although the viewer is not shown the grisly details of this elevator encounter, an inference about that action is encouraged by way of the gap, the cut, the editorial leap in time and space that sparks spectatorial participation. In this way, the film approximates the aesthetic and formal properties of the Japanese manga, even if—at the level of content—no such scene occurs in the original text.

While there are many examples of formalistic convergence and divergence that highlight the similarities as well as differences between the book series and the film, it is at the level of *content*—the fundamental "what" rather than the "how" of diegetic representation—where we detect the most compelling reasons to adopt a transcultural approach to cross-media comparison. Earl Jackson, Jr. has already noted the film's many departures from its source material, which focuses on a young Japanese man's search for his captor after his release from a ten-year (rather than fifteen-year) period of forced imprisonment.[23] However, the protagonist, named Goto Shinichi, is much less invested in the pursuit of vengeance than in solving the two related riddles that hang over him; namely, the questions of whom his adversary is and why the man has gone to such (expensive) extremes in making Goto's life a living hell. Only when his friends become victimized as a result of their relationship to him does Goto exude the same degree of rage that frequently flashes across Dae-su's pained face in the film.

One such acquaintance is Tsukamoto, a high-spirited bar owner with whom he had been pals prior to his incarceration. In Volume Two of the manga series, after reuniting with Tsukamoto at a horserace track, Goto follows his friend back to the Moon Dog, Tsukamoto's place of business in Shinjuku Golden Gai (significantly different from the Internet café in Seoul where Dae-su's friend, No Chu-hwan [Chi Tae-han], works). It is there, in the cramped Shinjuku dive, where Goto takes up temporary residence while attempting to solve the mystery that threatens to engulf him completely. It is also there where the hero comes face to face with his opponent, a former elementary school classmate named Kakinuma Takaaki (but who initially goes by the pseudonym Dojima). Eventually, in Volume Six, things take a terrible turn for Tsukamoto, who appears to have been murdered and dumped from a bridge over the Takahama Canal. Although a flashback—one of the manga series' many analeptic moments—reveals that Goto's unwitting friend was in fact *not* dead, but rather drugged and outfitted with a hidden life jacket (so that the floating body would look lifeless), the protagonist is so shaken by the sight that he grabs the collar of Kakunuma's trenchcoat and thrusts him over the side of the Rakusui Bridge, threatening to throw him into the water below. This series of panels, besides allowing the latent rage within an otherwise cool protagonist to bubble to the surface, is significant for the way that it anticipates a similar image at the beginning of Park's film, a rooftop scene in which Dae-su prevents a would-be jumper from committing suicide by grabbing the man's necktie. That opening scene is itself a harbinger of a later moment, a flashback toward the end of the film showing a teenaged Woo-jin struggling to save his sister from falling from a bridge into the river below.

The main point of contrast between these two texts concerns another of Goto's friends, this time a new acquaintance named Eri, whom the protagonist meets not long after being released from his private prison. He first encounters this young woman in a yakitori restaurant near Shibuya Station, where she works as a waitress. Noticing that he is bleeding (from having gotten into a fight with a group of hoodlums outside the restaurant), Eri applies a bandage to the stranger's face. Closing time comes, and the woman—putting her finger to his bandaged cheek—soon makes an unusual, forward request, asking Goto to accompany her back to her apartment for the night. The relationship that follows, peppered with sex scenes that indicate the couple's intensifying attraction to one another, momentarily distracts Goto from the threats closing in on him. However, just as Tsukamoto's life is threatened by Kakinuma and his henchmen, so too must Eri be protected if she is to survive. And so Goto, working with a former schoolteacher-turned-novelist named Kurata Yoko, conspires to shelter the young woman so that his nemesis cannot get to her, first hiding her at a pool hall near the district of Asakusa and later sending her outside Tokyo, to a rural family's farm. Eventually, once Kakinuma takes his own life (putting a bullet in his head after revealing the reason behind his plan to "ruin" Goto), the couple reunites. Theirs is a conventionally happy reunion, very different from the meeting that Dae-su has with his love interest at the end of Park's film, after the tragic truth of their relationship has been revealed by Woo-jin.

Mi-do (Kang Hye-jŏng), the young woman whom Dae-su falls in love with, is his daughter. Unwittingly committing incest, the two were brought together through the power of hypnosis, engineered by Woo-jin as a form of punishment. Although the villain in the manga series, Kakinuma, likewise employs a female hypnotist to ensure a romantic entanglement between Goto and Eri, their relationship is not incestuous. The villain in Park's film, Woo-jin, orchestrated the encounter between father and daughter as a form of cruel payback, ruining Dae-su's life in much the same way that the protagonist did to him years earlier, when they were high school classmates. Flashbacks in the second half of Park's film indicate that Dae-su had accidentally driven Woo-jin's sister,

Su-a, to suicide, after he had spotted the siblings in a carnal embrace. Because of this, Woo-jin has spent his adult years pursuing and enacting vengeance on Dae-su, imprisoning him for fifteen years before bringing the protagonist together with his young daughter, a virgin who would unknowingly give herself emotionally and sexually to her own father. In his discussion of the film's connection to the original Japanese manga series, Earl Jackson, Jr. argues that "the incestuous relationship between Woo-jin and his sister and the machinations of his revenge on Oh Dae-su make perfect sense, and answer all questions. In other words, the Korean film actually makes the story make sense in ways that it absolutely fails to do in Japanese."[24]

Beyond these obvious points of difference, a number of other textual elements deserve consideration for the way that they either strengthen the film's connection to the manga series or, conversely, lend the latter a greater degree of cultural specificity. Although, at times, the specific setting of Tsuchiya Garon's story—Tokyo—is rendered by illustrator Minegishi Nobuaki as a generic or nondescript backdrop, a few panels depicting this urban vista highlight the vibrancy of the city and its individual districts. For example, street signs and other place-designating iconography pepper the books, with locations such as the Kabukichō red-light district and Ikebukuro as well as landmarks such as Tokyo Tower visually represented in Volume Three of the series.[25] That same volume (encompassing Chapters 20–29 of the manga) presents the reader with a host of other Japanese signifiers, semantic elements that situate him or her in a city that is at once the largest metropolitan area in the world and a "hemmed-in," hermetically sealed universe where pachinko parlors, karaoke bars, and sushi restaurants outnumber transnational eateries and fast-food joints like McDonald's. Although a Dunkin' Donuts storefront is partially visible in a panel that appears in Volume Seven (and is furthermore situated opposite a panel in which Tsukamoto returns to his bar carrying "choice *hors d'ouevres* from a Taiwanese stall"), many pages of the manga series feature nods to Japanese cuisine, such as udon noodles and yakiniku (ironically, the latter—grilled barbeque—refers to Korea-originating meat dishes). This is in addition to the intermittent inclusion of pop culture references, including casual comments about the rock duo Puffy AmiYumi and a strong foregrounding of the famous folk song "Hana no Machi" ("City of Flowers") near the end of the unfolding narrative.

Volume Three is suffused with such Japanese-originating signifiers, ranging from cans of Asahi beer to the protagonist's surreptitious efforts to infiltrate one of Tokyo's most notorious yakuza gangs. Early on in that book, Goto is told by his unseen opponent (who, at this point in the narrative, communicates to the protagonist through a cell phone that was handed to him by a homeless man at the beginning of the volume) to "head to Kachidoki Bridge."[26] Taking a taxi, Goto makes his way to that bridge, a historically significant site that was completed in 1940, during World War II. The specificity of this reference, visualized over a series of panels that shows Goto crossing the river span only to come face-to-face with young Eri (rather than with his nemesis Kakinuma "Dojima" Takaaki), exemplifies Tsuchiya Garon's historically informed approach to his otherwise contemporary material. It also illustrates his eagerness to stage important, potentially confrontational scenes at sites where the metaphor of cultural mixing and the act of "crossing over" together attain special salience. Indeed, Kachidoki Bridge is merely one among several Japanese-specific references that, paradoxically, directs our attention away from the text into "adjacent" territories. Its present-day ability to conjure the past—its palimpsest-like hinting at a real confrontation, fought decades earlier—is not unlike Goto's insistence that the "game" that Dojima is playing is, in reality, a "war." Each is a rhetorical solicitation to the reader to imagine staged conflicts as a creative-agonistic exercise conducive to hybridization, if also as destructive clashes resulting in (cultural) loss.

In his book *Creative Destruction: How Globalization Is Changing the World's Cultures*, the economist Tyler Cowen ruminates on cultural loss as a tragic outcome of free market exchange, but one that need *not* transpire in societies where the dominant "ethos" (or "background network of worldviews, styles, and inspirations") is bolstered by "self-confidence" and is amenable to "cultural interpretation."[27] As Cowen states, "Cross-cultural contact often mobilizes the creative fruits of an ethos before disrupting or destroying it. In this regard trade plays a critical and neglected role in converting an ethos into creative artistic achievement."[28] It can be argued that South Korea's own comic-book (*manhwa*) industry has been enriched by local artists' exposure to Japanese manga, despite the latter's centrality to Japan's soft-power-style attempts to burnish its international image through the "diffusion and global consumption" of cultural productions that threaten to replace local productions. Historian Kyu Hyun Kim has remarked upon the Korean reception of manga, noting in particular the "rampant copying" of Japanese comics by *manhwa* artists that took place from the 1960s to the 1980s (a period when government bans severely limited the public's exposure to such works). But he sees this as "a consequence of the growth of the consumer market in South Korea, wherein mass production of comic arts has become an urgent necessity, accompanied by the ostensibly nationalistic practice of banning importation of Japanese cultural goods in the name of protecting domestic production." For Kim it is both ironic and logical that "once globalization really impacted the Korean market, copycat activities were no longer commercially urgent and died down."[29] After being serialized in the pages of the Japanese *seinen* (adult-oriented) magazine *Weekly Manga Action* beginning in 1996, Tsuchiya and Minegishi's *Oldboy* made its way to South Korea, where it circulated more freely than many previous cultural products from the former colonizer due to the Korean government's newly relaxed restrictions.

In looking at the transnational flow of Japanese comics, Wendy Siuyi Wong points out that one potential downside of that cultural spread (at least regionally, within East and Southeast Asia) is that "manga can be considered to represent the new image of 'Asian.'" Quoting the words of the anthropologist Harumi Befu, Wong postulates that "the similarity of the cultural assumptions and background . . . undeniably makes it easier for some Asian countries to understand and empathize with performances and characters,"[30] a facet of contemporary manga that is ironically undone, at least partially, in Tsuchiya and Minegishi's *Oldboy*. Despite the comic book series' many Japanese-specific references (including food products, such as udon noodles, that are voraciously consumed by Koreans), the uncanny appearance of the main character, Goto, who looks strangely "other" (in terms of his Caucasian features), hints at Japan's own susceptibility to Western influence. Significantly, the protagonist's questionable national heritage and ethnic background are foregrounded, if only briefly, in the third volume of *Oldboy*, a panel of which shows another character asking Goto if he is "South American."[31]

Even if, as Wong says, "locally produced Korean comics . . . mimic Japanese manga in style and technique," the increasingly "self-confident" industry of *manhwa* artists responsible for serialized hits such as *Priest* (*P'ŭrisŭt'ŭ*, 1998–2007), *The Royal Palace* (*Kung*, 2002–12), and *The Great Catsby* (*Widaehan K'aetch'ŭbi*, 2005) points toward a future in which the cultural flow between Japan and South Korea shifts more decisively (with products from the latter being consumed in greater numbers within the former). More importantly, a handful of comic book series such as *Blade of the Phantom Master* (a.k.a. *New Royal Secret Commissioner; Sin amhaengŏsa*) have fostered collaborative work between Korean and Japanese film artists when they are adapted for the big screen—a phenomenon that not only has occurred in the realm of animated shorts and features, but has also bled over into live-action film production. Indeed, cinematic partnerships between these two countries have grown steadily in number since the 2000 release of director E. J-yong (Yi Chae-yong)'s *Asako in Ruby Shoes* (*Sunaebo*), an important "Good Neighbor" coproduction about both fate and chance playing a part in the unlikely yet providential uniting of a young Korean man and an even younger Japanese woman. Like *Asako in Ruby Shoes*, which was funded by the Korean company Koo & Film and the Japanese company Shōchiku, the recent release *Genome Hazard* (a.k.a. *Nameless, Mumyŏngin*, 2013) is splayed between two nations, with equal contributions made by members of South Korea's and Japan's film industries. Tellingly, this sci-fi action thriller (directed by Kim Sŭng-su and adapted from Tsukasaki Shiro's 1998 novel *Genomu Hazado*) concerns a man who, after discovering that his wife has been murdered, endeavors to uncover the truth of his own identity despite memory loss—a theme that also emerges in *Oldboy*.

Trapped, Terrorized, Traumatized: The Transnational Meanings of *Oldboy*'s Detention Narrative

As discussed earlier, Park Chan-wook's *Oldboy* has received unprecedented attention in English-language film criticism in the past decade and has already generated several scholarly essays. While the film has been approached from diverse academic perspectives (including auteurism, psychoanalytic theory, narrative studies, adaptation studies, and sociological/cultural studies), none of the previous scholarship has offered a transnational interpretation of its abduction and detention narrative in the context of the US War on Terror and the Central Intelligence Agency (CIA)'s practice of extraordinary rendition. Extraordinary rendition refers to the CIA's program of abduction and extrajudicial transportation of foreign nationals suspected of terrorism to detention and interrogation facilities in Afghanistan, Egypt, Guantánamo, Iraq, Jordan, Pakistan, Syria, and elsewhere where torture is permitted.[32] In the second half of this chapter, we argue that *Oldboy* serves as a dual political allegory of South Korea's past military dictatorships and the post-9/11 New World Order, complementing local readings of the film by Joseph Junghyun Jeon and others who see the film as an expression of culturally specific class struggles between white-collar workers (so-called "salarymen") and conglomerate (*chaebŏl*) owners.

Released in South Korea in November 2003 (in the wake of news reports on prisoner abuses in Guantánamo prisons) and sent to the Cannes Film Festival the following spring (at the height of the Abu Ghraib scandals), *Oldboy* conjures South Korea's authoritarian political past while capturing the zeitgeist of a post-9/11 New World Order. As described previously, Oh Dae-su is abducted one night and imprisoned in a private cell for fifteen years without being informed why he is detained and when, if at all, he will be released. During his extrajudicial, long-term incarceration, not unlike indefinitely detained Guantánamo prisoners, Dae-su undergoes extreme mental duress which compels him to attempt suicide. Director Park makes explicit allusions to the global War on Terrorism through an image of 9/11 attacks on the Twin Towers in a montage sequence and Oh's voiceover narration referring to the Russian use of biological weapons against Chechen terrorists during the 2002 Moscow theater hostage crisis (a.k.a. the Nord-Ost siege).

Most daringly, the so-called "extreme cinema" auteur draws an implicit parallel between human rights abuses during the harshest period of the Korean authoritarian past—precisely fifteen years between Park Chung Hee's dictatorial *yushin* regime (1972–1979) and Chun Doo Hwan's equally oppressive military regime (1980–1987)—and those in overseas CIA black sites and US military-operated prisons after 9/11. While the decade-and-a-half period of imprisonment (which extends beyond the ten years in which Goto was held captive in the original 1997 Japanese manga) allegorizes Park Chung Hee's and Chun Doo Hwan's military dictatorships, which abducted and tortured political dissidents and student protesters without due legal process, it is noteworthy that Oh's imprisonment begins in 1988, the transformative year when partial democratization was launched in South Korea. Oh is imprisoned throughout an optimistic political renaissance in his nation, which eventually returned to civil rule in 1993, and inexplicitly released by his unidentified, offscreen captor in 2003. Ambiguously timed after the end of South Korea's military dictatorships and encompassing the immediate aftermath of the September 11, 2001 World Trade Center attacks, when the US expanded its covert CIA program of extraordinary rendition and "enhanced (overseas) interrogation,"[33] the extrajudicial abduction/detention narrative in *Oldboy* can be read as a transnational political allegory aimed at both South Korea's past regimes and the US's current foreign policy.

In *Firestorm: American Film in the Age of Terrorism*, Stephen Prince provides an exploration of post-9/11 cinema, positioning cultural productions such as *7 Days in September* (2002), *Operation: Dreamland* (2005), and *The Kingdom* (2007) in relation to "the responses of the administration of President George W. Bush in its efforts to fight what it referred to as a global war on terror." As he states,

> In this context, the wars in Afghanistan and Iraq are part of this aftermath, as are the controversies over the administration's policy of designating terrorist subjects as illegal enemy combatants and holding them beyond the reach of civil and military law. The administration's use of torture, forcible renditions, and secret prisons belong to the legacy of 9/11, as does the expansion of domestic and foreign surveillance by the FBI, CIA, and NSA, often conducted without warrants. The Constitutional issues that arise from these novel policies are also part of the new climate of the post-9/11 world. . . . For filmmakers concerned about any aspect of 9/11 or its aftermath, the attacks and their legacy offer a tremendously rich and challenging body of material. The resulting films range from those that seek simply to exploit 9/11 for entertainment purposes to those that seek to understand, explain, and interpret this recent history.[34]

While Prince primarily investigates the latter type of films, including Spike Lee's *25th Hour* (2002), Oliver Stone's *World Trade Center* (2006), James Longley's *Iraq in Fragments* (2006), Mike Nichols's *Charlie Wilson's War* (2007), Brian De Palma's *Redacted* (2007), Alex Gibney's *Taxi to the Dark Side* (2007), and Errol Morris's *Standard Operating Procedure* (2008), he also acknowledges the way in which the post-9/11 cultural context has shaped American genre films with no overt political subtexts.

According to Prince, the terrorist attacks of 9/11 and the Iraq War "gave American film a new means for inflecting the conventional elements of existing genres," from zombie films and revenge films to war films and ancient epics.[35] For example, Prince evaluates the recent "torture porn" phenomenon sparked by horror films like *Saw* (2004) and *Hostel* (2005) as a response to public debates surrounding extrajudicial detention and torture in US military-operated prisons in Abu Ghraib and Guantánamo Bay. It is not coincidental that, in *Hostel*, Americans are presented as the most expensive victims to procure for wealthy patrons of a sadistic pleasure establishment in Slovakia, where kidnapped tourists are detained, tortured, and killed for monetary gain. As Prince points out, "This plot conceit can be seen as a transposition into horror film terms of the animosity that the Bush administration's policies—the attack on Iraq, the extraordinary renditions and torture, the extra-legal prisoner limbo in Guantánamo and the CIA's black prison—elicited around the world."[36] Following Prince's lead, we offer a transnational interpretation of *Oldboy* that argues that its abduction/detention narrative resembles the premise and aesthetics of post-9/11 American horror films such as *Saw* and *Hostel.* Like these latter films, *Oldboy*'s early detention sequence highlights "the dark, dirty, squalid conditions in which [a captive is held and his] anguish at being cut off from all communication with the outside world and subjected to the power of others who have control over [his] bodies."[37] Thus, as Prince concludes about the "torture porn" variety of horror films, "the association of the imagery with conditions and events at Abu Ghraib prison, and at Guantánamo, is difficult to avoid."[38]

When interviewer Cameron Bailey asked Park if "the stark, extreme vengeance of a man imprisoned for fifteen years stands as any kind of political allegory for the generation that survived Korea's dictatorship in the 1980s," the director replied, "*Oldboy* has no political subtext . . . but it's not purely a genre film either."[39] In another interview (at the 2004 Edinburgh International Film Festival), the director reaffirms this position, stating that the political allusion to South Korean military dictatorship of the past was not what he intended, although he could understand why people would make that connection.[40] However, in his 2006 interview with Esther K. Chae for *BOMB* magazine, Park admits,

> The anger that accumulated in the 1980s during our *gongpo* [fear] era is significant, because our artistic expression, especially with regard to politics, was limited, and violence was an everyday phenomenon that we had to deal with. You'd take the bus to work, and passing through the student demonstration area you'd witness bleeding protestors on the street. Reading

> the daily newspapers you'd learn about yet another person jumping off a building or bridge or someone lighting themselves on fire and committing suicide for political reasons or someone dying due to unjust torture. All these things happened in our daily life growing up in Seoul, and so we feared violence and thought the only way to deal with it was through perseverance and avoidance. The recent explosion of anger, I think, comes from the years of it being pent up inside. And the more democratized Korea became, the less reason for us to bottle it up. Even though my films don't deal with any specific political agenda, the reason I have this through-line of violence is due to the events I witnessed as a college student, and the fear and pain I felt during those times.[41]

Oldboy was not intended by its director as political commentary on Korean military dictatorship of the 1970s and 1980s or the post-9/11 US policy of extraordinary rendition and extrajudicial detention. Nevertheless, it serves as an indicator of the political unconscious in a culture of fear and violence, linking two geopolitical contexts of different eras.

Persuasive evidence for a nonauteurist, sociopolitical reading of *Oldboy* can be found in the words of several South Korean journalists. For example, Yi Chi-ŭn opens her 2005 report on hunger strikes in the Guantánamo Bay detention camp for the leftist online newspaper *Voice of People* (*Minjung ŭi sori*) by referring to the space of Oh Dae-su's imprisonment in *Oldboy*: "It is a space where the protagonist, an ordinary company man who had been secretively kidnapped, was breathing for over a decade without knowing when, if ever, he would be released. The image of that cinematic room of terror is similar to that of real-life jail cells out of our sight. There are in fact many prisons in which inmates are incarcerated in more wretched conditions than the motel room in the film and are not even allowed to ask the simple question 'Why am I here?' Guantánamo is one of those prisons."[42] As a part of travelogue series on Cuba for the online newspaper *OhMyNews*, Yi Kyu-bong makes reference to the fate of Guantánamo prisoners,

> After the September 11, 2001 terrorist attacks, the United States government established a detention camp within Guantánamo Bay Naval Base and detained hundreds of terrorist suspects. Muslim prisoners were tortured sexually, mentally, and physically. . . . Despite the US military's strict suicide watch, there had been thirty-four suicide attempts by early 2005 and three prisoners took their lives in 2006. The United States, a champion of democracy and human rights, incarcerated these kidnapped suspects for years with no court procedures or concrete evidence. Their families or the media have not been allowed to visit these prisoners. Their hearts must have been far more tormented than that of Oh Dae-su who becomes imprisoned for fifteen years without knowing why in

> Park Chan-wook's *Oldboy*. At least, Oh was not brutally beaten or tortured like Guantánamo prisoners.[43]

It is notable that both journalists evoke *Oldboy* as a "local" point of reference to understand the desperation and misery of Guantánamo prisoners whose situation is even worse than that of Park's unfortunate hero.

Aryong Choi, a Korean-speaking interviewer, makes a different association, gesturing toward South Korea's repressive political period of the 1980s. Drawing attention to the color of Oh Dae-su's internment room, Choi states, "It reminded me of Im Ch'ŏr-u's novella *The Red Room*. The protagonist [in this novel] is an English teacher who helps a political activist by giving him shelter for a while. One day he is kidnapped by the police, imprisoned in the red room, and tortured."[44] Once again Park denies any such authorial intent, saying, "I didn't intend to make the room red. The pattern is more important than the color. I wanted to say, 'There are no exits, we can't get out of here.'" Not coincidentally, Im's 1988 novella *The Red Room* (*Pulŭn pang*) is an inspirational literary source for the Korean New Wave filmmaker Chung Ji-young (Chŏng Chi-yŏng), whose 2012 political drama *National Security* (*Namyŏngdong 1985*) is based on the memoir of a real-life student activist-turned-politician Kim Kŭn-t'ae. The latter individual was kidnapped and tortured for twenty-two days at the National Police Headquarters (now National Policy Agency) during Chun Doo Hwan's military regime. Prior to reading the late National Assemblyman Kim's memoir and deciding to film it, Chung considered adapting Ch'ŏn Un-yŏng's 2011 novel *Ginger* (*Saengang*). The latter's story revolves around a troubled relationship between an ex-professional torturer named An (based on the real-life "torture technician" of Chun's regime, Yi Kŭn-an, who serves as the chief antagonist in *National Security*) and his daughter Sŏn, who despises her father hiding in the attic as a fugitive from the law. The veteran director quickly gave up the idea of adapting Ch'ŏn's novel, as he found the material "made for Park Chan-wook" rather than himself.[45] Although Park has not made films that explicitly confront the legacy of South Korea's authoritarian past, Chung's association of the novel about a police torturer from Chun's regime and the younger director further solidifies our interpretation of *Oldboy* subtextual meanings.

Kidnapping and Detention: Analyzing *Oldboy*'s Transnational Imagery

The first shot of *Oldboy* is a close-up of Oh Dae-su's hand pulling the necktie of an offscreen man who is about to jump from the rooftop of an apartment complex. The camera tilts up to reveal the protagonist's shadowy face, starkly contrasting the blinding sunlight that engulfs the scene. A reverse shot shows a man in business attire with a puppy in his arms. He leans back precariously, suspended in midair thanks to Dae-su's firm grasp on his tie. Dae-su says, "I said I want to tell you my story." Baffled, the suicidal man asks, "Who the fuck are you?" The camera zooms in to a tight close-up of Dae-su, who slowly speaks, "My name is . . ." Cutting on the dialogue, the next shot presents the viewer with a flashback, regressing back to 1988 and transitioning to a close-up of a younger, drunken Dae-su in a disheveled suit being detained in a police station for "flirting" with a stranger's girlfriend. The inebriated man shuttles between aggression and passivity; he denies the charge being brought against him, and attempts to urinate on the floor only to become apologetic the next moment, when he shows a police officer a photo of his family and tells him that today is his daughter's birthday.

The bulletin board behind the clownish character shows a poster of the 1988 Seoul Olympics—an image (fronted by Hodori, the tiger mascot of the Games) that reveals the precise time frame of this flashback. After behaving in a disorderly way (yelling, cursing, taking off his shirt, and getting physical with the police officers who are trying to calm him), Dae-su is eventually handcuffed to the wall. However, his best friend, No Chu-hwan, an Internet café owner, comes to his rescue and bails him out. Facing the camera, which occupies the place of the police officer, Dae-su bows and says that he will visit the station soon to pay his courtesy. The offscreen officer responds indifferently, telling him, "Don't ever come back." Dae-su curses the cop, yelling, "That's up to me, you assholes," before dashing out of the station. The next shot shows a public telephone booth, where the released man calls his daughter. He promises to come home soon, only to step out of the booth after passing the handset to his friend, who wants to talk to the birthday girl. As Dae-su recedes into the shadowy background, the camera circles the phone booth in which Chu-hwan engages in small talk with the offscreen girl, who hands the phone over to her mother. At the request of Dae-su's wife, Chu-hwan turns around to pass the handset back to his friend, who is nowhere to be seen. The camera cuts to an overhead shot of a rainy, nocturnal street scene. Dae-su has disappeared without a trace. Chu-hwan calls out for his missing friend to no avail. After the latter exits from the frame, a group of passers-by with umbrellas walk past the phone booth. As the camera cranes up to reveal a wide, high-angle overview, a stranger with a purple umbrella (whose face is hidden) can be seen standing in front of the booth. The camera cuts to a close-up of the abstract patterned umbrella and then on an object that the stranger—presumably Dae-su's kidnapper—drops on the asphalt: a brown bag with costume angel wings that Dae-su had bought as a gift for his daughter.

This economically edited, enigmatic precredit sequence in *Oldboy* seamlessly stiches together a temporal gap of fifteen years, highlighting Dae-su's transformation before and after the imprisonment. Here, Park Chan-wook employs a kind of "lightning mix," a reference to Orson Welles's trademark sound technique wherein "images separated from one another by vast gaps in time and space are seamlessly melded together by continuity on the soundtrack, usually by using the dialogue."[46] In Welles's masterpiece *Citizen Kane* (1941), a temporal ellipsis of fifteen years is conveyed via sound montage, cutting from one holiday greeting ("Merry Christmas") to another ("And Happy New Year!"). The sliver of space between these shots, covering a vast period of time in the life of the titular protagonist, connects a scene of childhood to one of adulthood. In Park's film, a similar sound bridge is used to travel backward, not forward, in time, an aural cue that reveals the mysterious protagonist's name as well as his previous self: an alcoholic man whose petty misdemeanor is too pathetic—indeed, too petty—to be taken seriously by the police. As Joseph Jonghyun Jeon points out, "When we see the drunken Dae-su in the police station, we see a typical salaryman who has overindulged in a typical activity for his type: excessive drinking in an effort to relieve himself from the stress of corporate life."[47] Ironically, had Dae-su opted to remain a cog in the financial-industrial complex of a conglomerate (*chaebŏl*), he would have become a prime target for massive layoffs in the wake of the IMF Crisis in 1997—a financial meltdown which forced the South Korean government to resort to a $57 billion bailout package from the International Monetary Fund. Although viewers do not learn anything about the background of the suicidal businessman on the rooftop (Dae-su leaves abruptly at the end of the extended flashback without giving his listener a chance to tell *his* story), one can conjecture that he is a victim of the IMF Crisis—a bankrupt small business owner or a laid-off worker—and a soon-to-be archetypal figure in the ensuing economic recession in South Korea.

While Jeon's analysis of the film, focusing on the class warfare between exploited white-collar workers and their ruthless *chaebŏl* employers (represented by Dae-su's nemesis, the wealthy business owner Lee Woo-jin), is certainly persuasive, we cannot help but notice the subtle political subtexts of the police station scene and the following detention sequence. One of the recurring motifs in Park's cinema in general and the "Vengeance Trilogy" in particular is his apparent lack of faith in law enforcement. All three vengeance-seeking protagonists in the trilogy (including an industrialist whose daughter is kidnapped and killed in *Sympathy for Mr. Vengeance* and a wrongly convicted woman who serves jail time for a crime she did not commit in *Lady Vengeance*) take the law into their hands and seek personal justice, a single-minded quest which eventually leads to the demise of their nemeses. While Dae-su is not the least bit political (in the traditional sense) and apparently cares little, if at all, about the social issues of his time, his irreverent attitude toward police officers—contrasting sharply with his friend's genuflectory gestures—is somewhat subversive. In *Sympathy for Mr. Vengeance*, a similar sentiment is expressed in the lovemaking scene in which a mute-deaf factory worker-turned-kidnapper named Ryu (Sin Ha-kyun) and his anarchist girlfriend/accomplice Yŏng-mi (Bae Doona [Pae Tu-na]) copulate for the first time in front of a life-size dummy police officer, a mocking decoration in the latter's apartment.

According to Kyung Hyun Kim, in the world of Park Chan-wook, "the police are useless." Kim elaborates that idea, stating, "Although this police station sequence [in *Oldboy*] lasts more than two and half minutes . . . uniformed policemen are rarely seen in the frame. Only their voices are heard, presaging the absence of the police throughout the narrative."[48] Kim finds it odd that the police let Dae-su go unscathed despite his insulting behavior. For him, this law enforcement unit of 1988 acts like South Korea's democratized police of the twenty-first century. However, the absence and indifference of the police during this transitional era—moving from Chun Doo Hwan's dictatorship to Roh Tae Woo (No T'ae-u)'s nominally "democratic" government installed by general elections following the massive civil protests of June 1987—is a satirical jab at the perpetual failures of law enforcement regardless of regimes (authoritarian, transitional, or democratic). If the authoritarian police forces on view in Lee Chang-dong (Yi Ch'ang-dong)'s *Peppermint Candy* (*P'akha sat'ang*, 2000), Bong Jun-ho (Pong Chun-ho)'s *Memories of Murder* (*Salin ŭi ch'uŏk*, 2003), and Chung Ji-young's *National Security* fail morally and professionally by torturing mistaken suspects and coercing false confessions, their post-authoritarian counterparts in Na Hong-jin's *The Chaser* (*Chu'gyŏkja*, 2008) are shown to be equally incompetent by letting correct suspects walk away in fear of government audits on police brutality and abuse of power.

In *Oldboy*, Dae-su's booze-fueled bravado of gesturing obscenely with his clenched fist to police officers quickly dissipates in the scene that follows, set in a private jail cell. The scene begins with an extreme low-angle close-up of the small dog door near the floor of Dae-su's detention room, captured from the perspective of someone looking in from the outside corridor. This low-key shot emphasizes the squalor and darkness that viewers typically associate with prison spaces. We then see a pair of legs approach the door's small opening, which is suddenly flung open. A desperate captive, Dae-su is seen laying on the floor, poking out his face through the tiny door in an attempt to catch the guard's attention. He beseeches the latter, saying, "*Ajŏssi* (Uncle). Wait, let's talk. I won't ask you to let me go again. Just tell me why I'm here, please. I have a right to know why. Fuck, I've already been locked in here for two months." The offscreen man thrusts a tray of fried dumplings—the only type of food that Dae-su will eat for the next decade and a half—inside and walks away. The protagonist pulls his leg, asking, "What is this place? Please, just tell me how long I should be here. One month? Two months?" The guard kicks the prisoner's head back into the room and shuts the steel door.

FIGURE 7.1. *Oldboy*'s abduction/detention narrative resembles the premise and aesthetics of post-9/11 American horror films such as *Saw* and *Hostel*.

The next shot is an interior long shot of the detention room. It resembles a dingy, cheap motel room despite an exposed, doorless bathroom. Dae-su's voiceover intones, "If they had told me then that it would be fifteen years, would it have been easier or not?" The camera then cuts to a close-up of an expressionistic oil painting with a semi-abstract portrait of a bleeding yet smiling man's face. The caption at the bottom reads: "Laugh, and the world laughs with you. Weep, and you weep alone." A reverse shot shows a bearded Dae-su with a creepy grin plastered on his haggard face. Then, white gas begins to pour into the room with a diegetic sound cue. The voiceover explains, "When the music begins, gas is released. When the gas is released, I fall asleep. Later on, I found out that it was the same valium gas that Russian soldiers used on Chechen terrorists." After drugging Dae-su with chemicals, his captors give him a haircut, change his clothes, and clean the room. Permanently dressed in an inmate's blue uniform and perpetually subjected to a disciplinary gaze (twenty-four-hour CCTV surveillance), Dae-su has no connection to the outside world other than the television set that sits opposite his bed. He surfs through various news, fitness, religion, education, and entertainment programs on this one "luxury item" in his prison cell. One day, he learns through a TV news report that his wife has been brutally murdered and that he is being framed for her death with implanted fingerprints and blood at the scene of the crime. While watching this horrific report, albeit with no emotional reaction on his face, Dae-su begins to hallucinate. Ants appear to crawl out of his skin. With this, he starts screaming like a madman. His body shakes uncontrollably, as if undergoing an electrocution. The scene culminates with a series of shots depicting broken mirror and fallen glass pieces on the floor, followed by a long shot of Dae-su's body (with bloody wrists) being dragged out of the room. This last shot is repeated in the flashback sequence when he makes a second suicide attempt years later.

Joseph Tomkins and Julie A. Wilson describe the extended imprisonment sequence, framed as Dae-su's flashback, in the following way:

> Dae-su is made to forget his former life as a middle-class businessman . . . forced as he is to capitulate to a life of solitary confinement. Echoing the transformation and serialization of bourgeois and worker alike into interchangeable consumers, Dae-su's intensified leisure space—complete with bed, toilet, and cable TV—reflects middle-class self-internment in a world of commodity goods. . . . Through these nuanced depictions of the urban prison, Park effectively portrays in Orwellian fashion the inordinate atomization of a populous and the accompanying helplessness of a citizenry rationally segregated from each other by simulated reality—or in other words, life experienced as mere spectacle. . . . Dae-su's incarceration simultaneously figures the rationalized system of exploitation instinct to twentieth-century modernization, and, on the other hand, deterritorializing possibilities amidst late capitalism where intensification of economic standardization gives way to qualitatively new knowledges and discursive regimes, as well as latent relationships to oneself and to others.[49]

Although Dae-su praises the versatility of television as a "clock, calendar, school, home, church, friend, and lover" in his voiceover, his subaltern existence as a suicidal captive indefinitely detained in an underworld prison (with no access to the amenities of daily comfort, let alone the companionship of his family and friends) is simply too harsh, too severe, to be read as an allegory of a self-confined, middle-class consumer lifestyle.[50]

According to Park Chan-wook, in an earlier script Dae-su's character is abducted at the airport, not in front of a telephone booth. The director/co-writer explains his original premise, "As an employee of a travel agency Dae-su is someone who does a lot of overseas travel. . . . He's also the kind of a man who politely propositions the white woman sitting next to him on the plane coming back from Paris, and he gets kidnapped at the airport. It started with more of a Hollywood-film atmosphere than it does now. . . . [Actor] Choi Min-sik complained a bit about that. 'What, it doesn't really even seem like a Korean movie. . . .' Choi gave some suggestions, and I switched to what you see in the movie now."[51] Dae-su's capture at the airport in the original scenario calls to mind an actual case of extraordinary rendition on the part of the CIA that occurred in September 2002, one year and two months prior to *Oldboy*'s domestic release in South Korea. According to a November 2007 editorial of the *New York Times*, a Syrian-born Canadian named Maher Arar "was stopped at Kennedy Airport in 2002 while returning from a family vacation. After being held in solitary confinement in a Brooklyn detention center and interrogated without proper access to a lawyer, he was spirited off to Syria." In the months that followed, Maher Arar was tortured on several occasions. Eventually, the officials in his detainment "decided that their suspicions that he was a member of Al Qaeda were mistaken and let him go." The editorial sums up this abuse of human rights by stating that "Mr. Arar was a victim of extraordinary rendition, America's notorious program of outsourcing interrogations to governments known to use torture."[52]

Although the total number of victims for the CIA's program of extraordinary rendition since 9/11 has not been declassified, a 211-page comprehensive report published by Open Society Foundations in 2013 provides a few details (names and bios) of 136 known detainees who have been subjected to secret detention under the smokescreen of national security.[53] Another innocent victim of the practice, Khaled El-Masri, is a German citizen of Lebanese descent who was erroneously captured at the Macedonian border in December 2003. According to a 2012 report by Amrit Singh, a contributor to the *Guardian*:

> He was held incommunicado and abused in Macedonian custody for twenty-three days, after which he was handcuffed, blindfolded, and driven to Skopje airport, where he was handed over to the CIA and severely beaten. The CIA stripped, hooded, shackled, and sodomized El-Masri with a suppository—in CIA parlance, subjected him to "capture shock"—as Macedonian officials stood by. The CIA drugged him and flew him to Kabul to be locked up in a secret prison known as the "Salt Pit," where he was slammed into walls, kicked, beaten, and subjected to other forms of abuse. Held at the Salt Pit for four months, El-Masri was never charged, brought before a judge, or given access to his family or German government representatives. The CIA ultimately realized that it had mistaken El-Masri for an Al-Qaida suspect with a similar name. But it held on to him for weeks after that. It was not until 24 May 2004, that he was flown, blindfolded, earmuffed, and chained to his seat, to Albania, where he was dumped on the side of the road without explanation.[54]

Although the main character in *Oldboy* is not subject to physical torture, beatings, and abuses, the overall process of abduction, secret transport, arbitrary detention, and unexplained release in these two high-profile cases bear striking resemblance to the Korean protagonist's experience in Park's thriller. El-Masri was even detained in a Macedonian hotel room (not unlike Dae-su in *Oldboy*) before being rendered to the CIA and sent to Afghanistan. As the *New York Times* columnist Paul Krugman explains, extraordinary rendition is "a Kafkaesque system under which suspects can be sent, at the government's whim, to Egypt or Syria or Jordan, and to fight such a move, it's up to the suspect to prove that he'll be tortured on arrival."[55] The fictional hero in *Oldboy* likewise forcefully undergoes a Kafkaesque transformation, becoming a larger-than-life warrior of vengeance who, after his unexplained release on the rooftop in an oversized suit case, tracks down the private prison complex and defeats dozens of thugs single-handedly (in a celebrated two-and-a-half-minute long-take fight scene).

Confronting Dae-su face-to-face for the first time, the mastermind of his imprisonment, Lee Woo-jin, calls his victim "the monster that I have created," obliquely alluding to Mary Shelley's *Frankenstein* (1818). At one point, Woo-jin proposes an absurd game to Dae-su, telling him that he will kill himself if the latter discovers the motive for his imprisonment within the next five days. If his opponent fails, he will kill Dae-su's love interest Mi-do, a young sushi chef whom he becomes intimate with after the release. Lee's engineering of Dae-su's fate as well as his proposal of a Russian Roulette-style, life-or-death game evokes the image of the Coen Brothers' coin-flipping villain, Anton Chigurh (Javier Bardem), in the neo-noir/revisionist Western *No Country for Old Men* (2007). As Camilla Fojas points out in her article "Hollywood Border Cinema: Westerns with a Vengeance":

> As a figure of terrorism, Chigurh is everywhere and nowhere at once. . . . He operates freely with no rules or limits. He is the nightmarish symptom of a renegade capitalism without limits, boundaries, or borders. . . . The man sent by corporate headquarters to rein him in . . . describes him concisely, "He's a peculiar man. You might even say he has principles, principles that transcend money or drugs or anything like that." This comment resonates with the constant iteration of US ideology as the pursuit not of economic gain (or oil) but of "democracy" as well as the imperious power of US policies to drive the state directives of other nations.[56]

This description applies almost word-by-word to Park Chan-wook's villain, who is not only a wealthy capitalist but also an Americanized Korean who studied in the United States and, while there, had a motor implanted in his failing heart thanks to a special surgery. In other words, Lee's ruthless heart is literally propelled and sustained by US technology. If this character information, conveyed through dialogue, is not sufficient in communicating the allegorical dimensions of the film, then consider the fact that at one point Park positions his antagonist against a telling backdrop: a wall-to-wall image of a vintage black-and-white portrait of American businessmen. This image, which occurs during a brief exposition flashback from Woo-jin's perspective, shows him spying on Mi-do as if he were seated among those men, an all-Caucasian grouping that casts a collective gaze toward the camera, as if breaking the fourth wall.

FIGURE 7.2. As if representing the arrogance of US exceptionalism, Woo-jin (background) shares the frame with a wall-to-wall portrait of American businessmen.

Like Anton Chigurh, Woo-jin, who lives in a finely appointed Manhattan-style penthouse, is a symptom of both limitless global capitalism and the arrogance of American exceptionalism, which the Senator J. William Fulbright once defined as the malady of a powerful nation that takes upon itself a "special responsibility [to remake other nations] in its own shining image."[57] The Senator, in a 1966 speech, cautioned that "power confuses itself with virtue and tends also to take itself for omnipotence."[58] This statement resonates with Park's deliberate highlighting of the relationship between Dr. Frankenstein and the Monster in the aforementioned Shelley novel. That relationship, denoted by the inclusion of a televised image of Boris Karloff's monster in the Universal horror classic *Bride of Frankenstein* (1935) in the detention sequence, is an analogy for the way Woo-jin "makes" Dae-su. As it turns out, the film's villain has undertaken an elaborate scheme—imprisoning Dae-su, having the man's wife murdered, overseeing Mi-do's upbringings, and hypnotizing both Dae-su and Mi-do to fall in love with each other—in order to refashion his nemesis in his "own shining image." He makes Dae-su into an incestuous father who eventually learns, to his dismay and the audience's shock, that he has slept with his own daughter. When Woo-jin triumphantly discloses this crucial information to Dae-su in the confrontation/exposition scene set in the former's penthouse, the latter kneels and begs his nemesis not to tell the truth to Mi-do. Dae-su addresses Woo-jin with the honorific *hoejannim* (Chairman), offers to be his *ttonggae* (mutt), and even licks the latter's shoes. As Joseph Jeon argues, "At this crucial point in the film, Dae-su addresses Woo-jin in the very manner that the salary man would address the chairman of the *chaebŏl*, revealing in stark terms his understanding of their relationship and of the specific type of authority that Woo-jin wields despite the fact that Woo-jin was never his actual employer."[59]

While we are not opposed to this interpretation of the master/slave relationship, we find it hard to overlook Woo-jin's symbolic embodiment of imperialist ideology, specifically bringing to mind the discourse of American exceptionalism which suffused the US Invasion of Iraq, the CIA's extraordinary renditions, "enhanced interrogation," and indefinite detention of untried suspects in Guantánamo and other foreign prisons. Presented through a transnational lens, Dae-su's humiliating impersonation of a dog in front of the film's sadistic antagonist, who bursts into audible laughter, is a disturbing reminder of Abu Ghraib prisoner abuse photos, in particular the famous image of Lynndie England holding a dog leash attached to the neck of a naked prisoner on the floor.

Discontinuous History: The Performative Temporality of *Oldboy*'s Montage Sequence

The most obvious, yet crucial image that supports our positioning of *Oldboy* as an allegory of the post-9/11 zeitgeist is that which depicts a hijacked plane striking the second World Trade Center tower as the first tower begins to collapse. These oft-replayed images are juxtaposed with various local and global events from 1996 to 2002, depicted in split-screen format—a time-passing montage sequence that plays out during Dae-su's imprisonment period. That sequence, which showcases multiple events televised for a literally captive audience, can be read as a kind of instructional rhetorical maneuver on Park Chan-wook's part, "teaching" the audience how to read *Oldboy* as a transnational text laden with both local and global meanings.

Six years into his solitary imprisonment, Dae-su gets a lucky break and is accidentally given an extra metal chopstick in addition to his usual fried dumpling dinner. He secretly keeps the metal piece and uses it as a tool to gradually dig through the brick wall behind the bed. After three years of labor, the prisoner succeeds in removing a brick and making a passage into the concrete cavity inside the wall. Soon, the screen splits and a montage of television news footage depicting major world events fills the right side of the frame. On the left side are images of Dae-su digging through the wall and training for imaginary fist fights. This fast-paced montage alternates between national and international news coverage: Chun Doo Hwan's arrest and trial in 1996 is shown, followed by China's takeover of Hong Kong in 1997; Princess Diana's funeral in 1997; South Korea's signing of the IMF bailout package in 1997; the long-time political dissident Kim Dae Jung (Kim Tae-jung)'s presidential inauguration in 1998; the first inter-Korea summit in Pyongyang in 2000; the 9/11 terrorist attacks on the World Trade Center Twin Towers in 2001; South Korea's advance to the semi-finals at the 2002 World Cup Games; and the ex-human rights lawyer Roh Moo Hyun (No Mu-hyŏn)'s inauguration as President in 2003. In the director's audio commentary, included as a supplementary part of Tartan Video Region 1 DVD release of the film, Park Chan-wook explains, "I did not exclusively include the news footage that speaks only to Koreans. I also mixed [Korean events with] international events that could give foreign audiences a sense of passing time."[60]

Previous commentators of *Oldboy*—Joseph Jeon and Kyung Hyun Kim, in particular—emphasize Dae-su's separation from history, insinuated by this time montage and literally suggested by the four walls that segregate him from the rest of the world (a structural means of containment further hinted at by the quadrilateral cage of the film frame, split in half, with the protagonist on one side and televised events on the other). As Jeon puts it, "Dae-su is forgotten by history, which progresses at a speed and magnitude that render Dae-su's diligent scratching in the wall irrelevant. The competing montages dramatize how the scale of history dwarfs the scale of Dae-su's efforts. The split in the screen constitutes the impenetrable boundary that Dae-su's efforts . . . cannot breach. And though he can watch history on his television set, he is decidedly erased from it, leaving him to record time by tattooing lines on the back of his hand."[61] Although Kim does not refer to the montage sequence in particular, he nevertheless puts forth a related interpretation:

> Because he had been locked up alone in the private jail, the dumpling [the key clue which leads the protagonist back to the prison complex] is Dae-su's only significant memory from the critical years between 1988 and 2003, when South Korea became a democracy, as well as one of the most economically successful and technologically advanced countries in the world. Dae-su does not remember the deaths of numerous demonstrators throughout this period of democratization, or the workers fired during the so-called IMF bailout crisis. What matters most to him is the unforgettable taste of

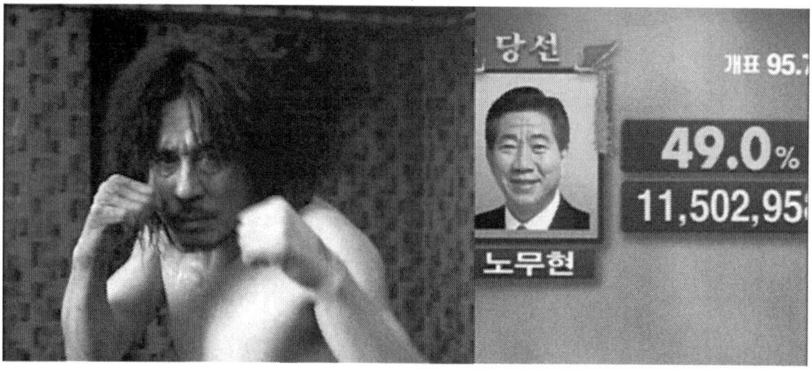

FIGURE 7.3. The split screen in *Oldboy*'s montage sequence juxtaposes the protagonist's solitary pursuits with major local and global events such as South Korea's presidential elections.

excessive buchu [leek] that he has struggled to find again, so he can put his trauma behind him.[62]

While we wish to acknowledge the validity of both interpretations (Dae-su's erasure from history as well as his lack of memory or interest), we would like to propose a third hermeneutic line, positioning the Korean protagonist as an intermediary between the local and the global. He is literally excavating an interstitial space between the interior of the prison room and the exterior of the building. As a would-be-threshold-crosser who embodies the cinematic act of border-crossing in Park's time montage, Dae-su is a deterritorialized subject snagged in a dialectics of locality and globality. As someone who lives in the "liminality of the nation," Park's protagonist enacts the "repetitious, recursive strategy of the performative" in lieu of the "continuous, accumulative temporality of the pedagogical," to borrow Homi K. Bhabha's terminology.[63] Bhabha resists Benedict Anderson's "naturalized, nationalized space of the imagined community" as, to him, the celebrated concept "fails to locate the alienating time . . . produced within the process of transcultural negotiation."[64] Dae-su's disembodied voiceover in this time montage sequence overthrows the pedagogical, continuous temporality of official history, for his own count of imprisonment years does not match the historical events depicted in news footage.

For example, an image of Chun Doo Hwan's arrest for a bribe scandal in 1996 is shown over Dae-su's voiceover counting "eleven years." Since his imprisonment began in 1988, the correct count should be eight years. Chun's televised appearance is followed by footage of the handover ceremony in Hong Kong, Princess Diana's funeral at Westminster Abbey, and the Minister of Finance Im Ch'ang-yŏl's signing of the IMF Agreement. Although the latter three events took place one year after the Korean ex-dictator's arrest, there is no voiceover separating 1996 and 1997. As if alluding to this temporal gap, on the left side of the split screen Park's protagonist pokes his head out of the chopstick-dug opening in the wall and looks around the empty tunnel inside the concrete structure. Over his count of "twelve years," we see three different events, which took place in 1998, 2000, and 2001 respectively: Kim Dae Jung's presidential inauguration, Kim's visit to Pyongyang for a historical inter-Korean summit, and the 9/11 attacks on New York's World Trade Center. His voiceover reference to year "thirteen" is accompanied by images of South Korean soccer players wowing spectators at the 2002 World Cup Games co-hosted in Seoul. The final historical images of Roh Moo Hyun's presidential election (2002) and inauguration (2003) are identified as belonging to year "fourteen."

It is easy to attribute this mismatch between personal and official histories to continuity errors. But one could also speculate that, while Dae-su watched these momentous events on television, because of his extraordinary circumstances he is unable to remember their exact dates or their proper placement in world history. Park's hero might, therefore, be labeled as an unreliable narrator who mixes up personal time (the performative) and official time (the pedagogical). Intentional or not, this significant gap between Dae-su's counts of his imprisonment years and the chronology of history adds new layers of meaning to the already deep diegetic world of *Oldboy*. The discontinuity of split-screen temporality between left-side (personal) and right-side (public) images aptly symbolizes "the tension between the pedagogical and the performative . . . in the narrative address of the nation."[65]

While both Sanjay Gupta's Bollywood remake *Zinda* and Spike Lee's *Oldboy* have similar temporal montages, neither of them recreates the fissures and discontinuities of Park's film. In the Indian film, the montage is interspersed with shots of Balajeet Roy (Sanjay Dutt) practicing samurai swordplay with a curtain rod and digging through the brick wall in a fashion that recalls Dae-su's actions. Four split-screen images are intercut in the sequence, which consists of various shots depicting Balajeet watching a Japanese samurai film and world news (reporting Princess Diana's death, the 9/11 World Trade Center attacks, the Indian Ocean Tsunami, etc.) on television. These split screens provide a point of contrast for Balajeet's emotionless face (on the left) and images of four news events (on the right): the Indo–Pakistani War of 1999; the 2000 New Year celebration in Paris; the 2003 fall of Saddam Hussein's statue in Baghdad; and Australia's 2003 win of the Cricket World Cup. Like the Korean original, Gupta's borrowed text alternates between global events (9/11, the US invasion of Iraq, etc.) and local/regional events (Indo–Pakistani conflicts, the Cricket World Cup, Tsunami, etc.). However, the Bollywood remake does not include the protagonist's voiceover (mis)matching his detention years and the historical dates. Moreover, *Zinda* makes the demarcation between the diegesis proper (Balajeet's story) and the televised images (on the screen-within-the-screen) clear by inserting several shots of the protagonist watching television. His viewing, therefore, becomes an embedded figuration of the film spectator's activity.

Devoid of voiceover narration (unlike its predecessors), Spike Lee's remake of Park's film does away with the split-screen technique and presents a series of news footage images as enlargements of the diegetic television screen that the protagonist, Joe Doucett (Josh Brolin), is watching, or rather being distracted from while focusing on solitary pursuits of body building and wall digging. The momentous historical events depicted include: Bill Clinton's second presidential inauguration in 1997; the 2000 New Year's celebration; the 9/11 attacks on the World Trade Center; the 2003 Invasion of Iraq; the 2005 Hurricane Katrina wreckage of New Orleans; and Barack Obama's second presidential inauguration in 2013. While Lee's film notably "Americanizes" the time montage, the US director also puts his auteurist spin on it by highlighting events such as Hurricane Katrina and Obama's reelection, both of which carry a special resonance for many African American viewers. It is noteworthy that the only event that is featured in all three films is the 9/11 attacks, attesting to the primacy of that tragic event in the collective unconscious of global audiences.

History Repeats Itself: The Enduring Political Relevancy of *Oldboy*

Although the Korean *Oldboy* is itself a migratory, cross-cultural adaptation of a Japanese manga (written prior to 9/11), the former's recasting of the Japanese original as a transnational distillation of extraordinary rendition—presenting phantom references to ghost prisoners in the Global War on Terror—is a significant contribution. We are therefore in agreement with Iain Robert Smith, who argues that, "rather than positioning *Oldboy* as the 'original' text framed in terms of its South Korean background, it is more productive to consider the film within a broader global context."[66] As professors of film and media studies at a university where few courses are offered in the areas of Korean language, history, and/or culture, we cannot help but be pleasantly surprised by the persistent way in which several of our undergraduate students name *Oldboy* as their favorite example of world cinema. We have each incorporated Park's thriller in our broader contemporary film survey courses, not because we feel that it is the most representative example of contemporary Korean cinema, but rather due to its ability to underscore the transnational connections between South Korea's authoritarian past and post-9/11 US foreign policies.

Unfortunately, *Oldboy*'s detention narrative is as relevant today as it was in 2003. As the historian Alfred W. McCoy reminds us, there is a strong continuity between the Bush and Obama administrations in terms of their policy on the War on Terror:

> As the CIA expanded covert operations inside Somalia under Obama, its renditions of terror suspects from neighboring East African nations continued just as they had under Bush. In July 2009, for example, Kenyan police snatched an Al-Qaeda suspect, Ahmed Abdullahi Hassan, from a Nairobi slum and delivered him to that city's airport for a CIA flight to Mogadishu. There he joined dozens of prisoners grabbed off the streets of Kenya inside "The Hole"—a filthy underground prison buried in the windowless basement of Somalia's National Security Agency. . . . Obama also allowed the

> continuation of a policy adopted after the Abu Ghraib scandal: outsourcing incarceration to local allies in Afghanistan and Iraq while ignoring human rights abuses there. Although the US military received 1,365 reports about the torture of detainees by Iraqi forces between May 2004 and December 2009, a period that included Obama's first full year in office, American officers refused to take action, even though the abuses reported were often extreme.[67]

In a recent article on contemporary "torture documentaries" such as *Taxi to the Dark Side* and *Standard Operating Procedure*, Julia Lesage likewise condemns the Obama administration's smoke-screen policy, which simply stopped sending additional prisoners to the controversial Guantánamo camp only to reroute them to Afghanistan (the military interment facility of Bagram Airfield) and elsewhere.[68] Immediately after his inauguration in 2009, President Obama issued an order to close the CIA's black sites permanently and end the use of harsh interrogation techniques by American agents. However, as of 2014, his administration has continued to practice extraordinary renditions and indefinite detention of prisoners (who are now being sent to foreign dungeons run by allied governments on behalf of the CIA, which funds those facilities). Moreover, the Obama administration has largely replaced the controversial detention/torture complex with a hassle-free, cost-effective "take-no-prisoner-alive" policy of drone strikes and targeted killings, which have claimed the lives of as many as 2,400–3,800 (inclusive of an estimated 420–1,000 civilians) in Pakistan alone between 2004 and 2014.[69] As McCoy points out, "Washington has slid down torture's slippery slope to find . . . at its bottom lies the moral abyss of extrajudicial execution."[70]

At the end of his canonical essay "An American Dilemma," which examines Civil Rights-era race-related commentary in John Ford's Western *The Searchers* (1956), Brian Henderson quotes Reverend Jesse Jackson—"Racism is the curse of the American soul"—and closes his piece by concluding, "As long as this remains true, *The Searchers* is likely to retain its power."[71] We close our chapter in much the same vein, echoing Henderson's insightful statement about Ford's mid-century masterpiece. As long as prisoners of the War on Terror continue to be subjected to abduction and extrajudicial incarceration without due process, the power of *Oldboy* will not diminish. In this aspect, and despite its status as a genre production popular with cult film aficionados, Park Chan-wook's shock-filled thriller retains greater global political relevancy than most contemporary South Korean films, especially in the context of current world affairs. However, the director did not stop there, but has continued to use genre conventions as a means of tackling socially relevant subject matter. In *Thirst* (*Pakjwi*, 2009), for example, Park alludes to the plight of immigrants within the generic framework of a vampire film. It is to that blood-filled text that we turn briefly in the next chapter, which takes as its focus a relatively new trend of "multiculturalist film" productions that directly and indirectly confront South Korea's long history of human rights violations.

Chapter 8

A *Thirst* for Diversity

Recent Trends in Korean "Multicultural Films," from *Bandhobi* to *Where is Ronny?*

In recent years, moviegoers and television viewers have not had to look far to find examples of vampire-themed fiction in US popular culture. In addition to such post-*Buffy* TV series as *True Blood* (2008–2014), *The Vampire Diaries* (2009–), and *Being Human* (2011–2014), several big-budget Hollywood films such as *Underworld* (2003), *Ultraviolet* (2006), *30 Days of Night* (2007), *Twilight* (2008), and *Daybreakers* (2009) have been vying for the eyes of audience members while expanding the representational schemas of this perennial, if critically derided, subgenre of horror. Amidst this rising tide of vampiric narratives, an influx of international productions has further diversified the kinds of archetypal characters and stories that are unique to the subgenre, the roots of which can be traced back to Bram Stoker's 1897 novel *Dracula* and to that Expressionistic classic of German cinema, F. W. Murnau's *Nosferatu* (1922), a silent film starring Max Schreck as the Transylvanian bloodsucker Count Orlok. A more recent European production, Swedish director Tomas Alfredson's 2008 film *Let the Right One In* (*Låt den rätte komma in*), is just one example of the global rerouting of cultural flows that has resulted in subtle generic shifts at the semantic and syntactic levels, with conventional iconography as well as plotlines changing, however slightly, to accommodate regionally or nationally specific variations on the Dracula mythos.

But of these recently released international productions, South Korean director Park Chan-wook (Pak Ch'an-uk)'s 2009 film *Thirst* (*Pakjwi*, which literally translates as "Bat") is perhaps the most fascinating for the manner in which it mobilizes visible signs of cultural and ethnic difference for the purpose of measuring the protagonist's fluid positioning vis-à-vis *another* "Other"—a Filipina character whose initially marginalized place within the text belies her ultimate centrality as a figure of irreducible alterity. As a cross-cultural adaptation of French novelist Emile Zola's *Thérèse Raquin* (1867), *Thirst* puts a nonnaturalistic spin on its nineteenth-century literary predecessor, incorporating fantastic, supernatural elements associated with vampiric fiction and allegorizing contemporary social problems associated with immigration and the alienation of foreign brides in South Korea. This chapter uses Park's auteurist take on the global vampire genre—an "alien" element within the decades-old history of Korean supernatural horror filmmaking, which is more often populated with long-haired female ghosts rather than Dracula-like bloodsuckers[1]—as a starting point for an investigation into the representation of multiculturalism and "otherness" in recent South Korean productions.

Until recently, images of foreigners in South Korean cinema have largely been limited to Japanese and Americans: colonial and neocolonial others, respectively, who took the spotlight, if only temporarily, in our previous chapters. The presence of these figures was marginal yet instrumental in solidifying the cinematic construction of Korean unity through nationalist narratives. The term "multiculturalism film" (*tamuhwa yŏnghwa*), which we are utilizing throughout this chapter, refers to a relatively new phenomenon: the emergence of new ethnicities in South Korean cinema, nationalities as diverse as Filipinos, the Vietnamese, Bangladeshis, Bhutanese, Urzbeks, Pakistanis, Indians, Burmese, Russians, Turks, and Ghanans. Although many other films dealing with Korean–Japanese conflicts and Korean immigrants in the United States or Europe have been produced, we wish to define *tamunhwa yŏnghwa* as films featuring (undocumented) migrant workers and multicultural families in accordance with the current discourse surrounding the Korean neologism *tamunhwa* ("multi- or plural culture") outside colonial or postcolonial relationships.

In the second half of the chapter, we apply the French philosopher Jacques Derrida's theory of hospitality to deconstruct the questionable ethics of "multiculturalism films," a pedagogically inclined cycle of cultural productions aiming to raise civic consciousness about diversity and educate Korean audiences to become better hosts for immigrants and foreign guest workers. By shifting our earlier-established "host" metaphor from the site of cities (Seoul and Tokyo in particular), which we discussed in Chapter Six, to the place of citizens (who are often situated opposite migrants from Southeast Asia and other underdeveloped regions), we seek to underscore both the progressive politics and representational limitations of new multiculturalism discourses in contemporary Korean cinema, which exposes social prejudices against migrant workers, foreign brides, and multicultural children for the purpose of civic enlightenment.

Cultural Differences and Blood Metaphors

Focusing on both the ethical and physical transformations of a Catholic priest, Sang-hyŏn (Song Kang-ho), who becomes a vampire after being given a resuscitating transfusion of tainted blood, *Thirst* charts this tortured protagonist's descent from his vaunted position as a devout man of the cloth to his literally supine place on a hospital floor, sipping the blood of an ailing patient through an IV. This movement from spiritual commitment to physical fulfillment, from lofty ideals to lowly pursuits of the flesh leading to sexual gratification (hinted at by a shot of him descending the steps outside the monastery), might suggest an irreversible declination into moral turpitude. However, when compared to the depraved state of another vampiric figure—a newly undead woman named T'ae-ju (Kim Ok-bin) whose titular craving for blood can only be satiated by the killing of several innocent people—Sang-hyŏn comes to embody a relative degree of rationality and respect for the living, deciding in the end to commit double suicide with her in the glow of early-morning, skin-lacerating sunlight. Moreover, the former priest's decision to spare the life of Evelyn (Mercedes Cabral), a woman from the Philippines whose Korean husband has been murdered by T'ae-ju, indicates a return to absolution, something earlier given to Sang-hyŏn by another, older priest at the monastery that had been his isolated home for so many years. That is, audiences are invited to "forgive" the main character for his various transgressions, including his killing of an innocent man (Kang-u [Sin Ha-gyun], the sickly, bed-ridden husband of T'ae-ju), in light of his desire to right the wrongs of his past and ensure that this *other* outsider figure is given a chance at having a future.

We have opted to begin our discussion of cultural difference in contemporary South Korean cinema by way of a genre film that, on the surface, might appear to offer little in terms of its politics of representation, its nearly exclusive focus on Korean characters and settings. However, the occasional appearance of Evelyn (a woman who can be said to "mirror" the redeemable male monster at the heart of this story), as well as Sang-hyŏn's own status as an outsider brought into a tightly knit community, disrupt the text even as these so-called "foreign" elements conform to some of the conventions of vampiric fiction. Although several other vampire films lay bare the obstacles that make the movement from exclusion to inclusion difficult, if not impossible, *Thirst* complicates matters by gesturing toward the challenges faced by ethnic

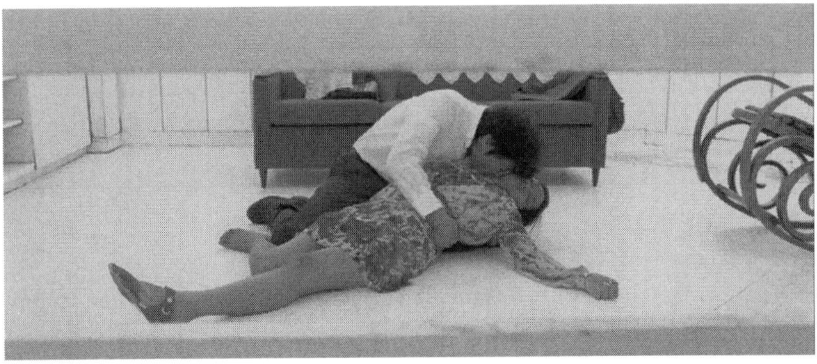

FIGURE 8.1. The vampire Sang-hyŏn pretends to suck the blood of a Filipina woman named Evelyn in a scene from Park Chan-wook's *Thirst.*

minorities in South Korea, a country frequently described by historians, social scientists, demographers, and even geneticists as being racially homogenous and fiercely nationalistic.

For instance, in Nancy L. Fisher's edited volume *Cultural and Ethnic Diversity: A Guide for Genetics Professionals*, Sechin Cho writes, "Ethnically, Korea is the most uniform country in the world. It is populated almost exclusively by a single ethnic group, the Han."[2] Although lacking in contextualizing nuance and missing the kind of statistical data or empirical evidence that might lend credibility to her claim, Cho's blanket pronouncement echoes much of the research being carried out in this area. This is perhaps best expressed by the sociologist Gi-wook Shin, who has written about "the strong sense of unity and national pride displayed by Koreans" during the 2002 FIFA World Cup, held in Seoul, Daegu, Pusan, and other Korean cities in addition to Japanese venues that year. As Shin states, such a combination of pride and unity "arises in large part from an identity based on a common bloodline and shared ancestry."[3] Significantly, one of the surveys cited by Shin in his book *Ethnic Nationalism in Korea: Genealogy, Politics and Legacy* "found that 68.2 percent of the respondents in South Korea consider 'blood' the most important criterion of defining the Korean nation."[4]

Blood is quite literally in abundance throughout *Thirst*, a motion picture that recalls director Park Chan-wook's earlier works (including the three films comprising his "Revenge Trilogy": *Sympathy for Mr. Vengeance* [*Poksu nŭn na ŭi kŏt*, 2002], *Oldboy* [*Oldŭ poi*, 2003], and *Lady Vengeance* [*Ch'ingŏlhan Kŭmjassi*, 2005]) in terms of its unrelenting imaging of hemorrhaging bodies. Blood flows freely in this film, spurting from manufactured gashes as well as natural orifices and serving as the temporary "cure" for Sang-hyŏn's physical ailments—the blisters and sores that disappear with each ingestion only to reappear hours later. But the figurative "blood" referenced in the previously-mentioned survey (conducted in December 1999 by the Korean Broadcasting System [KBS] and Hallym University), and frequently mentioned in subsequent polls since that time, is also present in Park's film. Stated another way, as an allegorical "bloodline narrative" that seems to privilege Korean national identity only to shift spectatorial attention toward sites of irreducible otherness, *Thirst* distinguishes itself from other vampire movies by acknowledging the rise of multicultural citizenship during the first decade of the twenty-first century. If indeed Evelyn can be said to stand in for over 60,000 people from the Philippines currently living in South Korea,[5] then her complicated relationship to the monster might be indicative of the difficulties associated with the implementation of social programs designed to remedy rights violations of the past and create equitable relations among persons from different cultural backgrounds.

If Park's film differs in this respect from the many American and European vampire narratives currently glutting movie theaters, it is consonant with the general tenor of contemporary cultural production in South Korea, a country whose government (under the presidential administrations of Roh Moo Hyun [No Mu-hyŏn] and Lee Myung-bak [Yi Myŏng-bak]) has sought to broaden the scope of citizenship over the past decade while transforming the image of Seoul and its satellite environs into that of a cosmopolitan space attractive to foreign investors and multinational corporations. Filmmakers in particular have been instrumental, if not necessarily complicit, in lending audiovisual support to the government's policies, perhaps unwittingly perpetuating the unifying myth of open-mindedness and cosmopolitanism even as they narrativize the plights of immigrant workers, foreign brides, and other ethnic minorities whose very presence signals the country's embrace of globalization (*segyehwa*) as well as its liminal status as a sub-imperial "middle-man" nation. Indeed, local film and television industries have participated in the enactment of a "contradictive policy agenda," one that strives to heighten public awareness of social problems (through educational programs as well as popular entertainment) but unfortunately provides little more than empty rhetoric and political sloganeering, according to the cultural anthropologist Han Geon-soo.[6]

In a recent article entitled "Multicultural Korea," Han highlights several recent television series that, on the surface, seem to promote a progressive vision of plurality. The 2007 national celebration of Ch'usŏk (Harvest Moon Festival) was accompanied by a slew of holiday-themed programs that, for the first time, showcased "diverse types of foreign migrants as . . . legitimate constituents of Korean society."[7] One, a weekly KBS talk show entitled *Chatting with Beauties* (*Minyŏdŭl ŭi suda*, 2006–2010), featured a group of foreign-born female residents of South Korea discussing societal perceptions of ethnic minorities. A Ch'usŏk holiday special episode entitled *Chatting with Hunks*

(*Minamdŭl ŭi suda*, 2007) was devoted to a set of male perspectives on cross-cultural interactions and obstacles to widespread acceptance. Around that time, rival network MBC programmed a holiday special entitled *Finding the Best Foreign Daughter-in-Laws* (*Ch'oegang! woegukin myŏnŭri yŏljŏn*), which, according to a writer for *Sports Chosun*, gave viewers "an opportunity to think about the preciousness of the family through foreign daughters-in-law who nurture healthy homes by overcoming cultural differences."[8] As Han Geon-soo suggests, the institutional entrenchment of "healthy multiculturalism"—the idea that Ch'usŏk is no longer a "single-nation festival" but rather one that speaks to "people of diverse races and countries"—can be partly attributed to these and other TV programs, which frequently "stress the female marriage migrants' mastery of dialects" and skillful adaptation to Korean culture. That is, the potentially edifying content of minority-themed television series is offset by the focus on immigrants' successful assimilation, their ability and/or willingness to dissolve into a supposedly multiethnic morass of unified national identity.

At the time of these programs' broadcast, a press release issued by the Ministry of Justice indicated that a record number of foreign residents were living and working in South Korea. For the first time in the nation's history, that number broke the 1 million mark. Nearly three-fourths of those individuals (724,967 people) established long-term residency by staying in South Korea for more than ninety days. This marks a steep increase from the number of long-term residents documented in 1995 (110,028 people), when the country was at the very bottom of international lists tracking relative levels of "fractionalization," a term used by economists and social scientists to measure ethnic and linguistic heterogeneity in developed or developing nations. With a fractionalization number of .0020, South Korea scored lower than North Korea (.0392), the runner-up for least ethnically diverse country in a list of 189 others. Although still quite low on the list, South Korea has witnessed a significant change in its demographic makeup, with foreign residents in 2007 comprising 1.48% of the entire population (of 49.1 million people).

Even though it is not cited by Han, *Kamgeun's Mom* (*Kkamgŭn-i ŏmma*), another Korean television program broadcast on October 7, 2006 (the day after Ch'usŏk), is significant as a site of convergent yet contradictory discourses concerning the prejudicial attitudes directed at ethnic minorities—attitudes that sometimes manifest as moments of physical and/or verbal abuse. Aired on the SBS network, and distributed to neighboring countries in the region, this winner of the Best Drama category at the 2007 Asia Pacific Broadcast Union tackles the serious issue of racial discrimination, focusing on the plight of a half-Filipino, half-Korean boy, Myŏng-gŭm (played by Kim Chi-han, a first-time child actor born to a Korean mother and a Bangladeshi father), who struggles to fit in as a new student at an elementary school overrun with bullies. Derisively nicknaming the nine-year-old boy "Kkamgŭn" (a word that roughly translates as "blackie" or "darkie"), Myŏng-gŭm's classmates express a level of hostility that is second only to that of his new stepmother, To-sun (Kyŏn Mi-ri), a Korean woman who visibly blanches at the sight of his dark skin upon first meeting him and later refuses to help him with his homework while his father serves time in prison (for involuntary manslaughter). Interlaced through the program's frequently melodramatic, *sinp'a*-filled scenes is a critique of deeply engrained racial bias, directed toward the many men, women, and children who marginalize Myŏng-gŭm and make a mockery of his physical difference. Here too, though, the potentially progressive aspects of a television production firmly rooted in multicultural discourses are counterbalanced by a curious focus on the titular character's feelings—the stepmother's mounting frustrations as a working-class woman burdened with a "mixed-blood" youngster whose nasty pranks push her to send him away.

Preparing to put the boy on a plane bound for the Philippines, where his birth mother presumably lives, To-sun shares a heart-to-heart conversation with a female friend at the restaurant where the two work. Revealing that Myŏng-gŭm's mother, Teresita, is actually dead (a sad truth that she only recently discovered), the put-upon stepmother shrugs her shoulders and suggests that the boy's grandparents (whom he has never met) might better serve his familial needs. When her friend reminds her of the language barrier that separates Myŏng-gŭm and his Filipino grandparents, To-sun responds by stating that "blood will tell." More accurately translated as "blood will pull," the slang expression *pitjul i ttaenggida* is deployed here to indicate the supposedly magnetic attraction that will bring together disparate people connected only by birth. It is one of several occasions in which a reference to blood is brought to bear on the interrelated topics of multicultural citizenship, ethnic diversity, and the underlying belief (articulated throughout *Kamgeun's Mom*) that national belonging hinges on "dark" people's willingness to "whiten" their skin in order to "fit in." Significantly, the Korean word for "mixed blood," *honhyŏl*, has been a point of contention for human-rights activists and nongovernment al organizations seeking to replace such outdated expressions with new, politically correct terms that reflect a forward-thinking shift in emphasis away from perpetuators toward *victims* of rights violations, including second-generation members of multicultural families.[9] As Han Geon-soo explains, this seemingly praiseworthy emphasis on the "politics of naming" in South Korea, this rejection of derogatory or offensive terms such as "Kosian" (which refers to mixed-race Korean children who have blood ties to other Asian ethnicities), problematically deflects attention away from the legal and material obstacles that prevent the amelioration of discriminatory policies, spotlighting instead the kind of spoken and written discourses that enflame prejudice, intolerance, or xenophobia.

Among Koreans, the expression *tanil minjok*, or "one-blooded people," has long been used to strengthen national identity and solidarity in the face of colonial or neocolonial threats. However, if one were to ask a twentysomething or thirtysomething today what "Koreanness" connotes, he or she would likely point to the development of a fully democratic political system or to the adherence to fair laws as being important conditions for citizenship endowment. Nevertheless, blood continues to seep into the narrative universes of these filmic and televisual responses to government policies and demographic changes, never more so than in *Thirst*, a film that stages a seemingly deadly, cross-cultural encounter between vampire and victim only to reveal, in the penultimate moments, that Sang-hyŏn has *not* bitten the neck of Evelyn. Hoping to steer T'ae-ju away from the Filipina woman, he only pretends to suck her blood, dropping a sports coat onto her still-breathing body so as to mislead the thirsty female vampire. Significantly, Sang-hyŏn's act of kindness in this otherwise grisly scene, besides serving to ensure his forgiveness if not salvation according to the ethical terms of enlightened vampirism, is linked to his refusal to imbibe the blood of an ethnic minority, someone whose very presence in the text disturbs the homogeneity of the Korean family and its small network of friends, but whose "freedom" at the end marks a return to the "pure" blood ties connecting these ill-fated characters.

Like the Russian hitman Mikhail in Kim Jee-woon (Kim Chi-un)'s neo-noir film *Bittersweet Life* (*Talch'omhan insaeng*, 2005), or the unnamed French woman who briefly appears in Hong Sang-soo (Hong Sang-su)'s metatextual film *A Tale of Cinema* (*Kŭkjang chŏn*, 2005), or the Pakistani picnickers who gawk at the titular river monster in Bong Joon-ho (Pong Chun-ho)'s *The Host* (*Goemul*, 2006), or the Indian woman and child who magically spring up in Lee Chang-dong (Yi Ch'ang-dong)'s *Oasis* (2002), or the trio of dock workers from Myanmar who express an interest in Korean women only to be turned away by the main characters in Jeong Jae-eun (Chŏng Chae-ŭn)'s *Take Care of My Cat* (*Koyangi rŭl put'akhae*, 2001), Evelyn can be thought of as "matter out of place." She is a foreign body whose sudden entrance into and exit from the text gel into a punctum-like moment of uncanny otherness. Indeed, Evelyn's presence can be likened to the accidental dropping of blood into a fruit shake made by T'ae-ju in *Thirst*, a pinprick of plasmic intensity and associative complexity that at first might suggest contamination or the "soiling" of something pure. However, the mixing of blood in this scene, which culminates with T'ae-ju's stepmother ([Kim Hae-suk] who is in a paralytic state due to the shock of her son's death) ingesting the tainted beverage and slowly regaining her strength, suggests that such "unholy" mergers or plasmic interminglings might lead to a more potent form of cultural embodiment. It is doubly noteworthy, then, that Sang-hyŏn opts *not* to kill Evelyn, a woman whose blood, if mixed with his, might engender a new relational understanding of the vampire–victim dyad unique to the subgenre. Although honorable, his decision can also be interpreted as a symptomatic feature of seemingly outdated, yet persistent cultural attitudes about the diluting or mixing of Korean national identity through the infusion—or intraregional "transfusion"—of foreign elements.

Sang-hyŏn's apparent benevolence and restraint in refusing to suck the Filipina woman's blood can thus be read as both a sign of his redemption and respect for human lives as well as an unintended expression of xenophobic fear concerning the mixing of Korean and non-Korean blood. From a humanistic point-of-view, one is tempted to explore the deeper religious connections between Sang-hyŏn and Evelyn as fellow-Catholics. If the act of sparing Evelyn's life is admirable from the perspective of their shared religion (which connects them on a deeper spiritual level distinct from the blood ties of Koreans), it is ironic that the next act he commits is double suicide, a mortal sin for Catholics, surpassing other transgressions throughout the narrative (attempted rape, illicit sex affairs, adultery, murders, etc.). As pointed out by the Korean critic Mun Sŏk, *Thirst* is a text of paradoxes and ironies wherein contradictory elements (including the mixing of Western iconography related to vampirism and Catholicism along with Japanese architecture, Korean traditional costumes, Chinese mahjong games, Russian vodka, and Filipina brides) come into contact while subverting genre conventions in the process.[10] According to the director Park Chan-wook, while his film might at first seem to lack "authenticity" as a cultural text, it is all the more "Korean" because of the "impure" mishmashing (*chapsŭrŏum*) that he and others see as the core of contemporary Koreanness.[11]

As we have endeavored to point out in each of this book's preceding chapters, over the last two decades South Korean films have become increasingly "transmigratory," not only in terms of their global dissemination via international festivals but also at the level of narrative itself. A number of Korean films made in the past twenty years reveal a thematic obsession with travel, escape, immigration, border crossing, and cross-cultural encounters. *Asako in Ruby Shoes* (*Sunaebo*, 2000), *Anarchists* (*Anak'istŭ*, 2000), *The Warrior* (*Musa*, 2001), *Fighter in the Wind* (*Param ŭi P'aitŏ*, 2004), *Rikidozan: A Hero Extraordinaire* (*Yŏkdosan*, 2004), *R-Point* (*Al p'ointŭ*, 2004), *Antarctic Journal* (*Namgŭk ilji*, 2005), *Typhoon* (*T'aep'ung*, 2005), *Daisy* (*Taeiji*, 2006), *Muoi: The Legend of a Portrait* (*Mui*, 2007), *The Good, the Bad, the Weird* (*Chotŭn nom, nappŭn nom, isanghan nom*, 2008), *Night and Day* (*Pam kwa nat*, 2008), *With a Girl of Himalaya* (*Himallaya, param i mŏmunŭn kot*, 2008), *A Good Rain Knows* (*Hou sijŏl*, 2009), *Amen* (2011), *My Way* (*Mai wei*, 2011), *Papa* (*P'ap'a*, 2012), and *The Berlin File* (*Perŭllin*, 2013) are only a few examples of contemporary South Korean films set partially or entirely outside of South Korea's national borders. Perhaps this is not unusual, given the sometimes-stifling conditions in which Seoulites are forced to live, as well as the always-intoxicating whiff of adventure wafting in from distant shores. What is perhaps less easily resolved is the attendant trend toward ethnic diversity, diasporic consciousness, and new, intraregional cultural flows that reveal how seemingly heterogeneous this East Asian nation has become in recent years. Indeed, racial, ethnic, and cultural minorities have been emerging in narratives of great national import—stories allegorizing the plight of low-wage workers, underclass immigrants, and other marginalized figures. Examples include the Chinese "illegals" in *Failan* (*P'airan*, 2001), the Filipino brides in *You Are My Sunshine* (*Nŏ nŭn nae yunmyŏng*, 2005), and the North Korean defectors in *Crossing* (*Kŭrosing*, 2008), *Over the Border* (*Kukkyŏng ŭi namjjok*, 2006), and *My Wedding Campaign* (*Na ŭi kyŏlhon wŏnjŏnggi*, 2005). This latter film, produced in 2005, is significant for the way that it combines the two recent trends, showing first a farmer's journey out of Korea (in search of a bride) and then an attempt, on the part of a female North Korean defector working as a marriage facilitator in Uzbekistan, to seek political asylum in the south.

As the closing film of the 2005 Busan International Film Festival (formerly, Pusan International Film Festival), this directorial debut from newcomer Hwang Pyŏng-guk sparked critical commentary about the topic of international marriages, a growing trend in South Korea, particularly in rural areas and farming communities where there is a gender imbalance within the rapidly aging population of potential brides and grooms. As the sociologist Kim Hyun Mee states, migrant women, as the first "settler type" immigrants to come to Korea, "have paved the way for reconsidering the 'pure blood' ideology or 'ethnic nationalism.'"[12] Moreover, "as the most easily mobilized resource to solve the various family crises" plaguing parts of the country, they have also played a vital part of the government's attempts to address South Korea's low birth rates, operationalized by the Ministry of Education and Human Resources as the "Plan for Promoting the Social Integration of Migrant Women, Biracial People, and Immigrants," announced in April 2006, a year after the theatrical release of *My Wedding Campaign*.

This film tells the story of two unmarried men in their thirties who, unlucky in love and not likely to find matrimonial bliss among the womenfolk of their village in Kyŏngsang Province, sign up for a ten-day "wedding campaign" in Uzbekistan, where much of this motion picture was shot. One of the bachelors in question, Man-t'aek (Chŏng Chae-yŏng), has been pressured by his widowed mother to find a bride, someone who can help her take care of the grandfather's funeral rites once he dies. Before he and his best friend, Hŭi-ch'ŏl (Yu Chun-sang), board a plane for Uzbekistan, Man-t'aek's grandfather is shown speaking to a neighboring village woman. During their conversation, the old man discovers that her daughter-in-law is actually from that landlocked country of the former Soviet Union, a place whose name they both struggle to pronounce ("U-zoo-beck-ist" is the best that they can produce). When the Uzbek woman finally appears, both the old man and the audience can see that, behind her basket full of laundry, she is pregnant. Man-t'aek's grandfather looks on in wonder as she approaches her mother-in-law and begins speaking in Korean. This brief encounter between a slack-jawed Korean villager and a Caucasian woman whose birthplace is some 3,000 miles away plants the seeds for his grandson's cross-continental journey, his trip to a country where professional matchmakers will attempt to pair him up with ethnic Korean women.

Not long after he and Hŭi-ch'ŏl arrive, they meet potential mates through a shady marriage broker. Sheepishly shy and almost pathologically insecure, Man-t'aek struggles to break the ice with the ladies, stuttering during his interviews and running to the restroom every few minutes due to an upset stomach. Helping him throughout the arduous process is a translator, Kim Lara (Su Ae), who patiently works to turn Man-t'aek into an acceptable marriage partner in the eyes of each woman that he meets. It is probably not a surprise to most audiences that these two develop a romantic relationship, which presents a problem for Lara insofar as her unscrupulous boss expects her to put her professional responsibilities before her personal desires, going so far as to prevent her from getting the forged South Korean passport for which she has worked long and hard. The film's representation of the marriage broker as a man who profits from the illegal trafficking of women (including prostitutes) and stops at nothing to assert his power over female underlings is indicative of the trend toward social consciousness in contemporary Korean cinema—a trend that unfortunately comes up short in terms of overlooking the structured violence and human-rights abuses that migrant women often face upon their arrival in South Korea.

One scene that reveals Lara's perilous position occurs not long after she and Man-t'aek venture out into the streets of Tashkent, the capital of Uzbekistan. Two local police officers pass in and out of a crowd of people gathered outside a national monument. As they begin checking passports, Lara—an illegal alien who, having overstayed her work visa, cannot risk being caught—asks Man-t'aek to draw their attention and run away. With the cops in hot pursuit of him, Lara sneaks away, staving off the threat of deportation, at least for a short while. A few days later, after Man-t'aek has declared his love for Lara, another, similar encounter takes place. Only, this time, having discovered the truth of her predicament and learning that she is originally from Sinuiju City in North Korea, he pleads with *her* to run away, thus taking the sacrificial fall and being slapped with a minor infraction after a fight breaks out. It is Man-t'aek who is sent home by South Korean embassy officials, a forced ejection that would seem to make his union with Lara a near-impossibility.

However, the narrative concludes with a conventional happy ending, once Man-t'aek has returned to his hometown. There he receives news from two National Intelligence Service agents that Lara has jumped the gate of an embassy and won political asylum in South Korea, information that sends a dazed, half-dozing Man-t'aek to his feet and rushing toward the camera in a burst of euphoric anticipation, a moment that marks the official end of his titular campaign to get married.

Significantly, *My Wedding Campaign*, like the aforementioned *You Are My Sunshine*, dangles the prospect of cross-cultural romance and international marriage before the audience only to assert a more traditional form of narrative closure and heterosexual union at the end. In both cases, two Korean characters—male and female—are brought together as mutually enriched beneficiaries of romantic desire, arising ironically out of the struggles involved in finding a partner from another country (Uzbekistan in the case of the former film, the Philippines in the case of the latter). Prior to that conventional coupling of Korean characters, both films establish that the "country bumpkin" protagonists (Man-t'aek in *My Wedding Campaign*, Sŏk-jung [Hwang Chŏng-min] in *You Are My Sunshine*) either suffer from nocturnal emissions ("wet dreams") or resort to masturbation, the source of much frustration for their mothers, who must wash their grown sons' underwear. As signs of a stunted adolescence, such crises in masculinity are eventually overcome once the "appropriate" partnership with a Korean woman comes into narrative focus. *You Are My Sunshine* even accelerates the drive toward this culturally homogenous form of coupling, with early scenes set in the aftermath of the main character's unsuccessful and unsatisfying attempt to find a Filipina bride. Although another unnamed woman from the Philippines appears during these passages (someone who is shown being carted through a field in a wheelbarrow by her husband, a friend of the protagonist), ethnic minorities are largely invisible in this film, a suppressed part of Sŏk-jung's failure to connect with someone across cultural lines.

Not coincidentally, among these early moments in the film is a revealing scene set inside a country clinic, where Ŭn-ha (Jeon Do-yeon [Chŏn To-yŏn], the self-described "princess" who will soon meet and grow to love Sŏk-jung), is having blood tests. Although the physical examination is being performed so as to test the Korean woman for sexually transmitted diseases (foreshadowing the sex worker's infection with HIV/AIDS), a curious close-up of medical blood vials might remind audiences of the insistence with which cultural producers tend to single out determining factors in the forging of onscreen romances, including those between members of the same ethnicity or nationality. While it is commendable that such films reflect the many steps taken by the South Korean government and its citizenry in the advance toward a more rights-oriented, multicultural society, one cannot help but feel that considerable progress is still needed before the harsh realities of immigrant life in a largely mono-ethnic culture become the stuff of mainstream cinema.

Becoming Better "Hosts" through Multicultural Films

As discussed earlier, in recent years, *tamunhwa* ("multi- or plural culture") has become a buzzword in South Korean society, thanks partly to government campaigns to raise public awareness of "multicultural families" (*tamunhwa kajŏng*) and end any discriminations that might be directed against them.[13] In fact, it is customary today for corporations and private schools to offer preferential treatment to multicultural families, in terms of benefits-allocation for employees as well as slots available for schoolchildren. According to official statistics of the Ministry of Security and Public Administration, as of January 2014, 1.57 million foreigners (3.1% of the total population) reside in South Korea.[14] Excluded from this statistical assessment are illegal immigrants, whose population is estimated to be as many as 280,000.[15] While upwardly mobile mixed families comprised of a Korean parent, an immigrant parent (usually mother), and bicultural children have been the key beneficiaries of state-sponsored multicultural initiatives, policy makers and industrialists alike have done little to protect the basic rights of economically deprived, undocumented migrant workers and their non-Korean children. Between 2008 and 2010, 33,000 illegal immigrants were deported from South Korea, and those who are "fortunate" enough to linger as liminal subjects of the state (with no official status) are routinely abused in the workplace and denied their basic human rights such as minimum wage earnings, medical care for work-related injuries, and education for their children.[16]

Given the ambivalent state of Korean multiculturalism (*tamunnhwa chuŭi*), which celebrates mixed (half-Korean) families on the principle of assimilation while excluding migrant workers forced to take undesirable "3-D" (dirty, dangerous, demeaning) jobs at meager wages, the increased presence of the latter group in recent Korean films is an unexpected yet welcome, if not unproblematic, trend. Core media texts in the latest cycle of *tamunhwa yŏnghwa* (multicultural films) include Sim Sang-guk's *Where Is Ronny?* (*Roni rŭl ch'ajasŏ*, 2008), Shin Dong-il (Sin Tong-il)'s *Bandhobi* (*Bandubi*, 2009), Kim Min-sŏk's *Haunters* (*Ch'onŭngrŏkja*, 2010), Yuk Sang-hyo's *He's on Duty* (*Pangga? Pangga!*, 2010), Cho Yong-gyu's *Punch* (*Wan-dŭk-i*, 2011), and Kim Sŏng-hun's *A Wonderful Moment* (*Mai Rit'ŭl Hiŏro*, 2012). Despite the seemingly progressive message of inclusion and tolerance shared by all of these films, only one film, *Punch*, centrally positions the *tamunhwa* (multicultural) hero as an agent of narrative change: a rebellious half-Korean, half-Filipino high school student who trains to become a kickboxer thanks to the support of his homeroom teacher ([Kim Yun-sŏk] who, it turns out, moonlights as an advocate for migrant workers). Ironically, this ascendancy of the multicultural hero is made possible through the cross-ethnic casting of a popular television/film actor, Yu A-in, in the lead role. And tellingly, in an early part of the film, his character Wan-dŭk is unaware of his own dual heritage and "passes" as a full-blooded Korean in school.

The other films comprising this well-meaning *tamunhwa yŏnghwa* cycle tell stories of soul-searching Korean heroes or heroines who forge deep friendships or romantic relationships with foreign characters from Bangladesh (*Where Is Ronny?* and *Bandhobi*), Ghana and Turkey (*Haunters*), and Vietnam (*He's on Duty*), as well as a dark-skinned, half-Filipino child (*A Wonderful Moment*). Despite variations in film genre—*Where Is Ronny?* is a road movie, *Bandhobi* is a coming-of-age youth film, *Haunters* is a superhero action film, *He's on Duty* is slapstick comedy, and *A Wonderful Moment* is a musical drama—most of the foreign characters in these films are virtually eliminated by the end of each multicultural narrative. In *Where Is Ronny?* and *Bandhobi*, undocumented Bangladeshi workers who develop rocky yet warm relationships with Korean characters are deported. In *He's on Duty*, the Vietnamese love interest for the clownish Korean hero ([Kim In-wŏn] who passes as a Bhutanese to get a job in a factory) barely escapes deportation but disappears as a fugitive. And in *Haunters*, the righteous superhero (Ko Su)'s loyal Ghana-born and Turkish sidekicks (Abu Dad and Enes Kaya) are killed by the sadistic villain (Kang Tong-wŏn). While sympathetically-oriented against discriminatory attitudes and the oppression faced by migrant laborers and mixed race children, these films ultimately privilege the Korean subject position and foreground positive changes experienced by that central character, facilitated by his or her acceptance of multiculturalism and alterity as opportunities for personal growth and edification.

As mentioned earlier, the theme of multiculturalism in the country's new millennium cinema directly reflects the South Korean government's policy to raise public awareness about a growing immigrant population and improve the treatment of non-Koreans by Koreans. This progressive policy is partly propelled by self-interest on the part of the South Korean government, just as the US government actively sought to improve race relations at home in order to win the Cold War abroad during the 1950s and 1960s. First, Korean society is in desperate need of migrant workers and foreign brides in order to sustain its national economy and raise the low birth rate. Second, the image of new, multicultural, and global Korea is in itself a lucrative commodity in an era of the Korean Wave (*Hallyu*), as South Korean films and television shows are gaining popularity not only in East Asian neighboring countries but also in Southeast Asia, South Asia, Central Asia, the Middle East, and Africa. Given these socioeconomic factors, it is reasonable to suspect that the emerging discourse of multiculturalism in contemporary South Korean cinema is little more than an extension of state-sponsored, self-promotional propaganda. As Asian American scholar Lisa Lowe persuasively points out in her book *Immigrant Acts: On Asian American Cultural Politics*, multiculturalism oftentimes serves as a hegemonic ideological apparatus that "levels the important differences and contradictions within and among racial and ethnic minority groups according to the discourse of pluralism, which asserts that American culture is a democratic terrain to which every variety of constituency has equal access and in which all are represented, while simultaneously masking the existence of exclusion by recuperating dissent, conflict, and otherness through the promise of inclusion."[17] Lowe ideologically counters a more humanistic interpretation of multiculturalism as a liberal discourse, as represented by Robert Stam's definition: "Radically egalitarian, polycentric multiculturalism sees world history and contemporary social life from the theoretical perspective of the fundamental equality of peoples in status, intelligence, and rights. . . . Its task is double, at once one of deconstructing Eurocentric and racist norms and of constructing and promoting multicultural alternatives."[18]

Out of the aforementioned films comprising the multicultural film cycle, *Punch* and *A Wonderful Moment* are examples that represent the illusionistic discourse of pluralism and inclusion, as critiqued by Lowe. The multicultural heroes in both films succeed as a kickboxer and a musical star, respectively, against all odds and hardships, not only through their perseverance and natural gifts but also thanks to an apprenticeship and support from their native Korean mentors. In a way that is reminiscent of many immigrant stories in American cinema (e.g. *America America* [1963], *The Godfather: Part II* [1974], *Moscow on the Hudson* [1984], *Far and Away* [1992], *The Joy Luck Club* [1993], *An American Rhapsody* [2001], *My Big Fat Greek Wedding* [2002], *Spanglish* [2004], *The Namesake* [2006], and *A Better Life* [2011]), these underdog heroes end up achieving "The Korean Dream" and their success is a testament to the ideal of South Korea as a land of opportunities (as opposed to their immigrant mother's poorer country of origin). However, other entries in this cycle of films depart from the familiar formula and instead focus on life-altering, intercultural friendships between local protagonists and foreign characters, creating "multicultural alternatives" to "racist norms," as in Stam's idealistic view.

Not unlike Classical and New Hollywood's socially conscious race-problem films, such as *Pinky* (1949), *No Way Out* (1950), *Guess Who's Coming to Dinner* (1967), and *In the Heat of the Night* (1967), recent Korean multiculturalism films made by liberal young filmmakers—particularly, Sim Sang-guk's *Where Is Ronny?* and Shin Dong-il's *Bandhobi*, which will be analyzed in detail in the next few pages—concentrate their efforts in exposing xenophobia and racial/ethnic discrimination in Korean society and heightening the public's consciousness about undocumented migrant workers and their rights. These films are not celebratory about the current state of multiculturalism in South Korea, nor are they entirely progressive in their representational strategies, since migrant stories tend to be focalized through the eyes of Korean protagonists. Rather, they should be understood as "pedagogical films" which advocate inclusion and tolerance and aim to educate Korean audiences about the challenges faced by foreign guests. By teaching an ethics of inclusion to would-be "hosts," these recent multiculturalism films evoke the French philosopher Jacques Derrida's notion of unconditional hospitality.

In the opening paragraph of his book *Of Hospitality*, Jacques Derrida makes an intriguing distinction between "the question of the foreigner" (*la question de l'etranger*) and "the foreigner's question" (*la question d'etranger*). The former phrase presupposes the undesirable status of the foreigner as someone who is subject to debate, interrogation, and control by the suspecting host society. The latter phrase, on the other hand, elevates the status of said subject to that of an insightful enunciator who poses the question to the insider, someone who interrogates rather than faces interrogation. Drawing upon Plato's dialogues, Derrida states, "The Foreigner shakes up the threatening dogmatism of the paternal *logos* . . . As though the Foreigner had to begin by contesting the authority of the chief, the father, the master of the family, the 'master of the house,' of the power of hospitality."[19] Derrida goes on to quote Socrates' speech, stating, "If I were a foreigner, here in the court . . . you would tolerate not only my accent, my voice, my elocution, but turns of the phrase in my spontaneous, original, idiomatic rhetoric. There is thus a foreigner's right, right to hospitality for foreigners at Athens."[20] Derrida's two opening propositions in his book—the foreigner's freedom to ask the probing question and to challenge the *logos* of the father/nation as well as the foreigner's right to tolerance and hospitality in the host community—raises ethical questions about the current state of (undocumented) immigration not only in developed Western countries such as England, France, Germany, and the United States, but also in industrialized East Asian societies including Hong Kong, Taiwan, Japan, and South Korea.

Notably missing in today's late-capitalist global metropolises, from Paris and London to Tokyo and Seoul, is what Derrida calls "absolute or unconditional hospitality" wherein the host is unconditionally welcoming and offers his home to the "absolute, unknown, anonymous other" with no expectation of reciprocity.[21] What is practiced in reality is a highly compromised form of "conditional hospitality," which reaffirms a sovereignty of the host that "can only be exercised by filtering, choosing, and thus by excluding and doing violence [against the guest]."[22] The pursuit of pure, unconditional, absolute hospitality—hospitality of *visitation* rather than of *invitation*—is crucial to Derrida's notion of ethics.[23] To borrow his words, "*ethics is hospitality*; ethics is so thoroughly coextensive with the experience of hospitality."[24] As Judith Still states, "Hospitality is both the genre and substance of Derrida's public political commitment and solidarity with immigrants, with or without appropriate documents."[25] As an Algerian-born Jewish philosopher, a marginalized subject himself despite his towering stature in contemporary Western philosophy, Derrida called for "a hospitable extension of citizenship beyond legal definitions which exclude 'undocumented aliens' or those of a different race."[26]

Derrida's Concept of *Hôte* and the Question of Hospitality in *Bandhobi*

Perhaps no other South Korean film in recent years epitomizes Derrida's philosophy of hospitality as emphatically as Shin Dong-il's third feature film *Bandhobi.* This 2009 release is the final installment of the up-and-coming director's "relationship trilogy," along with *Host & Guest* (*Pangmunja*, 2005) and *My Friend & His Wife* (*Na ŭi ch'ingu, kŭ ŭi anae*, 2008). From his debut film, Shin's oeuvre exudes a Derridean concern for the interdependent, dialogical relationship between host and guest. The English title of his debut film itself evokes Derrida's reversible concept of *hôte*, a French word which can be translated as both host and guest, "the one welcoming . . . or the one being welcomed."[27] Along with such words as *pharmakon* (neither remedy nor poison), *supplement* (neither a plus nor a minus), and *hymen* (neither the inside nor the outside), *hôte* is another Derridean deconstructionist signifier of undecidability "that can no longer be included within philosophical [binary] opposition, but which, however inhabit[s] philosophical opposition, resisting and disorganizing it, *without ever* constituting a third term, without ever leaving room for a solution in the form of speculative dialectics."[28]

In Shin's debut film, a recently divorced, underemployed film-studies lecturer named Ho-jun (Kim Chae-rok), who hides his depression behind a veneer of aggression and cynicism, is one day visited by a kind-hearted, mild-mannered Jehovah's Witness named Kye-sang (Kang Chi-hwan). When the young evangelical arrives at the door of Ho-jun's apartment in hopes of converting its occupant, he hears a faint scream seeking help from the offscreen antihero who has been locked in the bathroom (due to a doorknob failure). The visitor breaks into the studio and saves the life of the host who has passed out by exhaustion and the cold. This fortuitous event brings two figures of opposite personalities together and leads to the formation of an initially rocky and ultimately life-altering friendship. The film's Korean title, *Pangmunja* ("Guest"), attests to the outsider status of both protagonists, who do not fit in within an ultracompetitive, capitalist society where one's worth is determined by material successes such as stable corporate employment and possession of high-value properties. Shin's original title for his debut film was *Pamungaek chuin i toeda* ("Visitor Becomes Host"), which further solidifies the connection between the film's central theme and Derrida's theory.[29]

Shin's film is a Derridean experiment wherein the *hôte* (host/guest) crosses over "thresholds or frontiers: between the familial and non-familial, between the foreign and the non-foreign, the citizen and the non-citizen . . . [and] the private and the public."[30] Toward the end of the film, Kye-sang forfeits his freedom for religious conviction and goes to prison for rejecting the mandatory military service as a conscientious objector. His heartwrenching anti-war speech in the courtroom apparently affects Ho-jun, who is seen as a kinder, more responsible person in later scenes (in which he impresses his ex-wife with a voluntary offer to take care of their son overnight and gives a helping hand to his next-door neighbor, who is folding laundry). The reformed man reciprocates Kye-sang's hospitality by visiting him in prison and consoling the prisoner with hopeful words: "This time it's my turn to let you out." Through the unconditional hospitality of his unselfish guest/visitor Kye-sang (who, in a Derridean inversion, takes the role of the hospitable host), Ho-jun is able to overcome his misanthropy and reintegrate himself into nonapathetic citizenry/community.[31]

In *Bandhobi*, director Sin develops the themes of *Host & Guest* further by foregrounding two characters—Min-sŏ (Paek Chin-hŭi), a seventeen-year-old Korean high school girl, and Karim (Mahbub Alam),[32] a twenty-nine-year-old Bangladeshi migrant worker—who are marked by a multitude of differences including gender, religion, nationality, race, ethnicity, and language. The film chronicles the unlikely duo's development of friendship and (semi-)romance after the initial antagonistic first encounter in which the Korean teen accidentally picks up the Bangladeshi worker's wallet on the bus and pretends that she has not seen it. Karim follows Min-sŏ when the latter gets off the bus and raids her unzipped backpack where the lost wallet is found. Caught red-handed, the Korean girl asks for a break in exchange for the promise of "granting him a wish" should they encounter one another again. The migrant worker takes up the high-schooler's half-hearted offer when their paths inevitably cross again inside a police station, where Karim is taken after being falsely accused of assaulting an inebriated, xenophobic Korean customer in the convenience store while Min-sŏ is interrogated for a similar charge after attacking her boss's son with a fueling hose (to stall his sexual advances at a gas station). A desperate Karim enlists Min-sŏ's help in locating his former boss (Chŏng Tong-gyu), who has evaded paying his deferred wages for an extended period.

After a series of unreturned phone calls and refusals to be received at the door, Karim finally confronts the unethical Korean entrepreneur during a business meeting in a coffee shop only to be humiliated and slapped in the face—a physical act of violence that is no more stinging than the xenophobic retort that accompanies it: "Go back to your country." The demoralized Bangladeshi worker's only source of joy between performing menial work in the industrial laundry factory and hunting for his elusive former boss is to befriend Min-sŏ and share his culture and food with the nonconforming Korean teen. Living with a single parent mother (Yi Il-hwa) and her unemployed, younger boyfriend ([Pak Hyŏk-kwŏn] whom she openly antagonizes and refuses to accept as a father figure), Min-sŏ is undergoing a rebellious phase of life and channels her angst through her transformative relationship with a fellow social outcast, Karim. His positive influence in life helps her quit her unsavory part-time job as a hand-job masseuse, a quick money-earning scheme to afford expensive English lessons with a native speaker instructor, and seek healthier employment in a bookstore. Min-sŏ's deepening relationship with Karim causes a concern for her anxious mother who, after her daughter steals her car for an overnight get-away trip with the Bangladeshi man, reports the immigrant to the authorities, resulting in his deportation. The film ends with a static long-take shot of Min-sŏ, eating Bangladeshi food alone in an ethnic restaurant in memory of Karim.

From its cross-cultural title (a Bengali word that translates as "female friend," phonetically spelled in Korean), *Bandhobi* foregrounds the language and experientially unique perspective of the migrant worker as a locus of filmic enunciation. In the precredit sequence, the audience is privy to Karim's private conversation with his offscreen wife in Bangladesh on a public phone in a subway station. The casually dressed migrant worker's tight medium close-up fills the foreground of the film's first shot, against the out-of-focus backdrop of a recessional underground passage where a couple of formally outfitted Korean businessmen can be seen walking. Karim's conversation is uncomfortably personal for such a transient, public space although his linguistic difference (speaking in his native tongue Bengali) protects his privacy when he responds to his wife who is apparently threatening to divorce him for his failure to send enough money back home: "Trisha, it's hard for me too. I'll get the money this time. I promise." The husband's desperate plea is to no avail as we hear his wife hanging up on the other end of the line. In the following long shot, a weary-faced Karim is seen emerging from the subway station and walking toward the camera against the backdrop of the reconstruction site of Namdaemun (South Gate), also known as "National Treasure Number 1," which was burned down by an arson attack in 2007.[33] The imagistic contrast between the 600-year-old traditional architectural site (in the background) and the recently arrived, racially marked Southeast Asian migrant worker (in the foreground) is deliberately jarring, inviting the audience to reflect on the relationship between Korean ethnic/historical pride and the contemporary predicament of foreign workers. In a documentary-like montage, the handheld camera continues to follow the Bangladeshi migrant worker as he roams aimlessly from the traditional market area (Namdaemum Market) to the modern shopping district

FIGURE 8.2. Karim's image against the backdrop of the reconstruction site of Namdaemun (a.k.a. "National Treasure Number 1") in the opening of *Bandhobi* invites the audience to reflect on the relationship between Korean ethnocentrism and migrant workers' predicament.

(Myôngdong), without the monetary power to participate in the zealous culture of consumption surrounding him. Unlike Ancient Athens's foreigners, whose right to linguistic difference, tolerance, and hospitality are cited in the aforementioned Socrates speech, Karim is a silenced subaltern in South Korean society, an exploited "permit worker" who has been robbed of wages from a previous employer.

Intraregional industrial migration from Southeast Asian countries to the Republic of Korea dates back to 1991, when the South Korean government launched the "Foreign Industrial Trainee System" (ITS: *Sanŏp yŏnsuje*), a temporary contract labor program, to cope with a growing labor shortage in the manufacturing sector. The number of trainees increased significantly from 50,000 per year between 1994 and 1997 to 145,000 per year between 1998 and 2002.[34] The ITS was an entirely pro-business model under which "trainees" were denied basic labor rights such as minimal wages, medical benefits, and the right to organize and bargain collectively. Because trainees were not authorized to switch workplaces under the system, many of them were forced to flee from their original contract employers and became illegal in the black labor market, due to low pay, poor working conditions, and human-rights abuses. In order to correct the ills and abuses of the ITS, the South Korean government introduced the improved "Employment Permit System" (EPS: *Koyong hŏgaje*) in 2004. According to the Korean Ministry of Employment and Labor website, under the new system, "National Labor Relations Acts such as Labor Standards Act, Minimum Wages Act, Industrial Safety and Health Act are applied to foreign workers and native Koreans equally."[35] Despite the improved legal status of "permit workers" (as opposed to "industrial trainees"), the discrimination and maltreatment of migrant workers persist. Under the new system, permit workers are allowed to work in South Korea for up to three years and change employers up to three times but only on "legitimate" grounds such as company bankruptcies, temporary business closures, and human-rights violations.[36] Such short-term, limited conditions of employment fostered the mass conversion of permit workers to "illegals," as many of them were seeking better opportunities and longer stay. As of 2009, the number of undocumented workers in South Korea is estimated to be 280,000.[37]

Shin Dong-il's film directly comments on the flaws of the EPS despite its benevolent intention to protect the minimal rights of foreign guest workers. When Karim's three-year contract expires, his boss in the factory (No Chin-u) grumbles, "Damn the Employment Permit System. You have to leave once you're trained." After Karim leaves the office, the Korean boss proposes a bet to his native employee, predicting that the Bangladeshi will return to them as an illegal job seeker. The boss's premonition proves to be prophetic, and Karim indeed returns, asking for reemployment, this time as an undocumented worker. While his smiling boss professes goodwill in his initial greeting, saying, "Karim, you're always welcome here," his hospitality quickly turns out to be conditional and is undermined by the following addendum: "Since we run the risk, we'll have to cut your pay." Karim's hard life as an illegal laborer is cut short by an immigration crackdown and deportation after Min-sŏ's mother reports him to the authorities to protect her daughter after the couple runs away for an overnight road trip to the beach (where the two loners express their budding romance with a coy first kiss). Karim's final scene in the film is set in the detention center where Min-sŏ visits him and faces him across the bars. The soon-to-be deportee is dressed in a state-manufactured T-shirt which has a logo on the back, labeling him a "protected foreigner" (*poho woegukin*). Min-sŏ makes a last attempt to keep her friend from being deported, pleading to Karim, who has recently broken up with his Bangladeshi wife, "Marriage [between us] will solve everything. It's not too late"—a proposition that she has already made during the impromptu road trip. The reaction shot shows the protagonist looking affectionately at the hospitable Korean teenager in an appreciative yet declining silence.

Karim's downward spiral from a permit employee to an illegal worker to a "protected foreigner" (a detainee-deportee) demonstrates the futility of Southeast Asian workers' Korean Dream and the unreliability of state promise of equal protection for migrant workers. In *Of Hospitality*, Derrida notes the fine line delineating guest and enemy as well as hospitality and hostility.[38] The philosopher elaborates:

> Wherever the 'home' is violated, wherever at any rate a violation is felt as such, you can foresee a privatizing and even familiarist reaction, by widening the ethnocentric and nationalist, and thus xenophobic circle . . . one can become virtually xenophobic in order to protect or claim to protect one's own hospitality, the own home that makes possible one's own hospitality. . . . I want to be master at home . . . to be able to receive whomever I like there. Anyone who encroaches my "at home," on my ipseity, on my power of hospitality, on my sovereignty as host, I start to regard as an undesirable foreigner, and virtually as an enemy. This other becomes a hostile subject, and I risk becoming their hostage. Paradoxical and corrupting law: it depends on this constant collusion between traditional hospitality, hospitality in the ordinary sense, and power. This collusion is also power in its *finitude*, which is to say, the necessity for the host, for the one who receives, of choosing, electing, filtering, selecting their invitees, visitors, or guests, those to whom they decide to grant asylum, the right of visiting, or hospitality.[39]

The South Korean government's EPS is illustrative of this self-serving, conditional hospitality, which is tightly regulated and controlled by state power and which inevitably leads to the violent exclusion and deportation of guest workers once their legal status is lost due to failures of immigration policy and labor relations. It is the state and its oppressive power that intervenes and breaks up the newly formed interethnic romantic couple without giving them a chance to move beyond puppy love and engage in genuine, unconditional hospitality.

The turning point of the relationship between Karim and Min-sŏ occurs forty-six minutes into the film when the former visits the latter's apartment and home cooks a full course of Bangladeshi food for his hostess (who, with a new pimple on her forehead, has made an excuse of sickness in order to avoid going out). In this scene, Karim is the Derridean *hôte* who both receives and offers hospitality in the Korean girl's house. The guest shows up with a bagful of groceries (ingredients of Bangladeshi food) as well as a gift of a beautifully embroidered blue *topi* (a Muslim prayer cap). When Min-sŏ offers a hand to Karim who is unpacking groceries, the guest tells her to sit and rest. The embarrassed hostess mumbles, "But you are the guest (*sonnim*)," to which the hospitable man replies, "Min-sŏ, you don't know Bangladeshi food." A montage of close-ups shows the elaborate preparation of authentic Bangladeshi dishes, from the chopping of fresh vegetables to the sautéing of meat in coconut curry. In a medium two-shot, Karim and Min-sŏ are seen sharing colorful home-cooked dishes complete with jasmine rice, naan, and lentil soup. However, their cultural difference is underscored when Min-sŏ hesitantly tries to imitate Karim and eat with her fingers but quickly opts to use a fork instead. Once bellies become full and the mood lightens, Karim introduces his culture of hospitality to his Korean friend, saying, "Bangladeshi people are very hospitable. When friends come over, we don't ask them when they'll leave for months or even years." Min-sŏ jokingly asks him, "Then can I stay with you when I go there for travel?" Karim gleefully replies, "You can just live in my house." After an exchange of laughter and playful banter, the Korean girl asks about her Bangladeshi friend's hometown, Chittagong, a beautiful seaside village. After noticing her friend's homesickness, Min-sŏ changes the subject and offers to show him her bedroom.

The next shot shows the Bangladeshi man awkwardly circling around the Korean girl's room, observing picture frames on the wall and books on the shelf while Min-sŏ sits on her bed, looking up at him with a resolved demeanor. The teenaged girl breaks the uncomfortable silence, inviting him to sit next to her and then lie down. In her ill-fated attempt to reciprocate Karim's hospitality with a trick she has learned in a massage parlor, Min-sŏ ends up offending the Muslim man who stops her hand job before it gets out of control and leaves her room silently. In the next scene, Karim is seen praying in his cramped trailer home and masturbating in bed. In order to make up with her friend, Min-sŏ visits Karim's factory with a carefully wrapped gift of a healing cream for his chapped hands. This gesture of kindness quickly expels a look of discomfort in Karim's face and the two go out on a date after his shift is over. Instead of agreeing to Min-sŏ's suggestion of an amusement park, Karim proposes an even more wholesome alternative: a ping-pong hall. His younger companion quickly becomes bored, however, and the Korean girl takes her friend to her mother's karaoke parlor, an impulse visit that triggers parental anxiety, which ultimately leads to Karim's deportation. The mother's boyfriend (who assists her with odd jobs) fuels her worry with a paternalistic yet prejudiced remark, saying, "I know Min-sŏ is a unique girl but isn't that too dangerous? People like him caused a lot of trouble lately. On the news, they reported that foreign workers raped and killed a runaway teenaged girl." While the adults are suspecting Karim's potential dishonorable intention for Min-sŏ, in the karaoke room, the two friends celebrate their interethnic friendship with a duet of the Korean punk band Crying Nut's "Luxemburg," a song about global citizenship with the following lyrics:

> A, A, Argentina
> Lux, Lux, Luxemburg
> A, A, Argentina
> Lux, Lux, Luxemburg
> Let's spread out the world map
> Let's spread out my dreams
> Let's find where the countries are
> Let's sing along, Luxemburg

Saudi, where oil is overflowing
China, where too many people are
Brazil, two consecutive World Cup triumphs
America, always waging war after war
Jamaica, where reggae plays all day
Sweden, where the sun always shines
Maldives, where many go on honeymoons
Korea, where it will become one nation soon
Let's go to the world hand in hand
Regardless of skin color and language
We are all proud people
Let's all sing along, Luxemburg
Let's all sing along, Luxemburg

Outside her mother's karaoke parlor, Min-sŏ invites Karim to a lunch gathering with her American English teacher, Haines, the next day. When Karim hesitates, the Korean girl tells him to "open [his] heart," repeating his advice to her regarding the mother's boyfriend whom she intensely dislikes. During this casual meeting between Karim and Haines, along with the latter's three female pupils from an English language institute (including Min-sŏ), the Koreans' discriminatory attitude toward different foreigners—adoration for Caucasian men vs. contempt for Southeast Asian men—is indicted, or at the very least questioned. Played awkwardly by an amateur French actor, Jean-Sebastian Bressy, who performs the role with a conspicuously non-American English accent, Haines comes off as an arrogant, narcissistic Westerner who apparently enjoys his "white man's privilege" in South Korea. After asking where Karim is from and if he is a Muslim, Haines probes into the migrant worker's love life: "Do you have a Korean girlfriend?" When Karim says "No," the American man grins and insinuates his own (sexual) familiarity with Korean women: "You don't? Korean girls are so sweet!" Haines then changes the subject and asks for Karim's opinion of Korean drinking culture (which he apparently partakes in with pleasure). The Bangladeshi stoically replies, "I don't drink alcohol. . . . Muslims don't drink alcohol."

To add insult to injury, Min-sŏ blames Karim after they part with Haines: "What's wrong with you? You look small-minded. Stuffy! Look at Haines. He's enjoying life in Korea. [Is it because] you're from a poor country?" Provoked by the teenager's insensitive comment, Karim talks back and poses a series of Derridean "foreigner's questions" to Korean society and its people: "Yeah, I'm from a poor country. So, I don't know how to enjoy myself. And I have no time either. But how ridiculous are you people? You brown-nose white people, and look down on us with contempt. You're hypocrites. Want some more? You know how dirty [Koreans] are? You all screw girls in Southeast Asia and

FIGURE 8.3. An arrogant American character named Haines (left) insults Karim (right) with insensitive questions in front of an oblivious Min-sŏ (middle).

bring them to tears." He goes on to (rather liberally) translate Haines's comment on Korean girls: "You know what that white guy said? 'Sweet.' He meant you looked like whores." Now Min-sŏ takes offense and showers more hurtful, xenophobic words on him: "So? Why don't you spit it all out while you're at it? Why'd you come here? You came here for money, right? You came here to be rich, didn't you? Just admit you're envious! Don't talk about people behind their backs."

Staged in depth with a gradating focus, the separation between Karim and Min-sŏ is dramatically visualized as the Bangladeshi man turns around and recedes into the blurry background while the Korean girl remains in sharp focus, walking forward with an angry expression on her face. This most tense, strained moment in Karim and Min-sŏ's relationship reconfirms Derrida's idea of permeability between guest and enemy as well as hospitality and hostility. Temporarily blinded by national pride and a self-inflicted neocolonial inferiority complex vis-a-vis the American other, Min-sŏ refuses to see the truth in the foreigner's indictment of his host's unjust attitude and behaviors. As Judith Still paraphrases Derrida's theory,

> Nevertheless the power is not simply on the part of the host; it is not just an act of generosity to allow those designated as "foreigners," rather than "citizens," to speak—even when these are not foreigners as honoured citizens of a respected country with whom we have reciprocal hospitality arrangements (*xenia*), but foreigners defined negatively as non-citizens, perhaps even state-less. For Derrida . . . there is a structural inevitability that the stranger will always already question. . . . It is critical to the fundamental question of hospitality that where we question

> the foreigner, the foreigner puts us in question, that where the host welcomes the guest, the host has always already been welcomed.[40]

As opposed to Karim, Haines is an "honored citizen of a respected country with whom [the Republic of Korea has] reciprocal hospitality arrangements." The United States has maintained long-term hegemony in South Korea since 1945 when it proposed a division of the country along the thirty-eighth parallel in an attempt to contain the Soviet expansion into the former Japanese country and secured its occupation right to the southern half of the peninsula. Although the three-year official military occupation ended in 1948, the outbreak of the Korean War triggered the return of US troops to South Korea in 1950 and its presence became semi-permanent with the signing of the Mutual Defense Treaty in 1953. Alongside 28,000 US troops stationed in South Korea today, as an American citizen Haines is a welcomed VIP of Koreans, many of whom are willing to pay exorbitant tutoring fees to learn English from native speakers (Caucasian Americans, in particular). Albeit stereotypical and caricatured, Haines is nevertheless a reasonable allegorical figure who embodies the ethos of US exceptionalism, which can be defined as "a long pattern of imperial arrogance and righteousness, backed by military force."[41] This sense of imperial entitlement is likewise alluded to in the aforementioned "Luxemburg" lyrics, which define the United States as a war-addicted nation. As a dark-skinned Muslim permit worker from an underdeveloped country with no influence or power over his host nation, Karim is unable to claim any of the national, racial privilege that Haines and his compatriots have enjoyed in US client states throughout the Cold War era and beyond. Even Min-sŏ, Karim's best Korean friend, his *bandhobi*, turns a deaf ear to his legitimate questioning of Korean racial discrimination between Caucasian Americans and Southeast Asians.

However, Min-sŏ shows her change of heart by visiting Haines in the private English school and confronting him about his comment on "sweet" Korean girls. Although the American teacher defends his choice of wording and defines it as being "gentle, kind, [and] cute," the Korean teen adds her own (or rather, Karim's) interpretation, "Easy to handle like a whore?," and precedes to grab the Caucasian man's groin area, squeezing it with her hand. Her ensuing reconciliation with Karim is partly facilitated by this admittedly heavy-handed symbolic act of rejecting the American exceptionalism represented by Haines. After quitting the English institute and severing her ties with Haines once and for all, Min-sŏ drops by Karim's factory presumably to apologize for what she has said to him the other day. The cross-cut scene shows Karim having a modest farewell party with a group of Bangladeshi workers who sing a doleful Bengali song and toast to his happy return to the homeland. The migrant workers opine that while they are worried about the conditions in Bangladesh, they do not see that their lives in South Korea are better off. One worker reports, "We work like dogs at the factory. The boss at the next factory still beats up the migrant workers." Another worker responds, "There is nothing much we can do but shut up and keep working," a comment which challenges the South Korean government's claim of equal labor rights protection under the EPS. A third man intervenes and reports that he recently met a Korean woman and marrying her will solve a visa problem. Another man replies, "Guys like you give Koreans bad images of us." Throughout the entire long-take conversation scene, Karim (relegated to the background) remains nonparticipatory and silent with his eyes cast downward at his plate on the dinner table.

The long-delayed reconciliation between the two protagonists occurs one hour and twenty minutes into the film, when Karim visits the bookstore where Min-sŏ works part-time. On a bench in a park, the two friends catch up with one another's missed news including Min-sŏ's punishment of Haines with her "magical hand" and Karim's breakup with his wife. Later that night, Min-sŏ steals her mother's car in order to take Karim to the beach so that it might remind him of his seaside hometown, Chittagong. Once they reach the destination, Karim rushes to the dark waterfront and screams in his native tongue, "I didn't come to Korea for this! What can I do now? I have been used like a dog. You crazy Koreans! You're all slaves like us. I just wanted to be happy. Allah! Is this the world you've created? I just wanted to be happy." Captured in an extreme long-shot and via hand-held camera with no artificial lighting, this documentary-like scene is all the more powerful as the actor who plays Karim, Mahbub Alam, came to South Korea as a migrant worker in 1999 and labored for twelve to fifteen hours a day in plastic and furniture factories.[42] Throughout the nearly two-minute long-take, Min-sŏ is seen silently observing Karim's desperate cry with her back turned toward the camera. When the camera cuts to her reaction in a close-up shot, the teenager's face is full of empathy and pathos as if she understood his anguish despite their linguistic difference. Her unconditional acceptance of the foreigner's pain and suffering in this confession scene, a far cry from her immature reaction after their meeting with Haines, is a pivotal prelude to her declaration of absolute hospitality in the following scenes.

As the ultimate gesture of hospitality, Min-sŏ "proposes" to Karim twice (ostensibly as a means to secure his legal status but perhaps also as an expression of her emotional attachment): in the car at the beach after the two share a first kiss and in the detention center where Karim awaits his deportation. This marriage proposal is highly unconventional not only because it is initiated by a woman but also because she is a minor who is unable to get married without parental consent. Given her mother's opposition to her relationship with the illegal immigrant, it is unlikely that their matrimonial union could have come to fruition even if Karim had given his consent. Regardless, the gift of a marriage that Min-sŏ offers is the consummation of her pure, unconditional, absolute hospitality for her best friend and soul mate. Karim reciprocates her kindness and generosity through his graceful, silent rejection of her gift. He refuses to take advantage of Min-sŏ's friendship for his personal gain and accepts deportation. Although Derrida emphasizes that reciprocity never be factored into consideration in offering unconditional hospitality, when Min-sŏ reciprocates Karim's hospitality (his offer of letting her stay in his Bangladeshi home permanently in an earlier scene) with a marriage proposal, their friendship reaches its highest level. Even though Karim has left the narrative (and South Korea) before the film's dénouement, Min-sŏ's elaborate ritual of eating Bangladeshi food with her fingers (as Karim did earlier in the film) in the final scene attests to his lingering influence. This static medium-shot, which lasts for four minutes over the end credits, furthermore invites the viewer to take the place of the absent *hôte* (host/guest), Karim, whose spirit is symbolically watching over her across the table.

Dressed in feminine business attire (a black cardigan, frilly skirt, and high heels), and adorned with longer, curlier hair, Min-sŏ looks nothing like the tomboyish, angry teenager who had earlier attacked a series of authority male figures throughout the film: the flirty boss's son whom she showered with a gas hose; her stepfather-to-be whom she openly cursed and scorned; crackdown immigration officers whom she hit to prevent Karim from being taken away from her; Karim's ex-boss whose house she raided after her friend's deportation to insult him in front of his family. Such a transformation may seem regressive from a feminist perspective, but Min-sŏ ultimately proves to be the most ethical character of the film, someone who is capable of learning to give unconditional hospitality that escapes the state and other adult characters. In this understated final scene, which suppresses directorial interventions such as close-ups, nondiegetic music, and camera movements, Shin Dong-il is perhaps giving the audience a much-needed pause, an opportunity to reflect on the rite of passage that Min-sŏ has taken throughout the narrative, from xenophobia to tolerance, from hostility to hospitality, and from solipsism to responsibility for the other. Perhaps too he is seeking to inspire the most cosmopolitan members of that audience to join in the process of building a better future of multicultural Korea.

A Smile: Multicultural Pedagogy in *Where Is Ronny?*

Released one year prior to *Bandhobi, Where Is Ronny?* is an understated yet effective drama of multiculturalism, one that has received little critical attention both inside and outside South Korea. Like *Bandhobi*, it is a low-budget independent film that revolves around the friendship between a native protagonist and a Bangladeshi migrant worker.[43] From the narrative's outset, the film cinematically connects Bangladesh (whose exotic landscape is featured in a series of traveling shots during the precredit sequence) and Ansan, a multicultural industrial city on the outskirts of Seoul, where an estimated 70,000 foreigners reside, approximately half of whom remain undocumented.[44] The film's protagonist Kim In-ho (Yu Chun-sang) is seen arriving in Ansan Station toward the end of the seamless, border-crossing montage that segues from the overcrowded Bangladeshi train to the Metro system connecting Seoul to its satellite cities. In-ho is introduced as the owner and coach of a provincial Taekwondo school (symbolically named *Hang'uk Ch'aeyukkwan*, or the "Korean Gym"), which is apparently struggling to stay afloat. In order to publicize his business and attract new recruits, Coach Kim prepares for the school's ten-year anniversary Taekwondo tournament. In the midst of mustering all his energy for the upcoming event, In-ho is offered a voluntary post as the captain of a new neighborhood watch (the "crime prevention watch," or *pambyŏmdae*), which purports to preempt the crimes that will be committed by migrant workers.

In a neighborhood meeting at the local Chinese restaurant, several residents vocalize their complaints. One person says, "When I run into them [foreigners] at night and our eyes meet, I feel scared out of my wits." Similar comments—"It's not good for [my daughter] to walk around at night" and "Ever since they've come here, our neighborhood's image has gone bad. Real estate prices are going down"—follow. At the same time that these xenophobic remarks are being spoken, a quiet and distracted Coach Kim, not unlike Karim in the farewell party scene in *Bandhobi*, is seen on the left side of the frame, mechanically nodding his head in the foreground. Even after being nominated as the captain of the proposed "crime prevention watch," he remains nonchalant and betrays no immediate commitment or rejection. The indecisive coach, however, reluctantly takes the job under peer pressure. On the first night of his patrol with two neighbors, In-ho cracks down on the makeshift street stand of a Bangladeshi jewelry peddler (Mahbub Alam, the same actor who plays Karim in *Bandhobi*) who does not speak Korean. Armed with a translator, his compatriot Duhin (Robin Shiek), the insulted Bangladeshi man whose name is later revealed as Ronny storms into In-ho's gym during the Taekwondo tournament and challenges In-ho to a fistfight. An initially confident Coach Kim ends up experiencing the biggest humiliation of his life in public, when he gets knocked unconscious by the foreign man's pile-driving punch.

After setting up this intriguing premise, the film follows In-ho's single-minded quest for the elusive Ronny, possibly seeking revenge or, at the very least, a redemptive rematch. Instead of finding the man responsible for ruining his reputation (the disastrous match results in In-ho's loss of the few remaining pupils at his school), the shamed coach accidentally reencounters Duhin,

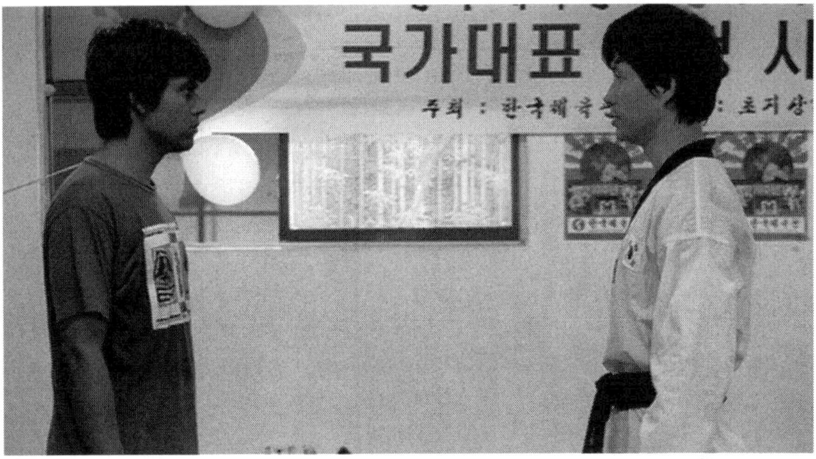

FIGURE 8.4. The Taekwondo coach Kim In-ho (right) encounters an unexpected challenge from a Bangladeshi peddler named Ronny (left) in *Where Is Ronny?*

the young man who accompanied Ronny at the tournament. Although the depressed In-ho is initially antagonistic toward the ever-cheerful Bangladeshi peddler (upon whom the former cruelly lavishes curses and scorn), his demeanor gradually softens and he comes to accept the illegal immigrant as a "friend" during their eventful yet futile journey together in search of Ronny. After procuring information that Ronny has returned to Bangladesh, an injured and hospitalized Duhin faces deportation, a fact that is unknown to In-ho, who is responsible for reporting to immigration authorities the whereabouts of a gang of Bangladeshi immigrants who have previously attacked him (without realizing that his friend is in their company). The film ends with In-ho's journey to Bangladesh in search of the titular character, returning to the temporality and location of the precredit, prologue sequence. In a dialogue-free epilogue, the man is seen undertaking one of South Korean cinema's many "movie migrations," traveling by riverboat until he reaches a remote destination where an old farm house stands. He cautiously knocks on its blue door and holds his breath for a response. In reverse shot, the offscreen occupant of the house (presumably Ronny) slowly opens the door, admitting a swath of natural light into the dark foreground. A static close-up shot fixates on In-ho's face, which brightens into a big smile before the screen fades out to the end credits.

Where Is Ronny? reiterates some of the narrative paradigms and ideological pitfalls of acclaimed art-house European or American films concerned with multiculturalism, such as Michael Haneke's *Caché* (2005), Ramin Bahrani's *Goodbye Solo* (2008), and Christian Zübert's *Three Quarter Moon* (*Dreiviertelmond*, 2011). In these latter motion pictures, the plight of marginalized immigrant groups (Algerians in Paris, Senegalese in North Carolina, and Turks in Germany, respectively) is evoked as a means of interrogating the troubled psyche of a native protagonist. Ultimately, what is searched for and found at the end of the Korean film is In-ho's once-unstable self, and Ronny remains an offscreen "other" who seems to be little more than a Hitchcockian MacGuffin. Despite this, however, *Where Is Ronny?* stands out among a small group of *tamunhwa yŏnghwa* released in South Korea over the past few years for its subtlety, understatement, and profundity. Kim In-ho is a deeply flawed yet relatable individual. He does not advocate illegal workers' rights like the eccentric high school teacher Tong-ju does in *Punch*; nor does he harass an "evil" industrialist who has robbed his foreign friend, as the sassy school girl Min-sŏ does in *Bandhobi*. He remains apathetic toward the neighborhood "problem" of immigrants yet reluctantly participates in police duty on behalf of his xenophobic neighbors. At one point, like Min-sŏ does in *Bandhobi*, In-ho betrays his own xenophobia outright when he tells Duhin, "If you came to make money, then work hard and go back to your country." He is not above reporting undocumented workers to authorities over a petty bar brawl and, as a result, becomes unwittingly responsible for Duhin's leg injury (caused by the latter's attempt to jump from a window to escape an immigration crackdown) and ensuing deportation. It is precisely because of In-ho's utter disregard for the politics of multiculturalism throughout the narrative that his subtle changes at the end speak volumes to ordinary moviegoers on both sides of the immigration issue.

In-ho's radiant smile, a smile epitomizing Derrida's notion of unconditional hospitality, in the final shot implies that he now sees Ronny—and perhaps, by extension, all Southeast Asian immigrant workers—as a friend (*ch'ingu*, an endearing term he uses to define his relationship with Duhin to a hospital administrator in an earlier scene) rather than as an enemy. Looking directly at the camera, In-ho invites viewers to smile back and also open their hearts, if only a little, toward undocumented immigrant workers living in the shadows of South Korean society. The character's facial response, his visual registering of emotion, might very well be the most persuasive call for multiculturalism committed to the Korean screen in recent years.

The self-reflexive final shot of *Where Is Ronny?* emulates the direct address technique often associated with Brechtian cinema, pioneered by maverick French New Wave filmmakers such as François Truffaut and Jean-Luc Godard. Both Truffaut's *The 400 Blows* (*Les quatre cents coups*, 1959) and Godard's *Breathless* (*À bout de souffle*, 1960), the seminal works of the Nouvelle Vague movement, conclude with direct-address shots in which each protagonist looks straight into the camera (at the audience), thus breaking the fourth wall and the fiction's illusion. But it is noteworthy that in *The 400 Blows*, the subject of the gaze represents social problems associated with juvenile delinquency and youth crimes. At the conclusion of *Where Is Ronny?*, the Korean social problem that the audience is ultimately confronted with is not "the question of the foreigner" (*la question de l'étranger*), but "the question of the host" (*la question de l'hôte*). It is the onscreen *Korean* self, not the offscreen Bangladeshi other, that is laid bare for collective scrutiny and interrogation. The structure of the point-of-view shot facilitates spectatorial identification with the impartial, non-Korean gaze and gives the Korean audience an opportunity for self-reflection while generating a subtle form of social criticism.

Liberal multiculturalism films such as *Where is Ronny?* and *Bandhobi* imagine a utopian space in which Koreans and non-Koreans learn to reciprocate Derridean absolute hospitality, despite the flaws and limitations of state immigration policies. These and other recent films exploring the lives of recent immigrants from Ghana, Turkey, and Bangladesh not only diversify the existing representational schemas by adding "new" ethnicities and nationalities to the mix, but also differ from the earlier cycle featuring foreign brides (such as *Failan, My Wedding Campaign, You Are My Sunshine*, and *Thirst*) by locating the no-longer frightening specter of "otherness" at the site of masculine, rather than feminine, identity formation. However potentially progressive these works are in the state-sanctioned project of cultural enlightenment, they offer only a taste of the tangy difference that has long been a part—suppressed though it was—of the Korean national character. As such, they are likely to leave the most forward-thinking audiences "thirsty" for more in-depth cinematic explorations of immigrant communities and far fewer blood-themed explanations for the nation's much-celebrated, yet deeply misleading, unity. However, the meager domestic box-office records of *Where Is Ronny?* and *Bandhobi*—1,478 and 7,687 admissions, respectively—as well as the xenophobic online backlash against the latter film (which received a controversial "Age 19 or Above Only" rating) forecast a gloomy outlook for the immediate future of Korean multiculturalism.[45]

Conclusion

Into "Spreadable" Spaces

Netflix, YouTube, and the Question of Cultural Translatability

There was a time, not long ago (in the mid-1990s), when the only South Korean film titles commercially available on home video (VHS or laserdisc) in the United States were director Pae Yong-gyun's *Why Has Bodhi-Dharma Left for the East* (*Talmaga tongkkot ŭro kan kkadakŭn*, 1989) and Pak Chŏl-su's *301/302* (*Samgongil, samgongi*, 1995). Categorized as a Buddhist-themed art-house film and a bizarre cult thriller, respectively, these two titles could only be found at specialty video stores known for exceptionally wide foreign selections, such as Kim's Video and Evergreen Video in New York City's East Village, certainly not at franchised national chains such as the now-defunct Blockbuster or Hollywood Video. Things have changed significantly over the past two decades. In fact, a number of Korean-language films, from big-budget genre flicks such as *Masquerade* (*Kwanghae: Wang i toen namja*, 2012), *The Tower* (*T'awŏ*, 2012), *My Way* (*Mai wei*, 2011), and *Woochi* (*Chŏn Uch'i*, 2009) to smaller auteur films including Kim Ki-duk (Kim Ki-dŏk)'s *Pieta* (*P'iet'a*, 2012), Lee Chang-dong (Yi Ch'ang-dong)'s *Poetry* (*Si*, 2010), and Park Chan-wook (Pak Ch'an-uk)'s *Thirst* (*Pakjwi*, 2009), can be rented at local video stores (those that still exist), purchased through Amazon's website, and streamed online via Netflix, Hulu, and other virtual spaces. Although South Korean cinema has not yet achieved massive commercial popularity in North

America or Europe and remains relatively marginalized compared with other East Asia cinemas (i.e. those of China, Hong Kong, and Japan), the increased visibility of Korean cultural products in US DVD/Blu-Ray and video-on-demand (VOD) markets is an important indicator of their ever-expanding global constituency outside the local/regional context.

In his book *Modernity at Large: Cultural Dimensions of Globalization*, Arjun Appadurai introduces five neologisms pertaining to "global cultural flows": ethnoscapes, mediascapes, technoscapes, financescapes, and ideoscapes.[1] The term "mediascapes," according to the author, refers both to "the distribution of the electronic capabilities to produce and disseminate information (newspapers, magazines, television stations, and film-production studios), which are now available to a growing number of private and public interests throughout the world, and to the images of the world created by these media."[2] In the age of global migrations of people, images, technologies, capital, and ideologies (as represented by the aforementioned five "scapes"), Appadurai believes that "the United States is no longer the puppeteer of a world system of images but is only one node of a complex transnational construction of imaginary landscapes."[3] Considering Hollywood's persistent dominance of the global film market (as of this writing, six major studios—Disney, Fox, Paramount, Sony, Universal, and Warner Bros.—hold 63% of the world's box-office share), it would be premature to characterize global mediascapes as an egalitarian cultural arena where the US film industry is an equal partner with its minion-like competitors. However, the ascendancy of South Korean popular culture (referred to as *Hallyu*, or the Korean Wave) in the Asia-Pacific region, as well as Hollywood's attempt to assimilate this regional leadership through cross-cultural, American remakes of Korean films, such as *The Lake House* (2007), *Mirrors* (2008), *My Sassy Girl* (2008), *The Uninvited* (2009), and *Oldboy* (2013), collectively point to a shift in transnational influence. While South Korean cinema has historically been nurtured and guided by external forces (American, Japanese, and Hong Kong in particular), the direction of the cultural flow has been reversed or become bilateral in the past decade and a half, a phenomenon that would have been unthinkable prior to the new millennium.

From *Dachimawa Lee* to *Gangnam Spy*: Disjunctive Cultural Flows

In an article entitled "Hong Kong Film and the New Cinephilia," David Desser attributes the availability of new technologies and communication platforms (e.g. the Internet, VCDs, DVDs) to the rise of what he calls a "new cinephilia" among young, "Asianized" Euro-American film buffs who are drawn to Hong Kong's gritty, often spectacularly choreographed action cinema.[4] If the since-eclipsed market of VCDs helped to disseminate Hong Kong films among Asian diasporic communities as well as Western cult film aficionados in the 1990s, a newer technology makes theatrically unreleased Korean films available to North American consumers today. Although it is rare to see Korean-language films in US theaters outside of large metropolitan areas or college towns, stateside audiences can readily access the latest Korean blockbusters such as *The Thieves* (*Todukdŭl*, 2012) and *War of the Arrows* (*Ch'oejong pyŏnggi hwal*, 2011) or, on the other end of the spectrum, recent Cannes Palme d'Or contenders such as Im Sang-soo (Im Sang-su)'s *The Housemaid* (*Hanyŏ*, 2010) and Hong Sang-soo (Hong Sang-su)'s *In Another Country* (*Tarŭn nara aesŏ*, 2012) through Netflix's instant streaming service. As of June 2014, the California-based, on-demand video powerhouse carries 135 Korean-language movies on Netflix Instant and 53 additional films for DVD-by-mail rentals. To put those numbers into perspective, Netflix carries 212 French films, 152 Chinese/Hong Kong films, 136 Indian films, 89 German films, 89 Japanese films, 85 Italian films, 55 Spanish films, and 25 Russian films for instant streaming.

Once only accessible in institutional venues such as museums, film festivals, and college campuses, contemporary South Korean cinema is now at the fingertips of audiences in the United States, Canada, Mexico, South America, the United Kingdom, Ireland, Netherlands, Norway, Sweden, Denmark, and Finland—countries covered by Netflix services. Even though the profile of South Korean cinema on Netflix Instant is impressive for a foreign film category, one should be mindful of the fact that such presence does not guarantee patronage. In *Spreadable Media: Creating Value and Meaning in a Networked Culture*, Henry Jenkins, Sam Ford, and Joshua Green contend: "Online retail and rental operations such as Amazon and Netflix . . . can maintain more extensive backlists of titles, many of which may get little circulation in any given week but which, over time, recoup their costs and may even turn significant profits. Further, for the distributor in such a model, even the titles which never turn a profit are valuable in building the company's reputation as a comprehensive source for material."[5] As one of twenty-one regional/national subcategories of "foreign movies" (along with African, Australian, Belgian, British, Chinese, Indian, Italian, Japanese, Latin American, Middle Eastern, New Zealand, Russian, Scandinavian, Southeast Asian, Spanish, Greek, German, French, Eastern European, and Dutch movies), Netflix's Korean film collection is a part of an inclusive branding strategy for the "world's leading internet television network with over 57 million members in more than 50 countries enjoying more than two billion hours of TV shows and movies per month, including original series."[6] In other words, contemporary South Korean cinema functions as an essential way for Netflix to enrich its extensive foreign title library, a means of achieving product differentiation for the online video rental service-turned-Internet television network, which recently ventured into producing original web television series such as *House of Cards*

(2013–) and *Orange Is the New Black* (2013–). As one of the newest discoveries for Western cinephiles, South Korean films can bring cultural cachet, if not huge profits, to Netflix, a company whose target demographic encompasses a wide array of young urbanites with diverse tastes in world cinema.

As Appadurai points out, global cultural flows across national borders inevitably hinge upon "disjunctures" and "chaos" rather than order and stability.[7] In order to recognize "the uneven nature of these flows," Jenkins, Ford, and Green replace the term "global" (used by Appadurai and others) with "transnational."[8] The uneven, transnational cultural flux from South Korea to the United States is exemplified by the fact that the highest-grossing Korean-language film in North America until recently is not Bong Joon-ho (Pong Chun-ho)'s CGI-infused monster movie *The Host* (*Goemul*, 2006), but rather Kim Ki-duk's meditative *Spring, Summer, Fall, Winter . . . and Spring* (*Pom yŏrŭm kaŭl kyŏul kŭrio pom*, 2003), a critically acclaimed yet esoteric art film seen by a mere 30,000 Korean theatergoers.[9] Surprisingly, Kim's film became an art-house hit in the US market, where it garnered 370,000 admissions and grossed $2.4 million for its distributor Sony Pictures Classics.

In her book *The South Korean Film Renaissance*, Jinhee Choi identifies Kim's Buddhist fable, which is set entirely in a forest setting severed from contemporary social realities, as a "festival-driven film," one that caters to "the demands of a specific audience" and effaces the distinctiveness of "Korean cinema as a national cinema."[10] However, the establishment of a clean-cut binary between "national cinemas" and "festival-driven films" may prove to be problematic. The Grand Bell (*Taejong*) Award's recognition of *Spring, Summer, Fall, Winter . . . and Spring* as the Best Picture of 2003, the highest honor for local films, as well as the South Korean government's submission of the same film to the Academy Awards competition attest to interlocking connections and mutually enforcing relationships between transnational/global and national/local forces. For art cinema trailblazers in South Korea and other nations, the Western art-house market is crucial for their professional well-being and survival since the size of the local, or even *regional*, market for noncommercial, alternative films is negligible and ever-shrinking, due to the perpetual push for vertical integration and conglomeration, modeled after the Hollywood industry. In other words, this different mode of transnational reception can provide options and opportunities to both local filmmakers and state bureaucrats who strive to preserve cultural diversity in the face of homogenization and commercialization.

An example of disjunctive trans-Pacific flow is found in Netflix's and Hulu's labeling of Ryoo Seung-wan (Ryu Sŭng-wan)'s 2008 Manchurian Western/espionage comedy *Dachimawa Lee* (*Tach'imawa Ri*) as *Gangnam Spy*, an overt allusion to the Korean rapper Psy's 2012 music video "Gangnam Style." The latter cultural phenomenon became the most-watched viral video in the history of YouTube with over 900 million hits generated in the course of a five-month period (as of June 2014, the video has generated more than 2 billion views). The US retroactive retitling of *Dachimawa Lee* is anachronistic on two fronts: Not only does Ryoo's film predate "Gangnam Style" by four years but also the titular district of Seoul (south of the Han River) was not even developed during the colonial era of the 1940s, the film's temporal setting. Although it is now Seoul's most affluent area, one that is packed with upscale apartment complexes, commercial skyscrapers, shopping centers, and entertainment zones, the urban development of Gangnam did not begin until the 1960s under Park Chung Hee's regime and its current reputation as South Korea's educational mecca (the coveted 8th School District) did not emerge until the 1980s. The film's Korean title is the phonetic inscription of the Japanese phrase *dachimawari* (literally translated as "standing and circling around"), referring to the "one vs. many" fight scenes that can be found in kabuki theater as well as samurai and yakuza films. Shortened as *dachimari*, the phrase was widely used as a shorthand for action scenes in South Korea's 1970s film industry. In the Korean film title, there is a gratuitous space between *dachimawa* and *ri*, and the final syllable of the Japanese phrase is misappropriated to signify the homophone Lee (Yi), the last name of the Korean protagonist—an Austin Powers-like secret agent who is entrusted with the mission of retrieving a stolen golden Buddha statute for a group of independence fighters battling the Japanese military in 1940s Manchuria. As a border-crossing action film whose settings include Shanghai, Manchuria, New Jersey, the Swiss Alps, and Tokyo (with Korean sets and locations standing in for foreign landscapes), *Dachimawa Lee* is a zany parody of not only the James Bond series, but also Korean action cinema of earlier decades characterized by postproduction dubbing, awkward dialogue, cultural inauthenticity, over-the-top fisticuffs, and excessive melodrama.

When transplanted into global digital spaces and repackaged for Western consumption, the fighting (*dachimawari*) Agent Lee (Im Wŏn-hŭi) has turned into the "Gangnam Spy," thus deracinating the comic hero's indebtedness to Korean and Japanese action cinema of earlier decades and recontextualizing him in relation to the contemporaneous YouTube-powered, K-pop craze which transformed Psy, a second-rate local pop singer, into an overnight global star in the second half of 2012. The anachronistic English title for *Dachimawa Lee* serves as a convergence point in which different eras (the 1940s, the 1970s, and the 2010s) and different digital platforms (Netflix, Hulu, and YouTube) intersect and interact, creating new meanings of a transnational text.

Korean Convergence Culture: Watching Cinematic Classics on YouTube

In her article "Cultural Studies and New Media," Caroline Bassett defines digital convergence as "a process through which previously discrete media forms, media industries and media contents are drawn together, so that many old media forms are re-mediated, and many new forms are produced, although distinctions between new, old and recombinant media are rarely absolute."[11] Media scholar Henry Jenkins has coined the phrase "convergence culture" to denote spaces "where old and new media collide, where grassroots and corporate media intersect, where the power of the media producer and the power of the media consumer interact in unpredictable ways."[12] According to Jenkins, "convergence" refers to "the flow of content across multiple media platforms, the cooperation between multiple media industries, and the migratory behavior of media audiences who will go almost anywhere in search of the kinds of entertainment experiences they want."[13] As an example of convergence culture, Jenkins cites the pretheatrical mobile phone release of the Bollywood film *Rok Sako To Rok Lo* (2004), which is reported to be the first full-length feature film to premiere on a wireless cellular network.[14] *Spreadable Media*, Jenkins's latest co-authored book, introduces the concept of "spreadability," which challenges the prevailing frameworks used to describe new/social media phenomena such as "memes" and "viral" forms of communication. Instead of being passively infected or contaminated by "viral media," according to this theory, audiences function as "grassroots intermediaries" and "play an active role in 'spreading' content" through social network platforms such as YouTube, Facebook, and Twitter.[15] For Jenkins and his co-authors, spreadable media not only facilitates activity within participatory fan cultures but also "represents a potential force for globalization, understood as 'an intensification of global connectedness' achieved through shifting the kinds of culture that people around the world can access."[16]

A case study through which to test Jenkins's theories of convergence culture and spreadable media is the state-subsidized nonprofit Korean Film Archive (KOFA)'s YouTube channel (www.youtube.com/user/koreanfilm). After debuting on May 10, 2012, this channel, which has been titled "Korean Classic Film Theater," captured the attention of audiences around the world, and today has generated approximately 5 million views in total. As of February 2015, more than 55,000 subscribers have accessed its content. It currently offers, free of charge, ninety-eight subtitled Korean classic and contemporary films, from the earliest surviving motion picture *Sweet Dream* (*Mimong*, 1936) to Hong Sang-soo's debut feature *The Day a Pig Fell into the Well* (*Toejiga umul ae ppajin nal*, 1996). Among the case studies singled out for textual analysis in this book, Yu Hyŏn-mok's *The Stray Bullet* (a.k.a. *Aimless Bullet*, *Obalt'an*,

1960), Shin Sang-ok (Sin Sang-ok)'s *Romance Papa* (*Romaensŭ ppappa*, 1960), Yi Pong-rae's *Third Rate Manager* (a.k.a. *A Petty Middle Manager, Samdŭng kwajang*, 1961), Yi Hyŏng-p'yo's *Under the Sky of Seoul* (*Sŏul ŭi chibung mit*, 1961), and Kang Tae-jin's *Mr. Park* (*Pak sŏbang*, 1960) and *The Coachman* (*Mabu*, 1961) are available for free streaming. On the Korean Classic Film Theater channel, films are classified according to seventeen different (and overlapping) playlists:

1. New arrivals (12 videos)
2. Liked videos (35 videos)
3. Top 10 (10 videos)
4. HD (31 videos)
5. 1930s (1 video)
6. 1940s (3 videos)
7. 1950s (13 videos)
8. 1960s (37 videos)
9. 1970s (11 videos)
10. 1980s (21 videos)
11. 1990s (11 videos)
12. Director Kim Su-yong (6 videos)
13. Director Lee Man-hee (Yi Man-hŭi, 7 videos)
14. Director Shin Sang-ok (8 videos)
15. Director Im Kwon-taek (Im Kwŏn-t'aek, 7 videos)
16. Director Kim Ki-young (Kim Ki-yŏng, 7 videos)
17. Director Chŏng Chin-u (3 videos)

It should be pointed out that the KOFA film channel was launched as a part of the "Korea Go Global" project agreement, which had been signed between Google Korea and the Ministry of Culture, Sports and Tourism in November 2011. The primary goal of this project is the worldwide circulation and promotion of Korean Wave (*Hallyu*) content—in particular, K-pop and K-drama (Korean television dramas)—via YouTube, a video-sharing social media platform owned by Google. Although the main agenda of the "Korea Go Global" project is to establish a YouTube channel devoted to K-pop (which was launched in December 2012), KOFA's Korean Classic Film Theater became the first tangible outcome of the collaborative partnership between Google and the South Korean government. Google Korea invested $70,000 in the project in order to cover the costs of English translation and the subtitling of Korean-language films to be posted on the channel. KOFA had already cleared copyrights of motion pictures not in public domain (post-1962) for the VOD service on its own website (where 380 Korean films can be streamed). Chang Kwang-hyŏn, manager of KOFA Media Services Department, points to the advantage of the YouTube channel, saying: "In the past, the only way to promote Korean film classics abroad was through international film festivals. But you can only send films that are requested [by festival organizers]. This usually meant films by famous directors, such as Im Kwon-taek and Kim Ki-young. There was no control on our part over which films to send and promote. YouTube gave us an opportunity to expose diverse Korean films to mass audiences worldwide without such limitations."[17]

In an article entitled "Re-worlding Culture?," Kent A. Ono and Jungmin Kwon argue that YouTube has "significantly altered the status of K-pop in the world as a cultural force."[18] According to Ono and Kwon, YouTube is K-pop friendly for three reasons. First, by foregrounding the visuality of music performances (putting emphasis on dance routines/choreography as well as the physical attractiveness of K-pop stars), YouTube enables the transmission of K-pop to international fans across language barriers. Second, as a new media platform with easy accessibility and global outreach, YouTube is an ideal marketing tool for K-pop producers and promoters. Finally, as an interactive social media site, YouTube allows K-pop fans to build cyber communities through comment streams and fan videos.[19] Although the popularity of KOFA's Korean Classic Film Theater channel may seem like "small potatoes" compared with that of the YouTube K-pop channel (www.youtube.com/music/kpop), which has over 808,000 subscribers (as of February 2015), this video-sharing website could become South Korean cinema's principal platform or launch pad in the coming years. Moreover, readers of this book might find that YouTube can serve as a useful audiovisual companion, for one can access full, subtitled videos of *Untold Scandal* (*Sŭk'aendŭl: Chosŏn namnyŏ sangyŏljisa*, 2003) and its star Bae Yong-joon (Pae Yong-jun)'s fan-subbed interviews; listen to the original soundtrack of *The Good, the Bad, the Weird* (*Chotŭn nom, nappŭn nom, isanghan nom*, 2008) and watch the original Korean ending (which has been cut from international releases); sample the best action scenes from *Oldboy* (*Oldŭ poi*, 2003) and watch fan video reviews comparing Park Chan-wook's original film with Spike Lee's remake; and legally purchase a digital copy of *The Host* provided by the film's US distributor Magnolia Pictures.

Jenkins, Ford, and Green state that spreadable media are "not just those texts which circulate broadly but also those that achieve particularly deep engagement within a niche community."[20] Although unavailable for mass consumption in multiplex theaters in the Western world, South Korean cinema has become a part of global spreadable media culture in recent years. Jenkins and his co-authors elaborate:

> Spreadability has increased diversity. . . . In theory, networked communication allows diverse groups to speak with each other. . . . [T]he online communities which grow up around fansubbing and the exchange of media content between

> different parts of the world have the potential to be context-rich sites, which can foster deeper understandings across cultural differences. . . . For the moment, this deep cultural empathy may be largely the stuff of the utopian imagination, yet the kinds of cultural practices we describe . . . represent perhaps our greatest hope for making such understandings a lived reality.[21]

A caveat attends such utopic visions of spreadable media and its capacity to foster cultural empathy across national borders. The concept of transnational cinema is instrumental to contemporary East Asian film criticism as national boundaries are made more permeable in the age of digital cinephilia (or what David Desser terms "new cinephilia"), when vast numbers of individuals around the world can access theatrically unreleased Asian films via Internet venues such as Netflix, Hulu, YouTube, and YesAsia.com (a Hong Kong-based online vendor for East Asian films and television series catering to the English-speaking market). The web-based circulation of media texts among techno-literate, younger audiences should be distinguished from the traditional, theater-based consumption of international art cinema in film festivals, where attendees are granted access to contextualizing information through catalog literature, prescreening introductions, and postscreening Q&A sessions. Whether or not intended by the filmmakers, their motion pictures are subject to transnational decoding by global audiences who might consume popular texts without cultural knowledge about the region in which they were produced.

Sassy Girls and Oldboys: Transnational Remakes

South Korean cinema is currently enjoying unprecedented global circulation, sparking passionate forms of fandom in "spreadable" digital spaces. Our aim in these closing pages, however, is not to celebrate the recent success of the Korean culture industry or its expanding footprint. Rather, we are interested in exploring lingering questions about the transnational translatability of South Korean cinema in a context of global consumption, industrial recycling, and fan remixing. Perhaps the most notable outcome of South Korean cinema's rising reputation in North America is Hollywood's recent attempts to remake Korean box-office hits. Over the past decade, major studios (including DreamWorks, Miramax, MGM, Paramount, Twentieth Century-Fox, Universal, and Warner Bros.) have purchased remake rights to nearly two dozen South Korean films, including *Il Mare* (*Siwŏlae*, 2000), *Joint Security Area* (*Kongdong kyŏngbiguyŏk*, 2000), *My Sassy Girl* (*Yŏpgijŏkin kŭnyŏ*, 2001), *Hi, Dharma* (*Dalmaya nolja*, 2001), *My Wife Is a Gangster* (*Chop'ok manura*, 2001), *Addicted* (*Chungdok*, 2002), *Phone* (*P'on*, 2002), *Jail Breakers* (*Kwangbokjŏl t'ŭksa*, 2002), *My Teacher, Mr. Kim* (*Sŏnsaeng Kim Pong-du*,

2003), *Into the Mirror* (*Kyŏul sok ŭro*, 2003), *A Tale of Two Sisters* (*Changhwa, Hongryŏn*, 2003), *Oldboy* (*Oldŭ poi*, 2003), *The Doll Master* (*Inhyŏngsa*, 2004), *A Moment to Remember* (*Nae mŏri sok ŭi chiugae*, 2004), *Sympathy for Lady Vengeance* (*Ch'iljŏlhan Kŭjassi*, 2005), *A Bittersweet Life* (*Talch'omhan insaeng*, 2005), *The Chaser* (*Ch'ugŏkja*, 2008), *The Yellow Sea* (*Hwanghae*, 2010), *Confession of Murder* (*Naega salinbŏm ida*, 2012), *Running Man* (*Rŏnningmaen*, 2013), and *New World* (*Sinsaegae*, 2013). Among these titles, *Il Mare, My Sassy Girl, Into the Mirror, A Tale of Two Sisters*, and *Oldboy* have already been remade into American versions, and a few additional titles (*A Moment to Remember, Sympathy for Lady Vengeance, A Bittersweet Life, The Chaser*, and *New World*) are currently in production.[22]

It is noteworthy that none of the Hollywood films based on Korean genre films have successfully achieved the cult status of the originals in both Asian and international markets. For example, Twentieth Century-Fox's *My Sassy Girl* (2008) failed to "Americanize" much of the culturally specific humor of the hit romantic comedy of the same title and ended up being relegated to the direct-to-DVD market in the United States. Paramount's *The Uninvited* (2009), adapted from Kim Jee-woon (Kim Chi-un)'s cult horror film *A Tale of Two Sisters* and produced by Walter F. Parkes and Laurie McDonald (who produced the American remake of the J-horror hit *Ringu* [1998]), fared only slightly better, grossing a modest $28 million at the US box office. However, the mediocre American remake disappointed many fans of Kim's original film, which, according to a *New York Times* reviewer, is deemed to be "one of the best, and most heartbreaking, weird-girl horror movies ever made."[23] Spike Lee's *Oldboy*, the most high-profile American remake of a Korean film to date, was likewise the recipient of some fairly damning reviews following its theatrical release in 2013. Examples of the negative discourse surrounding this Hollywood production include Stephanie Zacharek's comment that it is an "utterly unnecessary" remake, one that is "colorless and soulless in the extreme, [bearing] no one's fingerprints at all"; and Justin Chang's similar dismissal of the film as an uninspired, "disappointingly straight" remake that "feels content to shadow its predecessor's every move while falling short of its unhinged, balls-out delirium."[24] As a representative (if excessively vitriolic) voice of dissent aimed at the film's many presumed failings, Rex Reed sums up by stating that "Garbage never smells good, but you won't find a landfill anywhere more offensive than Spike Lee's stupid remake of *Oldboy*. . . . This one stinks at 10 below zero."[25]

We argue that the creative misfires and commercial as well as critical failures of recent Hollywood remakes can be attributed, at least in part, to the untranslatability of narrative circumstances and characterizations unique to South Korean culture. The elusive local cultural references in the Korean originals often fail to translate into Hollywood narratives, which frequently privilege clear-cut morality choices and unambiguous outcomes to those choices. To illustrate our point about cultural specificity, or what we term "untranslatables," we would like to briefly turn our attention to *My Sassy Girl*, a flagship example of *Hallyu* cinema, which offers textual moments whose meanings are accessible to Korean audiences but which might be untranslatable within a global gestalt of transnational media fandom. *My Sassy Girl* is a lighthearted youth comedy-cum-melodramatic romance which was the second highest-grossing domestic film of 2001 in South Korea. The film is based on an autobiographical Internet serial novel authored by an engineering student named Kim Ho-sik. Much of the film's humor derives from reversals of expected gender roles between the emasculated, goofy protagonist-narrator (named after Kim's social network ID, Kyŏn-u) and his boy-beating, sassy-mouthed girlfriend, who is simply referred to as "the Girl" in male voiceovers. Such seemingly liberating, countercultural rebellion apparently struck a chord with urban youths in neighboring Asian countries (including China, Taiwan, Japan, Thailand, and Vietnam) who share similar values and lifestyles to those of the mismatched college couple in the South Korean comedy.

Despite the fact that *My Sassy Girl* was never theatrically released in China, according to a 2004 survey conducted by the Korea Tourism Organization, approximately 85% of Chinese respondents in Beijing, Shanghai, and Guangzhou named it as "the most impressive Korean film" that they had encountered—a cultural production that they apparently accessed through new media forms such as VCD, DVD, and Internet streaming (proving that a "new cinephilia" is not a monopoly of Western [male] subjects).[26] In her focus group study of the South Korean film's influence on Chinese women's aggression in dating relationships in Beijing, Xiying Wang uses the term *ren xing* (willfulness) to define the many playful, childish, and insolent behaviors of the female protagonist in *My Sassy Girl* (oftentimes verging on physical and verbal abuse, such as habitual slapping, pushing, public humiliation, and death threats), which are quietly endured and indulged by her tolerant male partner.[27] As pointed out in Wang's study, some Asian men even regard *ren xing* as a positive, endearing attribute—a kind of theatrical foreplay that can increase affection between a couple, unlike negative male violence or aggression leading to domestic abuse or date rape. Although not quite the same thing, *ren xing* is indeed an appropriate Chinese reinterpretation of the Korean concept of *yŏpgi*, which is at the heart of *My Sassy Girl*'s cultural specificity.

The original title of the film—*Yŏpgijŏkin kŭnyŏ*—can be translated as the "Weird Girl" or "Gross-Out Girl." In fact, the Korean word *yŏpgi*, a combination of "weird," "gross," "grotesque," and "horrific," is hard to translate into English. The Korean title is striking because *yŏpgi* is not a word typically used to describe a person, much less a woman. Sometimes the word is used to describe graphic, disturbing scenes in horror or thriller films in the vein of the so-called "Asian Extreme" genre that is popular in the West, including the films of Kim Ki-duk (e.g. *The Isle* [*Sŏm*, 2000], *Address Unknown* [*Such'wiin pulmyŏng*, 2001]) and Park Chan-wook (e.g. *Oldboy, Thirst*). In the late 1990s, the original Internet novel of *My Sassy Girl* had sparked the trendy "*yŏpgi*" culture among Korean teens and twentysomethings, neutralizing and even subverting the negative original meanings of the word. In its film adaptation, the unnamed heroine's "*yŏpgi*" quality is established early on in the subway scene in which the drunken girl vomits on the wig of a geriatric male passenger (who mistakes the male protagonist Kyŏn-u as her boyfriend and forces him to clean up after her). This moment best encapsulates the female protagonist's corporeal "yŏpgi-ness," not her verbal "sassiness" (highlighted in the English title), which emerges only after she sobers up. The rule-breaking "yŏpgi girl" evinces not only bodily abjection but also a perverse imagination. As a would-be-screenwriter, the heroine habitually orders her reluctant boyfriend to read rough drafts of her preposterous scripts. In one of her amateur screenplays, the scenarist-hopeful transforms the Korean writer Hwang Sun-wŏn's canonical 1953 short story "Sonagi" ("Shower") into a *yŏpgi* horror story. In her revisionist, "postfeminist" adaption, the Girl (who is nameless just like the movie character) on her deathbed tells her parents a dying wish which is quite different from the one in the original short story. In the revisionist scenario, the female character asks that the boy she liked be buried alive along with her body rather than that she be buried in the clothes that she wore when the boy carried her on his back during a summer shower.

The rewriting of Hwang Sun-wŏn's story is significant because the "yŏpgi girl" refuses to be a traditionally encoded "Girl of Korean Melodrama." She directly challenges the sentimental, meek femininity prescribed in Hwang's famous tale, which, according to her boyfriend Kyŏn-u, is responsible for shaping Korean audiences' predilection for melodrama. When Kyŏn-u says that he couldn't sleep several nights because of the girl's sad last wish, the "yŏpgi girl" resolutely responds, "It should be changed." This resolution appears to be a feminist declaration of her corrective re-imaging of traditional (tragic) femininity typically linked to Korean melodrama. However, her will to rewrite the image of womanhood fails. It is Kyŏn-u who self-reflexively publishes her story on the Internet (under the same title as the film itself) and is invited by SinCine, the extradiegetic producer of *My Sassy Girl*, to make his autobiographical novel into a film. As in Yi Chŏng-hyang's *Art Museum by the Zoo* (*Misulkwan yŏp tongmulwŏn*, 1998), it is the male protagonist who finishes the story that the female character began.

Although the "yŏpgi girl" appears to exert considerable power over the emasculated male protagonist, it is only through his subjectivity (his spoken voiceover and his written words, in the form of his Internet novel) that her story can be told. Even in the only scene in which the Girl appears by herself without Kyŏn-u, her subjectivity is mediated through the presence of an old man who informs her that Kyŏn-u has replanted the tree at their rendezvous site, when it was felled by lightning a year ago. After hearing this story, the "yŏpgi girl" turns into a girl of melodrama (the role she once subversively rejected), someone desperately trying to locate Kyŏn-u and who cries over his absence. In fact, in her letter to Kyŏn-u in the time capsule, we see her as a sick, coy high school girl, a recalibrated femininity bearing commonalities with the female character in Hwang Sun-wŏn's "Sonagi." The audience comes to know that her sassiness and yŏpgi-ness is simply a defense mechanism for forgetting the death of her first love, who turns out to be Kyŏn-u's cousin. Her transgressive femininity is ultimately forgiven once she regains her old self and reappears womanly and mature in front of Kyŏn-u (as an "ideal" feminine image, no longer sassy or *yŏpgijŏk*). In the end, the "yŏpgi girl" finds her redemption despite all of her previous insolence and indulgent behavior.

According to linguist J. C. Catford, there are two types of untranslatability: one that is linguistic and one that is cultural. While linguistic untranslatability transpires when "there are no lexical or syntactical substitutes in the target language for a source language item," cultural untranslatability is caused by "the absence in the target language culture of a relevant situational feature for the source text."[28] Linguistic untranslatability of the word *yŏpgi* combined with the cultural untranslatability of the collective Korean readership of Hwang Sun-wŏn's short story (to which most South Korean teenagers and adults have been exposed due to its inclusion in middle school textbooks) and the original Internet novel (which many Korean bloggers prefer to the film version) create a gap in transnational reception. While cultural insiders might find the audacious parody of "Sonagi" the most humorous part in the entire film (therefore "getting" the self-reflexive reference to the original e-novel and its adaption process), regional and global audiences are momentarily displaced and might be discombobulated by such untranslatables.

It is particularly noteworthy that the two aforementioned scenes—the subway gross-out moment and the revisionist "Shower" story-within-the story—were replaced in the universally panned Hollywood remake, which was prematurely canned and relegated to the limited direct-to-DVD market in 2008. The failure of the American remake illustrates the difficulty of translating culturally specific humor and then fitting it into a mainstream Hollywood rom-com formula. As Jane Park points out, "the inability of the largely faithful adaptation in *My Sassy Girl* to capture the character types, motivations and performances that made [the Korean original] so popular speaks to the cultural difference between Korea and US with respect to what romance is and how it is represented in the movies." Park goes on to state that a "close examination of how and why some narratives fail to translate across cultures highlights not only gaps and disjunctions in the global mediascape but the continued existence of cultural and national differences in a supposedly swiftly 'globalizing' . . . world."[29]

The presence of what we call "untranslatables" renders the Korean rom-com *My Sassy Girl* as a culturally complex text despite its seemingly frivolous plotline, broad appeal, and transnational spreadability. As evidenced by the film's enormous regional commercial success, untranslatable textual moments do not necessarily diminish the spectatorial pleasures of non-Korean audiences who still appreciate slapstick humor and visual gags. However, they do provide differentiated viewing positions for local audiences capable of understanding "encoded" messages aimed at cultural insiders or in-group members. They also offer additional tasks for bilingual, bicultural critics working outside of South Korea to act as go-betweens deciphering or annotating these untranslatables for global audiences with limited cultural access. Movie migrations do, in fact, exist, but they cannot transpire exclusively within brick-and-mortar theaters or in spreadable spaces lacking such cultural interventions.

For educators who would like to bring old and new South Korean films to their classrooms, there has never been a better time than now. On their wireless mobile devices (laptops, tablets, and cellular phones), students around the world can instantly stream hundreds of films, from Golden Age classics of the 1950s and 1960s to contemporary blockbusters and art films. However, we do not believe that spreadability alone can "foster deeper understandings across cultural differences," as Jenkins and his co-authors optimistically predict. True cultural awareness requires work, and is a possible outcome of dedicated efforts to pursue critical enlightenment about a society that has remained relatively unknown in the Western world despite its crucial role in the making of the US Cold War Empire since 1945. As we have attempted to highlight in this book, film genre is a useful tool with which to chart out and comprehend various migrations (textual, cultural, ideological, anthropological) to and from South Korea. Without historical and cultural contextualization, however, those millions of "views" on YouTube will generate little more than untranslatable memes whose novelty wears off and will be forgotten once the next globally spreadable hit arrives.

Notes

Introduction South Korean Cinema's Transnational Trajectories

1 Kirsten Moana Thompson, *Crime Films: Investigating the Scene* (London: Wallflower Press, 2007), 4.
2 Daryl Lee, *The Heist Film: Stealing with Style* (New York: Wallflower Press, 2014), 5.
3 Ibid., 8.
4 Ibid.
5 Ibid., 10.
6 Françoise Lionnet and Shu-mei Shih, "Introduction," in Lionnet and Shih, eds., *Minor Transnationalism* (Durham, NC: Duke University Press, 2005), 5.
7 Ibid.
8 Coined by the Chinese media in 1999, this neologism denotes the contemporary inter-Asia phenomenon in which Korean entertainers are idolized and South Korean cultural products are consumed as never before, resulting in not only a wider circulation of television programs, films, popular songs, and fashion items across national borders but also the popularity of *Hallyu* tourism (the visiting of South Korea to tour location sites of movies or television shows featuring *Hallyu* stars).
9 Benedict Anderson, *Imagined Communities: Reflections on the Origin and Spread of Nationalism*, Revised Edition (London: Verso, 2006), 5–7.
10 Marshall McLuhan, *The Gutenberg Galaxy: The Making of Typographic Man* (Toronto: University of Toronto Press, 1962), 8.
11 Will Higbee and Song Hwee Lim, "Concepts of Transnational Cinema: Towards a Critical Transnationalism in Film Studies," *Transnational Cinemas*, Vol. 1, No. 1 (January 2010): 9.
12 Christine Gledhill, "Genre and Nation," in Brian McIlroy, ed., *Genre and Cinema: Ireland and Transnationalism* (New York: Routledge, 2007), 16.
13 Ibid., 17.
14 Ibid.
15 Christina Klein, "Why American Studies Needs to Think about Korean Cinema, or, Transnational Genres in the Films of Bong Joon-ho," *American Quarterly*, Vol. 60, No. 4 (December 2008): 871–898.

16 For definitions of film genres' semantic and syntactic elements, see Rick Altman, "A Semantic/Syntactic Approach to Film Genre," *Cinema Journal*, Vol. 23, No. 3 (Spring 1984): 6–18.

17 Kyung Hyun Kim, *Virtual Hallyu: Korean Cinema of the Global Era* (Durham, NC: Duke University Press, 2011), 183.

18 *Globalizing Torture: CIA Secret Detention and Extraordinary Rendition* (New York: Open Society Foundations, 2013), 13–15. http://www.opensocietyfoundations.org/sites/default/files/globalizing-torture-20120205.pdf. Accessed August 10, 2014.

Chapter 1 Toward a Strategic Korean Cinephilia: A Transnational *Détournement* of Hollywood Melodrama

1 In his documentary video version of *The Society of Spectacle*, Guy Debord mobilizes clips from Classical Hollywood films such as *The Shanghai Gesture* (1941) and *Johnny Guitar* (1954) to articulate a Neo-Marxist critique of mass-produced popular culture.

2 Although some Golden Age melodramas such as *Madame Freedom* (*Chayu puin*, 1956) and *Free Marriage* (*Chayu kyŏlhon*, 1958) center on bourgeois female protagonists, a greater number of films thematize the sorrows and conflicts of underclass families, as in *Mr. Park* (*Pak sŏbang*, 1960), *The Stray Bullet*, and *The Coachman* (*Mabu*, 1961).

3 Christine Gledhill, ed., *Home Is Where the Heart Is: Studies in Melodrama and the Woman's Film* (London: BFI Publishing, 1987), 11.

4 Korean film scholar Kyung Hyun Kim, for instance, notes that the "visual presentation and the thematic concerns of the film recall both the styles of German Expressionism and Italian Neo-realism." See Chungmoo Choi, ed., *Post-Colonial Classics of Korean Cinema* (Irvine, CA: Korean Film Festival Committee UCI, 1998), 17.

5 Yu Chi-na ed., *What Is Melodrama* [*Mellodŭrama ran muŏt in'ga*] (Seoul: Minŭmsa, 1999), 16–17.

6 Since 1897, the *sinp'a* drama developed in Japan, reaching its heyday between 1904 and 1910. The Japanese *sinp'a* drama was influenced by European literary and stage melodrama.

7 Soyoung Kim, "Questions of Woman's Film: *The Maid, Madame Freedom*, and Women," in Kathleen McHugh and Nancy Abelmann, eds., *South Korean Golden Age Melodrama: Gender, Genre, and National Cinema* (Detroit: Wayne State University Press, 2005), 190.

8 Over the past two decades, South Korean cinema has given rise to new *sinp'a*-style melodrama; exemplary films include *The Letter* (*P'yŏnji*, 1997), *My Heart* (*Chŏng*, 2000), *Kiss Me Much* (*Pesamemuch'yo*, 2001), and *Bitter but Once Again* (*Miwŏdo tasi hanbŏn*: a remake, 2002). Among recent American films, *Sweet November* (2001) was cross-culturally labeled as a *sinp'a* melodrama by South Korean critics.

9 See, for instance, Ahn Byung-Sup's "Humor in Korean Cinema," *East-West Film Journal*, Vol. 2, No. 1 (1987): 90–98; and Rob Wilson's "Melodramas of Korean National Identity," in Wimal Dissanayake, ed., *Colonialism and Nationalism in Asian Cinema* (Bloomington: Indiana University Press, 1994), 90–104.

10 For a more thorough English-language elucidation of *han*, see Michael Shapiro, *The Shadow in the Sun: A Korean Year of Love and Sorrow* (New York: Atlantic Monthly Press, 1990); Andrew Sung Park, *The Wounded Heart of God: The Asian Concept of Han and the Christine Doctrine of Sin* (Nashville: Abingdon Press,

1993); Jae Hoon Lee, *The Exploration of the Inner Wounds-Han* (Atlanta, Georgia: Scholars Press, 1994); and Uichol Kim and Sang-Chin Choi's "Indigenous Form of Lamentation (Han): Conceptual and Philosophical Analyses" in Ho-Youn Kwon, ed., *Korean Cultural Roots: Religion and Social Thoughts* (Chicago: North Park College and Theological Seminary, 1995): 245–266.

11 Quoted in Julian Stringer's "*Sopyonje* and the Inner Domain of National Culture," in David E. James and Kyung Hyun Kim, eds., *Im Kwon-Taek: The Making of a Korean National Cinema* (Detroit: Wayne State University Press, 2002), 171–172.

12 For an elaboration of the term "melodramatic imagination," see Peter Brooks, *The Melodramatic Imagination: Balzac, Henry James, Melodrama, and the Mode of Excess* (New York: Columbia University Press, 1985).

13 *Matthew's Chinese-English Dictionary* (Cambridge, MA: Harvard University Press, 1963), 310, quoted in Andrew Sung Park (1993), 180.

14 Donald Richie, *Ozu* (Berkeley: University of California Press, 1974), 52; and David Bordwell, *Ozu and the Poetics of Cinema* (Princeton, NJ: Princeton University Press, 1988), 28.

15 Deruoka Sojo, "Neighboring Land, Unknown Sentiment" ["Kakkaun nara, miji ŭi kamsŏng"], *Cine 21*, No. 244 (March 28, 2000): 68.

16 See Yu Hyo-in, "About Modernity in *Sinp'a*-Style Melodrama" ["Sinp'ajŏk mellodŭrama ŭi kŭndaesŏng e taehae"], *Korean Film Critiques* (*Yŏnghwa p'yŏngnon*), Vol. 7 (1995).

17 Kuan-Hsing Chen and Stuart Hall, "Cultural Studies and the Politics of Internalization," in David Morley and Kuan-Hsing Chen, eds., *Stuart Hall: Critical Dialogues in Cultural Studies* (London: Routledge, 1996), 393.

18 Gledhill, *Home Is Where the Heart Is*, 24.

19 KBS press kit (February 25, 1996).

20 *P'ansori* is a traditional operatic storytelling form in which a singer narrates folktales to the rhythmic accompaniment of a drummer.

21 *The Life and Death of the Hollywood Kid* was adapted into a film of the same title in 1994 by Korean New Wave director Chung Ji-young (Chŏng Chi-yŏng).

22 Ahn Junghyo, *The Life and Death of the Hollywood Kid* [*Hŏlliudŭ k'idŭ ŭi saengae*] (Seoul: Minjok kwa munhwasa, 1992), 88–91.

23 Ibid., 24, 80.

24 Anon., *Screen*, No. 45 (November 1987): n.a.

25 *Waterloo Bridge* was first released in the provisional capital Pusan in 1953 and *Love Is Many-Splendored Thing* was released in 1956, three years after the end of the war.

26 William Steuck, *The Korean War: An International History* (Princeton, NJ: Princeton University Press, 1995), 361.

27 During the Asia-Pacific War, over 360,000 Koreans were mobilized as soldiers, 240,000 as military personnel, and 2 million more as laborers. Between 100,000 and 200,000 women were also forcefully drafted as sex slaves (so-called "comfort women") for the Japanese military and sent to comfort stations (military brothels) across Asia. Chin Sung Chung, "The Origin and Development of the Military Sexual Slavery Problem in Imperial Japan," *positions*, Vol. 5, No. 1 (Spring 1997): 219–253.

28 R. Baird Shuman, *Robert E. Sherwood* (New York: Twayne Publishers, Inc., 1964), 77.

29 Lea Jacobs, *The Wages of Sin: Censorship and the Fallen Woman Film, 1928–1942* (Madison: University of Wisconsin Press, 1991), 5.

30 Joseph I. Breen's letter to Jack Warner, dated February 14, 1936, *Waterloo Bridge* PCA file, Margaret Herrick Library (MHL), Academy of Motion Picture Arts and Sciences (AMPAS), Beverly Hills, CA.
31 Joseph I. Breen's letter to David O. Selznick, dated October 5, 1939, ibid.
32 Toronto Film Society's "Film Buff Program 5" (Dec. 6, 1981), *Waterloo Bridge* clippings file, MHL, AMPAS.
33 Mary Ann Doane, *The Desire to Desire: The Woman's Film of the 1940s* (Bloomington: Indiana University Press, 1987), 119.
34 A direct translation of the Korean mantra "Kaja!" is "Let's go!" The authoritarian government suspected that it meant "Let's go to North Korea!" Director Yu defended his film against the charge, arguing that the line expressed a desire for a utopian society. Ho Hyŏn-ch'an, *Korean Film 100 Years* [*Han'guk yŏnghwa 100-nyŏn*] (Seoul: Munhaksasangsa, 2000), 124.
35 Exemplary works include *Hometown of Stars* (*Pyŏldŭl ŭi kohyang*, 1974), *Yŏng-ja's Heyday* (*Yŏng-ja ŭi chŏnsŏng sidae*, 1975), and *Miss O's Apartment* (*O-yang ŭi ap'at'ŭ*, 1978), each focusing on the exploits of heart-of-gold concubines, "hostesses" or prostitutes.
36 *Waterloo Bridge* clippings file, MHL, AMPAS.
37 Ibid.
38 Hyun Sook Kim, "Yanggongju as an Allegory of the Nation: The Representation of Working-Class Women in Popular and Radical Texts," in Elaine H. Kim and Chungmoo Choi, eds., *Dangerous Women: Gender and Korean Nationalism* (New York: Routledge, 1998), 178.
39 Katharine H. S. Moon, *Sex Among Allies: Military Prostitution in US-Korea Relations* (New York: Columbia University Press, 1997), 1.
40 André Bazin, *What Is Cinema?*, Vol. I, Trans. Hugh Gray (Berkeley: University of California Press, 1967), 35–36.
41 Laura Mulvey, "Visual Pleasure and Narrative Cinema," reprinted in Constance Penley, ed., *Feminist and Film Theory* (New York: Routledge, 1988), 57–68.
42 Doane, *Desire to Desire*, 119.
43 Ahn, *The Life and Death of the Hollywood Kid*, 40.
44 Chuanji Zhou also told us that when he criticized the film on television, many Chinese female audiences became upset because *Waterloo Bridge* was their favorite film.
45 See http://www.kmdb.or.kr. Accessed August 10, 2014.
46 Chŏng Chong-hwa, *Korean Film History through Primary Materials* 1955–1997 [*Charyŏ ro pon han'guk yŏnghwasa*] (Seoul: Yŏrhwadang, 1997).
47 Yi Tong-jin, "Movie-Moviemaker *The Stray Bullet*-Im Kwon-taek No. 1" ["Yŏnghwa–yŏnghwain *Obalt'an*-Im Kwŏn-t'aek 1wi"], *Chosŏn Ilbo* (July 16, 1998). http://www.chosun.com. Accessed August 10, 2014.
48 Ho, *Korean Film 100 Years*, 124.
49 Other films in the series included Yu Hyŏn-mok's *Daughters of the Pharmacist Kim* (*Kim yakkuk ŭi ttaldŭl*, 1964), *Martyr* (*Sun'gyoja*, 1965), *Rainy Days* (*Changma*, 1979), and *Son of Man* (*Saram ŭi adŭl*, 1980); Shin Sang-ok's *The Houseguest and My Mother, Sam Ryong, the Deaf-Mute* (*Pŏngŏri Sam-ryong-i*, 1964), *Dream* (*Kkum*, 1965), *Eunuch* (*Naesi*, 1968), and *Women of the Chosun Dynasty* (*Ijo yŏin chanhoksa*, 1969); and Im Kwon-taek's *Daughter of the Flames* (*Pul ŭi ttal*, 1983), *Kilsottŭm, Adada* (1987), *Ticket* (*T'ik'et*, 1986), and *Sopyonje.*
50 The "Three Korean Master Filmmakers" series introduced the film in its original title with the translation "Aimless Bullet" in parenthesis.

Chapter 2 The Mamas and the Papas: Cross-Cultural Remakes, Literary Adaptations, and Cinematic "Parent" Texts

1 Mi Hui Kim, "'Copywood' Ripoffs Pay Unwanted Homage to Popular US Titles," *Variety*, Vol. 391, No. 8 (July 14, 2003): 13.

2 According to a Korean Film Council report, the South Korean film industry has maintained 42–64% of the domestic market share between 2001 and 2013. In 2013, the industry's Korean film market share was 59.7%. *Korean Cinema 2013* (Seoul: Korean Film Council, 2013), 23. http://www.koreanfilm.or.kr/jsp/publications/books.jsp. Accessed August 10, 2014.

3 Byoungkwan Lee, and Hyuhn-Suhck Bae, "The Effect of Screen Quotas on the Self-Sufficiency Ratio in Recent Domestic Film Markets," *Journal of Media Economics*, Vol. 17, No. 3 (2004): 165.

4 Tony Rayns, "Sexual Terrorism: The Strange Case of Kim Ki-duk," *Film Comment*, Vol. 40, No. 6 (November–December 2004): 50–52.

5 Sang-Dawn Lee, *Big Brother, Little Brother: The American Influence on Korean Culture in the Lyndon B. Johnson Years* (Lanham, MD: Lexington Books, 2002), 71.

6 Gi-Wook Shin and Michael Robinson, eds., *Colonial Modernity in Korea* (Cambridge: The Harvard University Asia Center, 1999), 12.

7 Kim Yŏng-min, Foreword, in Pak Yŏong-jin, ed., *Korean Pŏnan Novel Series* [*Hang'uk pŏnan sosŏl sirijŭ*] (Seoul: Hyŏnsil Munhwa Yŏngu, 2007).

8 Pak Sŏn-hŭi, "Chonsun's Monte Cristo Begins His Revenge" ["Chŏnsŏn ŭi Mont'e Kŭrist'o poksu rŭl sijakhada"], *Donga Ilbo* (January 17, 2009). http://news.donga.com/3/all/20090117/8685427/1. Accessed August 10, 2014.

9 This marks a significant increase over the average of two films a year in 1960. For more information about attendance figures and the influence of American popular culture on Korean mass entertainment (films, radio programs, and television shows), see Lee, *Big Brother, Little Brother*, 69–87.

10 According to Sang-Dawn Lee, Korean cinema of the 1960s was as much "influenced by Japanese popular culture as by American . . . despite strong anti-Japanese feeling and a porous governmental ban on Japanese popular culture." Ibid., 69.

11 Initially established as a kabuki production company in 1895, Shōchiku transitioned into filmmaking in 1920, the same year that the Fox Film Corporation produced *Over the Hill to the Poorhouse* and screenwriter-director Ushihara Kiyohiko joined the Japanese film company. Two years later, one of the studio's most popular productions, Ushihara's *Where is My Mother?*, showcased many of the same themes found in the American film, laying the groundwork for subsequent adaptations and remakes. For more information about Shōchiku, see Chuck Stephens, "The Director's Studio," *Film Comment*, Vol. 41, No. 5 (September–October, 2005): 38–41.

12 A specialist in realistic yet sentimental melodramas and cross-cultural adaptations of Western texts, Ushihara directed the first Japanese version of Hugo's *Les Misérables*, a two-part epic titled *Ah, No Mercy* (*Aa Mujo*, 1923), before taking inspiration from Frank Capra's *Meet John Doe* (1941), the basis for the Japanese filmmaker's *A Popular Man in Town* (*Machi no Ninkimino*). See Joseph L. Anderson and Donald Richie, *The Japanese Film: Art and Industry* (Princeton, NJ: Princeton University Press, 1982), 175.

13 Eun-shil Kim, "The Cultural Logic of the Korean Modernization Project and its Gender Politics," *Asian Journal of Women's Studies*, Vol. 6, No. 2 (June, 2000): 58.

14 Mikhail Iampolski, *The Memory of Tiresias: Intertextuality and Film* (Berkeley: University of California Press, 1998), 36.

15 Upton Sinclair, *Upton Sinclair Presents William Fox* (Los Angeles, CA: author 1933), 61.

16 This 1908 short film directed by S.E.V. Taylor, scripted by D. W. Griffith, shot by famed cinematographer G. W. Bitzer, and starring a young Mack Sennett, is believed to be lost. It should be pointed out that another film bearing the title *Over the Hill*—a 1917 Astra Film production dealing with yellow journalism—bears no relation to Carleton's poem.

17 Jerry Fallon, *Will Carleton: Poet of the People* (Philadelphia, PA: Xlibris Corp, 2004).

18 Ibid. It seems fitting that Henry King's combined adaptation of Carleton's poem and remake of the 1920 silent film was released between the Stock Market Crash of 1929 and President Roosevelt's signing of the Social Security Act of 1935, two historical touchstones that defined the socioeconomic challenges of the Great Depression.

19 Sinclair, *Upton Sinclair Presents William Fox*, 59.

20 Ibid., 59–60.

21 Ibid., 60.

22 Ibid., 61.

23 For an example of this, see the motion picture advertisements in the *New York Times* (January 24, 1928).

24 Mordaunt Hall, "Sea Battles of 1914," *New York Times* (February 19, 1928): n/a.

25 Mordaunt Hall, "Fairbanks Travel Film," *New York Times* (November 29, 1931): n/a.

26 Sinclair, *Upton Sinclair Presents William Fox*, 15.

27 Yi Hyo-in and Chŏng Chong-hwa, *Traces of Korean Cinema from 1945–1959* [*Han'guk yŏnghwa ŭi p'unggyŏng 1945–1959*] (Seoul: Munhak Sasangsa, Inc., 2003), 187–188.

28 Pak Chi-yŏn, "Motion Picture Policies of Park Chung Hee's Modernization System" ["Park Chung Hee kŭndaehwa ch'eje ŭi yŏnghwa chŏngch'ek"], in Chu Yu-sin, ed., *Korean Cinema and Modernity* [*Han'gukyŏnghwa wa kŭndaesŏng*] (Seoul: Yŏlhwadang, 1996), 192.

29 Gregg Andrew Brazinsky, "Koreanizing Modernization: Modernization Theory and South Korean Intellectuals," in David Engerman, Nils Gilman, Mark Haefele, and Michael E. Latham, eds., *Staging Growth: Modernization, Development, and the Global Cold War* (Boston: University of Massachusetts Press, 2003), 252.

30 In the 1920 version, the father implicates himself in a horse-smuggling ring. Everything else that follows, from John's imprisonment on behalf of his father to his return from the west to discover his mother at a poor house, is like the 1931 version.

31 Andrew Horton, "Cinematic Makeovers and Cultural Border Crossings: Kusterica's *Time of the Gypsies* and Coppola's *Godfather* and *Godfather II*," in Andrew Horton and Stuart Y. McDougal, eds., *Play It Again, Sam: Retakes on Remakes* (Berkeley: University of California Press, 1998), 182.

32 Arthur Nolletti, Jr., "Ozu's *Tokyo Story* and the 'Recasting' of McCarey's *Make Way for Tomorrow*," in David Desser, ed., *Ozu's Tokyo Story* (Cambridge: Cambridge University Press, 1997), 27.

33 Robin Wood, *Sexual Politics and Narrative Film: Hollywood and Beyond* (New York: Columbia University Press, 1998), 154.

34 Clarke W. Sorensen, *Over the Mountains Are Mountains: Korean Peasant Households and Their Adaptations to Rapid Industrialization* (Seattle: University of Washington Press, 1988), 162.

35 Ibid., 192.

Chapter 3 The Nervous Laughter of Vanishing Fathers: Modernization Comedies of the 1960s

1 The retrospective showcased fifteen German and Korean films starring Emil Jannings and Kim Sŭng-ho: *The Last Laugh* (*Der lezte Mann*, 1924), *Faust: A German Folk Legend* (*Faust, Eine deutsche Volkssage*, 1926), *The Blue Angel* (*Der blaue Engel*, 1930), *Traumulus* (1936), *The Ruler* (*Der Herrscher*, 1937), *Robert Koch* (1939), *Uncle Kruger* (*Ohm Krüger*, 1941), *Bismarck's Dismissal* (*Die Entlassung*, 1942), *Independence Association and Young Syngman Rhee* (*Tongnip hyŏphŏi wa ch'ŏnyŏn Yi Sŭngman*, 1959), *The Coachman* (*Mabu*, 1961), *Romance Gray* (*Romaensŭ kŭrei*, 1963), *Kinship* (*Hyŏlmaek*, 1963), *The Sino-Japanese War and Queen Min* (*Ch'ŏngil chŏnjaeng kwa yŏgyŏl Minbi*, 1965), *Stone Heap* (*Tolmuji*, 1967), and *The Way of All Flesh* (*Yukch'e ŭi kil*, 1967).

2 Nancy Abelmann, *The Melodrama of Mobility: Women, Class, and Talk in Contemporary South Korea* (Honolulu: University of Hawai'i Press, 2003), 10.

3 Ho Hyŏn-ch'an, *Korean Film 100 Years* [*Han'guk yŏnghwa 100-nyŏn*] (Seoul: Munhaksasangsa, 2000), 117–118.

4 Yŏng-min Kong, et al., *Kim Seung-ho: Face of Father, Portrait of Korean Cinema* [*Kim Sŭng-ho: abŏji ŭi ŏlgul, han'guk yŏnghwa ŭi ch'osang*] (Seoul: Korean Film Archive, 2007), 24.

5 Ibid., 58–59, 66.

6 Sŏn-a Kim, "The Time of the Modern, The Time of Nation: 1960s Korean Cinema, Gender, and the Discourse of National Power," in Chu Yu-sin, ed., *Korean Cinema and Modernity* [*Han'guk yŏngwha wa kŭndaesŏng*] (Seoul: Sodo, 2001), 48–53.

7 Kelly Jeong, "The Quasi Patriarch: Kim Sŭng-ho and South Korean Postwar Movies," in Kyung Hyun Kim and Youngmin Choe, eds., *The Korean Popular Culture Reader* (Durham, NC: Duke University Press, 2014), 141.

8 Jinsoo An, *Popular Reasoning of South Korean Melodrama Films (1953–1972)*, Unpublished Ph.D. dissertation (Los Angeles: University of California, 2005), 144.

9 Ibid.

10 Jeong, *The Korean Popular Culture Reader*, 138.

11 Yi Hyŏ-in, *Korean Socio-Cultural History through Films* [*Yŏnghwa ro ilnŭn han'guk sahoemunhwasa*] (Seoul: Kaema Kowŏn, 2003), 109.

12 Abelmann, *The Melodrama of Mobility*, 189.

13 Ibid., 189–190.

14 Jinsoo An, "Anxiety and Laughter in Korean Comedy Films," in Chungmoo Choi, ed., *Post-colonial Classics of Korean Cinema* (Irvine: University of California, Irvine, 1998), 32.

15 Donald Richie, *A Hundred Years of Japanese Film*, Revised and Updated Edition (Tokyo: Kodansa International, 2005), 117.

16 The films in which Kim Sŭng-ho appears as working-class fathers include *Mr. Park* (1960), *The Coachman, A Bonanza* (*Nodagi*, 1961), and *Kinship*.

17 Yi Yŏng-il, *History of Korean Cinema* [*Han'guk yŏnghwa chŏnsa*], Revised and Expanded Edition (Seoul: Sodo, 2004), 274–276.

18 The mother's line that equates politicians with thieves is partially responsible for a suspension of the film's theatrical exhibition, following the May 16 coup and the new military regime's strengthening of political censorship. See Kong, *Kim Seung-ho: Face of Father, Portrait of Korean Cinema*, 43.

19 Yi Hyŏ-in, *Korean Socio-Cultural History through Films*, 109.

20 Homi Bhabha, *The Location of Culture* (London: Routledge, 1994), 85–92.

21 Chungmoo Choi, "The Magic and Violence of Modernization in Post-Colonial Korean Cinema," in Chungmoo Choi, ed., *Post-colonial Classics of Korean Cinema* (Irvine: University of California, Irvine, 1998), 5.

22 Despite their good intent, the National Motion Picture Ethics Committee faced many challenges during its short existence (August 5, 1960–May 16, 1961). As an independent civil organization with no connections to the government or the film industry, the committee had difficulty establishing its authority and enforcing concrete rules of regulation to producers—the same kinds of difficulty experienced by the Motion Picture Producers and Distributors of America (MPPDA) in the early thirties before the formation of the effective Production Code Administration (PCA) in 1934. For more info, see Ham Ch'ung-byŏm et al., *Korean Cinema and April 19 Revolution* [*Han'guk yŏnghwa wa 4.19*] (Seoul: Korean Film Archive, 2009), 22–28.

23 For more information about the American PCA censorship, see Thomas Doherty, *Hollywood's Censor: Joseph I. Breen and the Production Code Administration* (New York: Columbia University Press), 2007. After gradually losing power since the mid-1950s, the Production Code was abandoned altogether in 1968 and replaced by the MPAA (Motion Picture Association of America) ratings system.

24 *Korean Cinema '68* (Seoul: Motion Picture Producers Association of Korea, 1968). Film censorship guidelines were introduced in the first Motion Picture Law of 1962 and revised in 1966.

25 Yi Man-hŭi (Lee Man-hee) was probably the most high-profile victim of film censorship under the Park regime. In 1965, Yi was jailed for forty days after the authorities determined that his "anti-communist" film *Seven Women Prisoners* (*Ch'irin ŭi yŏp'oro*) was actually complimentary to North Korea. One particular scene in which the titular women from the South Korean army praise the soon-to-be-defecting North Korean officer who has rescued them from a Chinese rapist was the main cause for the director's predicament. When released from prison on suspension, Yi was assigned personally by the Director of the Korean Central Intelligence Agency (KCIA) to helm another anti-communist project *Soldiers without a Serial Number* (*Kunbŏn ŏpnŭn yongsa*, 1966). Yi came close to being scapegoated once again as his casting of good-looking matinee idol Sin Sŏng-il as a communist officer caused yet another controversy. However, the director was spared this time, since his film portrayed Sin's character (who orders an execution of his own anti-communist father) in an unambiguously brutal way. Kim Hak-su, *Offscreen Korean Film History* [*Sŭkrin pakkŭi han'guk yŏnghwasa*] (Seoul: Inmul gwa sasang, 2002), 112–113.

26 *Petty Middle Manager* DVD Booklet (Seoul: Korean Film Archive, 2007).

27 The wording of the anti-superstition clause became more specific and targeted in the revised second Motion Picture Law by changing the objectionable category from "films that respect superstition" (1962) to "films that justify or encourage superstition" (1966). Shin Sang-ok's 1963 film *Rice* (*Ssal*) epitomizes an anti-superstition "enlightenment" film encouraged by the Park Chung Hee regime. The story focuses on a crippled Korean War veteran (Sin Yŏng-gyun), Yong-i, who returns to his hometown, a poverty-stricken remote mountain village, and leads villagers to excavate a tunnel in order to establish a much-needed irrigation line for rice cultivation. A shaman becomes an obstacle to Yong-i's grand five-year plan for tunnel excavation (not so subtly allegorizing Park Chung Hee's Five-Year Economic Plan) as she adamantly opposes the construction because of her superstitious

worship of the mountain god. The film defines shamanism and superstition as the nation's ills, standing in the way of modernization and a prosperous future.

Chapter 4 Once upon a Time in Manchuria: Classic and Contemporary Korean Westerns

1 Thomas Schatz, *Hollywood Genres: Formulas, Filmmaking, and the Studio System* (New York: McGraw-Hill, Inc., 1981), 45.
2 As John Ford's elegiac, bittersweet farewell to the Westerner and his vanishing ideals, *The Man Who Shot Liberty Valance* offers a much-quoted line of self-criticism: "This is the West, sir. When the legend becomes fact, print the legend." Don Siegel's *The Shootist* opens with a montage sequence of John Wayne's images in previous Westerns, commenting on the history of the diegetic hero and on the genre itself.
3 Schatz, *Hollywood Genres*, 37–38.
4 Tag Gallagher, "Shoot-Out at the Genre Corral: Problems in the 'Evolution' of the Western," in Barry Keith Grant, ed., *Film Genre Reader III* (Austin: University of Texas Press, 2003), 273.
5 Steve Neale, "Questions of Genre," in *Film Genre Reader III*, 171.
6 Ibid., 168.
7 Ibid., 174–175.
8 Virginia Wright Wexman, *Creating the Couple: Love, Marriage, and Hollywood Performance* (Princeton, NJ: Princeton University Press, 1993), 101.
9 Brian Henderson, "*The Searchers*: An American Dilemma," *Film Quarterly*, Vol. 34, No. 2 (Winter 1980–1981): 20.
10 Schatz, *Hollywood Genres*, 79.
11 Henderson, "*The Searchers*: An American Dilemma," 22.
12 In the opening scene, Ethan appears in his brother's frontier home wearing Confederate uniform and carrying his sabre after missing three years since the end of Civil War, displaying his stubborn adherence to Confederate ideals.
13 William McClain, "Western, Go Home! Sergio Leone and the 'Death of the Western' in American Film Criticism," *Journal of Film and Video*, Vol. 62, Nos. 1–2 (Spring/Summer 2010): 57.
14 Ahn Junghyo, *The Life and Death of the Hollywood Kid* [*Hŏlliudŭ k'idŭ ŭi saengae*] (Seoul: Minjok kwa munhwasa, 1992), 91.
15 Yi Yŏng-il, *History of Korean Cinema* [*Han'guk yŏnghwa chŏnsa*], Revised and Expanded Edition (Seoul: Sodo, 2004), 355.
16 Ibid., 341.
17 Ibid., 340.
18 Jinsoo An, Popular Reasoning of South Korean Melodrama Films (1953–1972), Unpublished Ph.D. dissertation (Los Angeles: University of California, 2005), 145.
19 Ibid.
20 Ibid., 148.
21 "Films That Audiences Want to See Again" ["Sich'ongja ka ppobŭn tasi pogo sipŭn yŏnghwa"], KBS press kit (February 25, 1996).
22 Rick Altman, "A Semantic/Syntactic Approach to Film Genre," *Cinema Journal*, Vol. 23, No. 3 (Spring 1984): 10.
23 Rick Altman, *Film/Genre* (London: BFI Publishing, 1999), 210.
24 George Stevens, Jr. and Ivan Moffat, Audio Commentary, *Shane*, Paramount 2000, DVD.

25 Kim So-hŭi. "The Legend of 50 Years of Korean Cinema Resurrects" ["Han'guk yŏnghwa pansaegi ka puhwal handa]," *Cine 21*, No. 327 (November 13–20, 2001): 48.
26 Pak Haeng-ch'ŏl, *Interview Collections* [*Int'ŏbu charyojip*] (Seoul: Korean Film Archive, 2003), 189–190.
27 Ho Hyŏn-ch'an, *Korean Films 100 Years* [*Han'guk yŏnghwa* 100-nyŏn] (Seoul: Munhwasasangsa, 2000), 145.
28 Soyoung Kim, "If Only It Were Not Action for the Sake of Action: *The Bad, The Good, The Weird*" ["Aetsyŏn ŭl wihan aetsyŏn i aniŏt tŏramyŏn choatŭl *Chotŭn nom, nappŭn nom, isanghan nom*"], *Cine 21*, No. 663 (July 31, 2008). http://www.cine21.com/news/view/mag_id/52383. Accessed August 10, 2014.
29 Douglas Pye, "The Western (Genre and Movies)," in *Film Genre Reader III*, 208.
30 Although the Homestead Act stipulated minimal requirements for free land ownership of 160 acre-public land (adult citizenship, five year's residence on land to claim, a small filing fee), relatively few laborers and small farmers could afford to build and maintain a farm. As a result, most land went to speculators, railroads, cattlemen, and miners. Out of 500 million acres distributed by the General Land Office, only 80 million went to homesteaders. For more information, see Act of May 20, 1862 (Homestead Act), Public Law 37–64, May 20 1962, Record Group 11, General Records of the United States Government, National Archives. Available at http://www.ourdocuments.gov/doc.php?doc=31. Accessed August 10, 2014.
31 Barbara J. Brooks, "Peopling the Japanese Empire: The Koreans in Manchuria and the Rhetoric of Inclusion," in Sharon A. Minichiello, ed., *Japan's Competing Modernities: Issues in Culture and Democracy 1900–1930* (Honolulu: University of Hawai'i Press, 1998), 30.
32 Ibid., 28.
33 Bruce Cumings, *Korea's Place in the Sun*, Updated Edition (New York: W.W. Norton & Co., 2005), 162.
34 Schatz, *Hollywood Genres*, 56.
35 Matthew J. Costello, "Rewriting *High Noon*: Transformations in American Popular Political Culture during the Cold War, 1952–1968," in Peter C. Rollins and John E. O'Connor, eds., *Hollywood's West: The American Frontier in Film, Television, and History* (Lexington: The University Press of Kentucky, 2005), 179.
36 Ibid.
37 Costello identifies the morally upright, dutiful marshal Will Kane (Gary Cooper) in *High Noon* (1952) as an embodiment of the "virtuous individual." Ibid. The fact that supporting husband characters are positioned as official noble heroes for the community (as opposed to seemingly indifferent, titular antiheros) in both *Shane* and *The Man with No Home* attest to these films' significant departure from traditional codes of morality upheld by *High Noon*, the prototype of the "law-and-order" Western.
38 Neale, "Questions of Genre," 174–175.
39 Schatz, *Hollywood Genres*, 57–59.
40 Interview with Director Kim Jee-woon, *The Good, the Bad, the Weird*, MPI Home Video, 2010, DVD.
41 Yi Hyŏn-gyŏng, "*The Good, the Bad, the Weird*—Riding an Action Roller Coaster" ["*Chotŭn nom, nappŭn nom, isanghan nom*—Aetsyŏn ŭi rollŏ k'osŭt'ŏ ae t'apsŏng hada"], *Yi Tong-jin Dot Com* (July 9, 2008). http://news.naver.com/main/read.nhn?mode=LSD&mid=sec&sid1=106&oid=263&aid=0000000248.

Accessed August 10, 2014. Kim, "If Only It Were Not Action for the Sake of Action: *The Bad, The Good, The Weird.*"

42 Gi-Wook Shin and Michael Robinson, eds., *Colonial Modernity in Korea* (Cambridge: The Harvard University Asia Center, 1999), 4.

43 Ibid., 11.

44 Ibid., 9.

Chapter 5 Reinventing the Historical Drama, De-Westernizing a French Classic: Genre, Gender, and the Transnational Imaginary in *Untold Scandal*

1 Darcy Paquet, "An Interview with E. J-yong," *Koreanfilm.org*. http://www.koreanfilm.org/ejyong.html. Accessed August 10, 2014. Following the release of *Untold Scandal* in 2003, all three "poison" genres made reappearances at the box office, with varying degrees of success. Examples include *Mr. Gam's Victory* (*S'up'ŏsŭt'a Kangsayong*, 2004), *Marathon* (*Malat'on*, 2005), *The King and the Clown* (*Wang ŭi namja*, 2005), *Forbidden Quest* (*Ŭmran sŏsaeng*, 2006), *Hearty Paws* (*Maŭm-i*, 2006), *Scout* (*Sŭk'aut*, 2007), *Forever the Moment* (*Uri saengae ch'ogu ŭi sungan*, 2008), *Frozen Flower* (*Ssanghwajŏm*, 2008), *Woochi* (*Chŏnuch'i*, 2009), *Take Off* (*Kukka taepy'o*, 2009), *The Servant* (*Pangjajŏn*, 2010), and *War of the Arrows* (*Ch'oejongbyŏnggi hwal*, 2011).

2 *Memories of Murder, My Tutor Friend, Untold Scandal, Old Boy*, and *Oh! Brothers* tallied 5.1 million, 4.8 million, 3.3 million, 3.2 million, 3.1 million admissions respectively. Only two Hollywood blockbusters (*The Lord of the Rings: Return of the King* [2003] and *The Matrix: Reloaded* [2003] with 5.9 million and 3.6 million admissions) made the year's list of top ten films. The South Korean film industry's domestic market share in 2003 was 53%.

3 Soyoung Kim, "Question of Woman's Film: *The Maid, Madame Freedom*, and Women," in Kathleen McHugh and Nancy Abelmann, eds., *South Korean Golden Age Melodrama: Gender, Genre, and National Cinema* (Detroit: Wayne State University Press, 2005), 185–186.

4 "*T'osok ero*" can be translated as "indigenous eros."

5 Yun Mi Hwang, *South Korean Historical Drama: Gender, Nation, and the Heritage Industry*, Unpublished Ph.D. dissertation (St. Andrews: University of St. Andrews, 2011).

6 Kyung Hyun Kim, *Virtual Hallyu: Korean Cinema of the Global Era* (Durham, NC: Duke University Press, 2011), 209, 211.

7 Sim Yŏng-sŏp, "Harmony Blossomed out of Aesthetic Eroticism" ["T'ammi chŏk erot'isism esŏ p'iŏnan chohwa"], *Cine 21* (October 14, 2003): 106.

8 Hwang Hye-jin, "About the Fusion of the Historical Movies: New Temptation of Historical Movies, Beyond Communications between the Past and the Present," *Film Critiques* FIPRESCI Korea, Vol. 3 (Seoul: Happy House, 2004), 79.

9 Paquet, "An Interview with E. J-yong."

10 Ibid.

11 Choderlos de Laclos, *Les liaisons dangereuses*, Trans. Douglas Parmée (Oxford: Oxford University Press, 1995), 3.

12 Richard Frohock, "Adaptation and Cultural Criticism: *Les Liaisons dangereuses* 1960 and *Dangerous Liaisons*," in Robert Mayer, ed., *Eighteenth Century Fiction on Screen* (Cambridge: Cambridge University Press, 2002), 158.

13 For a feminist reading of the Marquise de Merteuil character, see Martine Debaisieux, "From Criminality to Hysteria: Translating the Marquise de Merteuil,"

Romantic Review, Vol. 78, No. 4 (1987): 461–470; Suellen Diaconoff, "Resistance and Retreat: A Laclosian Primer for Women," *University of Toronto Quarterly*, Vol. 58, No. 3 (Spring 1989): 391–408; Elizabeth Donvan and Lloyd Free, "*Les Liaisons dangereuses* and Contemporary Consciousness," in Lloyd Free, ed., *Laclos: Critical Approaches to* Les Liaisons dangereuses (Madrid: Studia Humanitatis, 1978), 259–296; Karen Hollinger, "Losing the Feminist Drift: Adaptations of *Les Liaisons dangereuses.*" *Literature Film Quarterly*, Vol. 24, No. 3 (January 1996): 293–300.

14 Frohock, "Adaptation and Cultural Criticism," 157.

15 Rey Chow, *Primitive Passions: Visuality, Sexuality, Ethnography, and Contemporary Chinese Cinema* (New York: Columbia University Press, 1995), 171.

16 Edward W. Said, *Orientalism* (New York: Vintage Books, 1979), 23.

17 Hyangjin Lee, "*Chunhyang*: Marketing an Old Tradition in New Korean Cinema," in Ch-Yun Shin and Julian Stringer, eds., *New Korean Cinema* (New York: New York University Press, 2005), 73–74.

18 See George Lukow and Steve Ricci, "The 'Audience' Goes 'Public': Intertextuality, Genre, and the Responsibilities of Film Literary," *On Film*, No. 12 (Spring 1984): 28–36.

19 Gérard Genette, *Paratexts: Thresholds of Interpretation* (Cambridge: Cambridge University Press, 1997); Jonathan Gray, *Show Sold Separately: Promos, Spoilers, and Other Media Paratexts* (New York: New York University Press, 2010).

20 Anon., "*Chunghyang*: A Film by Im Kwon Taek," New Yorker Films. http://www.newyorkerfilms.com/Chunhyang-(2000)/1/105/. Accessed August 10, 2014.

21 See Laura Mulvey, "Visual Pleasure and Narrative Cinema," in Leo Braudy and Marshall Cohen, eds., *Film Theory & Criticism*, Seventh Edition (Oxford: Oxford University Press, 2009), 711–722.

22 "Untold Scandal," Kino Lober. http://www.kinolorber.com/video.php?id=727. Accessed August 10, 2014.

23 Chŏng Sŏng-il, "Review: *Untold Scandal*," *Hankyoreh* (October 13, 2003): 20.

24 The "IMF Crisis" refers to South Korea's massive economic depression beginning late 1997 when the country was suddenly confronted with the possibility of national bankruptcy under the sway of the Asia-wide currency collapse and mounting foreign debts. The South Korean government resorted to a $57 billion bailout loan from the International Monetary Fund (the largest amount in the IMF's history).

25 Other offenses include disobedience toward the parents-in-law, adultery, theft, undue jealousy, grave illness, and extreme loquaciousness.

26 Martina Deuchler, "Tradition: Women during the Yi Dynasty," in Sandra Mattielli, ed., *Virtues in Conflict: Tradition and the Korean Woman Today* (Seoul: Royal Asiatic Society, 1977), 22.

27 For a detailed discussion of Missy images in 1990s Korean popular culture, see So-Hee Lee, "The Concept of Female Sexuality in Korean Popular Culture," in Laurel Kendall, ed., *Under Construction: The Gendering of Modernity, Class, and Consumption in the Republic of Korea* (Honolulu: University of Hawai'i Press, 2002), 141–164.

28 Yi Man-gyo's award-winning novel *Marriage Is a Crazy Thing* (*Kyŏlhon ŭn, mich'in chitida*, 2000) features a passage in which the libertine male protagonist, a bachelor college lecturer, recommends a list of novels and films thematizing extramarital affairs to one of his ex-girlfriends (who is married). When he mentions E. J-yong's *An Affair*, his partner in her early thirties exclaims, "Yi Mi-suk became much sexier

than before!," reflecting Korean female spectators' collective admiration for middle-aged Yi's revived screen persona. Yi Man-gyo, *Marriage Is a Crazy Thing* (Seoul: Minŭmsa, 2000), 189.

29 Feminist columnist O Suk-hŭi argues that the scene is provocative enough to provide "rebellious pleasure to a majority of Korean women suffering the stress of holiday rituals." O Suk-hŭi, "Now I Would Like to See 'Other' Women" ["Ije nŭn 'tarŭn' yŏja-dŭl ŭl pogo sipda"], *Cine 21* (September 21, 1999): 62.

30 It is debatable whether the servant sold his dead master's picture book simply for money or with the intention to punish Lady Cho (details of whose betrayal are not known to him).

31 Writer-director Hur Jin-ho (Hŏ Chin-ho) is known for his quiet, slow-paced melodramas focusing on emotional minutiae and understated sadness, such as *Christmas in August* (*8wŏl ŭi K'ŭrisŭmasŭ*, 1998), *One Fine Spring Day* (*Pomnal ŭn kanda*, 2001), and *April Snow* (*Oech'ul*, 2005). As Hur's first venture into a star-filled, big-budget mainstream production (costing $35 million), *Dangerous Liaisons* represents a departure from the director's predilection for realistic aesthetics (long shots and long takes). Loaded with at least 300 CGI shots, the film reportedly contains more shots than all of Hur's previous five films combined. Chŏng Han-sŏk, "Hur Jin-ho's New Film *Dangerous Liaisons*: An Interview with Actress and Director" ["*Hŏ Chin-ho sinjak Wihŏmhan kwangae*: Paeu-gamdok Intŏbyu"], *Cine 21* (June 12, 2012). http://www.cine21.com/news/view/mag_id/70157. Accessed August 10, 2014.

32 Kate Taylor, "Liaisons, Sure, But Not Enough Danger," *The Globe and Mail* (November 9, 2012): R5.

33 Stephen Dalton, "*Dangerous Liaisons*: Cannes Review," *The Hollywood Reporter* (May 29, 2012). http://www.hollywoodreporter.com/review/dangerous-liaisons-cannes-review-330339. Accessed August 10, 2014.

34 Laclos, *Les liaisons dangereuses*, 370.

35 For example, Sim Yŏng-sŏp grumbles, "Why do all of E. J-yong's films start with unrealistic signifiers—an airport video monitor (*An Affair*), a calendar picture (*Asako*), and a nude portrait (*Untold Scandal*)—and race toward yet another set of unrealistic signifiers such as Brazil, Alaska, and China in the end?" Sim, "Harmony Blossomed out of Aesthetic Eroticism," 107.

36 *Untold Scandal* evokes Korean audiences' nostalgia for the Yi Mi-suk of the 1980s on two fronts. Not only does the actress's unadorned face in the last scene remind them of earlier filmic images, but also her sultry embodiment of Lady Cho is an extension of her television roles in the 1980s, such as Chang Hŭibin, a power-hungry royal concubine (of King Sukjong) who was responsible for the unjust removal of Queen Min and was later ordered to take poison for her crime, and Chang Nok-su, a temptress who lured unsuspecting wives of high officials to the bedroom of King Yŏnsan (notorious for his debauchery) and was beheaded after the tyrant's dethronement in a coup. We are indebted to No Kwang-u for sharing his idea about the connection between *Untold Scandal* and 1980s television dramas.

37 Bae Yong-joon is commonly called "yon-*sama*" in Japan: yon is mispronunciation of the first half of Bae's given name (Yong) and *sama* is an honorific title that the Japanese often tag onto the name of their idols.

38 Fumiko Endo and Atsuko Matsumoto, "TV Dramas Melt Hearts, Thaw Japan-Korean Relations," *The Yomiuri Shimbun* (December 7, 2004): 4. When Bae Yong-joon made his much-anticipated cinematic debut in *Untold Scandal*, an estimated 20,000 Japanese tourists traveled to South Korea to see the film upon its Korean

release in October 2003. Released in 110 Japanese theaters in May 2004, *Untold Scandal* garnered 900 million yen and became the third highest grossing Korean film released in Japan to date, following *Shiri* and *JSA*. However, many Japanese female fans were reportedly disappointed at Bae's offcasting as an "immoral" character, departing radically from his gentle television persona in *Winter Sonata*. For a detailed discussion of Bae Yong-joon's star persona, see Robert Cagle, "Bae Yong-joon: The Image of South Korea," *The Korea Herald* (February 13, 2008): 11.

39 While Korean films featuring top *Hallyu* stars (including Bae Yong-joon, Jun Ji-hyun [Chŏn Chi-hyŏn], Jang Dong-gun, Lee Byung-hun [Yi Pyŏng-hyŏn], and Lee Young-ae [Yi Yŏng-ae]) tend to dominate Asian markets, Western attention to Korean cinema has primarily been directed to either art cinema (by award-winning auteurs such as Im Kwon-taek, Kim Ki-duk, and Hong Sang-soo) or genre films (particularly horror). Few Korean movie stars are famous outside of Asia with the exception of Yunjin Kim, who was cast as a substantial supporting character in ABC's ensemble drama *Lost* and one of the four lead characters in ABC's *Mistresses* (2013–), as well as Lee Byung-hyun and the pop idol Rain who have appeared in the recent Hollywood blockbusters *GI Joe: The Rise of Cobra* (2009) and *Ninja Assassin* (2009), respectively.

Chapter 6 From *Gojira* to *Goemul*: "Host" Cities and "Post" Histories in East Asian Monster Movies

1 Nikki J. Y. Lee, "Localized Globalization and a Monster National: *The Host* and the South Korean Film Industry," *Cinema Journal*, Vol. 50, No. 3 (Spring 2011): 47; see also Hye Jean Chung, "*The Host* and *D-War*: Complex Intersections of National Imaginings and Transnational Aspirations," *Spectator*, Vol. 29, No. 2 (Fall 2009): 50.

2 Christina Klein, "Why American Studies Needs to Think about Korean Cinema, or, Transnational Genres in the Films of Bong Joon-ho," *American Quarterly*, Vol. 60, No. 4 (December 2008): 887.

3 Kyung Hyun Kim, *Virtual Hallyu: Korean Cinema of the Global Era* (Durham, NC: Duke University Press, 2011), 47.

4 Darcy Paquet, *New Korean Cinema: Breaking the Waves* (New York: Wallflower Press, 2009), 106. For more information about the 1994 collapse of the Sŏngsu Bridge and other defining moments in South Korea during the 1990s, see Chang Kyung-Sup, "Compressed Modernity and Its Discontents: South Korean Society in Transition," *Economy and Society*, Vol. 28, No. 1 (1999): 30–55.

5 For more information about "*hibakusha* cinema" and the theme of atomic bomb paranoia in postwar Japanese film, see Donald Richie, "Hiroshima in Film," in Robert Hughes, ed., *Film: Book 2, Films of Peace and War* (New York: Grove Press, 1962), 67–86.

6 Richie, "Hiroshima in Film," 77.

7 Lawrence Wittner, *Confronting the Bomb: A Short History of the World Nuclear Disarmament Movement* (Stanford, CA: Stanford University Press, 2009), 52–53.

8 Ralph Lapp, *The Voyage of the Lucky Dragon* (New York: Harper & Brothers, 1958).

9 Chon Noriega, "Godzilla and the Japanese Nightmare: When *Them!* Is US," *Cinema Journal*, Vol. 27, No. 1 (Autumn, 1987): 68.

10 Alain Vezina, *Godzilla: Une métaphore du Japon d'après-guerre* (Paris: Harmattan, 2012), 34–35.

11 Besides Warner Bros.' *The Beast from 20,000 Fathoms*, another American production—Max and Dave Fleischer's animated short *The Arctic Giant* (1942)—showcases

iconography that is eerily similar to that of *Godzilla*. Near the mid-point of this nine-minute Superman cartoon, the ice encasing a recently discovered Tyrannosaurus (found in Siberia and put on display in Metropolis's Museum of Natural Science) begins to thaw, unleashing the titular beast. Like the Japanese monster, this awakened dinosaur takes to the streets, destroying buildings and bridges and sending citizens scurrying. The film culminates with the caped superhero subduing the monster and putting him on display in the city zoo.

12 That title would later be Anglicized to *Godzilla* by Tōhō's foreign sales department in anticipation of its 1956 release in the United States.

13 Peter H. Brothers, *Mushroom Clouds and Mushroom Men: The Fantastic Cinema of Ishiro Honda*, second printing (CreateSpace Independent Publishing Platform, 2013), 45.

14 Thomas Schnellbächer, "Has the Empire Sunk Yet? The Pacific in Japanese Science Fiction," *Science Fiction Studies*, Vol. 29, No. 3 (November 2002): 385.

15 Mark Siegel, "Foreigner as Alien in Japanese Science Fantasy," *Science Fiction Studies*, Vol. 12, No. 3 (November 1985): 255.

16 Maria Beville, *The Unnameable Monster in Literature and Film* (New York: Routledge, 2003), 6.

17 Jerome F. Shapiro, *Atomic Bomb Cinema: The Apocalyptic Imagination on Film* (New York: Routledge, 2002), 276.

18 William M. Tsutsui, "Through the Years with Godzilla and Tora-San: Film Series in Postwar Japan," in Jennifer Forrest, ed., *The Legend Returns and Dies Harder Another Day: Essays on Film Series* (Jefferson, NC: McFarland, 2008), 216.

19 Barak Kushner references Annalee Newitz's notion of "cultural cheese" in his recent study of the monster series, stating, "In Japan *Gojira* was not cheese." This comment reminds us that there is a cultural gap between the Japanese and non-Japanese reception of the movie monster, which can be appreciated by many American audiences only as an "artificial, exaggerated" screen icon framed by a "snide nostalgia." See Barak Kushner, "Gojira as Japan's First Postwar Media Event," in William Tsutsui and Michiko Ito, eds., *In Godzilla's Footsteps: Japanese Pop Culture Icons on the Global Stage* (New York: Palgrave Macmillan, 2006), 48.

20 Theodore Hughes, *Literature and Film in Cold War South Korea: Freedom's Frontier* (New York: Columbia University Press, 2012), 162.

21 Alison Peirse and Daniel Martin, "Introduction," in *Korean Horror Cinema* (Edinburgh: Edinburgh University Press, 2013), 5.

22 For example, the aforementioned *Mothra vs. Godzilla* opens with a coast-pounding sea storm followed by a scene of several onlookers standing atop a bridge, gazing out at the destruction caused by that unnaturally strong natural disaster.

23 Chung, "*The Host* and *D-War*," 54.

24 Jung Ji-youn, *Korean Film Directors: Bong Joon-ho* (Seoul: Seoul Selection, 2009), 10.

25 Lee, "Localized Globalization and a Monster National," 48. Hye Jean Chung also points out that, in addition to drawing inspiration from Japanese films, Bong was influenced by M. Night Shyamalan's film *Signs* (2002), "which also centers on a dysfunctional family's struggle against a monster (aliens in this case)."

26 Lee, "Localized Globalization and a Monster National," 56.

27 Chung, "*The Host* and *D-War*," 52.

28 Jung, *Korean Film Directors: Bong Joon-ho*, 17.

29 Quoted in Paquet, *New Korean Cinema*, 66

30 Samara Lee Allsop, "*Gojira/Godzilla*," in Justin Bowyer, ed., *The Cinema of Japan and Korea* (London: Wallflower Press, 2004), 63.
31 Ibid.
32 Ibid., 67.
33 Kim, *Virtual Hallyu*, 44.
34 Noël Carroll, "The Nature of Horror," *The Journal of Aesthetics and Art Criticism*, Vol. 46, No. 1 (Autumn 1987): 57.
35 Ibid.
36 Lee, "Localized Globalization and a Monster National," 55.
37 Slavoj Žižek and Glyn Daly, *Conversations with Žižek* (Cambridge: Polity Press, 2004), 7.
38 Anthony Lane, "Down by the River," *New Yorker* (March 12, 2007): 90.
39 Sean Burns, "Hole in Our Seoul," *The Improper Bostonian* (March 7, 2007): 58; Ella Taylor, "We Are What Eats Us," *LA Weekly* (March 9, 2007), 79.
40 Scott Foundas, "Critics' Picks," *LA Weekly* (Nov. 3, 2006). http://www.laweekly.com/2006-11-02/film-tv/critics-picks/. Accessed August 10, 2014.
41 Chung, "*The Host* and *D-War*," 51.
42 Beville, *The Unnameable Monster in Literature and Film*, 5.
43 Bruce Cumings, Preface to *The Origins of the Korean War* (Princeton, NJ: Princeton University Press, 2001), xxvi, xxix.
44 Adding intertextual richness to this first scene in *The Host* is the presence of actor Scott Wilson, best known to American TV fans for his performance as the character Herschel Greene in AMC's *The Walking Dead* (2010–). Although in Bong's film he plays a bossy lab technician who barks orders to a fellow medical specialist, Wilson provides a rare voice of reason and ethical understanding in the zombie series, another monster-filled narrative in which family members struggle to remain intact after an apocalyptic outbreak.
45 Jeffrey Burton Russell, Foreword, in Joseph Amato, *Dust: A History of the Small and the Invisible* (Berkeley: University of California Press, 2000), ix.
46 Ibid., 23.
47 Mary Douglas, *Purity and Danger: An Analysis of Concepts of Pollution and Taboo* (London: Routledge, 2003); paraphrased in Ibid., 21.
48 Scarlet L. Wynns and Lawrence B. Rosenfeld, "Father–Daughter Relationships in Disney's Animated Films," *Southern Communication Journal*, Vol. 68, No. 2 (2003): 91–106.
49 David Edelstein, "Stomach Virus," *New York* (October 25, 2007). http://nymag.com/movies/reviews/28907/. Accessed August 10, 2014.
50 In his review of *The Host*, Sean Burns states that the creature is "a weird reptilian thing, a tortoise-like version of H. R. Geiger's original *Alien*." Sean Burns, "Hole in Our Seoul," *The Improper Bostonian* (March 7, 2007): 58.
51 Chu Chin-suk and Kim Sŏn-a, eds., *Diversity and Coexistence* [*Tayang kwa kongjon*] (Seoul: Wulryŏk, 2011), 102.
52 Anon., "US Army Keeping Close Eye on Han River Monster," *Chosun Daily* (*Chosŏn Ilbo*), English Edition. http://english.chosun.com/site/data/html_dir/2006/08/11/2006081161014.html. Accessed August 10, 2014.
53 Bruce Wallace, "Who's the Monster?" *Los Angeles Times* (November 1, 2006). http://articles.latimes.com/2006/nov/01/entertainment/et-host1. Accessed August 10, 2014.
54 Bong Joon-ho, *The Host* Press Kit, Magnolia Pictures, 2006.

55 Mike D'Angelo, "Monster Imports," *Esquire* (February 2007): 31.

56 For example, Aidan Foster-Carter writes, "Knowing what to be scared of is, sadly, a skill we all need. But South Koreans seem a bit confused about this. . . . [A]re they scared of the menace from the north? Nope. . . . *The Host* is a monster movie . . . about a child-snatching mutant that rears up into Seoul out of the Han River, spawned by toxic fluid carelessly discharged from—guess where—an American military base. . . . Many of them [South Koreans] see North Korea as a slightly delinquent brother. . . . China, too, is viewed more positively than it is by most of its other neighbors. By contrast, American movies tend to be suspect." "Here There Be Monsters," *New York Times* (August 11, 2006): A13.

57 Chu and Kim, eds., *Diversity and Coexistence*, 87–88.

Chapter 7 Extraordinarily Rendered: *Oldboy*, Transmedia Adaptation, and the US War on Terror

1 Manohla Dargis, "The Violence (and the Seafood) is More Than Raw," *New York Times* (March 25, 2005): E14.

2 Darcy Paquet, *New Korean Cinema: Breaking the Waves* (New York: Wallflower, 2009), 96.

3 Terence McSweeney, "Memory as Cultural Battleground in Park Chan-wook's *Oldboy*," *Millennial Cinema: Memory in Global Film* (London: Wallflower Press, 2011), 227.

4 Ibid.

5 Liese Spencer, "Revenger's Tragedy," *Sight and Sound* (October 2004): 18.

6 McSweeney, "Memory as Cultural Battleground in Park Chan-wook's *Oldboy*," 222.

7 Ibid., 223.

8 Joseph Tomkins and Julie A. Wilson, "The Political Unconscious of Park Chan-wook: The Logic of Revenge and the Structures of Global Capitalism," *Post Script*, Vol. 27, No. 3 (Summer 2008): 76.

9 Kyung Hyun Kim, *Virtual Hallyu: Korean Cinema of the Global Era* (Durham, NC: Duke University Press, 2011), 181.

10 Kelly Y. Jeong, "Towards Humanity and Redemption: The World of Park Chan-wook's Revenge Film Trilogy," *Journal of Japanese & Korean Cinema*, Vol. 4, No. 2 (2012): 170.

11 Ibid., 177.

12 Ibid., 172.

13 Tomkins and Wilson, "The Political Unconscious of Park Chan-wook," 77.

14 Kim Young-jin, *Park Chan-wook* (Seoul: Korean Film Council, 2007), 45.

15 Steve Choe, "Love Your Enemies: Revenge and Forgiveness in Films by Park Chan-wook," *Korean Studies*, Vol. 33 (2009): 34.

16 Earl Jackson, Jr., "Borrowing Trouble: *Oldboy* as Adaptation and Intervention," *Transnational Cinemas*, Vol. 3, No. 1 (2012): 54.

17 See, for instance, Kate Taylor-Jones, *Rising Sun, Divided Land: Japanese and South Korean Filmmakers* (London: Wallflower Press, 2013), 138–145.

18 David E. Low, "'Spaces Invested with Content': Crossing the 'Gaps' in Comics with Readers in Schools," *Children's Literature in Education*, 43 (2012): 372.

19 Ibid.

20 Scott McCloud, *Understanding Comics: The Invisible Art* (Northampton, MA: Kitchen Sink Press, 1993), 66.

21 Thierry Groensteen, *The System of Comics* (Jackson: University Press of Mississippi, 2007), 22.
22 Noël Carroll, *Theorizing the Moving Image* (Cambridge: Cambridge University Press, 1996), 417–418.
23 Jackson, "Borrowing Trouble: *Oldboy* as Adaptation and Intervention," 58–60.
24 Ibid., 63.
25 Tsuchiya Garon, *Oldboy*, Vol. 3 (Milwaukie, OR: Dark Horse Manga, 2006), 120, 192.
26 Ibid., 34.
27 Tyler Cowen, *Creative Destruction: How Globalization Is Changing the World's Cultures* (Princeton, NJ: Princeton University Press, 2004), 47–72.
28 Ibid., 48.
29 Kyu Hyun Kim, "Fisticuffs, High Kicks, and Colonial Histories: The Ambivalence of Modern Korean Identity in Postwar Narrative Comics," in Kyung Hyun Kim and Youngmin Choe, eds., *The Korean Popular Culture Reader* (Durham, NC: Duke University Press, 2014), 40.
30 Wendy Siuyi Wong, "Globalizing Manga: From Japan to Hong Kong and Beyond," *Mechademia*, Vol. 1 (2006): 23–45.
31 Tsuchiya, *Oldboy*, 117.
32 For a more elaborate definition of the term and a full list of fifty-four foreign governments that reportedly participated in the program, see *Globalizing Torture: CIA Secret Detention and Extraordinary Rendition* (New York: Open Society Foundations, 2013). http://www.opensocietyfoundations.org/sites/default/files/globalizing-torture-20120205.pdf. Accessed August 10, 2014.
33 Although the US history of rendition (the transfer of a detainee across national borders without extradition process) dates back to 1886, as discussed in the Introduction, the CIA's "extraordinary" rendition program specifically targeting Islamic terrorist suspects reportedly began under the Clinton administration. According to Stephen Grey, the author of *Ghost Plane: The True Story of the CIA Rendition and Torture Program* (New York: St. Martin's Griffin, 2007), the first case of extraordinary rendition occurred in September 1995, with the CIA's kidnapping of Egyptian Abu Talal al-Qasimi, in Croatia, and his transfer to Egypt where he was executed. However, it was not until the immediate aftermath of 9/11 that the scope and extent of the program expanded significantly.
34 Stephen Prince, *Firestorm: American Film in the Age of Terrorism* (New York: Columbia University Press, 2009), 4.
35 Ibid., 286.
36 Ibid., 283–284.
37 Ibid., 284.
38 Ibid.
39 Cameron Bailey, "Vengeance Is His: Korea's Park Chan-wook Says Revenge Can Be Good for Your Health," *NOW*, Vol. 24, No. 33 (April 14–21): 2005. http://stage81.nowtoronto.com/movies/story.cfm?content=146864. Accessed August 10, 2014.
40 "Park Life," *Neil Young's Film Lounge* (March 23, 2004). http://www.jigsawlounge.co.uk/film/reviews/neil-youngs-film-lounge-park-life/. Accessed August 10, 2014.
41 Esther K. Chae, "Park Chanwook," BOMB, Iss. 96 (Summer 2006). http://bombmagazine.org/article/2827/park-chanwook. Accessed December 1, 2014.
42 Yi Chi-ŭn, "Hunger Strikes in the Guantánamo Detention Camp" ["Guantanamo suyongso aesŏ pŏlŏjinŭn tansik t'ujaeng"], *Voice of People* ["*Minjung ŭi*

sori"] (October 31, 2005). http://www.vop.co.kr/A00000031917.html. Accessed August 10, 2014.

43 Yi Kyu-bong, "The United States Usurps Guantánamo with $4,000 Annual Rent" ["Nyŏn 4000 imdaeryo ro Guant'anamo kangt'alhan Mig'uk"], *OhMyNews* (December 12, 2008). http://www.ohmynews.com/NWS_Web/View/at_pg.aspx?CNTN_CD=A0001799479. Accessed August 10, 2014.

44 Choi Aryong, "Sympathy for the Old Boy . . . ," *Ikonen* (June 8, 2008). http://www.ikonenmagazin.de/interview/Park.htm. Accessed August 10, 2014.

45 Ch'oe Yŏng-ju, "Interview: *National Security* Director Chung Ji-young" ["Int'ŏbyu: Yŏnghwa *Namyŏngdong 1985* ŭi kamdok Chŏng Chi-yŏng"], *PD Journal*, November 14, 2012. http://www.pdjournal.com/news/quickViewArticleView.html?idxno=36761. Accessed August 10, 2014.

46 Marilyn Fabe, *Closely Watched Films: An Introduction to the Art of Narrative Film Technique* (Berkeley: University of California Press, 2004), 91.

47 Joseph Jonghyun Jeon, "Residual Selves: Trauma and Forgetting in Park Chan-wook's *Oldboy*," *positions*, Vol. 17, No. 3 (Winter 2009): 720.

48 Kim, *Virtual Hallyu*, 182.

49 Tomkins and Wilson, "The Political Unconscious of Park Chan-wook," 77.

50 Ibid.

51 Kim Young-jin, *Park Chan-wook*, 98–99.

52 Editorial Board, "Rendition, Torture, Accountability," *New York Times* (November 19, 2007). http://www.nytimes.com/2007/11/19/opinion/19mon3.html. Accessed August 10, 2014.

53 *Globalizing Torture*, 29–60. Because the Open Society Foundations' study limits its scope to renditions to detention facilities run by foreign governments and excludes US military-operated prisons such as Guantánamo, the total number of extraordinarily rendered suspects is estimated to be considerably higher.

54 Amrit Singh, "European Court of Human Rights Finds against CIA Abuse of Khaled El-Masri," *The Guardian* (December 13, 2012). http://www.theguardian.com/commentisfree/2012/dec/13/european-court-human-rights-cia-abuse-khaled-elmasri. Accessed August 10, 2014.

55 Paul Krugman, "America's Lost Respect," *New York Times* (October 1, 2004). http://www.nytimes.com/2004/10/01/opinion/01krugman.html. Accessed August 10, 2014.

56 Camilla Fojas, "Hollywood Border Cinema: Westerns with a Vengeance," *Journal of Popular Film and Television*, Vol. 39, No. 2 (2011): 94, 100.

57 J. William Fulbright, *The Arrogance of Power* (New York: Random House, 1966), 3.

58 Ibid., 3–4.

59 Jeon, "Residual Selves," 726.

60 Park Chan-wook, "Special Features: Director Commentary," *Oldboy*, Tartan Video, 2007.

61 Jeon, "Residual Selves," 724.

62 Kim, *Virtual Hallyu*, 194.

63 Homi K. Bhabha, *Nation and Narration* (London: Routledge, 1990), 297.

64 Ibid., 311–312.

65 Ibid., 297.

66 Iain Robert Smith, "*Oldboy* Goes to Bollywood," in Alison Peirse and Daniel Martin, eds., *Korean Horror Cinema* (Edinburgh: Edinburgh University Press, 2013),189.

67 Alfred W. McCoy, "Impunity at Home, Rendition Abroad," *HuffingtonPost* (August 14, 2012). http://www.huffingtonpost.com/alfred-w-mccoy/extraordinary-rendition-torture_b_1775438.html. Accessed August 10, 2014.
68 Julia Lesage, "Torture Documentaries," *Jump Cut*, No. 51 (Spring 2009). http://www.ejumpcut.org/archive/jc51.2009/TortureDocumentaries/#top. Accessed August 10, 2014.
69 "Get the Data: Drone Wars," The Bureau of Investigative Journalism. http://www.thebureauinvestigates.com/category/projects/drones/drones-graphs. Accessed November 17, 2014. For more information on Obama's drone policy, see Jo Becker and Scott Shane, "Secret 'Kill List' Proves a Test of Obama's Principals and Will," *New York Times* (May 29, 2012). http://www.nytimes.com/2012/05/29/world/obamas-leadership-in-war-on-al-qaeda.html?pagewanted=all&_r=0. Accessed November 17, 2014.
70 McCoy, "Impunity at Home, Rendition Abroad."
71 Brian Henderson, "*The Searchers*: An American Dilemma," *Film Quarterly*, Vol. 34, No. 2 (Winter 1980–1981): 23.

Chapter 8 A *Thirst* for Diversity: Recent Trends in Korean "Multicultural Films," from *Bandhobi* to *Where is Ronny?*

1 Exceptions include exploitation horror films such Kim In-su's *The Female Vampire of the Night* (*Hŭphyŏlgŭi yanyŏ*, 1981), Yi Hyŏng-p'yo's *Dracula in a Coffin* (*Kwansok ŭi Tŭrak'ura*, 1982), and Sim Hyŏng-rae's *Young-gu and Count Dracula* (*Yŏng-gu wa Hŭphyŏlgŭi Tŭrak'ura*, 1992).
2 Sechin Cho, "Traditional Korean Culture," in Nancy L. Fisher, ed., *Cultural and Ethnic Diversity: A Guide for Genetics Professionals* (Baltimore: Johns Hopkins University Press, 1996), 134.
3 Gi-wook Shin, *Ethnic Nationalism in Korea: Genealogy, Politics and Legacy* (Stanford, CA: Stanford University Press, 2006), 2.
4 Ibid.
5 According to July 2014 statistics of Ministry of Security and Public Administration, the number of foreign residents from the Philippines reached 64,785, or 4.1% of the total foreign residents in South Korea. Ch'oe Yŏng-ho, "The Number of Foreign Residents is 1.57 Million, 3.1% of All Registered Nationals" ["Woegukin chuminsu 157man myŏng, chumindŭngrok ingu taebi 3.1%"], Press Release of Ministry of Security and Public Administration [Anjŏn Haengchŏngbu] (July 2, 2014). http://www.mospa.go.kr/frt/bbs/type010/commonSelectBoardArticle.do?bbsId=BBSMSTR_000000000008&nttId=42487. Accessed August 10, 2014. According to statistics announced by the Korean Immigration Service, as of February 2012, out of the 120,355 foreign brides residing in South Korea, Filipinas (8,315) make up 5.9%, the fourth largest population, following the Chinese (44%), the Vietnamese (26.1%), and the Japanese (7.7%). http://damunhwaedu.com/xe/menu1_1/723. Accessed August 10, 2014.
6 Han Geon-soo, "Multicultural Korea: Celebration or Challenge of Multiethnic Shift in Contemporary Korea?" *Korea Journal*, Vol. 47, No. 4 (Winter 2007): 32–63.
7 Ibid., 33.
8 Choe Sen-na, quoted in Han, "Multicultural Korea," 34.

9 Kim Hyun Mee, "The State and Migrant Women: Diverging Hopes in the Making of Multicultural Families in Contemporary Korea," *Korea Journal*, Vol. 47, No. 4 (Winter 2007): 103.

10 Mun Sŏk, "Deep Agony over Human Nature" ["Ingan ŭi ponjilae taehan kipŭn komin"], *Cine 21* (April 29, 2009). http://www.cine21.com/news/view/mag_id/55981. Accessed August 10, 2014.

11 Chu Sŏng-ch'ŏl, "Exclusive Interview with Park Chan-wook" ["Pak Ch'an-uk tandok int'ŏyu"], *Cine 21* (May 26, 2009). http://www.cine21.com/news/view/mag_id/56386. Accessed August 10, 2014.

12 Kim, "The State and Migrant Women," 101.

13 The Noh Moo Hyun administration introduced the "Basic Act for Improving Treatment of Foreign Residents" in 2007 and "Multicultural Families Support Act" in 2008, thus providing a basic legal framework to administer multicultural policies. See Kim Tong-hyung, "Multicultural Korea Needs New Legal Framework," *The Korea Times* (October 31, 2011). https://www.koreatimes.co.kr/www/news/biz/2013/06/123_97658.html. Accessed August 10, 2014.

14 Ch'oe Yŏng-ho, "The Number of Foreign Residents is 1.57 Million, 3.1% of All Registered Nationals," Press Release of Ministry of Security and Public Administration.

15 Yi Hyŏn-jŏng, *Our Future Depends on Multiculturalism* [*Uri ŭi mirae tamunhwa ae talryŏ itda*], (Seoul: Soul Mate, 2009), 85.

16 Min In-sik et al., ed., *Different Is Not Bad* [*Taerŭngae nappŭn kŏn anijanayo*], (Seoul: Kkumgyŏl, 2012), 109.

17 Lisa Lowe, *Immigrant Acts: On Asian American Cultural Politics* (Durham, NC: Duke University Press, 1996), 86.

18 Robert Stam, "Multiculturalism and the Neoconservatives," in Anne McClintock, Aamir Mufti, and Ella Shohat, eds., *Dangerous Liaisons: Gender, Nation, and Postcolonial Perspectives* (Minneapolis: University of Minnesota Press, 1997), 189.

19 Jacques Derrida, *Of Hospitality*, Trans. Rachel Bowlby (Stanford, CA: Stanford University Press, 2000), 5.

20 Ibid., 19.

21 Ibid., 25.

22 Ibid., 55.

23 For Derrida, hospitality of visitation (emphasizing the foreigner's right to visit) is synonymous with unconditional hospitality while hospitality of invitation (emphasizing the host's right to select and control his/her visitors/guests) is synonymous with conditional hospitality. For more info, see Jacques Derrida, *Acts of Religion* (New York: Routledge, 2002), 360–362.

24 Jacques Derrida, *On Cosmopolitanism and Forgiveness*, Trans. Mark Dooley and Michael Hughes (London: Routledge, 2001), 16.

25 Judith Still, *Derrida and Hospitality: Theory and Practice* (Edinburgh: Edinburgh University Press, 2010), 189.

26 Ibid.

27 Jacques Derrida, *Adieu to Emmanuel Levinas*, Trans. Pascale-Anne Brault and Michael Naas (Stanford, CA: Stanford University Press, 1999), 18.

28 Jacques Derrida, *Positions: Jacques Derrida*, Trans. Alan Bass (Chicago: University of Chicago Press, 1981), 43.

29 Personal interview with Shin Dong-il, June 4, 2014, Seoul, Korea.

30 Derrida, *Of Hospitality*, 49.

31 Although both Ho-jun and Kye-sang are native Korean men, their symbolic foreigner's status is expressed through their affiliation with European art cinema and Jehovah's Witnesses, both of which exist outside mainstream Korean culture. In an earlier scene, Ho-jun tries to convince a local grocery shop woman to watch Rainer Werner Fassbinder's *Ali: Fear Eats the Soul* (*Angst essen Seele auf*, 1974), a New German cinema masterpiece about the interracial, intergenerational love between an elderly German widow and a young Moroccan guest worker. This casual reference to the German film foreshadows Shin Dong-il's third feature which focuses on the friendship and love between a Korean woman and a Bangladeshi man who, like Ali, is a Muslim guest worker.

32 Mahbub Alam (a.k.a. Mustaque Ahmed Mahbub) came to South Korea as a migrant worker in 1999 before getting involved in the Migrant Worker's Trade Union in 2002 and founding Migrant Workers Television in 2005. As an activist, filmmaker, and actor, Alam also directed the Migrant Workers Film Festival, made several documentaries about immigration crackdowns and Bangladeshi migrant workers including *The Deported* (2007) and *Returnees* (2009) and appeared in several multicultural-themed films such as *Where Is Ronny?* and *Bandhobi.* He also appeared in a bit part in Shin Dong-il's sophomore film *My Friend & His Wife.* See Jenny Na, "Migrant Worker Film Festival Highlights Both Adversity and Change," *Hankyoreh Newspaper* [*Hankyŏrye sinmun*], English Edition (August 31, 2007). http://english.hani.co.kr/arti/english_edition/e_entertainment/232922.html. Accessed August 10, 2014.

33 The reconstruction was complete in May 2013 and cost the Korean Treasury US $24 million.

34 Joon K. Kim, "The Politics of Culture in Multicultural Korea," *Journal of Ethnic and Migration Studies*, Vol. 37, No. 10 (December 2011): 1581.

35 "Legal Status of Foreign Workers," Employment Permit System (Ministry of Employment and Labor). https://www.eps.go.kr/ph/index.html. Accessed August 10, 2014.

36 The restriction on migrant workers' freedom to change workplaces is one of the most contentious elements of the Employment Permit System (EPS). As recently as April 2013, various migrant workers' groups and Korean labor unions collectively demonstrated in Seoul, demanding the protection of labor rights for foreign workers and the abolishment of the EPS, which is deemed responsible for indenturing foreigner laborers to inhumane working conditions due to its prohibition of free labor mobility. Kim Ŭn-sông, "Migrant Workers Demand Labor Rights Protection and the Abolishment of the Employment Permit System" ["Iju nodongja nodong samgwôn pojang, koyonghôgajae paeji ch'okgu"], *Labor Today* [*Maeil Nodong News*] (April 28, 2013). http://www.labortoday.co.kr/news/articleView.html?idxno=117995. Accessed August 10, 2014.

37 Yi, *Our Future Depends on Multiculturalism*, 85.

38 Derrida, *Of Hospitality*, 45.

39 Ibid., 53–55.

40 Still, *Derrida and Hospitality*, 200–201.

41 Carl Boggs and Tom Pollards, "American Militarism, Hollywood, and Media Culture," Rhonda Hammer and Douglas Kellner, eds., *Media/Cultural Studies: Critical Approaches* (New York: Peter Lang, 2009), 462.

42 Na, "Migrant Worker Film Festival Highlights Both Adversity and Change."

43 Both *Where Is Ronny?* and *Bandhobi* were partly funded by the government-subsidized Korean Film Council.

44 Kim Ki-sŏng, "'Chakŭn kukjetosi' Ansan-si ŭi silhyŏm" ["A 'Small International City,' Ansan's Experiments"], *Hankyoreh Newspaper* [*Hankyŏrye sinmun*] (November 7, 2008). http://hani.co.kr/arti/society/rights/320489.html. Accessed August 10, 2014.

45 Director Shin Dong-il cites racist Internet blogs as well as the Korea Media Rating Board's harsh "Adults Only" rating (which he appealed unsuccessfully) as causes for the commercial failure of *Bandhobi*. Personal interview with Shin Dong-il, June 4, 2014, Seoul, Korea.

Conclusion Into "Spreadable" Spaces: Netflix, YouTube, and the Question of Cultural Translatability

1 Arjun Appadurai, *Modernity at Large: Cultural Dimensions of Globalization* (Minneapolis: University of Minnesota Press), 33.

2 Ibid., 35.

3 Ibid., 31.

4 David Desser, "Hong Kong Film and the New Cinephilia," in Meaghan Morris, Siu Leung Li, and Stephen Chan Ching-kiu, eds., *Hong Kong Connections: Transnational Imagination in Action Cinema* (Durham, NC: Duke University Press, 2005), 209–211, 219.

5 Henry Jenkins, Sam Ford, and Joshua Green, *Spreadable Media: Creating Value and Meaning in a Networked Culture* (New York: New York University Press, 2013), 239.

6 "Company Overview," Netflix Website: https://pr.netflix.com/WebClient/Login.jsp#. Accessed November 15, 2014.

7 Appadurai, *Modernity at Large*, 45–47.

8 Jenkins, Ford, and Green, *Spreadable Media*, 259.

9 *Spring, Summer, Fall, Winter . . . and Spring*'s record was broken by the medieval marine epic *The Admiral: Roaring Currents* (Myŏngryang) in 2014 when the latter film brought in $2.5 million in the US box office.

10 Jinhee Choi, *The South Korean Film Renaissance: Local Hitmakers/Global Provocateurs* (Middletown, CT: Wesleyan University Press, 2010), 181–182.

11 Caroline Bassett, "Cultural Studies and New Media," in Sue Thornham, Caroline Bassett, and Paul Marris, eds., *Media Studies: A Reader*, Third Edition (New York: New York University Press, 2009), 855.

12 Henry Jenkins, *Convergence Culture: Where Old and New Media Collide*, Revised Edition (New York: New York University Press, 2008), 2.

13 Ibid.

14 Ibid., 4.

15 Jenkins, Ford, and Green, *Spreadable Media*, 11, 21.

16 Ibid., 271.

17 Personal interview, Korean Film Archive, June 2, 2014.

18 Kent A. Ono and Jungmin Kwon, "Re-worlding Culture?: YouTube as a K-Pop Interlocutor," in Youna Kim, ed., *The Korean Wave: Korean Media Go Global* (London: Routledge, 2013), 207.

19 Ibid., 208.

20 Jenkins, Ford, and Green, *Spreadable Media*, 22.

21 Ibid., 288–290.

22 Jang Sung-ran, "Hollywood Remakes Korean Films," *Korean Cinema Today* (April 25, 2013). http://koreanfilm.or.kr/webzine/sub/feature.jsp?mode=A_VIEW&wbSeq=101. Accessed August 10, 2014.

23 Terrence Rafferty, "Cinema's Sisterhood of Spookiness," *New York Times* (January 25, 2009): AR18.

24 Stephanie Zacharek, "*Oldboy*: Spike Lee's Completely Unnecessary Remake," *Phoenix New Times*, November 28, 2013: http://www.phoenixnewtimes.com/2013-11-28/film/oldboy-review/full/; Justin Chang, "Film Review: *Oldboy*," *Variety* (November 26, 2013): http://variety.com/2013/film/reviews/oldboy-review-1200848857/#. Accessed August 10, 2014.

25 Rex Reed, "*Oldboy* is Oldhat," *New York Observer* (November 27, 2013). http://observer.com/2013/11/oldboy-is-oldhat/. Accessed August 10, 2014.

26 Shaoyi Sun, "From the Yupgi Girl to the "Super Girl": Toward a Reframed Inter-Asian Femininity," *Asia/Cinema/Network: Industry, Technology & Film Culture Conference Book* (Pusan: Pusan International Film Festival, 2005), 211.

27 Xiying Wang, "*My Sassy Girl*: A Qualitative Study of Women's Aggression in Dating Relationships in Beijing," *Journal of Interpersonal Violence*, Vol. 22, No. 5 (May 2007): 630.

28 Ke Peng, "Translatability vs. Untranslatability: A Sociosemiotic Perspective," *Babel*, Vol. 44, No. 4 (1999). http://dhost.info/pingke/T-P-Translatability.htm. Accessed August 10, 2014.

29 Jane Park, "Remaking the Korean Romcom: A Case Study of *Yeopgijeogin Geunyeo* and *My Sassy Girl*," in Daniel Black, Stephen Epstein, and Alison Tokita, eds., *Complicated Currents: Media Flow, Soft Power, and East Asia* (Melbourne: Monash University Press, 2010). http://books.publishing.monash.edu/apps/bookworm/view/Complicated+Currents/122/xhtml/chapter13.html. Accessed August 10, 2014.

Index

About the Authors

HYE SEUNG CHUNG is associate professor of film and media studies at Colorado State University. She is the author of *Hollywood Asian: Philip Ahn and the Politics of Cross-Ethnic Performance* (2006) and *Kim Ki-duk* (2012).

DAVID SCOTT DIFFRIENT is William E. Morgan chair of liberal arts and associate professor of film and media studies at Colorado State University. He is the author of *M*A*S*H* (2008) and *Omnibus Films: Theorizing Transauthorial Cinema* (2014) as well as the editor of *Screwball Television: Critical Perspectives on Gilmore Girls* (2010).

Available titles in the New Directions in International Studies series:

Niki Akhavan
Electronic Iran: The Cultural Politics of an Online Evolution

A. Aneesh, Lane Hall, and Patrice Petro, eds.
Beyond Globalization: Making New Worlds in Media, Art, and Social Practices

Dora Apel
War Culture and the Contest of Images

Daniel Leonard Bernardi, Pauline Hope Cheong, Chris Lundry, and Scott W. Ruston
Narrative Landmines: Rumors, Islamist Extremism, and the Struggle for Strategic Influence

Mark Philip Bradley and Patrice Petro, eds.
Truth Claims: Representation and Human Rights

Hye Seung Chung and David Scott Diffrient
Movie Migrations: Transnational Genre Flows and South Korean Cinema

Melissa A. Fitch
Side Dishes: Latina American Women, Sex, and Cultural Production

Elizabeth Swanson Goldberg
Beyond Terror: Gender, Narrative, Human Rights

Linda Krause, ed.
Sustaining Cities: Urban Policies, Practices, and Perceptions

Linda Krause and Patrice Petro, eds.
Global Cities: Cinema, Architecture, and Urbanism in a Digital Age

Andrew Martin and Patrice Petro, eds.
Rethinking Global Security: Media, Popular Culture, and the "War on Terror"

Tasha G. Oren and Patrice Petro, eds.
Global Currents: Media and Technology Now

Peter Paik and Marcus Bullock, eds.
Aftermaths: Exile, Migration, and Diaspora Reconsidered

Rebecca Prime
Intimate Strangers: Blacklisted Filmmakers in Postwar Europe

Freya Schiwy
Indianizing Film: Decolonization, the Andes, and the Question of Technology

Cristina Venegas
Digital Dilemmas: The State, the Individual, and Digital Media in Cuba